THE STAR
OF
REDEMPTION

THE STAR
OF
REDEMPTION

BY

Franz Rosenzweig

Translated from the Second Edition of 1930 by

WILLIAM W. HALLO

Holt, Rinehart and Winston

NEW YORK   CHICAGO   SAN FRANCISCO

Copyright © 1970, 1971 by Holt, Rinehart and Winston, Inc.

Published simultaneously in Canada by
Holt, Rinehart and Winston of Canada, Limited.

Library of Congress Card Number: 71-118091

First Edition

A portion of this book has appeared previously in *Great
Twentieth-Century Jewish Philosophers* edited by Bernard
Martin, published by The Macmillan Company.

DESIGNER: VINCENT TORRE
SBN: 03-085077-0
Printed in the United States of America

CONTENTS

TRANSLATOR'S PREFACE   vii

FOREWORD BY N. N. GLATZER   ix

PART I
THE ELEMENTS
or
THE EVER-ENDURING PROTO-COSMOS

INTRODUCTION: On the Possibility of the Cognition
    of the All   3

BOOK 1   God and His Being or Metaphsics   23

BOOK 2   The World and Its Meaning or Metalogic   41

BOOK 3   Man and His Self or Metaethics   62

    TRANSITION   83

PART II
THE COURSE
or
THE ALWAYS-RENEWED COSMOS

INTRODUCTION: On the Possibility of Experiencing
    Miracles   93

BOOK 1   Creation, or The Ever-Enduring
    Base of Things   112

BOOK 2   Revelation, or The Ever-Renewed
    Birth of the Soul   156

BOOK 3   Redemption, or The Eternal Future
    of the Kingdom   205

    THRESHOLD   254

PART III
THE CONFIGURATION
or
THE ETERNAL HYPER-COSMOS

INTRODUCTION: On the Possibility of Entreating
    the Kingdom   265

v

CONTENTS

BOOK 1 The Fire, or The Eternal Life   298
BOOK 2 The Rays, or The Eternal Way   336
BOOK 3 The Star, or The Eternal Truth   380

    GATE   418

INDICES

INDEX OF JEWISH SOURCES   427
INDEX OF NAMES   437
INDEX OF SUBJECTS   443

TRANSLATOR'S PREFACE

The Star of Redemption is no ordinary book, and its translation is no ordinary task. To do it justice, the translator must approach it more like poetry than like a work of prose. The present translation attempts to retain the rhythmic cadences of the original while, at the same time, reducing its intricate and sometimes almost interminable sentences to manageable proportions. It is faithful to the original, except where a literal translation threatens to introduce ambiguities not intended in the original. Pronouns, for example, have frequently been replaced with their appropriate antecedents to compensate for the loss of inflectional precision common in English. Where the ambiguities are inherent in the German the translation strives to preserve them when it cannot adequately resolve them.

Rosenzweig's magnum opus is, furthermore, a veritable mosaic of citations and allusions. Many of these were identified by Nahum Glatzer in the indexes appended to the second edition which are reproduced, with some additions, here. In particular, Rosenzweig spoke the language of Goethe's *Faust* and other German classics. This language, familiar and pregnant with meaning for his contemporaries, calls for occasional glosses in a modern translation.

Rosenzweig's choice of words was judicious, and many of his points are inextricably imbedded in elaborate figures of speech, including numerous plays on words. Nor was he above taking liberties with the German language. In confronting the peculiarities of style and diction thus presented, the translator may well be guided by Rosenzweig's own principles of translation as set forth in *"Die Schrift und ihre Verdeutschung,"* and other essays on the translation of the Bible by Buber and Rosenzweig. The attempt has thus been made, albeit within severe limits, to translate identical German words into identical English words, and their derivatives into English derivatives; to reproduce the plays on words; to render unusual German words and forms into equally conspicuous English equivalents, even when this results in such desperate neologisms as "selfication" or "factualize." Far as I am from attaining it, I have nevertheless striven for Rosenzweig's own ideal concept "that the translator, the one who hears and transmits, knows himself equal to the one who first spoke and received the word" (below, p. 366).

It is a pleasant duty to thank all those who have helped to make the translation possible: Mrs. Katharine S. Falk who, through the good offices of the National Foundation for Jewish Culture, provided the material support; Mr. Rafael Rosenzweig, who buttressed an old friendship with trenchant advice; the Franz Rosenzweig Fellowship of New York, which has long made the translation of the *Stern* its major objective; Prof. Maurice Friedman, who first encouraged me to undertake the project; Prof. Nahum N. Glatzer, who guided its progress; and Mr. Joseph Cunneen, who saw it into print. My wife Edith has been a patient and unfailing support throughout the four years that the translation was in preparation, and the three further years that it was in process of publication. Above all, my thanks are due to my mother, Dr. Gertrude Hallo, who read the entire manuscript and supplied numerous invaluable suggestions. Her intimate acquaintance with Franz Rosenzweig, his language and his thought, saved the translation from many errors. Those that remain are exclusively my own responsibility. Hopefully they do not subvert the translator's aim: in Rosenzweig's own sense to "Americanize" *The Star of Redemption*— not merely to translate it but to naturalize it in a new environment so that it may help once more to sow the seeds of a rebirth of thoughtful belief.

Some portions of this translation have previously appeared in *The Worlds of Existentialism: A Critical Reader*, edited by Maurice Friedman (New York, Random House, 1964), pp. 327–329; in *Christianity: Some Non-Christian Appraisals*, edited by David W. McKain (New York, McGraw-Hill, 1964), pp. 191–203; and in *Great Twentieth Century Jewish Philosophers: Shestov, Rosenzweig, Buber, with Selections from their Writings*, edited by Bernard Martin (The Macmillan Company, 1970), pp. 163–195; others are based on the rendition in *Franz Rosenzweig: His Life and Thought*, presented by Nahum N. Glatzer (New York, Schocken Books, 1953, 1961), pp. 292–341. These portions are reproduced here with minor modifications and by arrangement with the respective editors and publishers.

W. W. H.

New Haven
June, 1970

FOREWORD

by N. N. Glatzer

Franz Rosenzweig published his *Stern der Erlösung* without any explicatory matter; there was no introduction, no preface, no postscript, nothing that would give some inkling of the background and purpose of the work. Not even a publisher's note or jacket copy served to introduce, however briefly, the at-the-time-unknown author. The book, Rosenzweig felt, was to speak for itself; whoever was discontented with prevailing academic philosophies (and theologies) would find his way to it. Furthermore, he was deterred by prefaces to philosophical tomes and their authors' "clucking after having laid their egg and their discourteous, derogatory remarks directed to the reader who has done no wrong as yet, not even as much as reading the book." When, in 1925, four years after the publication of the *Stern*, Rosenzweig issued his "Das neue Denken" ("The New Thinking"), subtitled "Some supplementary remarks to the *Stern der Erlösung*," he forbade publication of this essay in any further editions of the *Stern*, either as introduction or postscript.

It was therefore with considerable trepidation that I yielded to the proposal by the publisher of *The Star of Redemption* to write a prefatory note. For, though several books and a good number of studies and essays on Rosenzweig are now extant, acquaintance with his life and background cannot be taken for granted. Rosenzweig himself abandoned his original position of considering the *Star* strictly as a *textus* when, shortly before his death, he asked me to prepare an extensive list of references to his Judaic sources to be included in the second edition of the work.

Franz Rosenzweig was born December 25, 1886 in Cassel, Germany, as the only son of a well-to-do, assimilated Jewish family. From 1905–1907 the highly gifted boy studied medicine, followed by several years of study (to 1912) of modern history and philosophy, mainly under Friedrich Meinecke, historian in the Ranke tradition, and Heinrich Rückert. In 1910, he began work on a major research project anent Hegel's political doctrines and his concept of the state. One section of the investigation served as a doctoral dissertation (1912); the two-volume work, *Hegel und der Staat* (*Hegel and the State*), completed

in 1914, appeared in 1920. In it, Rosenzweig, by means of the bio-
graphical approach, traces the dramatic development of Hegel's historical and political philosophy, a philosophy largely conditioned by
Hegel's own life. While working on this project, Rosenzweig discovered (1913) a manuscript page in Hegel's handwriting, marked
"Essay on Ethics." Close analysis proved the page to be the oldest
Systemprogramm of German Idealism, composed by Schelling rather
than by Hegel; he published his findings later, in 1917.

The work on Hegel was sufficient testimony to Rosenzweig's mastery of historical research, his mature grasp of the historic process, and
his grasp of the philosophical claim of German Idealism. And he was
fully aware of his power and the lure of a prestigious academic career.
The year 1913, however, marked a crucial turning point in his life.
With ever-increasing clarity he realized the ambiguity of the scientific
method and the hubris of philosophical Idealism to understand absolute
truth. Hegel's all-encompassing theory of world, history, spirit, and
man broke down before the individual asking the existential question:
Who or what am I?

For a proper understanding of all that was to come in Rosenzweig's
intellectual life and especially of what motivated the writing of *The
Star of Redemption*, it is essential to realize that this turning point was
determined not by objective, theoretical speculation but by a personal
need. In declining a university position in Berlin, he tried to explain his
stand in rational, academic terms. No wonder the explanation failed to
register with his teacher, Professor Meinecke. Overcoming his embarrassment, the young man wrote a letter to Meinecke, speaking "in a
very personal way." "In 1913, something happened to me for which
collapse is the only fitting name. I suddenly found myself on a heap
of wreckage, or rather I realized that the road I was then pursuing was
flanked by unrealities." The study of history satisfied only his "hunger
for forms," but no more. He began "to search for his self, amidst the
manifold for the One." By reexamining his Jewish heritage ("I descended into the vaults of my being, to a place whither talents could
not follow me"), he gained "the right to live." Academic scholarship
ceased to hold the center of his attention. "My life has fallen under
the rule of a 'dark drive' [a term Meinecke had used in his letter to
Rosenzweig] which I am aware that I merely name by calling it 'my
Judaism. . . .'

"The man who wrote [at the time as yet unpublished] *The Star of
Redemption* is of a very different caliber from the author of *Hegel and
the State*." He elucidates his new attitude to life and to people (which
is the theme of the "new thinking") by saying that now he is inquired

of by men rather than scholars, by men who stand in need of answers. "I am anxious to answer the scholar *qua* man but not the representative of a certain discipline, that insatiable, ever-inquisitive phantom which like a vampire drains him whom it possesses of his humanity. I hate that phantom as I do all phantoms. Its questions are meaningless to me. On the other hand, the questions asked by human beings have become increasingly important to me." Knowledge was to be service to men.

The disciple's radical break with the honored tradition of the academe again failed to convince the master, who explained the young man's position as an act of postwar disillusionment, though the letter clearly referred to events of 1913.

What Rosenzweig left unmentioned in his long letter was the religious element in his personal crisis; the reference to "the vaults of my being," "my Judaism" was a mere allusion to what had taken place.

The decline and fall of Rosenzweig's trust in academic scholarship and Hegelian thought was accompanied by the rise of a force of a different kind: religious faith. Rosenzweig discussed these issues with his cousins, Hans and Rudolf Ehrenberg (who had become Christians), and with Eugen Rosenstock-Huessy, a man widely learned in jurisprudence, sociology, and history. The latter's simple confession of faith and his position of full commitment to Protestant Christianity was especially instrumental in suggesting to Rosenzweig that faith was indeed a historically valid, intellectually admissible alternative. Judaism was only superficially known to him; besides, in the world of Christianity (as interpreted by his friends and now by himself) there "seemed to be no room for Judaism." During a highly decisive, soul-searching debate between the two friends in the night of July 7, Rosenstock-Huessy forced Rosenzweig to veer from a "relativist position into a non-relativist one." There seemed only one way out of the dilemma: acceptance of Christianity. Rosenzweig made only one "personal reservation"; he declared that he "could turn Christian only *qua* Jew," i.e., by remaining loyal to Judaism during the period of preparation and up to the moment of baptism—at which Rudolf Ehrenberg was to serve as godfather.

It is not known whether this reservation was motivated by theological considerations—the example of Paul's conversion—or by deep-seated, though undefined, allegiance to his ancestral Judaism that counteracted the daring, though rationally justified decision to convert. The weeks that followed must have been a period of anxious search in an attempt to do justice personally, to both forces—a rather impossible task.

The trying period came to an end after Rosenzweig, in the course of his "reservation," attended a Day of Atonement service in a traditional synagogue in Berlin (October 11). What he experienced in this day-long service can be conjecturally gathered from Rosenzweig's later reference to this most solemn day in the Jewish liturgic year: "Anyone who has ever celebrated the Day of Atonement knows that it is something more than a mere personal exaltation (although this may enter into it) or the symbolic recognition of a reality such as the Jewish people (although this also may be an element); it is a testimony to the reality of God which cannot be controverted." In the section on the Jewish liturgic calendar in the *Star*, Rosenzweig states anent the Day of Atonement that here "God lifts up his countenance to the united and lonely pleading of men. . . . Man's soul is alone—with God." And in a later work, again with reference to the Day of Atonement, he says: ". . . in this moment man is as close to God . . . as it is ever accorded him to be."

Prior to that memorable 1913 Day of Atonement, Rosenzweig had not thought it possible that the spiritual perception of the "reality of God," of "being alone with God," of the "closeness to God" could be experienced by a person within Judaism of his day. He thought that a true experience of faith calls for the mediator, Jesus. The thinker and theoretician in Rosenzweig needed time to scrutinize and examine what he had apprehended emotionally. "The reasoning process comes afterwards. Afterwards, however, it must come . . ." It was only several days later, on October 23, that he was able to write to his mother: "I seem to have found the way back about which I had tortured myself in vain and pondered for almost three months." And in a letter to Rudolf Ehrenberg (October 31), while acknowledging that to the Christian no one can reach the Father save through the "Lord," he claims "the situation is quite different for one who does not have to reach the Father because he is already with him." The Church knows that Israel will be spared to the last day, but what is admitted for Israel in general is denied the individual Jew. "So far as he is concerned, the Church shall and will test her strength in the attempt to convert him." Thus, in Rosenzweig's view, the Church is historically justified in her conversionist efforts, yet the Jew must live his own role in God's world. "Shall I become converted, I who was born 'chosen'? Does the alternative of conversion even exist for me?" he writes in 1916, looking back at the events of 1913.

This, then, was the basis of "my Judaism," which Rosenzweig mentioned in his letter to Meinecke without proffering any further information.

The academic year of 1913–1914 Rosenzweig devoted to an extensive study of the classical documents of Judaism. A major influence on him was Hermann Cohen, the founder of the neo-Kantian school of Marburg who, in 1912, had come to Berlin to teach Jewish religious philosophy at the liberal *Lehranstalt für die Wissenschaft des Judentums* (Academy for the Scientific Study of Judaism).

The first literary expression of his newly acquired stance in religious thought came in 1914, in an essay entitled "Atheist Theology" ("Atheistische Theologie"). In it he is sharply critical of both the stress on the humanity of Jesus in modern Protestantism (as opposed to the Christ of the traditional Church) and the emphasis on an idealized people of Israel (as opposed to Israel the recipient of the revelation at Sinai). Boldly, he characterizes both these theological views as atheistic since they obscure the reality of the divine and obfuscate the distinctness of God and man, "that terrible obstacle in paganism, both modern and ancient." What is needed is a renewal of "the offensive thought of revelation"; offensive, for it points to the divine breaking into (*Hereinstürzen*) the lowly, human, sphere, or, as he called it later (1916), the "intrusion of the spirit into the non-spirit." The event at Sinai cannot be replaced by (or interpreted into) the autonomous moral law; by the same token, for the Christian, incarnation cannot be replaced (or interpreted into) God's humanity. The essay is, in part, directed against Martin Buber's thinking at the time.

The radical meaning of revelation occupied Rosenzweig in his correspondence with Eugen Rosenstock-Huessy in 1916; it is lucidly discussed in his comprehensive letter to Rudolf Ehrenberg, dated November 18, 1917 (the so-called germ-cell [*Urzelle*] of *The Star of Redemption*), and becomes a most crucial tenet in that work's central section.

Rosenzweig had joined the German armed forces at the beginning of 1915 and from March 1916 onwards was assigned to an antiaircraft gun unit at the Balkan front. It was therefore during the war years that his intellectual position matured and became ready to be set forth in writing. At the end of August 1918 he started to write *The Star of Redemption*—on army postal cards. The bulk of the book he wrote after the retreat of the Balkan troops in September 1918 and upon his return to his native Cassel. As evidenced by the dates on the original manuscript (now in the care of the Franz Rosenzweig Archives in Boston), he wrote the sections of the book in quick succession; the final section bears the date February 16, 1919.

The work is a triumphant affirmation of the "new thinking": thinking that ensconces common sense in the place of abstract, conceptual philosophizing; posits the validity of the concrete, individual human being over that of "humanity" in general; thinking that takes time seriously; fuses philosophy and theology; assigns both Judaism and Christianity distinct but equally important roles in the spiritual structure of the world; and sees in both biblical religions approaches toward a comprehension of reality.

But before granting us a view of the affirmative aspects of his "new thinking," Rosenzweig prepares the ground by a polemical attack against Hegel and German Idealism as a whole, a philosophy that dared to ignore individual man, his anxiety, his fear of death, his loneliness, letting him vanish in the concept of the all-embracing World-Mind. The existentialist in Rosenzweig posits the priority of being before thought, contesting the Idealist assumption that all of existence, being based upon thought, can be grasped by thought.

The first part of the *Star* examines our knowledge of the three elements of existence: God, World, Man. The starting point is the negation of each. The "nothingness" is then dialectically overcome by a negation of the negation and an affirmation of what is not nothing. These are clearly conceptual constructions, a method from which Rosenzweig could not free himself, though he considered them to be mere "auxiliary concepts." Readers who found the theoretical, abstract, metaphysical sections heavy going, were advised by him not to stop but quickly to go on, since the main substance was to come later. He maintained that the first part of the book had only one intent: to demonstrate that the three concepts of thought—God, World, and Man—cannot be deduced one from the other, but that each one of them has an independent essence. "He who understands Part One does not need the rest—and *vice versa*."

Idealist philosophy considered language to be subordinate to thinking. Speech, its proponents argued, is but a means of expression. But already Schelling assigned to language a central position in his anti-Idealist system. "Language is the most adequate symbol of the absolute or unending affirmation of God," he said. And: "Without language not only no philosophical, but also no human consciousness can be thought of." He assumed existence of a primeval language, common to all humanity. Wilhelm von Humboldt saw in language "the craving for one speaking to the other"; "true speech (*Sprechen*) is colloquy (*Gespräch*)." To him, it is not the subject matter that connects the speaker with the listener, but the I confronting the Thou. The word is not only an expression of reality but also a means by which to explore it. The anti-Hegelian Ludwig Feuerbach opined that true dialectics "is not a monologue between a lonely thinker and himself but a dialogue between I and Thou." The true I "is only the I that confronts a Thou," whereas the idealist I does not recognize a Thou.

Rosenzweig's thinking is concerned with the renewal of this speech-thinking (*Sprachdenken*), which he made an integral part of his grand synthesis of philosophy and theology, reason and faith. He strives to replace the method of (abstract) thinking, adhered to by earlier philosophies, by the method of speech. Whereas abstract thinking is "a solitary affair," in an actual conversation something happens: you do not anticipate what the other person will say. The abstract, logical thinker knows his thoughts in advance. The speech-thinker, or as Rosenzweig, following a theory of Eugen Rosenstock-Huessy (*Ange-wandte Seelenkunde*), calls him, the "grammatical thinker," depends on the presence of a definite other person.

The centrality of language, word, dialogue, name, should be understood not only in its opposition to abstract, conceptual thinking, but also as countering trends in modern times that display a deep distrust of language. Bertrand Russell (*The Scientific Outlook*) views language as a series of abstract nouns, mirroring an atomized universe of sense data. No longer can speech be used as a vehicle of communication between men. To Henri Bergson (*Creative Evolution*) language, due to its "static" quality, cannot do justice to the dynamic continuity of reality; only intuition, being wordless, nonlogical, can do this. A. N. Whitehead (*Process and Reality*), too, criticizes language as being at odds with immediate experience. A universe of "events" and "activity" calls for a new language composed of verbs. In our own day, language is the least common and least trusted means of communication though the term dialogue is on the lips of many. Were he alive today, Rosenzweig would have continued to champion the cause of the word and of speech-thinking with ever-renewed vigor.

Rosenzweig is careful to point out (in the essay "The New Thinking") that his emphasis on speech does not imply a concentration on the so-called "religious problems" but refers as well to problems of logic, ethics, and aesthetics. The new theologian envisaged by him will have to be a philosopher "for the sake of his own honesty." The two disciplines, theology and philosophy, are to be dependent on each other. "God did not, after all create religion; he created the world." The fact that people speak to each and hear one the other points to "revelation."

Creation, Revelation, Redemption: these are the "paths" that link the "elements" Man, World, God. To be sure, these are terms taken from theological vocabulary, but Rosenzweig uses them in an attempt to construct a comprehensive view of reality. In Creation—a continuous process—God, hitherto hidden in the mythical beyond, appears and gives the world reality. It is a transitory, finite, mortal, mute world. Creation, however, is only the first contact between God and world; the second is revelation. Here God reveals his love to man, whom he calls by his name. This act of God makes man aware of his being an "I." Through the act of this love, man overcomes his isolation, his dumbness; now he becomes an individual able to speak and to respond to the first divine commandment: Thou shalt love. Love, ever present, is the foundation and the meaning of revelation. Now man translates his love for God into love for his "neighbor"—which is the first step toward redemption. Redeeming love liberates man from the finality of death. Complete redemption, the world in its perfection, eternity—this man encounters in prayer, in the rhythm of the holy days within the liturgic calendar. In living the sacred year, man "anticipates" eternity within time. Both Judaism and Christianity partake in eternity; both are grounded in the experience of love.

Creation, which Rosenzweig following Schelling identifies with the pagan world and with rational philosophy, is thus perfected in revelation—this, too, seen as a continuous process, not as a historical event— and revelation is consummated and fulfilled in redemption. Such a view of the world shows profound concern for the human person and the experience (never defined!) of the reality of God. Pictorially, God, World, and Man are represented by one triangle; Creation, Revelation, and Redemption, by another. Combined, they form a six-pointed star (a late symbol of Judaism) from which the book's title derives.

Despite his harsh criticism of the German idealistic tradition, its influence on Rosenzweig persisted both in the realm of philosophical issues and in writing style. He owes a great deal to Kant as interpreted by Schelling in his later period. On the problems of philosophy versus theology, his main debt is to Schelling's *The Ages of the World* (*Die Weltalter*). That a personal philosophy is the only one justifiable after Hegel, he finds confirmed by Kierkegaard, Schopenhauer, and Nietzsche, philosophers who made man the starting point of their thought. The influence of the poet Hölderlin and of the comparative philologist Wilhelm von Humboldt (in their concept of language) is a strong possibility, as is the direct or indirect influence of the philosopher Wilhelm Dilthey. And as indicated earlier, Rosenzweig's acquaintance with Rosenstock-Huessy and Hermann Cohen had decisive impact on his development. Yet, despite all these—and other—contacts with the works of both past and contemporary philosophers, he retained a remarkable measure of independence and full measure of freedom in confronting his partners in dialogical thinking.

The division of the *Star* into three "parts," each consisting of an introduction, three "books," and an epilogue (Transition, Threshold, Gate) was clearly outlined in Rosenzweig's mind when he commenced writing. The plan served as a blueprint constantly kept in mind; he had only to develop the preconceived scheme. The descriptive subtitles for the introductions, the "parts," and the "books" underwent revisions as the writing and rewriting went on. An early version of the Introduction to Part One (in pencil) has no subtitle; a later one (in ink) has, "On the possibility to think the All" (*das All zu denken*). The latter was revised to ". . . to know the All" (. . . *zu erkennen*—in the present translation, ". . . the Cognition of the All.") Part Two, Book Three has the original subtitle: "Redemption, or The Eternal Birth of the Kingdom"; a correction in the manuscript substitutes "future" for "birth."

Most Rosenzweig commentators find it significant that the *Star* begins with "from death" and concludes with "into life," thus indicating the work's major motif. However, it is of interest that the original beginning of the work was (in two copies, one in pencil, the other in ink): "Was not philosophy all full of presupposition?" (in the present version, section "The Philosophy of Totality," paragraph two). Then, following the text of the Introduction to Part Three, dated December 20, 1918, there is a text, entitled "Start of the Introduction to Part One," which became the celebrated overture to the *Star*. Clearly, this dramatic beginning occured to Rosezweig while the work was already in an advanced stage of preparation.

The concluding words of the work also underwent several revisions, apparently to give the message, "into life" the strongest possible appeal. The original wording reads: "To walk humbly with thy God: these are the words inscribed over the gate [leading] out of the mysteriously wonderful light of the divine sanctuary into life." The word "sanctuary" was then qualified by the addition of "in which no man can remain and live." "Into life" was removed from the sentence and a new one composed: "But to where do the wings of the gate open? Into Life." The last two words were again revised, with the final phrase now reading: "Do you not know? [They open] into life."

"Into life"—real life, returning to it after having partaken in what amounts to a vision of the divine, was the step to be taken after the argument—philosophical, existentialist, theological, humanist—was closed. "Everybody should philosophize at some time in his life," Rosenzweig wrote ("The New Thinking"), "and look around from his own vantage point. But such a survey is not an end in itself. The book is no goal, not even a provisional one. Rather than sustaining itself . . . it must itself be 'verified.' This verification takes place in the course of everyday life."

Rosenzweig realized that he had written an important and, at the same time, an unconventional work from the reader's point of view. He therefore welcomed the proposal of a publisher to present his thought in a more popular fashion. He wrote a short treatise (July, 1921) that was to be called *Das Büchlein vom gesunden und kranken Menschenverstand* (*The Little Book of Common Sense and Diseased Reason*). Here a patient, paralyzed by philosophy, is cured once he has learned to understand World, Man, and God as primary forms that underly reality, and to recognize their interrelationships. The application of "common sense" is to be adjudged not only as a corrective of the mind but as an expression of the health of man as a whole.

Again we encounter the major theme of *The Star of Redemption*, and the motifs of love, of language, and of the name. The three central chapters (VI–VIII) which describe the three stages of the cure, correspond to the three books of Part Two of the *Star*. Shortly after he completed the manuscript, Rosenzweig, dissatisfied with it, canceled its publication. It appeared a generation later, first in English in 1953, under the title *Understanding the Sick and the Healthy*, and in 1964, in the original German.

"Everyday life" imposed a severe test on Rosenzweig. Not long after his marriage to Edith Hahn (March, 1920) and his appointment as head of *Freies Jüdisches Lehrhaus* (Free Jewish House of Study) in Frankfurt am Main (August 1920), a medical checkup revealed amyotrophic lateral sclerosis with progressive paralysis of the bulba (February, 1922). In September 1922 his only son, Rafael, was born. In the years that followed, the gravely ill man defied his affliction and managed to continue living as an active scholar, writer, teacher, and friend to many—a man of faith, of love, of common sense, and a sense of humor. He died December 10, 1929.

PART
I

THE ELEMENTS
or
THE EVER-ENDURING
PROTO-COSMOS

INTRODUCTION

On the Possibility of the Cognition of the All

In philosophos!

Concerning Death

All cognition of the All originates in death, in the fear of death. Philosophy takes it upon itself to throw off the fear of things earthly, to rob death of its poisonous sting, and Hades of its pestilential breath. All that is mortal lives in this fear of death; every new birth augments the fear by one new reason, for it augments what is mortal. Without ceasing, the womb of the indefatigable earth gives birth to what is new, each bound to die, each awaiting the day of its journey into darkness with fear and trembling. But philosophy denies these fears of the earth. It bears us over the grave which yawns at our feet with every step. It lets the body be a prey to the abyss, but the free soul flutters away over it. Why should philosophy be concerned if the fear of death knows nothing of such a dichotomy between body and soul, if it roars Me! Me! Me!, if it wants nothing to do with relegating fear onto a mere "body"? Let man creep like a worm into the folds of the naked earth before the fast-approaching volleys of a blind death from which there is no appeal; let him sense there, forcibly, inexorably, what he otherwise never senses: that his I would be but an It if it died; let him therefore cry his very I out with every cry that is still in his throat against Him from whom there is no appeal, from whom such unthinkable annihilation threatens—for all this dire necessity philosophy has only its vacuous smile. With index finger outstretched, it directs the creature, whose limbs are quivering with terror for its this-worldly existence, to a Beyond of which it doesn't care to know anything at all. For man does not really want to escape any kind of fetters; he wants to remain, he wants to—live. Philosophy, which com-

mends death to him as its special protégé, as the magnificent opportunity to flee the straits of life, seems to him to be only mocking. In
fact, Man is only too well aware that he is condemned to death, but
not to suicide. Yet this philosophical recommendation can truthfully
recommend only suicide, not the fated death of all. Suicide is not the
natural form of death but plainly the one counter to nature. The
gruesome capacity for suicide distinguishes man from all beings, both
known and unknown to us. It is the veritable criterion of this dis-
engagement from all that is natural. It is presumably necessary for
man to disengage once in his life. Like Faust,[1] he must for once bring
the precious vial down with reverence; he must for once have felt
himself in his fearful poverty, loneliness, and dissociation from all the
world, have stood a whole night face to face with the Nought. But
the earth claims him again. He may not drain the dark potion in that
night. A way out of the bottleneck of the Nought has been determined for him, another way than this precipitate fall into the
yawning abyss. Man is not to throw off the fear of the earthly; he is
to remain in the fear of death—but he is to remain.

He is to remain. He shall do none other than what he already wills:
to remain. The terror of the earthly is to be taken from him only with
the earthly itself. As long as he lives on earth, he will also remain in
terror of the earthly. And philosophy deceives him about this "shall"
by weaving the blue mist of its idea of the All about the earthly.
For indeed, an All would not die and nothing would die in the All.
Only the singular can die and everything mortal is solitary. Philosophy has to rid the world of what is singular, and this un-doing of the
Aught is also the reason why it has to be idealistic. For idealism, with
its denial of everything that distinguishes the singular from the All, is
the tool of the philosopher's trade. With it, philosophy continues to
work over the recalcitrant material until the latter finally offers no
more resistance to the smoke screen of the one-and-all concept. If
once all were woven into this mist, death would indeed be swallowed
up, if not into the eternal triumph,[2] at least into the one and universal
night of the Nought. And it is the ultimate conclusion of this doctrine
that death is—Nought. But in truth this is no ultimate conclusion, but
a first beginning, and truthfully death is not what it seems, not
Nought, but a something from which there is no appeal, which is not
to be done away with. Its hard summons sounds unbroken even out
of the mist with which philosophy envelops it. Philosophy might well
have swallowed it up into the night of the Nought, but it could not

[1] Translator's addition.
[2] Isaiah 25:8. (Tr.)

tear loose its poisonous sting. And man's terror as he trembles before this sting ever condemns the compassionate lie of philosophy as cruel lying.

The Philosophy of the All

By denying the somber presupposition of all life, that is by not allowing death to count as Aught but turning it into Nought, philosophy creates for itself an apparent freedom from presuppositions. For now the premise of all cognition of the All is—nothing. Before the one and universal cognition of the All the only thing that still counts is the one and universal Nought. Philosophy plugs up its ears before the cry of terrorized humanity. Were it otherwise, it would have to start from the premise, the conscious premise, that the Nought of death is an Aught, that the Nought of every new death is a new Aught, ever newly fearsome, which neither talk nor silence can dispose of. It would need the courage to listen to the cry of mortal terror and not to shut its eyes to gruesome reality. Instead, it will grant precedence over the one and universal cognition only to the one and universal Nought which buries its head in the sand before that cry. The Nought is not Nothing, it is Aught. A thousand deaths stand in the somber background of the world as its inexhaustible premise, a thousand Noughts that are Aught precisely because they are many, instead of the one Nought which really would be nothing. The multiplicity of the Nought which is premised by philosophy, the reality of death which will not be banished from the world and which announced itself in the inextinguishable cry of its victims—these give the lie, even before it has been conceived, to the basic idea of philosophy, the idea of the one and universal cognition of the All. The millennial secret of philosophy which Schopenhauer spilled at its bier, namely that death was supposed to have been its Musaget, loses its power over us. We want no philosophy which joins death's retinue and deceives and diverts us about its enduring sovereignty by the one-and-all music of its dance. We want no deception at all. If death is something, then henceforth no philosophy is to divert our glance from it by the assertion that philosophy presupposes Nothing. Let us, however, look more closely at this assertion.

Was not philosophy itself already all full of presupposition, indeed all presupposition itself, through that presupposition that it presuppose nothing, its "sole" presupposition? Again and again, everything else that was possibly worthy of inquiry was attached to this question. Again and again, the answer to the question was sought in reasoning. It is as if this presupposition of the intelligible All, so magnificent in itself, threw the whole circle of other possible inquiries into the shade. Materialism and idealism, both—and not just the former—"as old as philosophy," have an equal share in this presupposition. One silenced or ignored whatever laid claim to independence in its face. One silenced the voice which claimed possession, in a revelation, of the source of divine knowledge originating beyond reason. Centuries of philosophical labors were devoted to this disputation between knowledge and belief; they reach their goal at the precise moment when the knowledge of the All reaches a conclusion in itself. For one will have to designate it as a conclusion when this knowledge encompasses completely no longer only its object, the All, but also itself, completely at least according to its own requirements and in its own peculiar manner. This happened when Hegel included the history of philosophy in the system. It seems that reason can go no further than to place itself visibly as the innermost fact known to itself, now as part of the system's structure, and of course as the concluding part. And at the precise moment when philosophy exhausts its furthest formal possibilities and reaches the boundary set by its own nature, the great question of the relationship of knowledge and belief which is pressed upon it by the course of world history seems now, as already noted, to be solved.

HEGEL

More than once, it already seemed as if peace were concluded between the two hostile powers, whether on the basis of a clean division of their respective claims, or on the basis of philosophy's supposing that it possessed in its arsenal the keys to unlock the secrets of revelation. In either case, therefore, philosophy allowed revelation to count as truth, inaccessible to it in the one case, confirmed by it in the other. But neither solution ever sufficed for long. The pride of philosophy very soon rose up against the first, unable to bear the thought of acknowledging a locked gate; belief, conversely, was bound to remonstrate against the second solution if it was not to be satisfied with being recognized, quite incidentally, as one truth among others by philosophy. What Hegelian philosophy promised to bring was, however, something entirely different. It asserted neither dichotomy nor mere congruity, but rather an innermost interconnection. The cognitive world becomes cognitive through the same law of reasoning which recurs as the supreme law of existence at the apex of the system. And this law, one and the same in thinking and being, was first annunciated, on the scale of world history, in revelation. Thus philosophy is in a sense no more than fulfilling what was promised in revelation. And again, philosophy carries out this function not merely occasionally or only at the zenith of its orbit; in every moment, so to speak with every breath that it draws, it involuntarily confirms the truth of what revelation has declared. Thus the old quarrel seems settled, heaven and earth reconciled.

KIERKEGAARD

Yet the [Hegelian] solution of the question of belief, as well as the self-fulfillment of knowledge, was more apparent than real—most apparently apparent, it is true, for if that aforementioned presupposition holds and all knowledge is directed toward the All, if it is all included in the All but at the same time omnipotent in it, then indeed that appearance was more than appearance, it was truth. Then anyone still wanting to raise an objection had to find an Archimedean footing, a "place where to stand" outside that cognitive All. A Kierkegaard, and not only he, contested the Hegelian integration of revelation into the All from such an Archimedean fulcrum. That fulcrum was the peculiar consciousness of his own sin and his own redemption on the part of Sören Kierkegaard himself or whatever might happen to be his first and last names. This consciousness neither needed a blending into the cosmos nor admitted of it, for even if everything about it could be translated into universal terms, there remained the being saddled with first and last name, with what was his own in the strictest and narrowest sense of the word. And this "own" was just what mattered, as the bearers of such experience asserted.

THE NEW PHILOSOPHY

At least this was a case of one assertion against another. Philosophy was accused of an incapacity or, more exactly, of an inadequacy which it could not itself admit since it could not recognize it. For if there was here really an object beyond it, then philosophy itself, especially in the conclusive form which it assumed under Hegel, had locked this and every Beyond from its view. The objection disputed its right to a sphere whose existence it had to deny; it did not attack its own sphere. That had to happen in another manner. And it happened in the philosophical period that begins with Schopenhauer, continues via Nietzsche, and whose end has not yet arrived.

SCHOPENHAUER

Schopenhauer was the first of the great thinkers to inquire, not into the essence but into the value of the world. A most unscientific inquiry, if it was really meant to inquire into its value for man, and not into its objective value, its value for some "something," the "sense" or "purpose" of the world, which would after all have been only another way of saying an inquiry into its essence. Perhaps it was even meant to inquire into its value for the man Arthur Schopenhauer. And so in fact it was meant. Consciously, it is true, he inquired only into its value for man, and even this inquiry was deprived of its poisonous fangs by ultimately finding its solution after all in a system of the world. System of course already implies in itself independent universal applicability. And so the inquiry of presystematic man found its answer in the saint of the concluding part produced by the system. Thus a human type and not a concept closed the arch of the system, really closing it as a keystone; it did not simply supplement it as an ethical decoration or curlicue. Even this was already something unheard of in philosophy. And above all, the enormous effect can be explained only by the fact that one sensed—and this really was the case—that here a man stood at the beginning of the system. This man no longer philosophized in the context of, and so to say as if commissioned by, the history of philosophy, nor as heir to whatever might be the current status of its problems, but "had taken it upon himself to reflect on life" because it—life—"is a precarious matter." This proud dictum of the youth in conversation with Goethe—it is significant that he said "life" and not "world"—is complemented by the letter in which he offered the completed work to the publisher. There he declares the content of philosophy to be the idea with which an individual mind reacts to the impression which the world has made on him. "An individual mind"—it was then after all the man Arthur Schopenhauer who here assumed the place which, according to the prevailing conception of philosophizing, should have been assumed by the problem. Man, "life," had become the problem, and he had "taken it upon himself" to solve it in the form of a philosophy. Therefore the value of the world for man had now to be questioned—a most unscientific inquiry, as already indicated, but so much the more a human one. All philosophical interest had hitherto turned about the cognitive All; even man had been admitted as an object of philosophy only in his relationship to this All. Now something else, the living man, independently took a stand opposite this cognitive world, and opposite totality there stood the singular, the "unique and his own," mocking every All and universality. This novum was then thrust irretrievably into the riverbed of the development of conscious spirit, not in the book so headed, which in the last analysis was only that— a book—but in the tragedy of Nietzsche's life itself.

NIETZSCHE

For only here was it really something new. Poets had always dealt with life and their own souls. But not philosophers. And saints had always lived life and for their own soul. But again—not the philosophers. Here, however, was one man who knew his own life and his own soul like a poet, and obeyed their voice like a holy man, and who was for all that a philosopher. What he philosophized has by now become almost a matter of indifference. Dionysiac and Superman, Blond Beast and Eternal Return—where are they now? But none of those who now feel the urge to philosophize can any longer by-pass the man himself, who transformed himself in the transformation of his mental images, whose soul feared no height, who clambered after Mind, that daredevil climber, up to the steep pinnacle of madness, where there was no more Onward. The fearsome and challenging image of the unconditional vassalage of soul to mind could henceforth not be eradicated. For the great thinkers of the past, the soul had been allowed to play the role of, say, wet nurse, or at any rate of tutor of Mind. But one day the pupil grew up and went his own way, enjoying his freedom and unlimited prospects. He recalled the four narrow walls in which he had grown up only with horror. Thus mind enjoyed precisely its being free of the soulful dullness in which nonmind spends its days. For the philosopher, philosophy was the cool height to which he had escaped from the mists of the plain. For Nietzsche this dichotomy between height and plain did not exist in his own self: he was of a piece, soul and mind a unity, man and thinker a unity to the last.

Man

Thus man became a power over philosophy—not man in general over philosophy in general, but one man, one very specific man over his own philosophy. The philosopher ceased to be a negligible quantity for his philosophy. Philosophy had promised to give him compensation in the form of mind in return for selling it his soul, and he no longer took this compensation seriously. Man as philosophizer had become master of philosophy—not as translated into mental terms, but as endowed with a soul, whose mind seemed to him only the frozen breath of his living soul. Philosophy had to acknowledge him, acknowledge him as something which it could not comprehend but which, because powerful over against it, it could not deny. Man in the utter singularity of his individuality, in his prosopographically determined being, stepped out of the world which knew itself as the conceivable world, out of the All of philosophy.

METAETHICS

Philosophy had intended to grasp man, even man as a "personality," in ethics. But that was an impossible endeavor. For if and as it grasped him, he was bound to dissolve in its grasp. In principle ethics might assign to action a special status as against all being; no matter: in practice it drew action, of necessity as it were, back into the orbit of the cognitive All. Every ethics ultimately reconverged with a doctrine of the community as a unit of being. Merely to distinguish the special nature of action, as against being, offered, apparently, insufficient guarantee against this convergence. One should have taken one more step backward and anchored action in the foundation of a "character" which, for all it partook of being, was nevertheless separated from all being. Only thus could one have secured action as a world to itself as against the world. But with the single exception of Kant, that never happened. And even in Kant's case the concept of the All again carried off the victory over the individual through his formulation of the law of morality as the universally valid act. With a certain historically logical consistency, the "miracle *in* the phenomenal world"—as he felicitously designated the concept of freedom—sank back into the miracle *of* freedom—sank back into the miracle of the phenomenal world with the post-Kantians. Kant himself serves as godfather to Hegel's concept of universal history, not only with his political philosophy and his philosophy of history, but already with his ethical fundamentals. And while Schopenhauer incorporated Kant's doctrine of intelligible character into his doctrine of the will, he debased the value of the former doctrine, and that in the opposite direction from the great Idealists. He made will the essence of the world and thereby let the world dissolve in will, if not will in the world. Thus he anni-

hilated the distinction so alive in himself, between the being of man
and the being of the world.

The new world which Nietzsche unlocked to reason thus had to
lie beyond the orbit described by ethics. One must acknowledge the
otherworldliness of the new inquiry as against everything which the
concept of ethics hitherto solely meant and solely was meant to mean,
the more so if one wants the spiritual achievement of the past to count
for everything which it accomplished rather than to destroy it in a
riot of blind destructiveness. A way of looking at life (*Lebensan-
schauung*) confronts a way of looking at the world (*Weltanschauung*). Ethics is and remains a part of the *Weltanschauung*. Its
special relationship with a life-focused point of view is only that of a
particularly intimate contradiction, just because both seem to touch
each other, indeed repeatedly claim mutually to solve the problems
of the other together with their own. It remains to be shown in what
sense this is actually the case. But the contrast of the life-centered and
the world-centered points of view comes down so sharply to a contrast with the ethical portion of the world-centered view that one is
inclined to designate questions of the life view as veritably metaethical.

The World

Personal life, personality, individuality—all these are concepts loaded
with the uses to which the philosophy of the world-centered point of
view has put them, and thus cannot be simply employed as is. What is,
however, more or less clearly so labeled, in other words the "metaethical" questions, cannot thus step out of the realm of the knowledge
of the world without leaving some traces in that knowledge. With
this establishment of an—as it were—indigestible actuality outside of
the great intellectually mastered factual wealth of the cognitive world,
a basic concept, nay the basic concept, of this world is dethroned.
It claimed to be the All; "all" is the subject of the first sentence spoken
at its birth. Now a self-contained unity rebelled against this totality
which encloses the All as a unity, and extorted its withdrawal as a
singularity, as the singular life of the singular person. The All can thus
no longer claim to be all: it has forfeited its uniqueness.

On what, then, does this totality rest? Why was the world not
interpreted, say, as a multiplicity? Why just as a totality? Apparently we have here again a presupposition, and again that afore-

mentioned one: the conceivableness of the world. It is the unity of reasoning which here insists on its right over against the multiplicity of knowledge by asserting the totality of the world. The unity of the logos establishes the unity of the world-as-totality. And the former unity proves in its turn the extent of its truthfulness by establishing the latter totality. Thus a successful resistance against the totality of the world implies at the same time a denial of the unity of reasoning. In "All is water," that first sentence of philosophy, there already lurks the presupposition of the possibility of conceiving the world, even if it remained for Parmenides to expressly identify being and reasoning. For it is not self-evident that one can ask "what is all?" with the prospect of an unambiguous answer. One cannot ask "what is much?" and expect an unambiguous answer. But the subject all is assured in advance of an unambiguous predicate. He who denies the totality of being, as we do, thus denies the unity of reasoning. He throws down the gauntlet to the whole honorable company of philosophers from Ionia to Jena.

This our times have done. True, one has always realized the "contingency of the world," its state of "that's the way it is." But the point is that this contingency had to be mastered. In fact this was precisely the function of philosophy. In the process of being thought about, the contingent changes itself into something necessary. This rational tendency attained its final conclusion in German Idealism, and again it was only thereafter that an opposite tendency emerged with Schopenhauer and the later philosophy of Schelling. "Will," "freedom," "unconscious," were able to hold sway over an accidental world as intellect had not been able to. Thus certain medieval tendencies, which asserted the "*contingentia mundi*" in order to secure the irresponsible caprice of the Creator, seemed to be reviving again. But precisely this historical memory leads us to question this conception. It fails to explain just that which calls for explanation: how the world can be contingent when it is supposed to be conceived as necessary. There is, to put it very crudely, a nonidentity of being and reasoning which has to show itself in being and reasoning themselves. It cannot be harmonized by a third party, will, stepping in as a *deus ex machina* which is neither being nor reasoning. And if the basis for the unity of being and reasoning is sought in reasoning, then the basis for their nonidentity should in the first instance be uncovered in reasoning.

METALOGIC

The reflection in which this happens takes approximately this course: granted that reasoning is the one and universal form of being, still reasoning has a content of its own, a specificity, which is nonetheless specific for being purely reasoned. It is precisely this "specification" of reasoning, this its ramification, which gives it the strength to identify itself with being, which likewise is ramified. Thus the identity of reasoning and being presupposes an inner nonidentity. Though reasoning refers throughout to being, it is at the same time a diversity in itself because it also, at the same time, refers to itself. Thus reasoning, itself the unity of its own inner multiplicity, in addition establishes the unity of being, and that insofar as it is multiplicity, not unity. And therewith the unity of reasoning, as concerned directly only with reasoning, not with being, is excluded from the cosmos of being-reasoning. With its intertwining of the two multiplicities, this cosmos itself thus has now a unity entirely beyond itself. In itself it is not a unity, but a multiplicity, no all-encompassing All, but an enclosed unicum, which may be infinite in itself but not completed. Thus, if one may say so, an excluding All. The relationship into which the unity of reasoning and the unity of reasoning and being thus enter could perhaps be compared with a wall on which a painting hangs. Indeed, the comparison is enlightening in several respects. Let us consider it more closely.

That wall, which otherwise is empty, symbolizes fairly well what remains of reasoning if one detaches its world-centered multiplicity: by no means a Nought, but still something quite empty, the naked unity. It would be impossible to hang the picture but for the wall, yet the wall has not the slightest connection with the picture itself. It would have no objection if other pictures were to hang on it in addition to the one picture, or another picture in its place. According to the notion prevailing from Parmenides to Hegel, the wall was in a certain sense painted alfresco, and wall and picture therefore constituted a unity. But now the wall is inwardly a unity, inwardly the picture is infinite multiplicity, outwardly it is exclusive totality. This, however, means not unity but unicum—"one" picture.

Now the old concept of logic no longer rests on anything but that unity, which knows nothing and acknowledges nothing outside of itself. It is too early to say where that unity belongs. At any rate that unity is not inside but outside the walls of the world, just because and insofar as it is the world "from Parmenides to Hegel." Reason is entitled to a home in the world, but the world is just that: a home; it is not totality. For its part, reason does not want to forget its nobler origin, which it knows without being able to trace it definitely in all its details. Indeed it may not forget it, even for the world's sake, for in the world its achievements on behalf of Being rest on the strength of that nobler origin. Thus the world is a beyond as against what is intrinsically logical, as against unity. The world is not alogical; on the contrary, logic is an essential component of the world, rather literally, as we shall see, its "essential" component. It is not alogical, but, to use the term coined by Ehrenberg, metalogical.

What this implies will become clearer, as far as this is at all possible and desirable in these preparatory remarks, if we cast a comparative glance backward at what, in connection with the concept of man, we called metaethics. Metaethical, too, was of course not intended to mean anethical. It was not meant to express absence of ethos but solely its unaccustomed placement, that is to say that passive position instead of the imperative one to which it was otherwise accustomed. The law is given to man, not man to the law. This proposition is demanded by the new concept of man. It runs counter to the concept of law as it appears in the realm of the world as ethical reasoning and ethical order. Accordingly this concept of man has to be characterized as metaethical. Now a similar relationship is also involved in the new concept of the world. Again it is not the intention to characterize the world as alogical. On the contrary: we absolutely maintain the position which, ever since the Ionians, has been reason's due in any philosophy worthy of the name. (Schelling dismissed Madame de Staël with a "*je méprise* Locke" when she played it English for him.) But in reasoning itself, insofar as it refers to the world, we discover a character which transforms it from the presumed to the actual form of the world, namely specification or, one might even say, contingency. Thus reasoning becomes—we have not hesitated to use the crude expression—a "component" of the world, specifically its essential component, just as we previously recognized ethos as the essential component of man. As long as one felt compelled of necessity to incorporate also and especially the unity of logic into the world, the conception of logic as form, law, validity had rested on it. We no longer regard this unity as anything but determining for logic, and not "logically" determining at that. To be sure, we here leave open the question of where this logic, commensurate with its own concept, may come to rest, in contrast to the previous case of ethics for which it was easy to fix a place proper to its concept because of the historical fulfillment of the philosophy of the world. Only that the world, the conceivable world, is metalogical precisely in its conceivability, this follows with certainty from this stepping out of it by what is logical on the one hand and the integration in it of what is logical on the other hand. For the world, truth is not law but content. It is not that truth validates [*bewährt*] reality, but reality preserves [*bewahrt*] truth.

The essence of the world is this preservation (not validation) of truth. "Outwardly" the world thus lacks the protection which truth had accorded to the All from Parmenides to Hegel. Since it shelters its truth in its lap, it does not present such a Gorgon's shield of untouchability to the outside. It has to expose its body to whatever may have happened to it, even if that should be its—creation. Yes, we might well grasp the concept of the world in this new metalogic sense rather completely if we would venture to address the world as a creature.

God

Unity had withdrawn from the All. On the analogy of the work of art, it was a single unicum outwardly, and no longer total except inwardly. Thus some room was left by its side. Logic and ethics had once, it seemed, been locked in ceaseless combat for pre-eminence: metalogic, however, left room beside itself for metaethics. The world as a multiplicity united into an individual unicum and man, by nature an individual unicum, now confronted each other and they could breathe side by side. This met the demand which we previously had to put in the interest of metaethics. The painting had been able to express its unconcern in the event that, say, a relief, too, should yet be hung on the same wall. A fresco could not have tolerated this, but the painting concerned itself about nothing outside of the four sides of its frame. But this mutual compatibility of picture and relief is purchased at a price—the painting's cool equanimity toward the wall without which it would, after all, not have taken place. The metalogical could be tolerant toward the metaethical only because it had previously shown the door to the logical. This, moreover, left the logical initially in a worse position than the ethical was with respect to the metaethical. For whereas the ethical knew at once where it had to seek shelter, the logical was initially without house or home. The world had relieved it of its duties insofar as it did not adapt to the world, that is, insofar as it claimed to be something "absolute," utter unity. The world had become utterly unabsolute. Not only man, nay even God, could find a place outside its limits if he was otherwise so inclined. But this metalogical world offered no protection against God, precisely because it was godless. From Parmenides to Hegel, the cosmos had been *securus adversus deos*. It was "secure against gods" because it itself encompassed the absolute. Again Thales had already said as much in the other traditional saying of his about the "All" to the effect that it was full of gods. The post-Hegelian cosmos did not enjoy this security. The creatureliness which we had claimed for the world in order to salvage the self-ness of man thereby allows God, too, to withdraw from the world. Metaethical man is the leaven which causes the logico-physical unity of the cosmos to fall apart into the metalogical world and the metaphysical God.

METAPHYSICS

There has long been a science of God called metaphysics. Indeed our two concepts of metalogic and metaethics are formed according to the meaning which the term metaphysics has assumed in the course of history. Accordingly we have to fear confusion with age-old philo-sophical concepts even more than before, and we are still harder put to avoid it already in this necessarily only allusive introduction. In discussing the metaethical self it was difficult to avoid confusing it with the moral personality. By way of analogy we had pointed to the lyric poet and the saint; we might have alluded likewise, say, to Richard III with his "Withal, what I have been, and what I am," in order to make evident that a complete liberation from the order of a moral realm of purposes is intended here. But that was done, as we are well aware, at the risk of unclarity and even the suspicion of philosophical dilettantism. It could not be avoided, not even by the attempt to disclose the threads between our concept and the post-Hegelian revolution in philosophy. That the metalogical concept of the world succumbed to, say, confusion with the concept of nature was equally unavoidable; indeed, the threat of this second confusion was an almost inevitable consequence of that first one. For if meta-ethical man, in spite of that designation, could be equated with the moral personality, then there remained for the metalogical cosmos only the equation with the critical concept of nature. Here, too, we had to turn to the questionable tool of analogy, questionable here, too, because here we were as yet unable to clarify the deeper truth of the analogy, its being more-than-analogy. We alluded allegorically to the inner self-containedness and totality and, for all that, outer singu-larity of the work of art. In the allegory of the wall on which the painting hangs, we also alluded to the external inadequacy of the work of art as it emerges everywhere—in the necessity of performance or publication or, in the final analysis, in the necessity of the observer, for a full existence of the work. Finally we ventured the allusion to the theological concept of the creature, an especially dangerous allusion because it anticipates at such a distance. We sought by all these allusions to distinguish our concept of the world from the critical concept of nature. Of the two, ours is by far the more comprehensive, for it encompasses on principle all the possible contents of a philosophical system, provided only they meet one condition: they are to appear as elements not of "the" but only of "an" All. These difficulties confront us now anew, and reinforced, as we turn to the metaphysical concept of God.

Metaphysical—not aphysical. All acosmism, whether Indian negation of the world or its Spinozist-Idealistic suspension, is nothing but a kind of pantheism in reverse. And it was precisely the pantheistic concept of the All which we had to abolish in order only so much as to catch sight of our metaphysical concept of God. The metaethical in man makes man the free master of his ethos so that he might possess it and not vice versa. The metalogical in the world makes the logos a "component" of the world entirely emptied into the world, so that it might possess the logos and not vice versa. Just so the metaphysical in God makes physis a "component" of God. God has a nature of his own, quite apart from the relationship into which he enters, say, with the physical "world" outside himself. God has his nature, his naturalistic, existential essence. This is so far from going without saying that, on the contrary, philosophy up to and including Hegel always disputed this existence-of-his-own with him. The ontological proof of the existence of God—another idea as old as philosophy—is nothing but the sublimest form of this dispute. Whenever theologians annoyed philosophers with their insistence on the existence of God, the latter withdrew to the side track of this "proof." Philosophy fed theology on the identity of reasoning and being as a nurse might prop a pacifier into the mouth of a babe to keep him from crying. With Kant and Hegel this centuries-old deception reaches a twofold terminus, with Kant because he criticizes the proof to death with his sharp distinction of being and existence, while Hegel, who praises the proof, deals it a deathblow in the eyes of theology by the very naïveté of his praise, although, philosopher that he is, he does not realize this. For he thinks that the proof coincides with the basic concept of the philosophic view of the world in general, with the idea of the identity of reason and reality, and that it therefore must be as valid for God as for everything else. Thus the way is clear for the establishment of divine existence independently of the intellection of the All and its being. God must have existence prior to any identity of being and reasoning. If any derivation is involved here, it were better the derivation of being from existence than the repeated attempt of the ontological proofs to derive existence from being. With such observations we are moving along the lines of the later philosophy of Schelling.

As long as God does not encompass his nature in himself, he is in the final analysis defenseless against nature's claims to encompass him in itself. It is only the natural element within God which provides him with a true independence against everything natural outside himself. But this natural element in God does not quite complete the description of the content of the metaphysical concept of God. That God has a nature—his nature—does not exhaust the metaphysical concept of God any more than it exhausts the metaethical concept of man to say that he has his own ethos, or the metalogical concept of the world to say that it has its own logos. What first makes man fully man is his assumption of this, his ethical inheritance and "gifts," be that assumption defiant, humble, or matter-of-fact. What first makes the world a creaturely world is not its intelligibility through the world's own logos but only the fullness and ramifications and ceaselessness of its configurations. In the same way, God becomes alive not simply by virtue of having his nature, but only when it is augmented by that divine freedom which we obscure almost more than we illuminate it with terms like Dante's "there where one can what one wills" or Goethe's accomplishment of the indescribable. God's vitality realizes itself only as it is augmented by this something as the actually divine. We may follow in Nietzsche's tracks for God's "freedom" as we pointed to Schelling for God's "nature."

The history of philosophy had not yet beheld an atheism like Nietzsche's. Nietzsche may not negate God, but he is the first thinker who, in the theological sense of the word, very definitely "denies" him or who, more precisely still, curses him. For that famous proposition: "If God existed, how could I bear not to be God?" is as mighty a curse as the curse with which Kierkegaard's experience of God began. Never before had a philosopher thus stood, as it were, eye to eye before the living God. The first real human being among the philosophers was also the first who beheld God face to face—even if it was only in order to deny him. For that proposition is the first philosophical denial of God in which God is not indissolubly tied to the world. To the world Nietzsche could not have said, "If it existed, how could I bear not to be it?" The living God appears to the living man. It is with a consuming hatred that the defiant self views divine freedom, devoid of all defiance, which drives him to denial because he has to regard it as license—for how could he otherwise bear not to be God? God's freedom, not his being, drives him to this self-assertion;

he could laugh off God's being even if he believed in it. Thus the metaethical, like the metalogical before it, disposes of the metaphysical within itself and precisely thereby renders it visible as divine "personality," as unity, and not like the human personality as unicum.

Mathematics and Symbols

But enough of preparatory remarks. One could enlarge on the historical as well as the conceptual connections without accomplishing more than—preparation. We recognized the presuppositional nature of the idea that reasoning had as its function to reason the All. Thereby the hitherto fundamentally simple content of philosophy, the All of reasoning and being, unintentionally split up for us into three discrete pieces which repelled each other in different but as yet not clearly apprehensible fashion. These three pieces are God, world, and man. As much as we have spoken of them, freely relying on the general consciousness of the present time, we know nothing of them in a strict sense. They are the Noughts to which the critique of Kant, the dialectian, reduced the objects of rational theology, cosmology, and psychology, the three "rational sciences" of his time. We mean to restore them, not as objects of rational science but, quite the contrary, as "irrational" objects. The method indicated by the prefix "meta" served us as a means for first staking out its loci, to wit, the orientation by the rational object from which the required irrational object propels itself in order to achieve its irrational being. In the case of man, this implies orientation by man as object of ethics; in the case of the world, by the world as object of logic; in the case of God, by God as the object of physics. This really could be no more than the means for a preliminary outlining. The disclosure of the areas thus staked out has to occur by other means. Our voyage of exploration advances from the Noughts of knowledge to the Aught of knowledge. We have not come very far when we reach the Aught, but at least Aught is more than Nought. From the point where we now find ourselves, we cannot even begin to fathom what may lie beyond the Aught.

That bare being, being prior to reasoning, is equivalent to the Nought in the brief, hardly apprehensible moment before it becomes being for reasoning, this, too, belongs to the insights that have accompanied the whole history of philosophy from its first beginnings in Ionia until its denouement with Hegel. This Nought remained quite as sterile as pure being. Philosophy started only when reasoning wedded itself to being. But it is precisely to philosophy, and precisely at this point, that we deny our allegiance. We seek what is everlasting, what does not first require reasoning in order to be. This is why we were not entitled to deny death, and this is why we have to admit the Nought wherever and however we may encounter it, and make it the everlasting starting point of the everlasting. "The" Nought cannot imply for us, as it did for the great heir to two millennia of the history of philosophy, unveiling of the essence of pure being. Rather it is necessary to presuppose a Nought, its Nought, wherever an existing element of the All rests in itself, indissoluble and everlasting. There is, however, a science which offers itself as guide for such a progression from a Nought to an Aught. This science, itself nothing but a continuous derivation of an Aught—and never more than some one Aught, any Aught—from the Nought and never from the empty universal Nought that belongs peculiarly to precisely this Aught, this science is mathematics.

ORIGINS

Plato already discovered that mathematics does not lead beyond the Aught and the any; it does not touch the real itself, the chaos of the This. At most it touches upon it. To this discovery, mathematics owes the respect which philosophers have accorded it ever since—or else, at times, their disdain, depending on whether the "universal" was in honor or in disgrace in the prevailing spirit of the times. This thus-far-and-no-further was already ordained for mathematics at its birth, but that it was not recognized until after that bimillennial movement had run its full course is no accident. Hermann Cohen, contrary to his own conception of himself and contrary to the impression his works make, was something quite different from a mere epigone to this movement, which had truly run its course. And it remained for him to discover in mathematics an organum of reasoning, just because it creates its elements out of the definite Nought of the differential, each time assigned to that required Element, not out of the empty Nought of the one and universal Zero. The differential combines in itself the characteristics of the Nought and the Aught. It is a Nought which points to an Aught, its Aught; at the same time it is an Aught that still slumbers in the lap of the Nought. It is on the one hand the dimension as this loses itself in the immeasurable, and then again it borrows, as the "infinitesimal," all the characteristics of finite magnitude with the sole exception of finite magnitude itself. Thus it draws

its power to establish reality on the one hand from the forcible negation with which it breaks the lap of the Nought, and on the other
hand equally from the calm affirmation of whatever borders on the
Nought to which, as itself infinitesimal, it still and all remains attached. Thus it opens two paths from the Nought to the Aught—
the path of the affirmation of what is not Nought, and the path of the
negation of the Nought. Mathematics is the guide for the sake of these
two paths. It teaches us to recognize the origin of the Aught in the
Nought. Thus even if Cohen, the master, would be far from admitting
it, we are continuing to build on the great scientific achievement of his
logic of origins, the new concept of the Nought. For the rest he may
have been, in the execution of his ideas, more of a Hegelian than he
admitted—and thereby as much of an "Idealist" as he claimed to be.
Here, however, in this basic idea, he broke decisively with the idealistic tradition. He replaced the one and universal Nought, that veritable "no-thing" which, like a zero, really can be nothing more than
"nothing," with the particular Nought which burst fruitfully onto
reality. There he took his stand in most decided opposition precisely
to Hegel's founding of logic on the concept of Being, and thereby in
turn to the whole philosophy into whose inheritance Hegel had come.
For here for the first time a philosopher who himself still considered
himself an "Idealist" (one more indication of the force of what happened to him) recognized and acknowledged that what confronted
reasoning when it set out in order "purely to create" was not Being
but—Nought.

For the first time—even if it remains true that here too, as everywhere, Kant, alone among all the thinkers of the past, showed the
way which we are now to follow, and showed it, as always, in those
comments to which he gave utterance without drawing their systematic
consequences. For he undermined those three "rational" sciences with
which he was confronted without himself by any means returning from
this undermining to a one-and-universal despair over cognition. Rather
he ventured on the great step—albeit hesitantly—and formulated the
Nought of knowledge as no longer uniform but triform. At the very
least, two discrete Noughts of knowledge are designated by the thing-
in-itself, the *Ding an sich* and the "intelligible character," the metalogical and the metaethical in our terminology. And the dark terms
in which he occasionally speaks of the mysterious "root" of both are
presumably attempts to grope for a fixed point for the metaphysical
Nought of knowledge too. Our reasoning did not see itself henceforth hurled back upon a one-and-universal *non liquet* when once a
totality had been presented to it as its one and universal object. The

Nought of our knowledge is not a simple but a triple Nought. Thereby it contains within itself the promise of definability. And the totality that we had to dismember we can therefore hope to recover, like Faust, in this Nought, this triple Nought of knowledge. "Be drownéd then! Or I might say: Arise!"

BOOK ONE

God and His Being

or

Metaphysics

Negative Theology

Of God we know nothing. But this ignorance is ignorance of God. As such it is the beginning of our knowledge of him—the beginning and not the end. Ignorance as the end result of our knowledge was the basic idea of "negative theology." This theology dismembered and abolished the existing assertions about God's "attributes," until the negative of all these attributes remained behind as God's essence. Thus God could be defined only in his complete indefifinability. This path leads from an existing Aught to Nought; at its end atheism and mysticism can shake hands. We do not take this path, but rather the opposite one from Nought to Aught. Our goal is not a negative concept, but on the contrary a highly positive one. We seek God, and will presently seek the world and man, precisely not within a one and universal total, as one concept among many. If that were our object, then indeed the negative theology of Nicholas of Cusa or of the sage of Koenigsberg would be the only scientific goal, for then the negative would already be established as the goal at the starting point of reasoning. One concept among many is always negative, at least vis-à-vis the others. And if it lays claim to unconditional validity, then science can only serve it with unconditional—nothingness! But precisely that presupposition of the one and universal All we have given up. We seek God, and will presently seek world and man, not as one concept among many, but rather for itself, dependent on itself alone, in its absolute actuality (if the expression is not subject to misunderstanding); in other words, precisely in its "positiveness." It is

23

for this reason that we must place the Nought of the sought-for concept at the beginning, must put it behind us. For in front of us there
lies as goal an Aught: the reality of God.

THE TWO WAYS

God is therefore initially a Nought for us, his Nought. Two paths
lead from the Nought to the Aught—or, more precisely from the
Nought to what is not Nought, for we seek no Aught—the path of
affirmation and the path of negation. The affirmation is the affirmation
of the *demonstrandum*, the non-Nought; the negation is the negation
of the given, the Nought. These two ways are as different from each
other, as opposite as—well, as Yea and Nay. Their end points, too,
are by no means identical with the one above designated as the
demonstrandum. Rather they differ from one another—again as Yea
from Nay. The Yea applies to the non-Nought, the Nay to the
Nought. Like every affirmation through negation, affirmation of the
non-Nought points to something infinite; negation of the Nought,
like every negation, points to something limited, finite, definite. Accordingly, we behold the Aught in twofold guise and in twofold
relationship to the Nought: once as its neighbor and once as its runaway. As neighbor of the Nought, the Aught is the whole fullness of
all that "is" not Nought. In God, therefore—for apart from him we
know of nothing here—it is the whole fullness of what "is" in him.
As a runaway who just now has broken out of the prison of the
Nought, on the other hand, the Aught is nothing more than the event
of this liberation from the Nought. It is entirely defined by this its one
experience; in God, therefore, to whom nothing can happen from
without (at least here), it is wholly and solely: action. Thus essence
issues forth from Nought without ceasing, while action breaks loose
from it in sharp delimitation. One inquires after origins in the case of
essence; after beginnings in the case of action.

METHODOLOGY

We have good reason not to go beyond these purely formal defini-
tions here for the time being; we do not wish to anticipate. What has
been said, however, will already become a little clearer if we regard,
solely for purposes of comparison, the opposite process, that of becoming Nought. Here, too, two possibilities are given; the negation
of the something—or, to replace this loaded expression with one

today less narrowly defined—the negation of the Aught and the affirmation of the non-Aught, the Nought. The reversal is so exact that the Nay appears on the outbound path where the Yea appeared before, and vice versa. For the emergence of the Nought through the negation of the Aught, German has an expression which we have only to free from its narrower connotations in order to be able to employ it here: *Verwesung* [decomposition, literally destruction of the essence] designates negation of the Aught, just like the mystical term *Entwesung* [sublimation; literally removal of the essence]. For the affirmation of the Nought, however, language uses the term annihilation [*Vernichtung*]. In decomposition, in sublimation, the Nought originates in its infinite indefiniteness; neither the decomposing body nor the disintegrating soul strives for the Nought as something positive but solely for dissolution of their positive essence, which is no sooner accomplished than they empty into the amorphous night of the Nought. Mephistopheles, on the other hand, who veritably wills evil and who loves the ever-void, craves the Nought, and so the whole is bound to come down to—"annihilation." Here, then, we behold the Nought, if not itself as something complex—for then it would be something definite and not Nought—yet as something accessible by several (different) paths and in opposite directions. And now perhaps we can better understand how different origins of the definite can exist in the undefined Nought, how the quiet stream of life can spring from the same darkly stagnant water as the gushing geyser of action.

Mark you, we are not speaking of a Nought in general, like the former philosophy which acknowledged only the All as its object. We know of no one and universal Nought, because we have divested ourselves of the presupposition of a one and universal All. We know only the individual Nought of the individual problem, a Nought which is therefore however not by any means defined, but only productive of definition. In our case this is the Nought of God. God is here our problem, our sub-ject and ob-ject. By beginning with his Nought we express just this, that he is to be for us initially nothing more than a problem. Thus we make of the Nought his presupposition and not perchance, as already noted at the beginning, the solution. We say as it were: if God exists, then the following is true of his Nought. By thus presupposing only that the Nought is the Nought of God, we are not led beyond the frame of this object by the consequences of this presupposition. To think that we have derived essence and action in general, say the essence of the world or the action directed to the world of man, in the welling forth of "essence" or the bursting forth of "action" would thus be quite wrong; it would be a relapse into the surmounted concept of the one and universal Nought. As long as we move within this hypothesizing limit of the Nought, all concepts remain within this limit; they remain under the law of If and Then without being able to step out of the magic circle. Essence, for example, can never mean anything but an essence within God; action can never refer to an object thought of as outside God. We do not get beyond pure reflections of God—as presently of the world and then of man—within himself. We have shattered the All: every fragment is now an All in itself. By immersing ourselves in this our fragmentary knowledge, we remain, in our journey into the Realm of the Mothers,[1] slaves to the first command, the command to submerge. The ascent will come later, and with it the fusion of the piecework into the perfection of the new All.

Divine Nature

Yea is the beginning. Nay cannot be the beginning for it could only be a Nay of the Nought. This, however, would presuppose a negatable Nought, a Nay, therefore, that had already decided on a Yea. Therefore Yea is the beginning. Moreover it cannot be the Yea of the Nought, for it is the sense of our introduction of the Nought that it is not to be the result but on the contrary and exclusively the point of departure. It is not even the beginning. At most it is the beginning of our knowledge. The point is, it is really only the point of departure, and therefore simply incapable of being itself affirmed. Admittedly it is equally incapable of being negated, as already stated. It lies equally before Yea and Nay. It would be located before every beginning if it were located. But it is not "located." It is only the virtual locus for the beginning of our knowledge. It is only the marker for the positing of the problem. We are careful to avoid naming it. It is no "somber basis" or anything else that can be named with Ekhart's terms, or Boehme's or Schelling's. It does not exist in the beginning.

In the beginning is the Yea. And since the Yea cannot, as we said, refer to the Nought, it must refer to the non-Nought. This non-Nought is, however, not independently given, for nothing at all is given except for the Nought. Therefore the affirmation of the non-

[1] See below, p. 87, note.

Nought circumscribes as inner limit the infinity of all that is not Nought. An infinity is affirmed: God's infinite essence, his infinite actuality, his Physis.

ARCHETYPAL WORD

Such is the power of the Yea that it adheres everywhere, that it contains unlimited possibilities of reality. It is the arch-word of language, one of those which first make possible, not sentences, but any kind of sentence-forming words at all, words as parts of the sentence. Yea is not a part of a sentence, but neither is it a shorthand symbol for a sentence, although it can be employed as such. Rather it is the silent accompanist of all parts of a sentence, the confirmation, the "sic!" the "Amen" behind every word. It gives every word in the sentence its right to exist, it supplies the seat on which it may take its place, it "posits." The first Yea in God establishes the divine essence for all infinity. And this first Yea is "in the beginning."

SYMBOL

This first Yea implies a step on the road to the perfection of God; we can attempt to capture the step in familiar logico-mathematical symbols. Initially we will confine ourselves to the use of algebraic letters and the equal-sign. In the equation $y=x$, for example, y would designate the subject and the content of the statement, y that is to say, the grammatical subject, and x the predicate. Now ordinarily the affirmative protasis designates the subject, and the negating apodosis the predicate; here, however, where we are dealing with origins, it is just the other way around. The affirmation becomes the criterion of the primeval apodosis. The predicate is in the individual case always something individual, and therefore negative, but the apodosis, according to its original concept, is precisely positive: the pure Then. This "Then" then becomes furthermore a "Thus and not otherwise," a fact that takes effect only when the "other" joins the original unicum. It is only by means of this transition to multiplicity that the apodosis turns into negation. And as the primeval apodosis occurs in the Yea, so the primeval protasis, the supposition of the original subject, occurs in the Nay. Each individual supposition of a subject is in itself merely a groundless position, but the original supposition, lying before everything individual, the presupposition, is negation, negation, that is, of the Nought. Every individual subject is simply "other," other, that is, than the Nought. In the equation which we have to erect here, the Nay will thus come to stand to the left of the equal sign, the Yea to its right. With the simple x or y we symbolize complete unrelatedness; with $y=$ we symbolize the relation of the subject to a predicate, the apodosis with a view to a protasis which is still to be assigned to it, with $=x$ we symbolize the protasis with a view to an apodosis which it still has coming to it. In this symbolic language, we would therefore have to designate God's physis, God's utter and endlessly affirmed being by A—by A and not, say, by B or C—for it is endlessly affirmed; within the sphere peculiar to it and conditioned by its Nought, nothing precedes it that it might have to follow; nothing *can* precede it, since it is posited as infinite and not as finite. It is utter actuality, dormant but infinite. As yet we do not know whether a storm will overtake this quiet ocean of the intra-divine physis and make its floodwaters swell, whether whirlpool and waves will form in its own lap to bring the placid surface into turbulent commotion. For the time being it is "A," unmoved, infinite being.

Divine Freedom

Are we really ignorant as to which of the two possibilities will bring the placid surface into commotion, the storm from without or the whirlpool from within? True, we cannot tell anything from looking at the surface itself. But let us remember how this unmoved essence originated for us in the Yea, and how we just now explained by way of anticipating that the Yea always assumed the right side of the equation $y=x$, the "x" side. Thereby the decision already falls in favor of the former of the two possible sources of motion. The Yea contains nothing which strives beyond the Yea itself; it is the "then." The commotion must therefore come from the Nay.

The Nay is just as original as the Yea. It does not presuppose the Yea. This or that derived Nay may make this presupposition, but the original Nay presupposes nothing but the Nought. It is the Nay of the Nought. Now of course it is true that it bursts forth directly from the Nought, bursts forth, that is, as its negation, and no Yea precedes it; but an affirmation does precede it. In other words: while it presupposes only the Nought, the Nought it presupposes is a Nought from which the Yea had to well forth, not a Nought with which it could have let the matter rest, not the eternal void which Mephistopheles cherishes. It is the Nought which was conceived of only as a Nought of knowledge, as a point of departure for reasoning about

God, as the locus for posing the problem; it was not conceived of as positively posited Nought, nor as a "somber basis," nor as the "abyss of the deity." The original Nay is preceded, though not by the Yea itself, yet by the Nought from which affirmation had to come forth. Thus the Nay, without prejudice to the immediacy of its origin, is "younger" than the Yea. *Non* is not *propter sic* but *post sic.*

Nay is the original negation of Nought. Yea could not have remained attached to Nought because the latter provided it, so to speak, with no point of contact; repelled by Nought, Yea therefore cast itself upon the non-Nought and, thus freed to infinity from its point of departure, it placed the divine essence in the infinite realm of the non-Nought. Nay, however, is intertwined in closest bodily contact with the Nought. This close contact is now possible because the Nought had been left behind as finite through the prior infinite affirmation of the non-Nought. Thus the Nay finds its opponent directly in front of itself here. But the metaphor of a pair of wrestlers is misleading. There is no pair. This is a wrestling match not of two parties but of one: the Nought negates itself. It is only in self-negation that the "other," the "opponent," bursts forth out of it. And at the moment of its bursting forth, the Nay is rescued and liberated from the self-negating intertwining with the Nought. Now it takes shape as free, original Nay.

At this point it is necessary to put the question into precise focus again. We are inquiring into God. The self-negating Nought was the self-negating Nought of God; the Nay born of this self-negation is a Nay of God. The Yea in God was his infinite essence. His free Nay, shooting forth out of the negation of his Nought, is not in itself essence, for it contains no Yea; it is and remains pure Nay. It is not a "thus" but only a "not otherwise." Thus it is always directed toward "otherwise," it is always and only the "one," the "one," that is, as the "one" in God, before which everything else that is in God becomes a mere "other." What is thus utterly "one," this utter Nay to everything that is "other" than itself—what should we call it if not freedom? God's freedom is born of the original negation of the Nought as that which is trained on everything else only *as* something else. God's freedom is intrinsically a mighty Nay.

God's essence, we have seen, was infinite Yea. That Yea left the Nought behind as something emptied of the infinite. The free Nay fought its way in original self-negation out of what had thus become finite. It bears the scars of the struggle during which it burst forth. It is infinite in its possibilities, in what it refers to, for it refers in the last analysis to everything. Everything is "other" for it, but it is itself ever "one," ever limited, ever finite, just as it first burst forth in the self-negation of the Nought-become-finite. It bursts forth into all eternity, for all eternity is merely "other" for it, is merely infinite time for it. Over against what is thus always "other" for it, it is for all time the solitary, the ever new, the ever initial. Divine freedom confronts infinite divine essence as the finite configuration of action, albeit an action whose power is inexhaustible, an action which can ever anew pour itself out into the infinite out of its finite origin: an inexhaustible wellspring, not an infinite ocean. Essence is constituted once and for all "as is"; it confronts the freedom of action, a freedom revealing itself ever anew, but a freedom for which we cannot as yet contemplate any object other than the infinity of that everlasting essence. It is not freedom *of* God, for even now God is still a problem for us. It is divine freedom, freedom *in* God and with reference to God. Even now we know, as yet, nothing about God. We are still engaged in the piecework of knowledge, still at the stage of inquiring, not of answering.

SYMBOL

The piece we have just gained is divine freedom. Let us attempt to capture it in a symbol even as, above, we captured the divine essence. We must place divine freedom, as original Nay, on the left side of the future equation. It is, moreover, a Nay which, as original subject, reaches beyond itself with unlimited power—albeit, as we must repeatedly emphasize, beyond itself only within God. Thus its symbol will have to be formed on the pattern "$y=$." And finally, although this freedom is finite in its ever-renewed uniqueness, it is infinite in its continuous novelty. Nothing can precede it for nothing exists beside it. It is ever unique but never a unicum. Therefore the symbol for this freedom turns out to be "$A=$." Let us now demonstrate how this symbol of divine freedom joins with that of divine essence and how we thereby first arrive at the equation and with it the first answer to the inquiry into God.

Vitality of the God

Freedom points to something infinite. As freedom it is finite; but to the extent that its concern is with an infinite, it is infinite, infinite power or, to put it bluntly, infinite caprice. Only essence is available to it as the infinite object of its craving. But essence, such as it was symbolized by a bare letter without the equal-sign, contains no explicit direction, whether an active or a receptive one, which might strive toward that force. The divine essence maintains the infinite silence of pure existence, of voiceless actuality. It exists. Thus caprice seems able to fall upon essence without being summoned or dragged in. But in approaching essence, caprice nevertheless ends up in the magic circle of its inert being. This being does not emit any force toward caprice, and yet the latter feels its own force ebbing. With every step that takes it closer to essence, the infinite power (of caprice) senses a growing resistance, a resistance which would become infinite at the goal, at essence itself. For here the "It exists" of essence is abroad throughout, its "It is thus" is stretched out inertly and would swallow up the expressions of that power. At the focal point of the infinity of the inert Yea, the infinitely weakened power of the infinitely active Nay would be extinguished. This power is now no longer the original, infinite Nay, but already that Nay on the way to exercising its power on the inert Thus of the Yea. We must therefore capture it short of the end of the movement, that is, before the inertia of Thus-ness can operate as infinite inertia. For at that point the infinite power of the divine act so to speak enters the magnetic field of the divine essence, and while this power is still predominant over the inertia of that essence, it is already constrained by it. We designate this point as the point of divine obligation and fate, in contrast to the point of divine power and caprice. As divine freedom takes shape as caprice and power, so divine essence takes shape as obligation and fate. An infinite movement, starting from freedom, courses over into the realm of essence, and out of it there originates, in infinite spontaneous genera-tion, the divine countenance which shatters broad Olympus with a quiver of its eyebrows, and whose brows are nonetheless furrowed with the knowledge of the saying of the Norns. Both infinite power in the free outpouring of *Pathos* and infinite constraint in the com-pulsion of *Moira*—both together form the vitality of the god.

ARCHETYPAL WORDS

We pause here a moment in order first to comprehend, if retro-actively, the evidently decisive step which we have here taken over and beyond the bare Yea and bare Nay. We took the movement which brought us from Nay to Yea as self-evident; we did not inquire after the archetypal term which, corresponding to the Yea and Nay of the first two steps, guided this third step. The archetypal Yea had been the term of the original supposition; as such it was the silent partner of the activities which each word carries on in the proposition as a whole. The archetypal Nay likewise is active in every word of the proposition, not however, to the extent that this term is a statement, but insofar as it is the subject of statements; thus its very own place in the sentence, as already demonstrated, is with the subject. As "Thus," the Yea confirms the individual word, that is, it assures it of an enduring "firm" value, independent of the relation which it assumes in regard to the other words within the sentence; the Nay, on the other hand, concerns itself precisely with this relation of the word to the sentence. As "not-otherwise" it "locates" this "locus" of the individual word, a locus which firmly fixes the peculiarity of each word over against the "others"—not its "firm" peculiarity but one dependent on the sentence as a whole, on the "other" components of the sentence. Let us take as an example initially two extreme cases, to wit, for the Yea, the statement nothing-but, the predicate adjective, and for the Nay the nothing-but subject of a statement, the subject noun. The word "free" has a specific sense regardless of whether it occurs in the sentence "man is created free, is free" or in the other sentence "man is not created to be free." This motionless sense is the work of the secret Yea. On the other hand the word "man" is something quite different in the statement that he is a citizen of two worlds and when he is called a political animal. This diversity, created each time by the other members of the sentence which the one subject confronts, is the work of the secret Nay. And now as a concluding example, one that is anything but extreme: the word "until" always means the conclusion of a successively envisioned quantity. But in "until tomorrow" it refers to a stretch of time, a stretch of time in the future, while in "distant until the stars" it refers to a stretch of space. Incidentally, it might easily seem as though the "secret Yea" therefore had to precede the "secret Nay" in reality and not merely in conceptual sequence (as a possibility or affirmation), as though the "secret Nay" were therefore less original. But this impression is dispelled by the simple consideration that those hard-and-fast meanings of the words are in reality only derived from their context in the sentence. Accordingly this "fixity" does not really exist in the individual case; on the contrary, every new sentence context into which a word enters transforms the "constant" character of the word. Language, therefore, constantly renews itself in living speech.

We have just been speaking, quite ingenuously, of sentence and context. Actually, however, Yea and Nay never prepare more than the individual word, albeit in the case of Nay, already in its relationship to the sentence. The sentence itself first comes into being, first originates by virtue of the fact that the remarking, establishing Nay seeks to gain power over the confirming Yea.[1] The sentence presupposes Yea and Nay, Thus and not-otherwise, and so does the smallest part of the sentence: the word in isolating languages, the combination of two words in agglutinative languages, the combination of stem and inflectional affix into one word in inflectional languages. Therewith we have the third of those archetypal words which, though not the equal of the other two in originality, for it presupposes both, yet for the first time helps both to a vital reality: the word "and." "And" is the secret companion not of the individual word but of the verbal context. It is the keystone of the arch of the substructure over which the edifice of the *logos* of linguistic sense is erected. We came to know a first test of strength of this third archetypal word in the aforementioned answer to the inquiry into God which we had posed when we determined the Nought of our knowledge of God.

SYMBOL

The equation symbolizes what is, at least for the present, conclusive in this answer, the equation in which the paths leading to the answer have become invisible. By looking at the equation $A=A$, one can no longer tell whether it is constructed from A, $A=$, $=A$, or A. One can recognize no more in it than the pure originality and self-satisfaction of the god. He is dependent on nothing outside of himself, and appears to require nothing outside of himself:

> God ethereal reigneth free,
> But his mighty appetites
> Nature's law doth hold in check

— the law of his own nature. The interplay of forces which produced this vital figure of a god is submerged. Just for that reason, the equation symbolizes the immediate vitality of this figure, the vitality of the god.

The Olympus of Mythology

Of the god—for the time being. For the gods of antiquity are vital too, not only him whom we today designate as the living God. They

[1] All the key verbs of this sentence represent etymological double-entendre's in the original German which are impossible to reproduce in translation. On this other level, then, the sentence may be rendered: The sentence itself first comes to stand, first stands forth, by virtue of the fact that the localizing, fast-laying Nay seeks to gain power over the firming Yea. (Tr.)

are even, if you will, much more vital. For they are nothing if not vital. They are immortal. Death lies under their feet. Though they have not conquered death, death does not dare approach them. They grant him his validity in his own realm, even dispatch one of their number out of the immortal circle to rule over that realm. This is, then, the most unlimited dominion which they exercise—indeed the only dominion in the stricter sense. In the world of the living they do not reign, though they may intervene in it; they are living gods but not gods of what is alive. For that they would have to truly step outside themselves, and that would not agree with the easygoing vitality, the "easy-living" liveliness, of the Olympians. They direct a certain amount of systematic attention only to the task of keeping death distant from their immortal world. For the rest these gods live by themselves. Even their much-cited relationship to the "forces of nature" changes nothing in this respect. For the concept of nature as a realm with its own legality in contrast to a possible "supernatural" one does not yet exist at all. Nature means always the gods' own nature. If a god is associated with a constellation or anything similar, he does not thereby become god of the constellation, as we would again and again imagine in a regressive application of our concept of nature; rather the constellation becomes a god or at least a part of the god. And if a magnetic field radiates outward from this divine sway of the constellations over all earthly occurrence, this occurrence is not thereby placed under the sway of the divine constellations, but rather it is, so to speak, elevated into that divine sphere, it becomes a part of this whole. It ceases to be independent, if ever it was independent; it becomes itself divine. The world of the gods remains a world unto itself forever, even if the gods encompass the whole world; the encompassed world in the latter event is not something unto itself, something into relationship with which the god must first enter, but, rather, precisely something divinely encompassed. Thus God is here without a world or, vice versa, this would be a world without gods, this world of gods who only live by themselves, if one would characterize this notion as a veritable *Weltanschauung*. And therewith we have enunciated the essence of what one may designate as the mythological conception of the world.

For this is the essence of myth: a life that knows nothing above and nothing beneath itself; a life—whether borne by gods, men, or things —without reigning gods; a life purely unto itself. The law of this life is the inner harmony of caprice and fate, a harmony that does not resound beyond itself, that constantly returns into itself. The freely flowing passion of the gods breaks on the internal dam of the somber law of his nature. The figures of myth are neither bare powers nor bare beings, for in neither form would they be vital. Only in the alternating current of passion and ordained fate do their highly vital traits emerge: baseless in hatred as in love, for there are no bases under their lives; without regard for man or thing, for there is no backward for them to glance at; their free outpouring unguided, constrained only by the verdict of fate; not absolved from their obligations by the free force of their passion; and withal, freedom and essence both one in the mysterious unity of the vital—this is the world of myth.

Asia: The Unmythical God

In the spirit of the mythological, God becomes a living god. This spirit draws its strength from that inclusiveness which itself is, in its turn, a consequence of the conclusiveness of this concept of God. Its weakness, too, is based on this conclusion, and its conclusive, product-like, but not productive, nature. But we must first emphasize its strength. The mythical was dominant in the religions of the Near East and Europe until their eclipse, and as a stage of development everywhere. As such it represents not a lower, but the higher form as against the "spiritual religions" of the Orient. It is not by coincidence that revelation, once it started on its way into the world, took the road to the West, not to the East. The living "gods of Greece" were worthier opponents of the living God than the phantoms of the Asiatic Orient. The deities of China as of India are massive structures made from the monoliths of primeval time which still protrude into our own times in the cults of "primitives." The heaven of China is the concept of divine power raised to world-encompassing proportions, a power which, without emptying itself over the divine essence and thus transforming itself into divine vitality, integrated the entire All into the massive globe of its dominant caprice, not as something other, but rather as something enclosed in it, "inhabiting" it. Nowhere is the graphic sense of the idea of immanence as clear as in this Chinese apotheosis of the vault of heaven, outside of which there is—Nought. China's god exhausts himself in the passage from the Nought to the all-encompassing power. Just so does India's god exhaust himself on the road between the Nought and the pure, all-pervasive silence of essence, the divine physis. Never has the sound of divine freedom penetrated the tacit circle of the Brahmin; thus it itself

remains dead, though filling all life and absorbing all life into itself.
Viewed from the living figures of the gods of myths, these "deities"—
a term favored by all those who flee the face of the living God for the
mists of abstraction—are retrogressions into the elemental. How
much this is the case is shown by a glance at the retroversions experienced by those same elemental foundations themselves. For, once
begun, this course of regression does not cease until it has arrived
near its outermost limit—near Nought.

The venerators of the Brahma profoundly enunciated his essentiality with the indefatigably repeated syllable of affirmation, which
was supposed to unlock all his secrets. At the same time they recognized this one undifferentiated essence as the absorber of all multiplicity, of the self of all things. In doing so, however, they already
witnessed the emergence of a new specification of essence behind the
one undifferentiated Yea. It was identical with Yea in its denotation,
but it connoted the infinite multiplicity that had been arrested in it.
It was the Nay Nay. Thus Yea was recognized as the negation of the
Nought. The infinitely countless "not thus, not thus" was therewith
inserted into the one infinite Thus. The negated Nought was the
essence of the deity. And from here there was only one more leap
backward. If the leap was not to come to grief on the rocks of the
Nought itself, it had to reach the last point still remaining between it
and that non-Nought. In this neither-nor of Nought and non-
Nought, however, we recogfinize once more that dizzying *ultima
ratio* of Buddhism, that Nirvana which takes its place beyond God
and gods and yet equally beyond the bare Nought, a place accessible
even in imagination only by a mortal leap. Evidently nothing further
exists here: it is something outermost; behind it there is only pure
Nought. The first stop on the path leading from Nought to non-
Nought is designated in this concept, however possible, by one last
sublimation of all essence.

CHINA

The power of heaven, in which classical China believes, freed itself
from Nought, like every active force, by simple negation. The multiplicity of things is not absorbed by this powerful, all-encompassing
entity as is the self, and every self, by the Brahmin's silence of the sea.
Rather, this heaven encloses all by holding sway over all. Its power
is action, its symbol the might which the male exercises over the
female. Thus it expresses itself not as an infinite Yea, but rather as a
Nay renewed with every moment against all and sundry enclosed

within it. Here, too, an abstraction dared to leap backward behind this elemental abstraction well-nigh to the limit of everything elemental in the Nought. This abstraction had to substitute for God and gods a concept of a supreme power as godhead, a power which was distinguished from Nought only in that it relates to act and effect. But this relationship itself was solely one of—doing nothing. The *Tao* thus effects without acting, it is a god who keeps "quiet as a mouse" so that the world can move around him. It is entirely without essence; nothing exists in it in the way that every self, for example, "exists" in the Brahma. Rather it itself exists in everything, again not in the way that every self "exists" in the Brahma, that is, to use the analogy of the Upanishads, in the way that salt crystals exist in a solution. Rather—and again the analogies are highly indicative—in the way that the hub exists in spokes, or the window in a wall, or the empty space in a vessel. It is that which, by being "nothing," makes a "something" usable, the unmoved mover of the movable. It is the non-act as the basis of the act. Here, too, we have again something outermost: the only possible form which atheism can assume if it is to be truly atheistic and if it is neither to become entangled in pantheism nor to be dissipated in pure nihilism, free of every special relationship to God and gods.

PRIMITIVE ATHEISM

To this day every structure into which reasoning about God may want to flee from the voice of the true God must thus be erected according to the plans here drafted in Nirvana and Tao. Only here is it secure from this voice—*securus adversus deos* as well as *adversus Deum*. There is no longer a path that leads back from here. The Nought is a firm peg: what is pegged to it cannot tear loose again. But this last abstraction about all divine life is unbearable for the living self of man and the living worlds of the nations and, accordingly, life in the long run ever regains its power over the escapist blandness of the abstraction. In short, it is the lot of the adherents of Buddha and Lao-tzu alike that a luxuriant heathenism again overtakes the adamantine monoliths of its non-ideas. And it is only for this reason that the ears of men, even within their sphere of influence, yet again become receptive to the voices from which those men once concealed themselves in the sound-proof chambers of Nirvana and Tao. For the voice of the living God echoes only where there is life, even if that life be intoxicated with gods and hostile to God. But the terror of God, which could not muster the courage to become fear of God, flees into the vacuum of the non-idea, and there that voice loses itself in the void. The gods of myth at least lived, albeit not beyond their walled-in realm. Even before the final sublimation into Nirvana and Tao, India's god, like China's, already shares this weakness of the gods of myth, this inability to live beyond oneself. But he is infinitely inferior to them in stopping halfway, in his incapacity for what breathes mightily out of the gods of myth: for life.

This wealth of life, full of contradictions, becomes possible through the self-containedness of the mythical world. For art it has remained operative outside of its original realm to the present day. Even today, all art is subject to the laws of the mythical world. A work of art must have that self-containedness unto itself, that indifference to everything beyond itself, that independence of higher laws, that freedom from baser duties which we recognized as peculiar to the world of myth. It is a basic requirement of the work of art that a tremor of the "mythical" emanate from its figures, even if they come clothed in our everyday habits. The work of art must be closed off by a crystalline wall from everything else that is not itself. Something like a breath of that "easy life" of the Olympian gods must hover over it, even if the existence that it mirrors is want and tears. Outer form, inner form, content is the threefold secret of the Beautiful; the first of these ideas, the miracle of outer form, the "what is beautiful, is blissful in itself," has its origin in the metaphysical spirit of myth. The spirit of myth is the foundation of the realm of the beautiful.

The Twilight of the Gods

If ever God was to proceed beyond the vitality he has hitherto reached and become the living God of life, then the result attained so far on the path from the Nought would itself have in turn to become a Nought, a point of departure. The elements of power and obligation, of caprice and destiny, which flowed together into the figure of the living God, would have to part company anew. The apparently final result would have to become a fountainhead. A certain unrest had overtaken even the mythically directed theology of antiquity. It pressed for progress beyond the self-satisfied sphere of myth, and thus appeared to demand that reversal of the merely living into the life-giving. But it is indicative of the power of the mythological view that the efforts in this direction, both on the part of the mysteries

and in the ideas of the great philosophers, always essayed the involvement of man and world in the sphere of the divine. Thus they ultimately had, just like myth, only the divine. The independence of the
human and the worldly spheres was suspended both in the mysteries of
apotheosis and in those concepts with which the philosophers bridged
the gap between the divine and the human, the worldly spheres, but
which led only from the latter to the former, never the other way
around: the concepts of longing and love. This is equally true of the
Greeks' loving longing for the perfect, as of the Indians' love of God.
Now to ensnare God once more in the passion of love would have
seemed a constriction of God, of the god whom one was proud to
have just elevated to all-encompassing status by heaping all the noble
qualities of the many gods on his one head. Though man might love
God, God's love for man could at most be an answer to man's love,
at most his just dessert. It could not be a free gift, gracious beyond all
measure of righteousness, nor the primeval force of the divine which
elects and need not be entreated, which indeed anticipates all human
love, and is the first to give sight to the blind, hearing to the deaf. And
even where man thought he was attaining the highest form of love by
renouncing all that was his own, all desires and appetites, as well as all
ascetic exertion for God and by awaiting God's grace in consummate
resignation—as it happened precisely in those circles of the Indian
Friends of God—then precisely this resignation was the achievement
which man offered; it was not itself first a gift of God. Putting it another way, God's love was not for the impenitent but for the perfect
man. The doctrine of resignation to divine grace counted as a dangerous "secret of secrets," never to be disclosed, it was taught, to those
who do not venerate God, who demur against him, who do not casti-
gate themselves. Yet precisely these lost, hardened, locked souls, these
sinners, should be sought out by the love of a God who is not merely
"amiable" but who himself loves, regardless of the love of man, nay,
on the contrary, first arousing the love of man. But of course to this
end it would be necessary for the infinite God to come more finitely
close to man, more face-to-face with him, more proper—name to
proper—name than any sense of sensible men, any wisdom of wise men
could ever admit. The gap between the human-worldly and the divine
is indicated precisely in the ineradicability of personal names. It is
beyond the power, ascetic or mystic, of men and the world to leap
over. It is deeper and more real than any ascetic's arrogance, any mystic's conceit will ever admit in his despisal of the "sound and haze" of
names earthly and heavenly. And it would, at the same time, have to
be recognized and acknowledged as such.

Thus the essence of this mythical god remained accessible to the yearning of man and world, but only at a price: that man ceased to be man and world to be world. Man and the world were borne aloft on the wings of yearning into the consuming fire of apotheosis. So too this yearning, while bearing toward the divine, left the human and the worldly far below and by no means led it into the divine with a deeper love. For India's Friends of God too, the act is only that which must not be evil, not that which must be good. And the divine nowhere overflows the limits of its individuality. Antiquity arrived at monism, but no more. World and man have to become God's nature, have to submit to apotheosis, but God never lowers himself to them. He does not give of himself, does not love, does not have to love. For he keeps his physis to himself, and therefore remains what he is: the metaphysical.

BOOK TWO

The World and Its Meaning
or
Metalogic

Negative Cosmology

Now what do we know of the world? It appears to surround us. We are in it, but it exists within us too. It penetrates us, but with every breath and every stirring of our hands it also emanates from us. It is for us the self-evident quantity, as self-evident as our own self, more self-evident than God. It is the evident pure and simple, the one thing specially suited and specially commissioned to be understood, to be evident from within itself, to be "self-evident." But philosophy long ago left this self-evidentness behind in favor of an agenda which would make now of the I, now of God the point of departure in one running start after another. Thus it has reduced the self-evidentness of the world to a virtual nil. What, then, remains of the self-evidentness of the world as knowledge of the *Ding an sic*—or whatever one chooses to call this infinitesimal residuum—would rather properly be the subject of a negative cosmology. It is due more to general cultural sympathies and antipathies than to objective reasons that this term has not been taken up with the same readiness as that of a negative theology. For the devotees of God are not always lovers of knowledge, and vice versa. No such contrast exists between the lovers of the world and those of knowledge; on the contrary, they are more or less dependent on each other, as indeed are also the concepts of world and knowledge themselves. Thus the "scientific conclusion" that one can know nothing of God was more palatable than the same conclusion with respect to the world. But we resist the one "conclusion" as well as the other. We will not let it remain conclusion. If science could lead to such a conclusion, then it has led itself *ad absurdum*. Though the conclusion need not then be wrong, the way in which it had to become a conclusion must be. Accordingly we consider this "conclusion," here as before with God, as a beginning.

METHODOLOGY

Of the world we know nothing. And here, too, the Nought is a Nought of our knowledge, a specific, individual Nought of our knowledge at that. Here, too, it is the springboard from which we are to take the leap into the Something of knowledge, into the "positive." For we "believe" in the world, as firmly at least as we believe in God or our self. Accordingly, the Nought of these three entities can be only a hypothetical Nought for us, only a Nought of knowledge from which we attain that Aught of knowledge which circumscribes the content of this belief. That we hold this belief is a fact from which we can free ourselves only hypothetically, by constructing it from the ground up, until we finally reach the point where we realize how the hypothetical must convert into the ahypothetical, the absolute, the unconditional character of that belief. This alone is what science can and must achieve for us. We cannot in the least expect that science free us from that threefold belief; science will teach us precisely that we cannot expect this and why. What appeared, according to earlier concepts, to be unscientific in this "belief" will thus be justified. The *de omnibus dubitandum* of Descartes was valid on the presupposition of the one-and-all universe. A one-and-all reasoning confronted this universe and, as tool of this reasoning, the one-and-all doubt *de omnibus*. But it was our initial endeavor to prove this presupposition untenable, to prove it, indeed, already invalidated for the conscious spirit. If, then, this presupposition falls, then the place of the one-and-all doubt, the absolute doubt, is taken by the hypothetical doubt which, just because no longer *de omnibus*, cannot regard itself any longer as end but only as means of reasoning. Thus we submerge once again into the depths of the positive.

World Order

Here, too, the original affirmation, the Yea of non-Nought, again wells forth out of the Nought, just because it cannot remain Nought. But this affirmation must affirm something infinite; hence the affirmed

Non-nought cannot in this case, as in God's, imply being. For the being of the world is not an infinitely static essence. We address the being of God as an ever-static essence, infinite in itself and in every moment. But the inexhaustible fullness of the vision, ever newly generated and newly perceived, the "being-full-of-form" of the world, is precisely the opposite of this. Thus the primeval Yea must here affirm something else; the primeval statement about the world must sound different. Only something "everywhere" present and "ever" lasting can be affirmed as something infinite—and only as such can the Non-nought be affirmed. The terms "everywhere" and "ever" would have only the meaning of an analogy as against the divine physis; they would be but the stammering expression for something inexpressible. But here in the case of the world they apply exactly. The being of the world really must be its Everywhere and Ever. Only in reasoning, however, is the being of the world everywhere and ever. The essence of the world is the logos.

Let us recall here what we premised about the relation of the world to its logos in the Introduction. Reasoning pours into the world as a system of individual stipulations with many ramifications. It is that which is valid in the world at all times and in every place. It owes its significance for the world, its "applicability," to that ramification, that diversity, on which it has decided. It has left behind the "simple word of truth," to use the language of tragedy. The force of its inclination to being springs from this very disinclination. The system of rational stipulations is a system by virtue not of a uniform origin, but rather of the unity of its application, its area of validity: the world. A uniform origin can and indeed must be presupposed by this reasoning, directed to being and only to being, but it cannot be proved. For by turning itself entirely into the applied reasoning at home in the world, it has renounced the capacity to demonstrate the unity of its origin. Since this uniform origin did not lie inside the world, the path from the "pure" — which was to be presupposed — to the "applied" came to lie outside the sphere of the power of applied reasoning. A merely presupposed reasoning may need to be reasoned about, but does not reason itself; only a real reasoning reasons, one that is valid for the world, applied to the world, at home in the world. Thus the unity of reasoning remains without; reasoning has to console itself for this with the unity of its application within the locked walls of the world. The infinite unity of divine being expressly precedes any identity of reasoning and being and thereby precedes both the reasoning which is valid for being and the being which can be reasoned out. It cannot possibly be proved here whether this unity is by chance the source whence the ramified system of logical irrigation issues into the tillable world; though it cannot be entirely excluded either, it remains here a mere assumption. No gate is barred against reasoning in the world in which it is at home, but— "the prospect 'cross the way is blocked to him."

ARCHETYPAL WORD, SYMBOL

The logos of the world is only applicable, but it is everywhere and ever applicable, and as such alone universally valid. With this concept of the universal we have sighted a new side of the effectiveness of the original Yea. Yea, we recall, was the wording of the original statement, the statement by which the "then" was fixed and confirmed—once and for all. Universal validity, therefore, is already inherent in the original Yea. Taken by itself, a predicate such as the word "free" has a meaning of its own ever and everywhere, regardless of the connotation it acquires through its use in the individual case of a particular statement. The universal is not what took shape in application, but rather the purely applicable entity itself. The Yea established applicability, but it is not the law of application itself. In the affirmation in which the divine essence issued forth from the Nought of God, the infinity of the affirmed non-Nought showed itself as infinite being of the divine physis. The infinity of the affirmed non-Nought of the world, on the other hand, shows itself as infinite applicability of the worldly logos. This logos is utterly universal and yet everywhere attached to the world, tied up in it. If we want a formulaic designation for it, then we would have to let it appear as the result of an affirmation on the right side of the equation; because of its universality, which allows for no free space next to it, we could only designate it by A; the trait of applicability which we recognized as essential here implies an allusion to the need for application really to occur to it: this passively attracting force which emanates from it was expressed symbolically by putting the equal-sign in front. Thus we arrive at "$=A$." This is the symbol of the world-spirit. For this would be the name which we would have to give the logos, poured as it is into the world, the so-called "natural" as well as the so-called "spiritual" world, and amalgamated as it is with the world at all points and all times. In using this name, of course, we would have to keep its Hegelian connotation, which lets the name lose itself in the deity, at a distance; it would be better to listen backward for the sound which the term, together with the related words "earth-spirit" and "world-soul," conjures up in the beginnings of the romantic philosophy of nature, in the young Schelling or again, say, in Novalis.

World Plenitude

But the disconcerting fact about the world is, after all, that it is not spirit. There is still something else in it, something ever new, pressing, overwhelming. Its womb is insatiable in conceiving, inexhaustible in giving birth. Or better yet—for both the male and the female are in it—the world as "nature" is equally the endless creatress of configurations and the indefatigable procreative force of the "spirit" inherent in it. Stone and plant, state and art—incessantly all creation renews itself. This plenitude of visions is just as original as the dancing circle of ideas. There is no precondition for its sprouting forth anymore than for the arrangement of that dance. The sun is no less a wonder than the sun-like quality of the eye which espies it. Beyond both, beyond the plenitude as well as the arrangement, there is immediately the Nought, the Nought of the world.

But the emergence of plenitude from Nought is here again something different from the previous emergence of the world-logos. The world-mind left the night of Nought behind it, and trod with calm and infinite Yea toward the Non-nought, the bright reality of the world. The plenitude of visions, however, breaks the nocturnal prison of the Nought in the ever-renewed constriction of procreation and birth; everything new is a new negation of Nought, a never-before, a new start unto itself, something unheard of, something "new under the sun." Here the force of the negation of Nought is infinite, but every individual effect of this force is finite; the fullness is infinite, the vision finite. The individual phenomena emerge from the night, baseless and aimless. Whence they are coming or whither going has not been inscribed on their foreheads: they simply exist. But in existing they are individual, each a one against all others, each distinguished from all others, "particular," "not-otherwise."

SYMBOL

Thus the intracosmic plenitude of distinctiveness confronts the intrasonic order of the universal. In the universal there reposed a need for fulfillment, an implication of application; nothing of the sort reposes in the distinctive. In fact no need whatever reposes in the distinctive, no direction, no force—not even against its own kind. Everything distinctive, it is true, distinctive with a view to everything other, but it does not experience this view; it is blind from birth, it is nothing but— existing. Its force is solely the blind dead weight of its existence. In our terminology its symbol is *B*, *B* pure and simple, the naked sign of individuality, without a sign indicative of equality.

Thus Nay here leads to a result just as characteristically at variance with previous results as did Yea. The warp of its "existence," which God had found in his physis, the world found in its logos; the woof of the fabric which divine freedom wove for God is supplied for the world by the inexhaustible well of phenomena. The free act in God, the phenomenon in the world—both are equally sudden, equally unique, equally novel revelations from the night of the Nought of, in the one case, God; in the other, the world. Both spring from the relentless close-quarter wrestling of Nay and Nought. Every divine action, every earthly phenomenon is a new victory over Nought, as glorious as on the first day. But while in God a boundless clarity breaks forth from the night of Nought, it is the birth of the individual, something colorful but itself still blind, which bursts from the dark womb of the world's Nought. This birth hurtles into the world, pro- pelled by its own gravity, not by any urge. But the world is already there, just as God's dormant physis was already in existence when the bright reveille of divine freedom burst in upon it. The world is there in the regal treasure of the vessels and implements of its logos, infi- nitely receptive, infinitely in need of "application." And the contents ceaselessly hurtle into these vessels from the spouting source. Above Yea and Nay, the And closes itself.

The Reality of the World

The distinctive is without drive, without movement in itself. It hurtles forth, and there it is. It is not the "given"—a misleading designation which mirrors the error of all pre-metalogical philosophies about the world; it is not for nothing that their systems come to a dead stop again and again precisely with this problem. It is not the given; much rather the logical forms are, once and for all, "given" in the simple, infinite validity of their Yea. The particular, however, is surprise, not a given, but ever a new gift or, better still, a present, for in the present the thing presented disappears behind the gesture of presenting. And

logical forms are not the spontaneous beasts—*sponteque se movent*—
which break into the gardens of the given to find their nourishment
there; rather they are the precious, age-old vessels that are ever ready
to store the wine of new vintages in their interiors. They are the
unmoved, "ever of yesterday," "universally common" which for all
that is still not the "wholly common," as the infuriated rebel apparently
would have it, though he correctly characterized it nonetheless as that
"which ever was and ever more shall be, valid today and therefore on
the morrow." The phenomenon, on the other hand, is ever new: the
miracle in the world of spirit.

The phenomenon had been the stumbling block of idealism, and thus
of philosophy as a whole from Parmenides to Hegel. Idealism had been
unable to comprehend phenomena as "spontaneous," for that would
have meant denying the omnipotence of the logos, and so it never did
it justice. It had to falsify the bubbling plenitude into a dead chaos
of givens. Basically, the unity of the intelligible All admitted of no
other conception. The All as one-and-universal can be held together
only by a reasoning which possesses active, spontaneous force. But if
vitality is thereby ascribed to reasoning, it must willy-nilly be denied
to life—life denied its liveliness! Nothing short of the metalogical
view of the world can restore life to its rights. For here the All no
longer figures as *the* one and universal All, but (only) as *an* All. Thus
the logos can fulfill it as the truth inherent in it without first having
to effect the unity. The intracosmic logos is itself a unity by virtue of
its relationship, however fashioned, to an extracosmic unity, wherever
at home. As such, it need no longer be burdened with an activity which
is the very antithesis of its worldly essence, its diversity and its applicability. It effects the unity of the world only from within, as its internal
form, so to speak, not its external form. This metalogical All already
possesses an external form by its very nature, by virtue of being *an*
All, not *the* All, intelligent, not intelligible, informed by spirit, not
created by spirit. The logos is not creator of the world as it was from
Parmenides to Hegel, but rather its spirit or, better yet perhaps, its
soul. Thus the logos has again become a world-soul and can now
give the miracle of the living world-body its due. The world-body
need no longer repose as an undifferentiated, chaotically undulating
mass of "given-ness," ready to be seized and shaped by the logical
forms; rather it becomes the living, ever renewed surge of the phenomenon, descending upon the quietly opened lap of the world-soul
and uniting with it to form the world.

Let us pursue the path of this descent of the particular upon the
universal more closely. The particular—let us recall the symbol "B"—

is aimless; the universal—"A"—is itself passive, unmoved, but by craving application, a force of attraction emanates from it. Thus an attracting field of force forms about the universal, and the particular plunges into it under the compulsion of its own gravity. We may distinguish in particular two points of this movement, here much as before within God, by way of describing more or less the entire curve of the process. After a piece of pure plunging, aimlessly and unconsciously blind, the particular becomes in a sense conscious of its attracted movement toward the universal, and thereby its eyes are opened to its own nature. This is the first point; at this instant what was previously blindly particular becomes altogether conscious of its particularity, and that means conscious of its direction toward the universal, particular (without qualification). The particular which "knows" about the universal is no longer merely particular; rather, without ceasing to be essentially particular, it yet has already stepped forward to the very edge of the sphere of influence of the universal. This is the "individual," the singular which bears the criteria of the universal on its body—not, however, of the universal in general, which after all has no distinguishing marks, but rather of its own universal nature, its species, its genus—and yet this individual is still essentially particular, though now precisely "individually" particular. Individuality is not somehow a higher degree of particularity, but rather a stop on the path from the purely particular to the universal. The other stop is situated at the point where the particular enters the decisive domination of the universal. Anything beyond this point would be purely universal and the particular would dissolve in it without a trace; but the point itself designates that instant in the movement where the particular can still be sensed through and despite the decisive victory of the universal. As the first point was occupied by the "individual" so this one is occupied by the "category" or whatever else one may wish to call this universal entity which is not universal pure and simple, but rather an individuated universal, a particular universality. For species and genus are concepts which are unconditional universalities only vis-à-vis their own particularity, and so are community, nation, and state if we may pass into the human sphere; for the rest, however, all these concepts are units which can very well unite among themselves into pluralities of categories, nations, states. Just so, for its part, the individuum too is an individuality pure and simple only vis-à-vis its category and for all that capable of representing a category—its category—only because it already represents a plurality vis-à-vis the naked, blind particular. This plurality consists

of at least two stipulations: the criterion of the species and its own
peculiarity.

Thus the structure of the world perfects itself in the individual and
the species, more specifically in the movement which carries the individual into the open arms of the species. With God, too, essence and
freedom were no more than conceptual extremes, and his vitality
created itself in the inner confrontations of divine power and divine
obligation, with the caprice of power confined by obligation, and the
constraint of obligation loosened by power. Similarly the world takes
shape, not immediately out of the distinctive's plunge into the universal, but more nearly out of the individual's penetration into the
species. The real "and" of the world is not the "and" of the world-
endowed-with-spirit and the spirit-inherent-in-the-world—these are
extremes—but much more immediately of the thing and its concept,
the individual and his genus, of man and his community.

There is one process which mirrors these two elements of the
cosmic essence in the strongest, most graphic, most meaningful terms.
The individual originates at birth; the genus, as the term itself already
suggests, at progeniture. The act of engendering precedes birth, it occurs
as an individual act without definite reference to birth as an individual
birth, yet strictly related and directed to it in its universal essence.
Birth, however, bursts forth in its individual result as a thoroughgoing
miracle, with the overwhelming force of the unpredicted, the unpredictable. There has always been progeniture, yet every birth is
something absolutely new. A consequence of truly "unspeakable,"
unthinkable individuality plunges over the most individual of all
human acts. The particularity of the newborn—his particularity,
mark you, as part of the world, not his self—collects itself together
entirely at the instant of birth. This is the profoundest meaning of
astrological belief, which fails because and to the extent of its delusion
of grasping man as self, when in fact it meets man only to the extent
that he is individuality, that is, a distinctive portion of the world like
every other extrahuman being or thing. Only for the demon of individuality is the astrological law really valid that "as on the day which
gave you to the world the sun arose, a greeting to the planets." Never,
therefore, is man and every individual part of the world more of an
individuality than at the instant when he precisely—individuates himself, when he makes his appearance as a part of the world himself refusing partition, when he "sees the light" of the world. Now this
individuality of his is, however, attracted by the power of its species
with somber might; it strives toward this focal point, always increas-

ing its distance from the day of its birth, full as that was with all possibilities. Thus it constantly forfeits its possibilities, its—individuality. In the end it surrenders it as completely as it can at the instant of engendering. At its birth, the individual is completely individual; it is downright concrete, free of connection and relationship, untouched by the reality if not by the concept of its species, at progeniture it penetrates just as completely into its genus. As it runs its perpetual course, this circular process proves a graphic representation of the metalogical essence of the world compared to Idealism's concept of generation.

SYMBOL

It is a circular process. We would have to symbolize it by $B=A$. The origins of the two terms of the equation have disappeared, but the equation itself is characteristically distinct from the one we have previously worked out. Whereas $A=A$, the formula for God, equated two equally original, equally infinite entities, the formula for the world asserts the equation of two unequals: the content of the world and its form. Initially, moreover, it asserts this identity explicitly as $B=A$, not by chance as $A=B$. That is to say, it asserts the passivity of form, the activity of content; to the concept it attributes a self-evident character, but the thing appears to it as a miracle. And thereby the world becomes self-contained for it, a whole exclusive of everything external, a vessel filled to saturation, a cosmos abounding in configurations. All basic relationships in the equation are such as lead from B to A, such, that is, as permit abundance, content, individuals to penetrate the order, the form, the categories. Any relationships running in the opposite direction are derivative, not original. Spirit can fashion a body for itself only because the body, amazingly enough, presses toward the spirit. The music of Apollo's harp can construct only a wall out of stones because the stones themselves are individuals miraculously endowed with souls—"filled with gods." This picture of the world is thus a decided counterpoise to the world of Idealism. For the latter, the world is not miraculous factuality, not, therefore, self-contained whole; it has to be all-encompassing universe. For it, the basic relationships must run from categories to individuals, from concepts to things, from form to content. The given matter must be present, chaotic, gray, self-evident, until the sun of spiritual form makes it sparkle colorfully with its rays, but the colors are only those of the light which radiates from this miraculous source of light. The chaotic gray matter itself produces no sparks. The formula of this world-view would not be $B=A$, but $A=B$, and so it really proves to be in the age of its completion. The $A=B$ of Idealism contains within itself the possibility of its "derivation" from an $A=A$. Thereby the profound paradox of the equation of two unequals, which after all is asserted here too, is broken. The idea of emanation leads almost imperceptibly over the gap which here too, after all, still yawns similarly between the universal and the distinctive. And only B can "emanate" from A, not A from B. B can only be "existing," not origin. Hence only the equation $A=B$ can be the equation of Idealism; only it can really be derived from a formally nonparadoxical equation. $B=B$, from which one would have to derive the equation $B=A$, would, it is true, be formally just as unquestionable, but materially it would be incapable of allowing anything to be derived from it, quite apart from the possibility of an equation $B=B$. But an immediate relationship, say, between $A=A$ and $B=A$ could not even be produced within the world. A paradoxical statement about B (to wit, $B=A$) does not become less paradoxical by virtue of a relationship to a nonparadoxical statement about A (to wit, $A=A$). On the other hand, a statement about A which is inherently paradoxical (to wit, $A=B$) diminishes perceptibly, if not precisely entirely, in its paradox by virtue of its relationship to a nonparadoxical statement about A (to wit, $A=A$). The fact is that here the unexplained residuum is nothing but the concept of the relationship, and this is a difficulty which applies equally to the possibility of a relationship between two equations as to that of a relationship within the individual equation. This difficulty, however, still lies entirely outside our purview, since we are still dealing solely with the individual equation; we have only had to allude to the path of Idealism by way of anticipation, only in order to elucidate the peculiarity of $B=A$ vis-à-vis $A=B$, or the difference between the metalogical and the idealistic views of the world. The path of Idealism leads to $A=B$ as an intracosmic path of emanation, of radiating forth, of idealistic generation. We will have much more to say about the significance of this intracosmic path later. Here we return to the simple equation $B=A$, or rather to its referent, the metalogical world.

The Plastic Cosmos

In contrast to the all-filling world of Idealism, the metalogical world is the wholly fulfilled, the structured world. It is the whole of its parts. These parts are not fulfilled by the whole, nor borne by it: the whole is simply not All, it is in fact only a whole. Accordingly many paths lead from the parts to the whole. Indeed, to be quite precise, every part—insofar as it is really a part, really individual—has its own path to the whole, its own trajectory. From the universe of the idealistic view, on the other hand, which fills all its members and bears every single one of them, only one single path leads to these members, to wit, precisely that path along which flows the current of the universe's force. The reason for a phenomenon which we mentioned in the Introduction becomes clear here. The Idealistic systems of 1800 display throughout a trait which we would have to designate as one-dimensional, most clearly Hegel's, but in outline also Fichte's and Schelling's. The individual is not derived immediately from the whole, but rather is developed through its position between the next highest and the next lowest in the system, as for example the "society" for Hegel in its position between the "family" and the "state." The force of the system as a whole courses through all the individual configurations as a one and universal current. This corresponds exactly to the Idealistic view of the world; the almost professionally impersonal quality of philosophers from Parmenides to Hegel mentioned in the Introduction also finds its explanation here. The unity of the All is a concept which admits of no other possible point of view than that which just happens to "have its turn" in the history of philosophical problems. And accordingly Hegel had to make of the history of philosophy itself the systematic conclusion of philosophy because thereby the personal point of view of the individual philosopher, the last thing which still seemed able to contradict the unity of All, was rendered harmless.

Now the metalogical view also creates, likewise of necessity in connection with the new view of the world, a new concept and type of philosopher. Here too the way, and a way of his own at that, leads from the individual philosopher, as before, from each individual thing, as individual, to the whole. Indeed, the philosopher is bearer of the unity of the metalogical system of the world. After all, this system itself lacks the unity of the one-dimensional, it is multi-dimensional in principle; threads and relationships run from every individual point to every other, and to the whole. The unity of these countless relationships, its relative conclusion, is the unity of the philosopher's point of view, personal, experienced, philosophized. It is only a relative conclusion, for though the idea of the cosmic whole must be strictly grasped in its metalogical peculiarity as a concept, nevertheless the individual system can never turn this idea into a reality except relatively. In the idealistic system, this relativity was conditioned by the status of the problem as it had been historically attained, as Hegel properly recognized. So too in the metalogical system it is conditioned by the subjective point of view of the philosopher. Even these remarks as yet do not exhaust the problem of the "philosopher," but we must save its further clarification for later.

ANCIENT COSMOLOGY

Category, although the fundamental "given" everywhere, was therefore overwhelmed by the miracle of individuality. Thus overwhelmed, the world of the metalogical view, not all-filling but all-filled, could be designated as the structured world, structured but not created. Createdness would have implied more than we were entitled to assert at this point. The living God of metaphysical theology was by no means "the" living God but "a" living god; just so the structured world of metalogical cosmology is not yet created but only structured. As the living gods symbolized the highpoint of ancient theology, so this structured world symbolizes the height of ancient cosmology, not alone the cosmology of the macrocosm but also and above all the microcosm, that is, of the "natural" as well as of the "spiritual" world. The relation is not even quite so clear for the natural world, since the identity of Existence and Reasoning—the basic idea of Idealism— had already occured to antiquity. But this idea remained without cosmological implementation in antiquity; it remained meta-physical. Even the idea of emanations awaited the Neoplatonic school, which already developed in response precisely to new ideas, not to ancient ones. Within the world, however, Plato himself as well as Aristotle teach no emanatory relation, no active relation at all, between idea and phenomenon, between concept and thing, between category and individual or whatever terms may capture the contrast. Rather we have here the odd idea that things "imitate" the idea, that they "look out" for it, "yearn" for it, "develop" into or toward it, though it is "purpose" not cause. The idea reposes; the phenomenon moves toward it—exactly, it appears, the metalogical relation.

PLATO AND ARISTOTLE

The difficulties of this conception, unsolved by the great thinkers of antiquity, are obvious. Some of them were articulated in Aristotle's polemic against his master, but he too did not overcome them. For the Aristotelian polemic mobilized the idea of infinity against Plato's doctrine of ideas: beyond concept and thing, it must in turn be possible to posit a concept of the relatability of the thing to the concept, and so on ad infinitum. But the metalogical view of the wholeness of the world of configuration is altogether defenseless against this concept of infinity: the Aristotelian cosmos is exactly as finite as the Platonic. The limit of the isolated metalogical idea simply comes into view at this point. Aristotle evades the problem with a breakneck leap into the metaphysical. For his divine "reasoning about reasoning" is reasoning only about reasoning. Expressly and on principle he rejects the possibility that it be thinking about the unthinkable as well. Divine reasoning can only think the "best," only, therefore, itself. But this a-cosmic quality of his metaphysics unfits it precisely for what it was meant to achieve. It was meant to expound the "principle" of the world as a doctrine of the purposeful cause. But because of its purely metaphysical character, this metaphysics is the principle only of itself. And if one disregards this stipulation of Aristotelian metaphysics as self-consciousness and tries to see it only as that which it is meant to achieve, without asking whether it really achieves it, then it becomes, as purposeful cause, a purely intracosmic principle. One can then direct against its relation to that which is caused everything that Aristotle had built up against the relation of idea and thing. Regarded theologically, Aristotle's metaphysics incurred the charge of a-cosmism; regarded cosmologically, that of atheism—a reproach in both cases, precisely because the claim is made of explaining the world. In the one case this is impossible because it disappears from the field of vision; in the other because it becomes a self-contained whole, a "here" whose prospect of the infinite, "the beyond" is barred. Thus even this great theologian of antiquity cannot free himself from the metalogical view of the macrocosm as a plastic configuration, outwardly limited, inwardly configured. The contradiction between reasoning's infinite claim to universality and unity, on the one hand, and the finite, but infinitely abundant wholeness of the world, which he sought to resolve, survived him, because he was incapable of replacing the either-or of theology and cosmology with a both-and.

THE POLIS

Thus the metalogical view could not be maintained vis-à-vis the macrocosm without internal difficulties. For the microcosm, on the other hand, it seemed easy enough to realize it, albeit only seemingly. It would seem that ancient humanity solved the problem of the relation of the individual and category, both theoretically and practically, in a metalogical sense. People state, or whatever else the ancient communities may have been, are lions' dens which the individual may see tracks leading into, but not out of. In a very real sense the community confronts man as a whole: he knows that he is but a part. He is but a part vis-à-vis these wholes, only a representative vis-à-vis these categories; they are absolute powers over his moral life, even though in themselves by no means absolute, themselves rather once more examples of the categories state and people in general. They are outwardly exclusive and inwardly unconditional and for just these reasons become those configured individual beings which, upon profound reflection, quite automatically evoked the comparison with a work of art. The secret of the ancient state is not organization. Organization is a thoroughly idealistic political formation. In the highly organized state, state and individual do not assume the relation of the whole to its part, but rather the state is the universe whence a uniform current of force flows through the members. Here everyone has his defined place and, by filling it, belongs to the universe of the state. Whatever the intermediate powers, classes or otherwise, that may occur in the modern organized state, they are at best and on principle no more than that; they mediate the relationship of the state and the individual, and define the place of the individual in the state; the state realizes itself in man, and generates him by means of his "class," his "place." The ancient caste is not an instrument of the state; rather it completely overshadows the state as a whole in the consciousness of the individual. For the individual, caste is the state itself wherever it exists. For the ancient state knows only the immediate relationship of citizen and state; the ancient state is simply the whole whose configuration absorbs its parts. The modern state, on the other hand, is the universe from which its members draw the force for their own configuration. It is for this reason that the medieval serf belonged to the state, and the ancient slave did not.

Thus the ancient individual loses himself in the community not in order to find himself but rather, quite simply, in order to construct the community; he himself disappears. The familiar distinctions between the ancient concepts of democracy and all more recent ones are fully justified. It also becomes clear now why antiquity never worked out the idea of representation. Organs can only belong to a body, while a building has nothing but parts. Indeed the idea of representation encounters very characteristic difficulties in ancient law. Every individual is only himself, only individual. Only in the cult is the idea of representation unavoidable, especially in sacrifice—both with regard to the sacrificer and the sacrificed person. Even here, however, this difficulty manifests itself, for we observe throughout the endeavor to provide the sacrificer with personal purity, and the sacrificed person with personal liability for death, whether for example as a criminal or at least as the object of a magically effective curse. Nothing could be further from ancient individualism than the idea that precisely someone personally impure is suitable for offering a sacrifice on behalf of all, or that one personally pure is suitable for suffering it, this idea of the absolutely communal surety for man-kind by all men—nothing, that is, except the idea of the common surety of mankind.

THE OECUMENE

For that is the final characteristic of the metalogical ethic of the ancient world: the whole made up of parts can itself never be more than part of a whole, can never be All. The community as his community is something ultimate for the individual, beyond which all is barred from his view. The thing too knows only its own concept. The categories themselves, as individuals in their turn, construct a higher category, but of this the individual at the lower level is not conscious; it can only be drummed into him each time by action, and even then it does not, as a matter of course, enter his consciousness. The ancient empires accomplish at most the political disintegration of their national components; a positive sense of world empire eludes them. The doctrine of the Stoa encompasses only the equality of the original human quality in all individual men, not any community of renewed humanity. On the other hand, wherever it seems to man that his own community is the power which generates him, wherever as an individual in it he knows himself to be a member of a universe, not just an individual of his category, there the community, too, is pressed to know itself a member of an All. For while the whole reposes in itself and has no drive to progress to higher wholes, totality will not rest until it has found rest in the All. As a result, there is more world-consciousness in the smallest cell of the idealistic organization, in a guild, for example, or in a village commune, than in that empire of the Emperor Augustus which was always precisely that: a self-contained whole, a world both pacified and appeased within itself, with no urge to carry its peace beyond its borders. What lay beyond, remained beyond; with clearest conscience the world of Augustus identified itself with the world as—oecumene.

THE SOPHISTS

Now antiquity itself rebelled against this metalogical view of communal life, whose limitations we have here demonstrated in juxtaposition to the idealistic view. It rebelled, not with an alternative doctrine of communal life, but simply from the point of view of the individual person, who is not ready to admit that he is only part of a whole. The Sophists' revolution is so instructive precisely because it fails to go beyond this basic idea, profound and correct as it is in itself. It proclaims the free glory of man against all things and over all systems—and stops. It is incapable of explaining how this free nature of man is to prevail in all things and systems. It makes man the measure of things. But to the things it is a matter of complete indifference how they are measured or by whom or with what kind of scale; what impresses them is who moves them, not who measures them. And thus the Sophists' revolution remains a tempest in a teapot. It is not true that it uprooted antiquity's political consciousness. The *polis* remained what it was, indeed it became even more so, and the great centuries of Rome, the greatest *polis*, already transpire in the full light of the Sophists' political critique, which could find little fault with it. The Sophists' concept of man with its deficient activity is just as incapable of a new solution to the problems of the metalogical microcosm as the philosophical concept of God, with its inactivity, of a solution of the macrocosmic problem.

Asia: the Non-Plastic World

INDIA

The fact is that the metalogical view of the world retains something unsolved just as did the metaphysical view of God considered earlier. Yet for all that, "it is the Greeks," in this case as in that, who drove the idea forward to the highest development possible for it in its isolation—once more they and not the legendary peoples of the Orient. Here too, the latter come to a halt in the forecourts of Yea and Nay, of dream and ecstasy, while the Greeks stepped forth to the And, to the plastic structure. And again India and China each developed one side of the elemental, prestructural existence in enforced self-discipline to the highest degree. Indian thought, mad with spirit, covered the fullness of the world with the veil of the Maya; in all things it allowed only the "self" to count and dissolved this self in turn in the solitude of the Brahmin. But long before this, in its first beginnings, Indian thought already deviates from the definiteness of the particular and seeks something universal supposedly standing behind it. In those old hymns which accompany sacrifice, it has been noted, the individual god easily assumed the traits of the supreme and unique god for the poet, forfeiting his own peculiar visage. Hymns which begin with entirely individual strains lose themselves in colorless generalities. Divine figures of purely allegoric origin insert themselves into the oldest, naturalistic clan of gods at an early date, as similarly later in Rome. But here in India this is only the symptom of an intellectual disintegration of the world as a whole. The problem of the origin of the world is solved by countless learned pseudo-myths, which exist side by side and each of which in reality develops a system of categories in the guise of a myth of origins. Water, wind, breath, fire, or whatever else they may be are not elements of any reality; rather they assume, at an early date, the countenance of basic, prescientific concepts for clarifying the world, a world, moreover, which is not accepted and experienced, but above all "clarified." What the priest offers up is not real things but rather the essence of things; only because they are essence can they be equated with the essence of the world and thus extend an immediate effect into it. Thus everything is prepared for the world to become a system of concepts, a system of world, it is true, of reality, but without any of the independent right of the particular, which is ascribed only to "illusion." And now the doctrine of Buddha reaches behind even this objective world of concepts, and designates the concepts of cognition as the essence of these essences; whatever was still concrete in this world, already sublimated into concepts, was dissolved in a succession of epistemological concepts. And as the cognitive and volitive I is suspended, the entire world generated by this cognition and volition, including its gods and its essence, is at last suspended into the Nought. The Nought? No, here too we prefer to avoid a term which yet contains a residuum of positivism, and to speak instead of a realm beyond cognition and noncognition. Again we have reached a point just short of the limit of the Nought and withal far to the rear of the infinite universality of cognition, which negates the Nought and thus infinitely affirms itself.

CHINA

Spiritual powers alone were recognized as the essence of the world in India, and even their suspension still had to occur spiritually. China, for its part, denied these same powers of concept with equal decisiveness. For China it is precisely the fullness of the world which alone counts as real. All spirit must be material, specific, in order to qualify for place and existence here. Spiritual powers retreat before earthly interests. The Confucian system, freest of metaphysics of all systems of national ethics, has shaped and colored the life of the people down to the present day. To the extent that it still plays a role, the spiritual has become a matter of spirits. The spirits become entirely individual individuals, endowed with their own names and distinctly tied to the name of the worshiper: the spirits of his ancestors. Sacrifice is intended for them; they are present, in the midst of the living, visible, indistinguishable from them. Unhesitatingly the fullness of the world is filled to overflowing with their fullness. The question of the whereabouts of the deceased and why the world is not filled to overflowing with them was at least one of the stumbling blocks which in India significantly enough led to the doctrine of the transformation of the person through alternating forms; this type of unity of concepts above the diversity of phenomena is totally strange to the original China. Here the throng of spirits multiplies without concern, each immortal for itself, new ones ever added to the old, each distinguished prosopographically from the other. In India the individual was deprived of his distinctiveness by a caste which enclosed him, if not as a community, yet as a superior universality. In China, on the other hand, the chain of ancestors constitutes the community into which the individual is immediately inserted. This insertion, so far from robbing him of his distinctiveness, on the contrary confirms him in his external distinctiveness as the final link in the chain which runs his way. And it is only a distinctiveness in the world of which he is part. In India, Buddhism reached even behind the universal concepts for comprehension itself, and attained redemption from the world in the suspension of comprehension.[1] In China, however, Lao-tzu reached behind the all-too-visible, all-too-busy, all-too-industrious, all-too-regulated world of Confucius and, without denying its essential reality, seeks the root and source of all this headlong industry. All the fullness of action springs from this source of in-action. The immeasurable fullness of beings arises from this arch-base of the one. The secret of governing is enclosed in this: not to govern, not to prescribe and proscribe in busy calculation, but rather in being, like the root of things, oneself "without action and without inaction"; thus the world is supposed to take shape "by itself." Buddha teaches his followers to suspend the world, already become concept, in comprehension and beyond that in the

[1] In the original, there is a play on the words for reach behind, concept, and comprehension, all of which are derived from the root "to grasp."

comprehension of comprehension and thus beyond comprehension; Lao-tzu, similarly, teaches his adherents to overcome the material full-ness of occurrence by a deed-lessly tacit absorption in the nameless arch-base of noisy and denominated occurrence.

PRIMITIVE PHENOMENALISM

Here again: closest proximity to the Nought and yet not the Nought itself. Here again—and also in that outermost point gained by the Indian spirit. They are the two poles of the worldliness which cannot muster that courage for clarity of vision to which alone the configuration of things is revealed. For the world disappears when one turns one's back on it as well as when one submerges in it; only with open eyes and head held high can one behold configuration. The cool void of escape from the world, the ardent depth of love for the world —one and the other alike make India and China heirs of primeval man who escapes into the illusory world because he lacks the courage for a real inspection of the world—India, the nation dreaming with closed eyes, and China, dreaming with eyes open. And again the Greeks, that nation of discoverers, guide our species to the path of clarity. For the configuration outlined with worldly clarity is after all destined to triumph over the "supramundanely grand, rich in configurations and devoid of them by turns."

Esthetic First Principles: Inner Form

At one point, moreover, configuration already triumphed under the Greeks, and has prevailed since: in the work of art. The work of art, initially at least, does not, after all, experience those problems of transcendant interconnection which appeared to endanger the meta-logical view of the world in the last analysis. Its interconnection is initially only within itself. The mythical had already demonstrated its force as the eternal law of the realm of the beautiful, independent within itself against everything external to it, as the law, therefore, of outer form. Just so the world as configuration provides the second fundamental law of all art: self-containedness, the thoroughgoing in-terconnection of every part with the whole, of every individual detail with every other. This interconnection cannot be reduced to a unity in any logical manner, and yet it is thoroughly uniform. In it each part is inserted into the whole without an intermediary, without the

mediation of any other part. It is the law of inner form which has
its basis, once and for all, here in the metalogical view of the world.
True, the law of outer form, though it too is operative in a work of
art, reaches further yet, by substantiating the realm of the beautiful,
the "idea of the beautiful." But the law of inner form is peculiarly the
law of the work of art and of the individual thing of beauty altogether, of the beautiful configuration, of: Hellas.

The Slumber of the World

But it did not go beyond configuration, a world inwardly infinitely
wealthy, a colorfully irradiated, overwhelming cascade which, ever
renewed, ever renews its clarity and placidity in the still depths
which gather it in, but a world outwardly weak and impoverished.
Is there an Outward for it? Well, it must answer affirmatively. But
it has to add that it knows nothing of this outside and, worse yet,
wants no part of it. It cannot deny the outside, but it has no need of
it. A God there may be, but as long as he remains outside and does
not become a part of this world itself, just so long this existence of his
is invisible to its macrocosm. Man there may be, but as long as he can
only be a measure laid against this world from outside, and not a
moving force within it, just so long its microcosm is deaf to his existence, this "being there." And truly, it is entitled to remain blind and
deaf as long as God does not strive and man does not speak. As yet
the world may be satisfied to bear within itself its logos, its entire and
adequate basis. As yet it may remain what it is, its own basis and base,
inspired with its own spirit, resplendent with its own splendor; as yet
it may be—metalogical.

BOOK THREE

Man and His Self

or

Metaethics

Negative Psychology

Of man—do we really know nothing even of him? The knowledge by the self of itself, self-consciousness, has the reputation of being the most assured knowledge of all. And normal common sense bristles almost more vigorously yet than scientific consciousness if the foundation of knowledge, to him truly and literally "self"-evident, is to be pulled out from under him. And yet this occurred, albeit at a late date. It remains one of the most amazing achievements of Kant to have turned this most self-evident quantity, the I, into the most questionable object, into the problem *par excellence*. He teaches that the cognitive I can be recognized only by its fruits, by its relation to cognition, not "per se." He even knows, concerning the volitive I, that credit and blame, the actual morality of deeds, even of our own, always remains concealed from us. Thereby he constructs a negative psychology which gave an entire century, the century of a psychology *sans* soul, room for reflection. We need hardly emphasize that here too the Nought counts as starting point for reasoning for us, not as its result. Once, presumably, the absurd had to be thought. For it is the profound meaning of the much abused *credo quia absurdum* that all belief requires an absurdity of knowledge as its presupposition. Thus if the content of belief is to become self-evident, it is necessary to stamp the apparently self-evident part of knowledge as an absurdity. That is what happened in turn with the three elements of this content: with God, the world, and man. It happened with God as early as the beginning of the Middle Ages, with the world at the beginning of modern times, with man at the beginning of the nineteenth century. Thus knowledge left nothing simple and clear, and only thereupon could belief take the Simple, expelled by knowledge, under its protection and thereby become itself completely simple.

METHODOLOGY

Man is no more capable of proof than are the world and God. If knowledge nonetheless tries to prove one of these three, then it necessarily loses itself in the Nought. It cannot escape these coordinates between which every step that it takes, every move it makes is silhouetted—not even if it "took the wings of the morning and dwelt on the outermost sea." For it cannot jump the tracks defined by those three elements. Thus the Nought of evidential knowledge is here never more than a Nought of knowledge or, more exactly, a Nought of evidencing. Fact, on the other hand, which helps to lay the basis of the space wherein knowledge itself lives, works, and exists, remains unmoved in its entire and utter factuality. And knowledge can, accordingly, do no more here than to follow in the path from the Unprovable, the Nought of knowledge, on to the factuality of fact—to do, in short, for a third time what we have here already done twice.

Human Idiosyncracy

Of man too we therefore know nothing. And this nothing too is but a beginning, is indeed but the beginning of a beginning. In him too the primeval words awaken: the Yea of creation, the Nay of generation, the And of configuration. And here too the Yea creates the true existence, the "essence" in the infinite non-nought.

What is this true existence of man? The existence of God was an existence pure and simple, an existence beyond knowledge. The existence of the world existed within knowledge, it was known, universal existence. What is the existence of man in the face of God and the world? Goethe has provided the answer: "What distinguishes gods from men? That many waves walk before the former—us the wave lifts, the wave swallows, and we sink away." And Ecclesiastes teaches it: "One generation passeth away, and another generation cometh, but the earth endureth for ever." Ephemerality, that quality foreign to God and gods, to the world the perplexing experience of its own force as it ever renews itself, is to man the everlasting atmosphere which surrounds him, which he inhales and exhales with every breath that he draws. Man is ephemeral, his essence is to be ephemeral as it is the essence of God to be immortal and unconditional, or of the world to be universal and necessary. The existence of God is an existence in the unconditional, the existence of the world is an existence in the universal, the existence of man is existence in the distinctive. Knowledge reposes not below him as in the case of God, not about him and within him as in the case of the world, but rather above him. He exists, not beyond the universal validity and necessity of knowledge, but this side of it. He exists, not when knowledge ceases, but before it begins. And it is only because he exists prior to knowledge that he exists afterward too, that he again and again announces his triumphant "I am still there" to all knowledge, no matter how completely it has deluded itself with having captured him in the vessels of its universal validity and its necessity. Precisely this is his essence: that he will not be tapped into bottles; that he is eternally "still there"; that he ever exults over the peremptory dictate of the universal in his distinctiveness; that for him his own distinctiveness is not, as the world would presumably like to grant, an incident, but rather just his self-evident quality—his essence. His first word, his primeval Yea, affirms his peculiarity. This affirmation establishes his distinctiveness, his idiosyncrasy, as his essence in the boundless Not of its Nought. He is an individual, but not an individual like the Individual of the world, which momentarily shoots forth from an uninterrupted sequence of individuals. Rather he is an individual, in the boundless void of space, an individual, therefore, that knows of no individuals beside himself, that in fact knows of no "beside himself" at all because he is "everywhere," an individual not as act, nor as event, but as everlasting essence.

This idiosyncrasy of man is therefore something different from the individuality which he assumes as individual phenomenon within the world. It is not an individuality which sets itself apart from other individualities. It is not a part—whereas the individual thing confesses that it is itself a part precisely in boasting of its immunity to partition. It is "in" the infinite even if not itself infinite; it is individual and withal universal. The infinite silence of human non-Nought surrounds it. It is itself the sound which sounds in this silence, finite yet boundless.

ARCHETYPAL WORD

Here the way is clear to our symbolic language. The original affirmation, which the right side of our equations always posits, was the original "Thus." In the physis of God it had effected its absoluteness, in the logos of the world its universal validity. Thus the force which assures the individual word a meaning in the first place had become effective in the first case; that which assures it the identity of its significance in the second. Here the direction of the primeval Yea comes into force. This direction lays the basis for the meaning of the individual word, not only one and the same meaning every time, but rather its own distinctive meaning. This distinctiveness is inherent in each word prior to any application, in contrast to that distinctiveness which each particular case of application determines anew. The distinctiveness which finds its place in the personal ethos of man is one of existing character, not of surprise of the moment, of the *coup d'oeil.* "Only man is capable of the impossible, he alone can endow the moment with permanence." He can do so because he himself bears within himself as his permanent essence precisely that quality which lets the moment "hover in vacillating appearance": distinctiveness. For him alone, distinctiveness becomes the limitless peculiarity of "character," not a partitive "individuality."

SYMBOL

Peculiarity as something distinctive can only be designated by B. We have been unable to ascertain an aim in it. It is just as aimless, as far beyond active and passive, as utterly existent as the infinite existence of God. It confronts the simple, undenoted A of God as an equally simple B, equally without plus or minus. In this case one existence opposes the other. With the all-form and no-content existence of the world, however, the existence of man, wanting nothing and boundlessly distinctive, is not in contrast; rather it is wholly separate from it. No relationship at all is valid between $=A$ and B. If it were merely a question of essence, then "enmity would be placed" between God and man, while world and man, on their different levels, could not even be linked by enmity. But it is not merely a question of essence, though something of this relationship of the elements yet remains in the final form of the equation. Rather this equation reflects the fact that, on the other hand, a particularly close relation exists, after all, precisely between world and man. This is the similar occurrence in both of an aimless, absolute distinctiveness: B. Of course this B occurs as "Nay" in the case of the world, as "Yea" in that of man, as the ever new miracle of individuality with the world, as the permanent essence of character with man. But at least it is the first time, and as we shall see the only time, that a term appears more than once in our equations. The significance of this circumstance can only be recognized later.

Human Volition

The matter does not rest with the Thus of character either, any more than with a previous Thus.[1] The force of the Nay may now try itself out on the Nought of man too, after this has proved itself, as to its character, as a Nought whence affirmation could issue. Again, it is in order to wrestle the Nought to the ground in a struggle at close quarters with finiteness; again, to let a well of living waters flow from this barren rock. The Nought of the world capitulated to the triumphant Nay in the gushing fullness of manifestations. God's Nought shattered before his Nay into the ever new divine freedom of action. For man likewise his Nought discloses itself, in negation, as a kind of freedom, his freedom, though a very different one from God's. For God's freedom was infinite power without more ado, since its object was the infinite and wholly passive divine essence; it was, in fact, freedom for action. Man's freedom, on the other hand, will encounter something finite, albeit boundless, in the form of the unconditional. Already in its origin, it will thus be finite, not merely, like God's freedom, finite in the ever renewed instantaneousness of its eruption —that would be the finiteness already demanded by the immediate propulsion from the negated Nought, for all negation posits something determined, finite, as far as it is not simply the infinite affirmation which occurs in the form of negation—not merely of such a finiteness, then, as God's freedom also possesses. The finiteness of human freedom, rather, is a finiteness which, apart from its emergence, is inherent in freedom itself. Human freedom is finite freedom, but as a consequence of its origin immediately out of the negated Nought it is unconditional freedom, presupposing nought and only nought and no manner of thing, no-thing. It is thus freedom for volition, not, like God's, freedom for action; it is free will, not free power. Human freedom in contrast to divine freedom is denied capability in its very origin, but its volition is as unconditional, as boundless, as the capacity of God.

---

[1] Original emended to "*Auch bei dem 'So' des Charakters hat es nicht sein Bewenden, sowenig wie bei einem früheren So.*" from the First Edition. (Tr.)

SYMBOL

This free will is finite and momentary in its manifestations, as is the fullness of worldly phenomena. But in contrast to the latter, it is not simply satisfied with its existence; it knows another law than that of its own gravity. It does not fall headlong: it has direction. Therefore its symbol is a B on the left side of the equation, as in the case of the fullness of phenomena, but by way of differentiation a $B=$ not a simple B. Thus the symbol has the same form as the $A=$ of divine freedom, but the opposite content: (human) free will is as free as divine free action. God has no free will, man no free capability. "Being good" means, for God, doing good, but for man: willing the good. And the symbol has the same content as that of worldly manifestation, but the opposite form: in the world of phenomena, freedom appears as one content among many, but it is the "miracle" within this world, it is distinguished from all other contents.

The Independence of Man

Thus Kant, whom we just cited, secured the nature of freedom with undeniably magnificent intuition. Further developments, too, will again and again lead us close to him, albeit again and again close only to his intuitions. For the time being we will again follow the way which leads from the free will to peculiarity and on which man, who as free will and as peculiarity was but an abstraction, for the first time gains a self. For what is free will as long as it only has direction and not yet content? And what is peculiarity as long as it merely exists, merely—is? We seek the living person, the self. The self is more than volition, more than existence. How does it become this something more, this And? What happens to human volition when, following its inner direction, it enters on the path to human existence?

From the first it is finite, and consciously so, since it has direction. It wants nothing other than what it is; like God's freedom, it wants its own essence. But this own essence that it wants is a finite essence, not an infinite one in which freedom might recognize itself as power. Still entirely within its own realm, then, but already sighting its object from afar, free will recognizes itself in its finiteness without, however, in the least surrendering any of its unconditionality. At this point of its way, still entirely unconditional and yet already conscious of its finiteness, it changes from free will to defiant will. Defiance, the proud withal, is to man what power, the lofty Thus, is to God. The claim of defiance is as sovereign as the privilege of power. The abstraction of free will takes shape as defiance.

As defiance it continues to run its course—let us recall that we are dealing only with internal movements within man; relationship to things is not at all at issue—up to the point where the existence of peculiarity makes itself so noticeable to it that it can no longer proceed without paying attention to it. At this point peculiarity comes to lie—to step would already be saying too much—across the path of free will in all its tacitly existing factuality. This point is designated by a term which we have previously, anticipating somewhat, already utilized more than once for elucidating the concept of peculiarity vis-à-vis "individuality": character. Volition would dissolve into Nought in peculiarity; Mephistopheles humbles it with an allusion to peculiarity: "You still stay ever what you are." But if volition meets with annihilation in peculiarity, defiance does not do so in character; rather, it still remains thoroughly preserved as defiance. It finds its content here, its determination, not its termination. Defiance remains defiance, it remains unconditional in form, but it takes character for its content; defiance defies all with character. This is the self-consciousness of man or, putting it more briefly, his self. The "self" is what originates in this encroachment by free will upon peculiarity as the And of defiance and character.

The self is utterly self-contained, owing to its being rooted in character. Were it rooted in individuality, that is if defiance had thrown itself upon the distinctiveness of man vis-à-vis others, upon his indivisible portion in universal mankind, then that which originated would have been not the self-contained self which does not look beyond itself but rather the personality. As the origin of the term already implies, personality is man playing the role assigned to him by fate, one role among many in the polyphonic symphony of mankind. It is indeed the "greatest gift of mortal men," of every last one of them. Self has no relation to the children of men, only and always to one individual man, in short to the "self." At best a group too can have a self, if it considers itself utterly unique, like a people, for example, for whom all other peoples are "barbarians." But there is no plural of "self." The singular "personality" is only an abstraction which draws its life from the plural "personalities." Personality is always one among many; it may be compared. Self does not compare itself and is not comparable. The self is not a part, not a type case, nor a zealously guarded portion of the commonweal which it might be meritorious to "give up." All these are ideas which can only be entertained for personality. The self cannot be given up—to whom? After all there is no one available for it to "give" anything to. It is alone; it is none of the "children of men"; it is Adam, Man himself.

SYMBOL

Many predications are possible about personality, as many as about individuality. As individual predications they all follow the scheme $B=A$, the scheme in which all the predications about the world and its parts are conceptualized. Personality is always defined as an individual in its relation to other individuals and to a Universal. There are no derivative predications about self, only the one, original $B=B$. Just so there was no plurality of predications about God or the world, only the two original ones symbolized by the equations. In itself, character is just as individual as individuality. Consequently it is, in itself at least, designated by the same bare symbol B. But in contrast to individuality it appears on the right side of the equation and is therefore totally distinct from it. By appearing on the left side of the equation, individuality is characterized as subject. Character, standing on the right side of the equation, proves to be its predicate, assertion. That character is distinctive is not again mentioned, as is shown by this very place in the equation. For the distinctive develops its distinctiveness by allowing itself to become the subject of predicates. This is true of everything distinctive in the world including also individuality. A distinctive entity which itself goes over to the predicate side of the equation foregoes the possibility of having predications made about it; it foregoes the development and demonstration of its distinctiveness. It turns itself into the content of predications about something else. Of all distinctive entities only one, character, does this. Character is the predication which "defines" free will "more closely." What does free will will but a character of its own? Thus free will become defiant will, and the defiance of volition coagulates with character to shape the self.

Thus self, symbolized by the equation $B=B$, takes its stand directly opposite the God. We see how the total external contradictoriness of content, together with an equally total identity of form, is equally evident in the finished equation as it was in the equation in the making. The finished equation designates a pure self-containedness together with an equally pure finiteness. As self, assuredly not as personality, man is created in the image of God. In contrast to the world, Adam is really exactly "like God," only unadulterated finiteness where God is unadulterated infinity. The serpent has good reason to turn to man alone of all creation. As finished self man no longer stands in the same complicated relationship to the world as did the elements before they came together in the And, but rather very simply as an equal, of which, however, an opposite is predicated. The subject B can either be A or B. In the first case, $B=A$, it is world, in the second $B=B$, it is self. Apparently man can be both, as the equations teach us; in Kant's words he is a "citizen of two worlds."

Of course this expression, in itself forceful, at the same time betrays Kant's entire weakness, which initially caused even the imperishable truth of the expression to be forgotten. This weakness is the identification of both spheres as "worlds." The fact is that only one of them is world. The sphere of the self is not world, nor does it become world by being called world. "This world must perish" so that the sphere of the self can become "world." The analogy which integrates the self into a world misleads into confusion of this "world" of the self with the extant world, already with Kant and quite openly in the case of his successors. The struggle of irreconcilables, the obduracy of space and the tenaciousness of time—all these it passes over deceptively. It erases the self of man even as it means to outline it. Our equation, which emphasises the formal difference so strongly —by equating two unequals in one case, two equals in the other— does not run this danger; accordingly it can without concern exhibit the parallelism of content: that predications, albeit opposite predications, are made about one and the same thing in both cases.

The Heroic Ethos

LINES OF LIFE

Viewed from without, therefore, the self cannot be distinguished from personality. Internally, however, they are every bit as different —indeed as contradictory—as character and individuality. This will become evident at once. We have described the nature of individuality as a world phenomenon, on the basis of its orbit through the world. Natural birth was also the birth of individuality; in progeniture it died its way back into the genus. Here natural death adds nothing; the orbit is already exhausted. It is inconceivable, precisely from the side of individuality, that life should endure beyond the generation of progeny. And the endurance of individual life even beyond the years of procreativeness into old age is a completely incomprehensible phenomenon for a purely natural view of life. Right here, then, we should be led to the inadequacy of the ideas of individuality and personality for comprehending human life.

But the concepts of self and character bring us further here. Character, and therefore the self which bases itself on it, is not the talent which the celestials placed in the crib of the young citizen of the earth "already at birth" as his share of the commonweal of mankind. Quite the contrary: the day of the natural birth is the great day of destiny for individuality, because on it the fate of the distinctive is determined by the share in the universal; for the self, this day is covered in darkness. The birthday of the self is not the same as the birthday of the personality. For the self, the character, too, has its birthday: one day it is there. It is not true that character "becomes," that it "forms." One day the self assaults man like an armed man and takes possession of all the wealth in his property. This day is always a definite day, even if man no longer knows it. Until that day, man is a piece of the world even before his own consciousness; no later time of life ever attains again the objectivity of a child. The self breaks in and at one blow robs him of all the goods and chattel which he presumed to possess. He becomes quite poor, has only himself, knows only himself, is known to no one, for no one exists but he. The self is solitary man in the hardest sense of the word: the personality is the "political animal."

Thus the self is born in man on a definite day. Which day is this? It is the day on which the personality, the individual, dies the death of entering the genus. This very moment lets the self be born. The self is a *daimon*, not in the sense of Goethe's orphic stanza where the word designates just the personality, but in the sense of the Heraclitan saying "*Daimon* is for man his ethos." This speechless, sightless, introverted *daimon* assaults man first in the guise of *Eros*, and thence accompanies him through life until the moment when he removes his disguise and reveals himself to him as *Thanatos*. This is the second, and, if you will, the more secret birthday of the self, just as it is the second, and, if you will, the first patent day of death for individuality. Personality must depersonalize itself, what is individual must regenerate itself—this is made manifest even to the most obtuse imagination by natural death. That part of man over which (the idea of) genus had not yet been able to assert its rights falls prey in death to the naked, suprageneric Universal, to nature itself. But while the individual thus renounces the last remnants of his individuality at this moment, and returns home, the self awakes to an ultimate individuation and solitude: there is no greater solitude than in the eyes of a dying man, and no more defiant, proud isolation than that which appears on the frozen countenance of the deceased. Whatever of the self becomes visible to us lies between these two births of the *daimon*. Can there be anything prior, anything posterior? The visible existence of these configurations is tied to the life orbit of individuality; it is lost in the invisible at the point where it dissolves in this orbit. But it is tied to it only as if to a material on which it makes itself visible. This we already learn from the opposite direction which it maintains vis-à-vis the orbit in the decisive points. The life of the self is no orbit but a straight line leading from one unknown to another; the self knows neither whence it comes nor whither it goes. But the second birth of the *daimon*, his rebirth as *Thanatos*, is no mere epilogue like the death of individuality. This provides a status of its own to life beyond the limits of generation, to that life which in the light of the belief in personality is vain and senseless, to—old age. The aged no longer have a personality of their own; their share in the common concerns of mankind has paled to a mere memory. But the less they are still individualities, the harder they become as characters, the more they become self. This is the essential transformation which Goethe works in Faust: he has already forfeited all his rich individuality at the beginning of the Second Part and just for that reason appears at last, in the final act, as a character of consummate hardness and supreme defiance, really and truly as a self—a faithful portrait of the ages of man.

True, ethos is content for this self and the self is the character. But it is not defined by this its content; it is not self by virtue of the fact that it is this particular character. Rather it is already self by virtue of the fact that it has a character, any character, at all. Thus personality is personality by virtue of its firm interconnection with a definite individuality, but the self is self merely by its holding fast to its character at all. In other words, the self "has" its character. Precisely the nonessentiality of the definite character is after all articulated in the general equation $B=B$. In the equation $B=A$, distinctiveness is an individuality, subject of all predicates, goal of every interest; this same distinctiveness must here be satisfied to be, in its distinctiveness, the general substratum on which the structure of the individual self, ever individual and yet constantly the same, is raised.

LAWS OF THE WORLD

Thus the self makes the distinctiveness of individuality merely into its merely "distinctive presupposition." But by the same token the whole world of ethical universality which depends on this ethical distinctiveness of individuality is simultaneously relegated to this mere background of the self. Together with individuality, therefore, genus too sinks to the level of mere presupposition of the self—communities, nations, states, the whole moral world sink to this level. All this is for the self only something which it possesses, not the very air of existence which it breathes. It does not, like personality, live in it. The only atmosphere of its existence is—itself. The whole world, and in particular the whole moral world, lies in back of it; it is "beyond it," not in the sense of not needing it, but of not recognizing the laws of this world as its laws. It recognizes them merely as presuppositions that belong to it without its having to obey them in return. For the self, the world of ethics is merely "its" ethos; nothing more is left of it. The self does not live in a moral world: it has its ethos. The self is metaethical.

CLASSICAL MAN

The self in its mountainously taciturn solitude, in its freedom from all the relationships of life, its lofty restriction to itself—whence is it familiar to us, where have we already seen it with our own eyes? The answer is simple if we recall where we laid eyes on the metaphysical God and the metalogical world as configurations of life. Metaethical man too was a living configuration in antiquity, and again principally in the truly classical antiquity of the Greeks. There the forces of genus, which literally consume personalities, took shape in the phenomenon of the polis, unrestrained by counterforces. And precisely there the configuration of the self, elevating itself above all the privileges of genus, also took possession of its royal throne. It did so not only in the claims of Sophist theories, which made of the self the measure of all things, but even more so, and with the impetus of visibility, in the great contemporaries of those theories, the heroes of Attic tragedy.

Asia: Non-Tragic Man

INDIA

The tragic hero of antiquity is nothing less than the metaethical self. Therefore the tragic sense came to life only where antiquity went the whole way to the erection of this human image. India and China stopped along the way, before the goal had been reached; they attained to the tragic neither in drama nor in its prototype, the popular tale. India never arrived at the defiant identity of the self in all characters; Indian man remains mixed in character, and no world is more rigid in its characters than that of Indian poetry. Nor is there an ideal of humanity that remains as intimately tied to every organization of natural character as the Indian. A distinct law of life applies not only, say, to the generations or the castes, but even to the ages of man. Nothing is more important than that man obey this law of his distinctiveness. Not everyone has the privilege or even the duty to be a holy man; on the contrary, it is veritably prohibited to a man who has not yet founded a family. Holiness too is here one distinctiveness among many. The heroic, however, is an inner Must, universally and equally, for each and every life. Again it is the asceticism climaxing with Buddha which first reaches back of this distinctiveness of character. The perfected one is freed from everything except from his own perfection. All conditions of characters have ceased, neither age nor caste nor sex counts here. What remains is the one unconditional character, to wit, the character freed of every condition, in short, that of the redeemed one.

True, this too is still character: the redeemed is separated from the unredeemed, but the separation is altogether different from that which otherwise separates character from character; it lies behind these conditional separations as the only unconditional one. Thus the redeemed are characters at the instant of their emergence from the Nought—or more correctly: of their immersion into the Nought. Nothing really lies between the redeemed and the Nought but that admixture of individuality with which character is alloyed in consequence of the participation in the world of all living things as long as they are alive. Death makes this bit of individuality ebb back into the world; it removes this last partition separating the redeemed from the Nought and even strips him of the character of being redeemed.

CHINA

If India attributes too much to character and distinctiveness, China attributes too little to it. Here the world is rich, too rich, in individuality; the inner man, however, man, that is, to the extent that he is not regarded, as it were, from without, as a part of the world, is veritably without character. The concept of the sage, as it is once more classically personified by Confucius, passes lightly over any possible distinctiveness of character. He is truly the man *sans* character, the average man. It may indeed be said, to the honor of humankind, that nowhere except only here in China could such a tedious person as Confucius have become the classical model of the humane being. What distinguishes Chinese man is something quite different from character; it is a wholly elemental purity of feeling. Chinese feeling is without the least relation to character, without any relation, as it were, to its own bearer; it is purely objective. It exists at the instant that it is felt and it exists because it is felt. The lyric poetry of no other nation is so pure a mirror of the visible world and of the impersonal feeling released from the I of the poet, nay veritably tapped from him. There are verses by the great Li Po which no translator would dare to render without the word I; yet the original text phrases them, as the peculiarity of the Chinse language permits, without any allusion to any kind of personality, that is to say purely, as it were, in It-form. The purity of what is, after all, an entirely momentary feeling—what is this other than volition which was not privileged to materialize in a character, an agitation which remains mere agitation without any substrate. Again Lao-tzu, the great sage who overcame China in China itself, reaches behind this purity and guilelessness of feeling. Feeling still had content, no matter how elemental it was, how stripped of character. Thus it could still be seen, articulated, designated. Of Lao-tzu, however, it is said that he wanted to remain nameless. It is this "concealment of the self" which he prescribed for his perfect one too: to be unnoticeable, unattested, to let things go. Man, too, like the primeval fundament itself, must be beyond action and inaction. He does not look out the window: consequently he sees heaven; he helps all beings to their action by himself practicing inaction; his love is nameless and concealed like himself.

PRIMITIVE IDEALISM

Thus the complete dissolution of the self in Buddha's self-control and in Loa-tzu's self-effacement is a twofold one, like the complete denial of God and the complete negation of the world. All of them must be twofold, for the living gods will not be denied, nor the world of configuration negated, nor the defiant self extinguished. The powers of annihilation and of disintegration are masters only of the bare elements, the halves which have not yet coalesced into the unity of configuration. In self-control and self-effacement, then, there occurs at all times the extinction of the self, the only extinction which leads close to the complete Nought of the self without, however, disappearing in it; for in self-control and self-effacement it is, after all, still man who controls and effaces. The last of the elemental powers of primeval times takes its place beside the fear of God and the illusion of the world: the human conceit of the Magician, who knows how to escape a fate having mastery only over the self by force or guile, and who thus spares himself the defiance of the hero. Again India as well as China have shown the only two ways by which man can at all times elude his self if he cannot muster the courage to become tragic. Strictly speaking this may be true only for the redeemed of Buddhism and the perfect one of Lao-tzu, those last two superlatives of this aboriginal conceit; historically, however, neither India's soil nor China's produces the plant of tragedy at all. In India the distinction of character is too conditional, in China feeling too impersonal, and both are too separated from each other to allow tragedy to grow forth, for that presupposes an interlacing of volition and essence into the established unity of defiance. Instead of a tragic hero, this soil at most produces a pathetic situation. In pathos, the self suffocates in its misfortune; in tragedy, misfortune loses all independent power and significance. It belongs to the elements of distinctiveness on which the self stamps the seal of its defiance, that ever self-same seal: *si fractus illabatur orbis*—"may my soul die with the Philistines!"

The Tragic Hero

GILGAMESH

Even before the tragic defiance of Samson and Saul, the ancient Near East erected the archetype of the tragic hero in Gilgamesh, that figure who stands on the border of the divine and the human. The curve of Gilgemesh's life leads through the three fixed points: its beginning is the awakening of the human self in the encounter with Eros; there follows the straight line of the journey full of exploits which breaks off abruptly in the last and decisive occurrence, the encounter with Thanatos. This encounter is here made powerfully graphic: it is, initially, not his own death which directly confronts the hero, but the death of his friend; in the friend's death, however, he experiences the terror of death in general. In this encounter his tongue fails him; he "cannot cry, cannot keep silent," but neither does he submit. His whole existence becomes the enduring of this one encounter; his life gets death, his own death, which he beheld in the death of his friend, as its sole content. It is a matter of indifference that death in the end will gather him in too: that which actually counts already lies behind him at that point. Death, his own death, has become the sovereign event of his life. He himself has entered that sphere where the world becomes strange to man with its alternation of screaming and silence, the sphere of pure and lofty speechlessness, the self.

ATTIC TRAGEDY

For that is the criterion of the self, the seal of its greatness as well as the stigma of its weakness: it keeps silent. The tragic hero has only one language which completely corresponds to him: precisely keeping silent. It is thus from the beginning. Tragedy casts itself in the artistic form of drama just in order to be able to represent speechlessness. In narrative poetry, keeping silent is the rule; dramatic poetry, on the contrary, knows only of speaking, and it is only thereby that silence here becomes eloquent. By keeping silent, the hero breaks down the bridges which connect him with God and the world, and elevates himself out of the fields of personality, delimiting itself and individualizing itself from others in speech, into the icy solitude of self. The self, after all, knows nothing outside itself: it is inherently solitary. How is it to manifest this solitude, this stubborn self-reliance, other than precisely by keeping silent? And so it does in the tragedies of Aeschylus, as his contemporaries already noticed. The heroic is speechless. In Aeschylus, the dramatis personae can keep silent through a whole act; if these great silences are not found in the later dramatists, then this gain in "naturalness" is purchased at the cost of a greater loss in tragic force. For it is by no means true that the speechless heroes of Aeschylus acquire speech, the speech of their tragic self, in Sophocles and Euripides. They do not learn to speak, they only learn to debate. The dramatic dialogue luxuriates here with its artful disputations which today strike us as hopelessly frigid. Rationally it analyzes the content of the tragic situation in endless twists and turns. Thereby it withdraws the self, defiant beyond all situations, the essence of tragedy, from view until such time as it is once more restored to the center of attention by one of those lyric monologues to which the existence of the chorus again and again gives rise. The enormous importance of these lyrico-musical passages in the economy of the drama as a whole is based on the fact that Attica did not find in dialogue the dramatic technique *par excellence* —*the* form for expressing the heroic–tragic. For the heroic is volitive, while Attic dialogue is "dia-noetic," to use the expression of its earliest theoretician, of Aristotle himself; it is rational altercation.

Nor is this limitation of Attic drama a purely technical one. The self can only keep silent. At the very most, it can still seek to express itself in lyric monologue, although even this expression, *qua* expression, is no longer altogether suited to it; the self does not express itself, it is buried within itself. As soon as it enters into conversation, however, it ceases to be self. It is self only as long as it is alone. In dialogue it thus forfeits even the small headstart on speech which it had made in monologue. Dialogue does not create any relation between two wills because each of these wills can only will its isolation. Technically, the pièce de résistance of modern drama is the persuasion scene in which one will breaks the other and steers it. Such a scene, like the one which has a "woman in this humor woo'd" is therefore unknown to Attic drama. So is the love scene, as has often been observed, and this fact here finds its ultimate explanation, at once technical and spiritual. Love at most can appear in monologue as unfulfilled yearning. Phaedra's misfortune—unrequited feeling—is feasible for the ancient stage; Juliet's fortune—reciprocally augmented giving and having—is not. No bridge leads from the will of the tragic self to any kind of an exterior even if this exterior is another will. Its will gathers every impetus within itself as a defiance directed against its own character.

Thus the self lacks all bridges and connections; it is turned in upon itself exclusively. And this in turn drenches divine and worldly things with that peculiar darkness in which the tragic hero moves. He does not understand what befalls him, and he is conscious of being unable to understand it; he does not even attempt to penetrate the enigmatic rule of the gods. The poets may pose Job-like questions of guilt and fate, but to the heroes themselves, unlike Job, it never even occurs to pose them. If they did, they would have to break their silence. But that would mean stepping out of the walls of their self, and they would rather suffer in silence than do this, rather ascend the steps of the inner elevation of the self like Oedipus, whose death leaves the enigma of his life entirely unsolved and even untouched and yet, just for that, encompasses and confirms the hero entirely in his self.

This is the meaning of the hero's demise altogether. Tragedy readily creates the impression that the demise of the individual necessarily restores some kind of equilibrium to things. But this impression is based only on the contradiction between the tragic character and the dramatic argument. As a work of art, the drama needs both halves of this contradiction in order to survive, but the actual tragic element is thereby obscured. The hero as such has to succumb only because his demise entitles him to the supreme "heroization," to wit, the most closed-off "selfication" of his self. He yearns for the solitude of de-

mise, because there is no greater solitude than this. Accordingly the
hero does not actually die after all. Death only cuts him off, as it were,
from the temporal features of individuality. Character transmitted into
heroic self is immortal. For him, eternity is just good enough to echo
his silence.

PSYCHE

With immortality we touch on an ultimate yearning of the self.
Personality does not demand immortality for itself, but the self does.
Personality is satisfied with the eternity of the relations into which it
enters and in which it is absorbed. The self has no relations, cannot enter
into any, remains ever itself. Thus it is conscious of being eternal; its
immortality amounts to an inability to die. All ancient doctrines of
immortality come down to this inability of the disengaged self to die.
Theoretically, the only difficulty consists in finding a natural bearer
of this inability to die, a "something" that cannot die. This is the
origin of ancient psychology. The psyche is supposed to be the
natural something that is incapable of death by its very nature. Thus
it is theoretically separated from the body and becomes the bearer of
the self. But this linkage of the self with what is in the final analysis
still only a natural bearer, in short with the "soul," makes of immortality a most precarious possession. The soul, it is asserted, cannot
die, but being intertwined with nature, its inability to die becomes an
indefatigable capacity for transformation; the soul does not die, but
transmigrates through the bodies. Together with immortality, the self
is thus presented with the double-edged gift of transmigration, and
thereby immortality is rendered valueless precisely for the self. For if
the self, proud of the boundlessness of its transitory essence, demands
immortality at all, it demands an immortality without transformation
and transmigration. It demands self-preservation, preservation of the
self. But the "soul" in the ancient sense of the word expressly designates only a "part" of man, the one incapable of dying, not his
entirety. By being linked to this soul, the self is granted its demand
but only as if in mockery. The self remains itself, but it passes
through the least-known configurations, for not one of them becomes
its property. Even what is its very own, its character, its peculiarity,
it retains in name only. In truth no recognizable portion of it remains
to it in its passage through the configurations. It remains self only in
its complete speechlessness and unrelatedness. These it retains even in
its transformation; it always remains the sole and solitary speechless

self. It would have to renounce precisely this speechlessness, it would have to turn from solitary self to speaking soul—but soul here in a different sense, meaning a human whole beyond the contrast of "body and soul." If the self were to become a soul in this sense, then it would also be sure of immortality in a new sense, and the spectral idea of the transmigration of souls would lose its force. But how this is to happen, how one is to free the tongue and unlock the eye of the self, that is quite beyond the imagination of the self as we know it hitherto. No paths lead from $B=B$, immersed in itself to the resounding open air; all the paths only lead deeper into the silence of the interior.

Esthetic First Principles: Content

And yet there is a world where this silence is already speech—not, of course, the speech of the soul, but speech nonetheless, a speech before speech, the speech of the unspoken, the unspeakable. In the exclusive seclusion of outer form, the mythical element founded the realm of the beautiful for metaphysical theology; in the self-containedness of inner form, the plastic component established the work of art, the thing of beauty, for metalogical cosmology; just so, the tragic factor in metaethical psychology lays the foundation of the wordless understanding by which art can first become reality on the eloquent silence of the self. What originates here is content. Content bridges the gap between artist and observer, indeed between the artist as a living person and the artist who sends his *oeuvre* into the world over and beyond his own lifetime. And this content is not the world, for in the world, though it is common to all, each one has his own individual share, his distinctive point of view. Content must be something immediately equal, something which men do not share with one another like the common world but rather something which is equal in all. And that is alone the human quality per se, the self. The self is what is condemned to silence in man and yet is everywhere and at once understood. It need only be rendered visible, "acted out," in order to awaken the self in every other one as well. Itself it feels nothing at the time, it remains exiled into tragic soundlessness, it stares unflinchingly into its interior; but whoever sees it awakens, as it was once again formulated with profound foresight by Aristotle, to "terror and compassion." These awake in the spectator and at once direct themselves to his own interior, making a self out of him. If they were to awake in the hero himself, he would cease to be speechless self: *phobos* and *eleos* would disclose themselves as "awe and love," the soul would acquire speech, and the newly granted word would pass from soul to soul. There is no such rapprochement here. Everything remains speechless. The hero, who arouses terror and compassion in others, remains himself an unmoved, rigid self. In the spectator, again, the same emotions at once move inward and turn him too into a self-enclosed self. Everyone remains by himself, everyone remains self. No community originates. And yet there originates a common content. The selves do not converge, and yet the same note sounds in all: the feeling of one's own self. This wordless transfer of the identical occurs, even though no bridge as yet leads from man to man. It does not occur between soul and soul: there is no realm of souls yet. It occurs from self to self, from one silence to the other silence.

This is the world of art, a world of tacit accord which is no world at all, no real, vital, back-and-forth interconnection of address passing to and fro and yet, at any point, capable of being vitalized for moments at a time. No sound punctures this silence and yet at every instant each and everyone can sense the innermost part of the other in himself. It is the equality of the human which, prior to any real unity of the human, here becomes effective as content of the work of art. Prior to any real human speech, art creates, as the speech of the unspeakable, a first, speechless, mutual comprehension, for all time indispensable beneath and beside actual speech. The silence of the tragic hero is silent in all art and is understood in all art without any words. The self does not speak and yet is heard. The self is perceived. The pure speechless glance completes in every beholder the introversion into its own interior. Art is not a real world, for the threads which are drawn from man to man in it run only for moments, only for the short moments of the immediate glance and only at the place of the glance. The self does not come alive by being perceived. The life aroused in the beholder does not arouse the beheld to life; it at once turns inward in the beholder himself. The realm of art provides the ground on which the self can grow up everywhere; but each self is in turn a wholly solitary, individual self; art nowhere creates a real plurality of selves, although it produces the possibility for the awakening of selves everywhere: the self that awakes nevertheless only knows of itself. In the make-believe world of art, in other words, the self ever remains self, never becomes—soul.

Solitary Man

And how should it become soul? Soul would mean stepping out of the introverted confinement. But how should the self step forth? Who should summon it—when it is deaf? What is to lure it out when it is—blind? What is it to do out there when it is—speechless? It lives altogether inwardly. Only the magic flute of art could bring off the miracle of making the unison of human content resound in the discrete selves. And how limited was even this piece of magic! How it remained a world of make-believe, a world of mere possibility, this world that originated here. The same sound resounded and yet was everywhere heard only in one's own interior; no one felt the human element as the human element in others, each one only immediately in his own self. The self remained without a view beyond its walls; all that was world remained without. If it possessed the world within itself, it did so as personal property, not as world. The only humanity of which it was aware was that within its own four walls. It itself remained the only other one that it saw; every other one wishing to be seen by it had to be contained in this its field of vision and to forego being regarded as another. The ethical norms of the world thus lost all their own meaning in this field of vision of the self-willed self; they became the mere content of his self-inspection. Thus it had, presumably, to remain what it was: elevated above any world, fixing its own interior with a defiant gaze, incapable of sighting anything alien except there in its own sphere and therefore only as its own property, hoarding all ethical norms within its own ethos so that the self was and remained lord of its ethos—in short: the metaethical.

TRANSITION

Retrospect:
The Chaos of the Elements

Mythic God, plastic world, tragic man—we hold the parts in our hand. Truly we have smashed the All. The deeper we descended into the night of the positive in order to snatch up the Aught immediately upon its origin out of the Nought, the more the unity of the All shattered for us. The bric-a-brac of knowledge which now surrounds us looks passing strange to us. These are the elements of our world but we do not know them thus; it is what we believe in but we do not believe in it in the way in which it confronts us here. We know of a living movement, a circuit in which these elements swim; now they have been torn from the current. In the orbit of the constellation which shines over our life they are familiar to us and worthy of our faith in every sense; released from this orbit, reduced to mere elements of a calculated orbital construction, we do not recognize them. And how are we to recognize them? The mystery of the elements cannot be brought out into the open except by and at the curvature of the orbit. Only this curvature leads out of the merely hypothetical of the elements into the categorical of visible reality. And if the elements were more than mere "hypotheses," it remains for their capacity for constructing a visible orbit to prove as much.

THE SECRET "IF"

Hypothetical—that is the word which clarifies that strange appearance of the pieces of the universe for us. Not one of these pieces has a secure, an unalterable place; a secret If is inscribed over each. Behold: God exists and is existing life; behold: the world exists and is inspired configuration; behold: man exists and is solitary self. But don't ask how these three elements find their way to one another. How *does* man in all his solitude take his place in a world driven by spirit? How can God in all his limitlessness endure beside himself a world enclosed within itself, a mankind solitary within itself? How does this world in all its serene figurativeness still leave room for an infinite life of God or for an independent existence of man? If you ask such questions, a whole swarm of If's overpower you by way of an answer. Before you inquire, the three elements may appear to lie side by side in calm fixity, each with a one-and-all feeling about its own existence that is blind to whatever is outside. In this respect they are all three mutually equivalent. Not man alone but God too and so too the world are each of them a solitary self, each staring fixedly into itself and knowing of no Without. Not God alone but man and the world too live in the internal vitality of their own nature, without requiring any existence other than their own. Not merely the world but man and God too are configurations enclosed within themselves and inspired with their own spirit.

THE PATENT "PERHAPS"

Thus all boundaries and distinctions appear to blur; each part posits itself monistically as the whole. But what erupts here side by side are after all *three* monisms, three one-and-all consciousnesses. Three Wholes were still possible; three Alls are unthinkable. And so the question of their relationships must be asked after all. But precisely this question compounds the confusion to the highest degree. For no relationship is excluded here. There is no fixed order among the three points God, world, and man; there is no above and below, no right and left; no order of the three receives the decisive yes or no of the heathen consciousness. Each one is tried out and tested. From the If's issue forth the Perhaps'. Is God the creator of the world, the one who himself communicates himself to man in revelation? Perhaps. Plato, and with him many a mythologist of Europe and the Near East, teaches creation. In hundreds of oracular sites, on thousands of altars, in the twitching entrails of the sacrifice, in the flight of birds, in the silent progress of the stars—everywhere the mouth of the gods speaks to men, everywhere the deity descends and makes his will known. But behold: perhaps after all it is not so. Are not the gods parts and progeny of the eternal world? Thus speaks Aristotle and numerous theogenies in all manner of places with him. And the old earth's mouth —does it not reveal to man everything which it avails him to know? All of heathendom does not finish the struggle between Gaea and the celestials for the rights to the oracles. And the very gods themselves descend to seek counsel at the Earth's lips; they inquire into their divine destiny at the pronouncement of the old mother's wise and prescient son. And as for him: who knows but that he himself—he, the measure of all things—is not the true creator, and everything constituted as his specifications ordained. Have not men, by human dictum, been promoted to the stars? Become gods? Indeed, are not perhaps all those who today are venerated as gods deceased humans of another age, kings and heroes of prehistory? Is not perhaps everything divine simply elevated human self? But no—human life crawls along in all its weakness, tied to earth and of gods in awe; with humble prayer it attempts to bend the will of the celestials; it en-counters the coercion of the external with the counterforce of magical powers. But it is never capable of crossing the limits of the human; the somber power of earth and of unfathomable fate press down his proud neck: how is he to presume himself master of earth and destiny?

Perhaps, perhaps. . . . We have ended in a maelstrom of contradictions. One moment it seems as if God, the creator and revealer, thrones above, man and the world at his feet; the next as if the world occupied the throne, with God and man its progeny; and then again as if man stood uppermost, himself the measure of all things, meting out the laws of his nature to gods and the world. There is after all no drive in any of the three to come together; each one originated only as a result, as conclusion, self-contained, eyes directed inward, each an All to itself. In such a situation only caprice, only Perhaps, can assert—no, not assert, at most surmise—interconnections, and any one interconnection, one order, will do as well as any other. Perhaps, perhaps—there is no certainty, only a rotating wheel of possibilities. If piles on If, Perhaps under Perhaps.

And Perhaps reigns even within each of the three. Nothing less than number and order remain uncertain here. If each is an all unto itself, then it harbors the possibility for unity as well as for plurality. In mere existence, everything is possible, and no more than possible. And what we have found so far has been pure existence, pure "matter-of-factness": the factuality of the divine, the human, the worldly—a major matter vis-à-vis the pure incertitude of doubt, a trifle compared to the claim of belief. Belief cannot be satisfied with the mere factuality of existence. Its demand goes beyond this existence in which everything is still possible under the single presupposition of existing; it demands unambiguous certainty. But this is what existence is no longer able to provide. The relationship which, as reality, mediates between the facts of existence—this and this alone establishes an unambiguous number, an unambiguous order. This is true even of the simplest relationships. Whether the number 3, for example, is a unit or a multiple is determined only by the equation which relates it to other numbers. Only its equation with 1×3, for examples, defines it as a unit, or with 3×1 as a multiple. Prior to the equation it is mere existence and, as such, integer, universality, universal possibility; it can be determined only through the product of infinity and zero—a product which is absolutely indeterminate, which contains within itself all possibilities. As with number, so with order: whether the individual existence, the point x_1, say, or y_1, or z_1, is an element of a straight line, a curve, a plane, or a solid, and, if so, of which straight line, which curve, which plane, which solid, this can only be determined by the equation which brings the point into differential relationship with x_2, y_2, z_2. Previously, the point is universal possibility, precisely because, as firm "factuality," it has existence in space. So too the three elements of the universe can be recognized, each in its inner potentiality and structure, in its number and rank, only when they enter into a real and unambiguous relationship with one another which is removed from the maelstrom of possibilities.

THE PREVALENT "WHO KNOWS"

While antiquity was thus in lively possession of the factuality of man, world, and God, it nevertheless failed to extract their mutual relationships from the mists of the Perhaps, pregnant with configurations, into the clear and unambiguous light of reality. Therefore it was unable to achieve clarity on any question which leads beyond mere factuality. One God or many gods, a realm of gods or several realms, quarrelling with one another or allied against one another or succeeding one another in the succession of the ages?

Who knows, who knows, who knows . . . One world or many worlds, juxtaposed or superimposed or succeeding one another—in a straight line or in circles returning upon themselves in eternal recurrence? Who knows, who knows, who knows . . . One and the same self in all humanity or many selves, humanity following humanity in generations, assembled against one another in aggregates, subdivided into individual selves ad infinitum, or heroes grouped together into a heroic community of a Valhalla or an Elysium—into a battle of Achaians and Trojans, a succession of patriarchal history and epigonic revenge, or again the solitary hero, performing his deeds in a world without heroes, and ascending to the gods, alone in the flaming pyre? Who knows, who knows, who knows . . .

A glittering shimmer of Perhaps covers gods, worlds, and men. Paganism perfected the structure of the monism of each of these three elements in the consummate feeling, one and universal, of their factuality. And precisely for this reason it is not merely "polytheism" but also "polycosmism," and "polyanthropism." Precisely for this reason it fragments the universe, already broken down into its factualities, once more into the splinters of its possibilities. The factuality of the elements, substantial but lackluster, is dissipated in the ghostly mists of possibility. Above the gray Realm of the Mothers,[1] paganism celebrates its classic Witches' Sabbath with a chromatic dance of the Spirits.

Prospect: *The Cosmic Day of the Lord*

MOVEMENT
Thus the chaotic mix-up of the Possible is but the externally visible appearance of the elemental internal fragmentation of the real. If we wish to bring order, clarity, nonambiguity—in short, reality—into this dizzying whirl of the Possible, then it is necessary to cure those elements of their subterranean fragmentation, to articulate them, to transport them out of their mutual exclusiveness into a free-flowing interrelationship, to "emerge" upward once more instead of "submerging" in the night of positivism where every something would like to assume the gigantic proportions of the All. But the one and only river of cosmic time alone carries us upward, back into the one and only All of reality. This river itself carries with it those seemingly static elements in a rolling movement in which it brings these elements, separated by their plunge into the darkness of the Aught, back together again from cosmic morn via cosmic noon to cosmic eve in the one and only cosmic Day of the Lord.

But how are the elements to begin their course? Are we to conduct a current to them from without? Never! For then the current itself would be an element and the three elements no longer its elements. No, the path of the coursing movement must originate in the elements themselves, and wholly and only in the elements. Otherwise they would not be the elements, and our belief in their factuality, on which we have so far bravely based ourselves, would not be confirmed by the picture of the mobile reality in which we live. The elements

[1] The primordial forces of Goethe's *Faust*. (Tr.)

themselves must harbor the potential whence movement originates and the reason for the order in which they enter the current.

TRANSFORMATION

They are to bear within themselves the force whence movement springs? But how are they to do this? We found them precisely in their factuality, in their blind introversion: how are they to direct their gaze outward? What does this demand mean? How are the results to become origins? They are to do so, but how? Let us recall how they became results for us. We let them "originate" from the Nought of knowledge, conducted by the belief in their factuality. This origin is not a matter of originating in reality, but rather it is a passage in space prior to all reality. The reality of the three results does not border on anything real, nor did they originate out of anything real for us; rather they are neighbors of Nought, and their origin is the Nought of knowledge. Thus the forces which in the end converge in the result—in God they are the deed of power and the compulsion of destiny; in the world, birth and category; in man, defiance of will, and peculiarity—these forces are not forces of visible reality. Rather they are mere stopovers on the path of us, the cognitive ones, from the Nought of our knowledge to the Aught of knowledge. Or, if a "real Nought" corresponds to the Nought of our knowledge, as we presumably must admit, then they are mysterious for us beyond any reality that will ever be visible to us, occult powers that are at work inside God, world, and man before ever God, world, and man are revealed. But in becoming revealed, all those mysterious generative powers now become a thing of the past, and what appeared to us hitherto as result becomes itself beginning. And similarly too, even if we would rather regard the Nought only as a Nought of knowledge, while we gingerly make our way along the tightrope of the consciousness of cognition, even then reality only begins with the finished result, and thus here too the result becomes a beginning vis-à-vis the Real. But what we took for secret generative forces before the birth into the manifest, or for last stages on the road of the cognitive construction, that will emerge out of them as first revelation of their interior at the point when the results convert into origins. That which made them real, converging in them beyond reality, will thus flow from them into the Here of reality as first testimony to their turning toward effectiveness. It is a turning, a conversion. What converged as Yea will radiate forth as Nay; what entered as Nay will issue as Yea. For be-

coming manifest is the converse/conversion of becoming. Only becoming is secret, but becoming manifest is—manifest.

ORDER

   Thus the purely factual transforms itself into the origin of real
movement. From finished rings they become links in a chain. But how
do the links range themselves? Is there some indication at least of their
rank and order for the chain of the route in the elements themselves,
in spite of their blind introversion, just as the precondition for their
conversion into the manifest already existed in them themselves, in
spite of their introversion? Let us see. We found God, world, and
man in those forms in which a mature heathendom had believed them
to be: in the living god of myth, in the plastic world of art, in the
heroic man of tragedy. But at the same time we presented these living
realities of a historical antiquity as the presence of an idea, by asserting
that the basic characteristic of the sciences of God, world, and man
consisted of the metaphysical, the metalogical, and the metaethical.
Indeed, in the prefatory introduction we attempted to demonstrate
that these basic characteristics of science were the specifically modern
and contemporary ones. An apparent contradiction—or could it be
that we wish to renew heathendom, perhaps immediately, with this
modernity of the metaphysical, metalogical, metaethical point of view?
Let us rather postpone the answer to the last question till later; the
apparent contradiction will resolve itself anyhow without it.

CONSEQUENCE

   The fact is that our demonstration did not always establish the same
relationship between modern science and its respective realization in
history in the three cases. In the case of the mythical God, the locus
of historical conception was the conception of God in which antiquity believed; in the case of tragic man, it was antiquity's vital self-
consciousness, in that of the plastic world its generated *Weltanschauung*. Apparently the difference does not go deep: in reality it
goes deeper even than we may demonstrate in these merely transitional
remarks. For the conception of God in the belief of antiquity contains
the heritage which came to it from an immemorial past; in its vital
self-consciousness we see the very air which it breathed, in the generated *Weltanschauung* the inheritance which it bequeathed to posterity.
Thus antiquity appears in a threefold temporal guise: a prehistory

which lies in the past for it too, a present which came and went with it, and an afterlife which leads beyond it. The first is its theology, the second its psychology, the third its cosmology. In all three we have learned to see only elementary sciences, for they mean to us no more than a doctrine of "elements" for all their modernity. Elementary sciences means to a certain extent sciences of prehistories, of the somber bases of origins: ancient theology, psychology, cosmology, that is, mean for us so to speak theogony, psychogony, cosmogony. Thus we have established the significant difference and we have established it without especially aiming at it, simply in carrying out our general objective. This difference is that theogony, the history of the birth of God, signified a past time to antiquity, while psychogony, or the history of the birth of the soul, signified a present life, and finally cosmogony, the history of the birth of the world, a future. This would, therefore, imply that God's birth had occurred before antiquity, the soul's birth happened during antiquity, and the birth of the world would be completed only after the decline of antiquity. And with this we would have an indication in these three births from out the dark depth, in these three creations (if we would once dare to use the term), of a distribution of the "elements" over the great universal day, the heavens on which their orbit will leave its mark. Let us formulate it briefly and leave the detailed description for later: God has been from the first, man became, the world becomes. Regardless of how we may yet distinguish these three births from the depths, these three creations—this their sequence in world-time we have already been able to recognize here. For what we have so far recognized of the All—by recognizing the everlasting elements—was nothing other than the secret of its everlasting birth.

A secret: for it is not yet manifest to us,
and cannot be manifest, that this everlasting birth out of the depth is—
creation. This becoming manifest of the everlasting mystery of creation is that
ever renewed miracle
of revelation. We are
standing   at   the
transition — the
transition from
the mystery
into the
miracle.

PART

II

THE COURSE
or
THE ALWAYS-RENEWED COSMOS

INTRODUCTION

On the Possibility of Experiencing Miracles

In theologos!

Concerning Belief

If miracle is really the favorite child of belief, then its father has been neglecting his paternal duties badly, at least for some time. For at least a hundred years the child has been nothing but a source of embarrassment to the nurse which he had ordered for it—for theology. She would have gladly been rid of it if only—well if only a degree of consideration for the father had not forbidden it during his lifetime. But time solves all problems. The old man cannot live forever. And thereupon the nurse will know what she must do with this poor little worm which can neither live nor die under its own power; she has already made the preparations.

If one may trust old reports, this was formerly a happy family life. What is it, then, that in relatively recent times broke it up so thoroughly that the present generation can hardly even recall those better days which transpired so recently? For once upon a time miracles were no embarrassment to theology, but on the contrary its most effective and reliable confederate. And it is a fact that today we are barely willing to believe that there was once such a time, and that it has only just passed into history. Just what has happened in the meantime? And how did it happen?

The timing of this about-face is the first observation which forces itself on our attention, and it is already quite remarkable. What had hitherto been the firmest and ultimate line of defense was transformed into a front-line trench, very lightly manned and immediately expendable on the first assault. And the timing of this transformation coincides with that moment which, in the Introduction to the preceding Part, we again and again recognized as critical for philosophy too.

93

It was the moment when the concept of the uniformly cognitive universe, the basic concept of philosophy, burst into pieces in philosophy's hands while they deemed it secure in their grasp. At that moment, philosophy had felt its ancient throne tottering. The dynasty which Thales and Parmenides had founded, and which—an exile of a thousand years included—was more than two millennia old, seemed, in a single greatest scion, headed for an extinction as brilliant as it was sudden. And at approximately the same time, theology too saw itself forced to undertake the aforementioned evacuation of a line it had held for centuries, and to occupy a new position further to the rear. A striking coincidence!

The Theology of the Miracle

THE MIRACLE BELIEVED

When Augustine or some other Church Father had to defend the divinity and veracity of revealed religion against heathen attacks and doubts, he scarcely failed to point to miracles. Although they were not claimed by revealed religion alone—Pharaoh's wise men had also certified their wisdom through miracles—they constituted the most powerful argument. For even if the heathen magicians might transform their rods into snakes—the rod of Moses consumed the rods of the idolators. One's own miracles were more miraculous than the miracles of the adversary. Thus the measure of miraculousness—which a rationalist mentality would have depressed as much as possible—was, on the contrary, raised as much as possible: the more miraculous, the truer. Although there existed a concept of nature such as today spoils the joy in the miraculous for the common consciousness, it did not then, strange to say, bar the way. The lawfulness of natural occurrence, this basic dogma of contemporary humanity, was thoroughly self-evident also to earlier humanity. For in our case it amounts, in practice, to the same thing, whether everything is guided and determined by forces operating in things by law, or by the influence of superior powers. Had it been otherwise, it would have to strike us as enigmatic just how miracles could become perceivable as such. To us today miracle seems to require the background of natural law before which alone it can, so to speak, be silhouetted. Herewith, however, we fail to see that, for the consciousness of erstwhile humanity, miracle was based on an entirely different circumstance, namely, on its having been predicted, not on its deviation from the course of nature as this had previously been fixed by law. Miracle is substantially a "sign." In a wholly miraculous world, wholly without law, an enchanted world, so to speak, it is true—and has already been remarked—that the individual miracle could hardly strike one as a miracle. It attracts attention by virtue of its predictedness, not of its unusualness. The latter is not its nucleus but only its "make-up," though as such often highly necessary for its effectiveness. The miracle is that a man succeeds in lifting the veil which commonly hangs over the future, not that he suspends predestination. Miracle and prophecy belong together. Whether a magic effect is operative in miracle at the same time may be left open and is left open; in any case it is not essential: sorcery and portent lie on different planes. Thou shalt not leave a sorcerer alive, the Torah commands. Of the prophet, on the other hand, it commands an examination as to whether his predicted portent makes its appearance. A wholly distinct evaluation manifests itself herewith. The magician turns on the course of the world in active intervention and in the judgment of the theocracy therefore commits a capital offense. He attacks God's providence and seeks by audacity, guile, or coercion to extort from it what is unforeseen and unforeseeable by it, what is willed by his own will. The prophet, on the other hand, unveils, as he foresees it, what is willed by providence. What would be sorcery in the hands of the magician, becomes portent in the mouth of the prophet. And by pronouncing the portent, the prophet proves the dominion of providence which the magician denies. He proves it, for how would it be possible to foresee the future if it were not "provided"? And therefore it is incumbent to outdo the heathen miracle, to supplant its spell, which carries out the command of man's own might, with the portent which demonstrates God's providence. This explains the delight in miracle. The more miracle, the more providence. And unlimited providence, the concept that in truth not a hair will fall from a man's head but by the will of God, precisely this is the new concept of God which revelation brings. It is a concept through which God's relationship with man and the world is established in an unequivocal and unconditional manner wholly foreign to heathendom. In its time, miracle demonstrated just that on which its credibility today seems to be coming to grief: the predestined lawfulness of the world.

Thus the idea of natural law, as far as it was present, comported excellently with miracle. Later that idea assumed the modern form of immanent legality in which it is familiar to us. From here too, at first, no shattering of the belief in miracle ensued as a result. On the contrary: the circumstance that the laws of nature fix only the inner interconnection of occurrence, not its content—in other words, that by saying that everything happens naturally, nothing is said about what exactly it is that "happens naturally"—this circumstance, which has virtually disappeared from today's common consciousness of natural law, was taken remarkably seriously by that epoch. Even there, then, miracle by no means appeared to contradict the unconditional validity of natural law as yet. From creation on, so to speak, miracle had been laid out along with everything else, to emerge one day with the inevitability of natural law. Thus the difficulties must have come from another direction.

THE CONFIRMED MIRACLE

In earlier times, then, the scepticism about miracles was not actually directed, as it is today, against their general possibility, but rather against their specific reality, against the credibility of the individual miracle. Miracle had to be proven, not like a general proposition, but as a particular occurrence. It required witnesses. The necessity of proving this and this alone was always acknowledged and so far as possible satisfied. We encounter every form of judicial proof here: from the weakest sort—circumstantial evidence—to the most substantial —the sworn witness and the trial by ordeal. Even in law, circumstantial evidence did not come into favor until very late, and for miracles too it plays only a slight role, a slighter one, at least, than one might expect here. This is because the circumstantial evidence for the miracle can be supplied by its success; but this success proves the miracle only for those for whom it is a "portent," that is, for those who as eyewitnesses attended the miracle in the entire course of its occurrence, including its prediction and its fulfillment, the two factors that are decisive for its miraculous character. Prediction, the expectation of a miracle, always remains the actually constitutive factor, while the miracle itself is but the factor of realization; both together form the "portent." To lend the character of a portent to their miracles of revelation is, accordingly, of supreme value both to Scripture and to the New Testament. The former does so through the promise to the patriarchs, the latter through the prophecies of the prophets.

Thus the proof of miracles must basically fall back on eyewitnesses. In taking their sworn testimony, their personal credibility will be decisive, as well as the estimate of their capacity for observation, and even their numbers. Thus, for example, ancient Jewish dogma by preference corroborated the greater credibility of the miracle of Sinai as against that of the empty grave (of Jesus) with the impressive number of the "600,000" eyewitnesses. But even the sworn deposition is still not the crowning proof. In spite of everything, it may be consciously or unconsciously false, without him who passes judgment noticing it. Only the testimony that is maintained through the tortures of an inquisition provides complete certainty. The Satan of the Book of Job already knew this: only he is a true witness who testifies with his life's blood. Thus the most cogent proof of the miracle is the appeal to the martyrs, in the first instance to those martyrs who had to corroborate the testimony of their eyes with their martyrdom, but beyond this also to the later martyrs. With their blood, these validated the steadfastness of their belief in the credibility of those who had transmitted the miracle to them, that is, in the last analysis, of the eyewitnesses. A witness for whose credibility others literally pass through the flames must be a good witness. The testimony of oath and the testimony of blood thus amalgamate and after several centuries both ultimately become a single proof in Augustine's famous appeal from all individual reasons to the present historical overall-manifestation, the *ecclesiae auctoritas*, without which he would not credit the testimony of Scripture.

The belief in miracles, and not just the belief in decorative miracles, but that in the central miracle of revelation, is to this extent a completely historical belief. Even the Lutheran reformation altered nothing in this respect. It only moved the path of personal confirmation from the periphery of the tradition, where the present is located, directly into the center, where the tradition originated. Thereby it created a new believer, not a new belief. Belief remained historically anchored, even though a kind of mystical eyewitness displaced the proof, cemented together out of the witness of oath and blood, from the visible Church. Least of all could anything be altered here, as already demonstrated, by the scientific Enlightenment which commenced at the same time or a little later. To make things difficult for this belief required another enlightenment than the scientific one—it required a historical enlightenment.

The Three Enlightenments

There is not just one enlightenment, but a number of enlightenments. One after another, they periodically represent for the belief which has entered the world that knowledge with which it must contend. The first enlightenment is the philosophical one of antiquity. All of

Patristic literature dealt with it. Its campaign against pagan mythology was taken over with complete equanimity. Its claim to omniscience was at first contradicted—what has the disciple of Greece in common with the disciple of Heaven? But step by step, albeit with ultimate reservations, this claim was gradually conceded. That which still branded Origen as a heretic approached that which Thomas Aquinas taught about belief a millennium later and which the Church accepted from him. At any rate it came closer to this than to the doctrine of the anti-Thomists. That Luther fought "Aristotle" when he rebelled against the medieval church was no accident. The epoch inaugurated by him has, in fact, a new enlightenment at its side in the form of the Renaissance, which also fights Aristotle, though from its own point of view. After the philosophical mists of its childhood have lifted, this enlightenment proves ever more clearly a scientific one. It enters the struggle against the rational knowledge of Scholasticism as an unsolicited ally of belief. Just like belief, it takes over essentially only the positive evaluation of nature as the legacy of Scholasticism. According to the view which matured in the Middle Ages, nature was superseded by the supernatural, but neither denied or rejected. This new concept of nature then coalesced into a reliance on experience and a demand for personal confirmation in belief as well as in knowledge. In its turn, it was overtaken by the new "enlightenment" of that period which we are accustomed to designate by this name in particular. The enlightenment of antiquity had directed its criticism against the dreams of mythology, that of the Renaissance against the webs of intellect. The new enlightenment directed it against the gullibility of experience. As critique of experience, it became, slowly but surely, a historical critique. And as such it now approached the hitherto unshattered belief in miracles.

The entire debate about miracles, beginning with Voltaire and continuing without interruption for an entire century, amazes us today by its almost total lack of principle. The major achievements of the critique—by Voltaire himself, by Reimarus and Lessing, by Gibbon—are always directed at a very specific segment of the miraculous event. The attempt is there made to demonstrate the tradition as incredible, the reasons hitherto advanced for its credibility as inadequate, whatever held out against the critique as explicable by natural causes, that is, without the assumption of a foreseeable and therefore foreseen evolution. But the general possibility of miracles is left entirely in suspension. Nor is this a conscious half-way measure, as we might initially think today, but rather honest uncertainty. As long as the arrested miracles of the past have not been proved with certitude not to have happened, just so long one also dare not, on principle, contest the possibility of miracles.

There is a transitional phenomenon which occurs regularly and which designates the moment when this examination appears, in essence, to be decided to miracle's detriment: the attempt to explain away miracles rationally. It begins in the later decades of the eighteenth century and reaches its zenith in the first decades of the nineteenth. Previously, one had felt no need for it. On the contrary, miracle had previously been in truth the favorite child of belief. The attempt to explain miracles away rationally is a confession that this belief is beginning to be ashamed of its child. Belief would rather have, precisely, as little of the miraculous to show for, and no longer as much as possible. The erstwhile crutch has become a burden which one strives to shake off. But it is time to seek a new crutch when the old one breaks. As we have seen so far, each enlightenment unintentionally supplied the advancing epoch with arms in its struggle against the epoch that had gone by. And so it is now, too. For it is a new epoch that advanced around 1800.

The Historical Weltanschauung

This time enlightenment meant historical enlightenment. As historical critique, it had rendered the eye-witness of miracle noncredible, and thereby miracle itself as a historical fact. The subject had begun to waver, not only for the transmitted faith of the visible Church, but also for Luther's faith which went back directly to Scripture as the ultimate source. But the new pietistic mysticism had already prepared, since the end of the seventeenth century, a new concept of belief which was virtually independent of the historical objectivity of miracles. And this new belief now received unexpected support from precisely that enlightenment which had undermined the old belief. The historical *Weltanschauung* grew directly out of the critique. Since the simple acceptance of tradition was no longer admissible, it was necessary to discover a new principle according to which those *disjecta membra* of the tradition which the critique had left in its wake could again be fused into one vital whole. This principle was found in the idea of "progress" of humanity. This idea emerged with the eighteenth century, and since 1800 has conquered the intellectual world along a broad front and in a variety of forms. Thereby the past was surrendered to cognition, but volition felt liberated from the past and turned to face present and future, for, to volition, progress seems harnessed between these two.

This orientation toward present and future was also inherent in the new direction which belief had assumed. Enlightenment connected present and future through its confidence in progress; the individual sustained himself on the certainty that, though the present century was not yet equal to his ideal, he could feel himself a citizen of the centuries to come. Just so, for its part, the new belief fastened the present moment of the inner breakthrough of grace to the confidence of its future implementation in life. It was a new belief even if it sought, at times, to speak the language of Luther. For on the one hand it surrendered Luther's mooring of the living belief in the firm bottom of the past, and tried to concentrate belief wholly into the present of experience. On the other hand it let this present experience merge into the future of "practical" life with an emphasis diametrically opposed to Luther's doctrine. Luther had tried to provide an objective support for belief by basing it on a past attested by Scripture; for his Paulinism, implementation in the future could at most be a consequence of belief. But the new faith even thought to provide that support through its hopeful confidence in that future implementation. This hope in the future realm of morality became the star to which belief hitched its world course. One has only to hear the Credo of Beethoven's *Missa Solemnis*. In it, the great son of this period triumphantly proclaims the words of the *vita venturi saeculi* in ever new repetitions as if they were the very crown of the whole belief, its sense and its confirmation. And the idea of progress born of the new *Weltanschauung* acted as a secular abettor—and also, it is true, as a competitor—precisely with respect to this hope of the new belief.

SCHLEIERMACHER

Thus the enduring value of the past was denied and the ever present experience of religious emotion was anchored in the eternal future of the moral world. In Schleiermacher this whole system found its classical representative. All subsequent theology has had to come to terms with him. His basic position has hardly been shaken. But in detail this intellectual construct was still quite questionable. True, it was possible to heave the past overboard, overburdened as it was with miracles and therefore now with doubts; without this ballast, it was possible to bring the ship of belief, already dangerously rammed, safely across the ocean of the present—or so one could delude oneself. But who was to say that what was dropped, really dropped? The past was far from obliging theology by really drowning. Rather it fastened itself to the outside of the vessel from which it had been thrown, and thus burdened it even more heavily than before when it had been suitably stowed away in the interior. The theology of the nineteenth century had to become historical theology not because of Schleiermacher but in spite of him—and yet again for the sake of Schleiermacher. For it was here that the durability of his fundamental idea, which after all had become the fundamental idea of the age, was in the last analysis decided.

HISTORICAL THEOLOGY

Historical theology set itself a task vis-à-vis the past. Of what did this task consist? Since it was sought by theologians, cognition was after all but a means to an end. But which end? The past was surely supposed to be unimportant to belief. Still, it was there, and thus it had to be interpreted so that, at the least, it would not become a burden to belief. And this is what happened in the fullest measure. Once this goal had been sighted, the path to it became extremely clear. The past has to assume the traits of the present. Only thus does it became completely harmless for the present. The idea of development is conjured up as a subservient spirit in order to arrange the material up to a certain culmination, the former miracle of revealed belief. Thereupon it is given its walking papers; it has "done its duty and may go." This culmination is simply equated with the content of the experience of the present, with the result that, in its unessential part, the past is neutralized by the idea of evolution. In its essential part, however, it is assimilated to the present experience to that point of confusion. Yet this is the only part which could claim to count as a yardstick of this experience. As a result only present and future exist for belief, precisely in line with the new fundamental attitude. The "Kantian" theology of Ritschl and his school had asserted the complete independence of belief from knowledge, doubtlessly in continuation of the fundamental idea of Schleiermacher, and this theology was left in full command of the field by historical theology. For it is the objectivity of knowledge which, in the last analysis, hides behind the concept of "the past." Historical theology is commissioned to intercept what has transpired, and partly to pigeonhole it, partly to clothe it anew, that is, in essence, to erect a Chinese wall against knowledge. As for knowledge itself, "liberal" theology expects an achievement of it which orthodox theology does not dare to demand of it: the claims of science, which have already been rejected in principle, are to be, in addition, turned down in each individual case by "scientific means." And lo and behold: historical theology achieved what was expected of it.

THE TURN OF THE CENTURY

With this achievement, however, historical theology hopelessly compromised its status as a science. Nor is it any wonder that no one today can therefore any longer repose any confidence in it. The procedure had after all been too transparent. In time the present had itself to pay its toll to time and become past. At that time, if not at once, it could hardly escape notice that these transformations of the present were promptly accompanied by transformations of the past caught in the "mirror" of science. About the turn of the century, the edifice of historical theology collapsed without hope of reconstruction under the immanent critique of Albert Schweitzer and under the audacious hypothesis of those who denied the historical Jesus on the one hand, and of the pan-Babylonianists on the other. A wholly new construction had now to be undertaken, far from the ruin heap. But one could not proceed in the same cavalier manner here as with historical theology. The present too wants to hold on to the fundamental position: the primacy of hope or, more precisely, the orientation of instantly experienced personal belief by the pole of the certainty that "the kingdom of the noble will eventually arrive." Precisely if one wants to do this the claims of knowledge must be satisfied more fundamentally and in particular more immediately than by simply applying new make-up to the past. Philosophy is a knowledge of the world in its systematic entirety for which no amount of knowledge of a simple part, be it ever so central, can be substituted, and it will have to prepare itself to collaborate with theology. And the weather vanes of the age already point throughout in this direction. The clamor for philosophy becomes audible in theology along its whole length. A new theological rationalism is advancing. The epigones and renovators of "German idealism" again prepare to "generate" belief out of ideal-istic intellect and thereby to "justify" it. At the same time, orthodox circles, likewise still easily satisfied, try to stake out belief's place exactly and to secure it. And the most determined systematic philoso-pher of the last generation nourishes the flame of a theology of his beliefs with a whole system, rather "like a fool in love who would explode sun, moon and all the stars for the diversion of his sweetheart."

TASK

The school of Ritschl asserted a separation between theology and philosophy which involved the neglect of "creation" and an over-emphasis on "revelation," to use the expressions of theology itself which this school employed, albeit but hesitantly. Thus creation has once more to be placed next to the experience of revelation in the full gravity of its substantiality. More than this: the only connection which hope is able to establish between revelation and redemption, and which today is felt to be the essential core of belief, is the trust in the coming of an ethical kingdom of eventual redemption; revelation itself, together with its involvement in and foundation upon this trust, must once more be built into the concept of creation. Both revelation and redemption are creation in a certain manner that cannot be analyzed as yet. Here, then, lies the point from which philosophy can begin to reconstruct the whole edifice of theology. It was creation which theology neglected in the nineteenth century in its obsession with the idea of a vitally present revelation. And precisely creation is now the gate through which philosophy enters into the house of theology.

The New Rationalism

The connection between knowledge and the concept of the past shows itself in this relationship to creation. Truth is always that which has been, whether as "a priori," or "towering in ancient sacred might" with Plato, or as object of "experience." Thus the trust in historical theology was unjustified from the start, but only because here no more than a segment of knowledge was allowed to come to terms with belief. Beyond that, admittedly, historical theology posed the wrong question and suffered accordingly; it denied to knowledge the right to realize its characteristic of being—just as the past alone can be—unalterable. Instead, it demanded that knowledge look out for, or rather look after, the experience of the present. It is the characteristic of knowledge to get "to the bottom" of things, and we therefore allow it to realize this characteristic by constructing it on the concept of creation. We make belief wholly the content of knowledge, but of a knowledge which itself lays its foundations on a fundamental concept of belief. This can only become apparent in the course of the procedure itself, for the fundamental concept of belief cannot be recognized as such until knowledge has arrived at the exposition of belief.

This new theological rationalism, however, here adumbrated in out-line—does it not conjure up again all the reservations which finished off its older brothers? Is not here too philosophy in danger of being reduced to the status of handmaiden of theology, or else theology in danger of being made superfluous by philosophy? How can we relieve this mutual distrust? Hardly otherwise than by demonstrating that both sides need something which in each case only the other party can supply. This is, after all, really the case. Philosophy found itself at a point where no further advance remained to it, where, indeed, every attempt to proceed further could only end in a plunge into the bottomless abyss. And at the very same historical moment, theology suddenly felt itself robbed of what had been up till then its firmest support, of miracles. We have to revert here once more to this con-spicuous fact. This simultaneity is more than coincidence. That is, in a sense, already attested by the relationships of personal history, and at times even personal union, which run back and forth between the bearers of the two about-faces. If, thus, it is more than a coincidence, then the reciprocal need must be demonstrable, and with it the base-lessness of the mutual distrust.

Philosophy and Theology

OLD PHILOSOPHY

About 1800, philosophy solved the problem of the cognitative cog-nition of the All, which it had posed to itself. (Here we must not hesitate to resume what has occasionally already been stated above.) By comprehending itself in the history of philosophy, nothing more was left for it to comprehend. It "generated" the truth-content of belief and discovered it to be its own methodological root, thereby overcoming the contradiction with that content. Thus it arrived at the goal of its material mission, and attested to this accomplishment by erecting the one-dimensional idealistic system which had been planned in it from the beginning but became ripe for realization only with this moment. Here the historical finale finds its right and fitting representation. The one-and-universal character of knowledge, in-cluding everything without exception, is formally one-dimensional. The ever multiple appearance of being is absolutely dissolved in that unity as in something absolute. A content may assume a particularly conspicuous position in this system, and belief makes such a claim for its content. But this position can only be that of the principle which, as method, consolidates the system itself as a unity. And precisely this position is accorded to the belief-content in Hegel's system. If we are to proceed another step beyond this peak without plunging into the abyss, then we have to shift the fundamentals; a new concept of philosophy must arise.

THE POINT-OF-VIEW PHILOSOPHER

We have already seen how this happened. The new concept of philosophy turned fundamentally against all those elements which had united at the peak of the old one. No longer is the objectively intelligible All its subject, or the intellection of this objectivity. Now it is *Weltanschauung*, the idea with which an individual mind reacts to the impression which the world makes on him. The content of belief is no longer its content. This now rebels against it in eternal paradox, powerfully brought out from both sides, the theological as well as the philosophical. Given an objective world and a one-and-universal reason, the one-dimensional form of the system may well have been the scientific one. But only a multi-dimensional form corresponds to the utter multiplicity of *Weltanschauungen*, which even within an individual person need by no means be a single one—a multi-dimensional form, even if it extend to the outermost limits of a philosophizing in aphorisms.

The new concept of philosophy at least has the merit of making any kind of philosophizing possible after Hegel. All its peculiarities come down to one: the old type of philosopher, impersonal by profession, a mere deputy of the naturally one-dimensional history of philosophy is replaced by a highly personal type, the philosopher of the *Weltanschauung*, the point of view. And here the questionable aspect of the new philosophy steps into plain view, and all serious philosophical efforts are bound to be accosted by the questions put to Nietzsche: Is this still science?

Indeed, is this still science? Is it still science when everything is viewed in its own right and in countless relationships, now from this point and now from that? The unity of such a view rests at best in the unity of the viewer, and how dubious is not this! We ask the question too. Everyone who regularly saw either the philosophical or the scientific part come off badly in the philosophical phenomena of recent times asks himself the same question with consternation. Thus we can sense here a requirement of philosophy which it evidently cannot meet out of its own resources. It owes its survival beyond that critical point of the solution of its original problem entirely to its new concept. How can it give that up again! Thus its support must come from another source, support, that is, precisely for its scientific status. Its new point of departure is the subjective, the extremely personal self, more than that: the incomparable self, immersed in itself. To this and to its point of view it must hold fast and withal attain the objectivity of science. The most extreme subjectivity, one would like to say deaf and blind egotism, on the one hand, on the other the lucid clarity of infinite objectivity—where is the bridge between them to be found?

THE NEW PHILOSOPHER

Our answer necessarily anticipates and yet stops halfway, with a hint: the bridge from maximum subjectivity to maximum objectivity is formed by theology's concept of revelation. As recipient of revelation, as experiencer of the content of belief, man bears both within himself. And whether the new philosophy wants to admit it or not, he is its given philosopher, indeed its only scientifically possible one. In order to rid itself of clichés, indeed for the sake of its very status as science, philosophy today requires "theologians" to philosophize—theologians, however, now likewise in a new sense. For as will now be seen, the theologian whom philosophy requires for the sake of its scientific status is himself a theologian who requires philosophy—for the sake of his integrity. What was for philosophy a demand in the interests of objectivity, will turn out to be a demand in the interests of subjectivity for theology. They are dependent on each other and so generate jointly a new type, be it philosopher or theologian, situated between theology and philosophy. Here too we must still save the last word about him for later. Coming back to our actual theme, we turn here first to the requirement which carries the new theology toward philosophy and which meets that requirement of philosophy which we have already treated.

Theology and Philosophy

OLD THEOLOGY

As we saw, theology had, since its new turn about a century ago, tried to live without *auctoritas*. If its living consciousness of the present was threatened, whether by the "dead past" of the *verbum scriptum* or of the *ecclesia visibilis*, then "historical" theology served as its police force against such attacks. But it did not count as the positive, cognitional establisher of theology's truth, as *auctoritas*. Thus historical theology played a role which might be compared to that of philosophy in Scholasticism. Essentially this had also enveloped belief from without, whether as *Summa contra gentiles* for defense against polemics, or as *Summa theologica* for new spiritual conquests by belief. But it was not *auctoritas*. That was the Church itself in its visible existence, like the *verbum scriptum* later for Luther, which "they must leave alone" as he scribbled on his table. Luther too surrounded his belief, which he had founded firmly on the new *auctoritas*, with a protective force from without. He energetically rejected philosophy as such a protective force, preferring instead the "temporal power." This assumed the same stance toward the Word and its apostles as had Scholastic philosophy to the visible church.

The theology of the new epoch had provided itself with a similar protectress from without, but it thought it could do without what was more important, the foundation of an *auctoritas*. Thus it hovered in suspension—which is what it actually wanted. For it zealously guarded the pure presentness of experience. This had to be protected from any contact with the hard, well-established earthly realm of truth and substantive reality. At most it could seek support at the anchor of hope cast over it on the starry heavens of the moral ideal. It did not want to feel itself on *terra firma*. It wanted to deny truth.

THE EXPERIENCE—THEOLOGIAN

But truth will not be denied, not for the sake of the ideal, least of all for the sake of experience. Truth is and remains the only soil in which the truthfulness of experience can grow, the only firm foundation on which the ideal can be verified. The miracle of the personal experience of revelation may confirm itself for the will in the certitude of its future verification through redemption. But cognition wants to see another basis under that experience, including even that anchor of hope which it drops.

THE NEW THEOLOGIAN

The contact of revelation and redemption is of central importance to contemporary theology which therefore, to put it theologically, calls upon philosophy to build a bridge from creation to revelation on which this contact can take place. From theology's point of view, what philosophy is supposed to accomplish for it is thus by no means to reconstruct the theological contents, but to anticipate them or rather, more correctly, to supply them with a foundation, to demonstrate the preconditions on which it rests. And theology itself conceives of its contents as event, not as content; that is to say, as what is lived, not as life. As a result its preconditions are not conceptual elements, but rather immanent reality. For this reason the concept of creation supersedes the philosophical concept of truth. Thus philosophy contains the entire contents of revelation, not, however, as revelation, but as precondition of revelation, as created contents, that is, and not as revealed contents. Revelation is providentially "foreseen" in creation—relevation in its entire contents, thus including, precisely in terms of current concepts of belief, also redemption. As practiced by the theologian, philosophy becomes a prognostication of revelation, in a manner of speaking the "Old Testament" of theology. But thereby revelation regains before our amazed eyes the character of authentic miracle—authentic because it becomes wholly and solely the fulfillment of the promise made in creation. And philosophy is the Sybilline Oracle which, by predicting the miracle, turns it into a "sign," the sign of divine providence. The enlightenment, not knowing what, critically, to make of its historical proof, had depressed miracle to the level of magic, conjurational if not cosmic; it appeared to be no more than a successful deception. It had thus robbed miracle of its authentic essence, bearing on its forehead the marks of its derivation from belief; it had turned miracle into something heathenish. Instead of its dearest child, this changeling was foisted on belief; it was only right if belief was ashamed of the paternity imputed to it. But today philosophy presses for collaboration with theology for its own sake. And the *auctoritas* of history, which was only a substitute, that is, apologetic not constitutive, has broken down. Theology for its part therefore looks longingly to philosophy as the authentic *auctoritas* suited to its new form. In these circumstances the authentic miracle, belief's dearest child, which it had given up for lost, is brought back to its arms by knowledge.

Grammar and Word

For the most part we have arrived at the goal which we intended to reach in this Introduction. It remains only to add a few words about the How of philosophical anticipation of the miracle of creation. It will necessarily be no more than inadequate and allusive, and will perhaps throw more light, retroactively, on what the previous Part offered than on what the present Part will offer. Questions of manner, of "method," should after all really never be discussed before the work has been done, only afterward. And it is a question of manner which concerns us here. How is one to recognize, within creation itself, the possibility of experiencing miracles, a possibility which dawned on us in creation? Or, to put it—at least apparently—in a more material way: where in the sphere of creation is the creature, where in the realm of philosophy is the "subject" which bears the visible seal of revelation on its countenance? Where in creation is the book which time has only to open to read in its pages the word of revelation? Where does the mystery disclose itself as miracle?

When we watched the elements of the All emerging speechless from the mysterious depths of the Nought, we had lent speech to their dumbness by giving them a language which they could make their own because it was no language. It was a language prior to language, just as that emergence is a creation prior to creation. From the point of view of the living language, it constituted the archetypal words which lie hidden under each and every manifest word as secret bases and which rise to the light in it. In a certain sense they are elemental words which constituted the manifest course of speech. Or again they are mathematical elements for developing a curve, and indeed the peculiarity of these elements could well be made graphic in mathematical symbols. In living speech, these inaudible arch-words became audible as real words, both they themselves and all real words with them. In place of a language prior to language, we see before us real language.

Those inaudible elemental words, standing side by side without relationship, were the language of the individual elements of the protocosmos, lying side by side. They were the language which is understood in the soundless realm of the Faustian Mothers, no more than the ideational possibilities of arriving at an understanding. Real language, however, is the language of the terrestrial world. The language of logic is the prognostication of this real language of grammar. Reasoning is mute in each individual by himself, yet common to all, and thereby the basis of speaking which is common to all. What is mute in reasoning becomes audible in speech. But reasoning is not speaking, that is, it is not "silent" speaking but rather a speech prior to speaking, the secret foundation of speaking. Its arch-words are not real words but rather the promise of the real word. But for its part the real word, which names the object and by which the object is named, gains a firm footing only by virtue of the fact that the arch-word has "given its word" to it. The mute becomes audible, the secret manifest, the occult disclosed; what was finished as thought reverts as word into a new beginning. For the word is mere inception until it finds reception in an ear, and response in a mouth.

Here, in the relationship between the logic of language and its grammar, we apparently already possess the object of our search, the link between creation and revelation. The mute, everlasting elements of the protocosmos, of creation, had been rendered perceptible for us by language in the arch-words of its logic. The resounding, ever self-renewing orbiting of the eternal contemporary cosmos will be rendered intelligible for us by language in the forms of its grammar. The prophecy of the arch-words of logic finds fulfillment in the public laws of the real words, the forms of grammar. For speech is truly mankind's morning gift from the Creator, and yet at the same time it is the common property of all the children of men, in which each has his particular share and, finally, it is the seal of humanity in man. It is entire from the beginning: man became man when he first spoke. And yet to this day there is no language of mankind; that will only come to be at the end. Real language, however, is common to all between beginning and end, and yet is a distinct one for each; it unites and divides at the same time. Thus real speech includes everything, beginning, middle, and end. It is the presently visible fulfillment of the beginning, for in its countless forms it is today the visible criterion of man whom, so we say, language makes human. And it includes the end, for even as the individual language of today, or as the language of the individual, it is dominated by the ideal of coming to a perfect understanding which we visualize as the language of mankind. Linguistic morphology became our organon of revelation as a real entity vis-à-vis the original idea of language, which had become our methodological organon of creation. Thereafter, however, the grammatical forms in their own turn thus again arrange themselves according to creation, revelation, and redemption. Revelation is after all at once revelation of creation and of redemption, for it is founded on creation in cognition, but directed toward redemption in volition. And language as the organon of revelation is at the same time the thread running through everything human that steps into its miraculous splendor and into that of its ever renewed presentness of experience.

THE MOMENT

But here we feel that we are venturing forth too far, as we had already feared. By speaking of the unknown, we are losing our way in the unintelligible. Thus we will break off here. The concept of experience in its inexhaustible youth is liable enough to mislead even a tempered reasoning into overenthusiastic aberration. Let us remain firm and confirm: language, for all it is all there, all created from the beginning, nevertheless awakes to real vitality only in revelation. And thus nothing in the miracle of revelation is novel, nothing is the intervention of sorcery in created creation, but rather it is wholly sign, wholly the process of making visible and audible the providence which had originally been concealed in the speechless night of creation, wholly—revelation! Thus revelation is at all times new only because it is primordially old. It makes the primeval creation over into an ever newly created present, because that primeval creation itself is nothing less than the sealed prophecy that God "renews day by day the work of creation." The human word is a symbol; with every moment it is newly created in the mouth of the speaker, but only because it is from the beginning and because it already bears in its womb every speaker who will one day effect the miracle of renewing it. But the divine word is more than symbol: it is revelation only because it is at the same time the word of creation. "God said, Let there be light"—and what is the light of God? It is the soul of man.

BOOK ONE

Creation

or

The Ever-Enduring
Base of Things

God spoke. That came second. It is not the beginning. It is already the audible fulfillment of the silent beginning. It is already the first miracle. The beginning is: God created.

God created. That is the novelty. Here the shell of the mystery breaks: whatever we had hitherto known of God was but knowledge concerning a concealed God, a God who concealed himself and his life in a mythical sphere of his own, a redoubt of the gods, a mountain of the gods, a heaven of God. This God of whom we knew had reached his end. But God the Creator is in the beginning.

In the beginning . . . God's vitality, which seemed the end, transforms itself into a beginning. Here too God's birth out of the ground, his creation prior to creation, will prove to be the prophecy of his manifestation. What is, after all, the difference between promise and fulfillment if not that the former remains stationary, finished, immovable while the latter happens, or, better, materializes. Thus nothing has changed on the way from promise to fulfillment. The content of the promise and the phases of the fulfillment are one and the same, only what was finished thus transformed itself into a beginning. Therewith, however, the constituent pieces which produce the finished product are transformed into predictions of the process which emerges out of the finished product become beginning again. This transformation, as already pointed out, can find expression only as interchange of the two first arch-words. What merged as Yea,

112

emerges as Nay, and vice versa, much like the contents of a traveler's trunk, which are unpacked in the opposite order from that in which they were inserted. As ludicrous as the analogy may appear, we may seriously use it nonetheless. For those acts into which the birth out of the ground is divided do not grow dialectically forth one out of the other, particularly not the second out of the opening act. The Nay is not the "antithesis" of the Yea. Rather, the Nay confronts the Nought with the same immediacy as the Yea. To come over to the side of the Yea, it presupposes not the Yea itself, but only that the Yea was derived out of the Nought. Both acts thus have an equally immediate relationship to their origin. This relationship, and thus the contrast between the dialectical method and that employed here, is enormously important. How important it is can only become clear in the course of the present Part. But the comparison with the packing and consequently also with the unpacking of a trunk is completely appropriate, and has its basis here.

The Creator

POWER

God's creating is the beginning of his self-expression. In it, then, the divine power which merged into his vitality with the arch-nay, expresses itself. But this power, which derived from divine freedom, from his arch-nay that is, now emerges anew no longer as Nay but as Yea. "As Yea" means not as an isolated "act," struggling to separate itself from God in the convulsion of self-negation, but as a still, infinite "attribute" of enduring essence. God's configuration, hitherto concealed in the metaphysical beyond of myth, emerges into visibility and begins to shine forth. God's configuration—for what but configuration allows us to say that he has an essential "attribute"? It is the only attribute; whatever else claims this designation does so, as we shall see, without justification. God can have no attributes at all prior to his emergence from himself. For attribute is the external factor, in the face of which the bearer of the attribute is something utterly internal, which simply does not express itself except in the attributes. Whatever else may properly be designated as divine attribute is, how-ever, included in this attribute.

What is power after it has become attribute? We have already stated it: no longer isolated deed, no longer caprice, but essence. God the creator is essentially powerful. His creativity is thus omnipotence without being caprice. God, he who is visible in creation, is capable of all that he wills, but he wills only what he must will out of his essence. This straightforward and self-evident formula which results for us here solves all problems which the idea of creation, as far as it concerns God, has ever posed.

CAPRICE AND COMPULSION

It is not so long ago that the difficulties found in the idea of creation were represented as a contradiction between God's "omniscience" and his "omnipotence." How can God be omnipotent, it was asked, if his wisdom, after all, continually limits him and prevents him from doing all that he is able to will? But this question demonstrates a misconception of power as deed, which it is, after all, only in the mystery of the inner self-configuration of God. In that configuration of God who is in the process of becoming visible, it is not deed but essence. There it is substantially incorporated into an inner necessity. And the concept of a wisdom peculiar to God means nothing else than such incorporation. The attribute of power, properly conceived, includes the notion of wisdom. Thus it is with the formula we have just found, the formula that the creator is capable of all that he wills, but that he wills only what he must will out of his essence. Thus power is grafted onto essence as an "attribute," and now the academic question of the relationship to wisdom is solved, but beyond this also the authentic and profound problem inherent in the concept of creation: does God create from caprice or from compulsion? The two possibilities seem irreconcilable. The concept of divine perfection and unconditionality seems to require us to affirm the former. God must not be dependent on anything, least of all on a need, be it external or internal. He must not have to create. He must not feel "lonesome," as Schiller asserted of the "Master of the World." Rather, in the words of the Koran, he must be "wealthy without any world." And indeed, the idea of the absolute caprice of the Creator is well represented precisely in Arabic Scholasticism, though also in earlier Christian and Jewish theology. But it is by no means as harmless as its advocates think. By making its God out to be in need of nothing, and by refusing to base his creativity in his essence, it threatens to release God from any necessary connection with the world. But thereby the creative emergence by God out of himself is turned into a mere factuality, unessential for him, and God's essence is removed to a height that is foreign to the world and suspended above it. Is this not also the doctrine of the heathens? What still distinguishes this God's suspension out of the world from

the cool apathy of the Epicurean gods who led a life of Olympian
serenity in the "interstices" of existence, untouched and unmoved by
it? In the authentic idea of revelation, the three "actual" elements of
the All—God world man—emerge from themselves, belong to one another, and meet one another, and this idea is in the final analysis effective in opposing the assertion of the caprice of the Creator. And so
it was precisely in this point that Maimonides, the great theoretician
of revelation, diverged from Arabic Scholasticism and, with utmost
decisiveness, asserted God's creativity as his essential attribute. He
even developed the whole doctrine of the attributes of divine essence
in clear methodological assimilation to this attribute of creative power.

Still, that emphasis on caprice was not wholly unjustified. This is
shown by the later fortunes of the idea of the creative act of power
as divine essence. It is always on the brink of being reinterpreted as
divine need. Creating the world is an essential necessity for God,
and so in creation the "lonesome master of the world" has, like the
artist, satisfied a need of his nature, has rid himself of an inner burden.
Indeed, not satisfied with the concept of necessity, one exaggerated
this still more by the admixture of a drop of passion. Creation was
turned into an act of love, of yearning love, not overflowing love,
though this too would have meant a shift of emphasis. Such formulations must be rejected, if not for God's sake, then assuredly for the
world's. For in them God is robbed of his inner freedom, and the
world forfeits its inner cohesiveness within itself, its ability to stand
by itself. Out of all the myriad possibilities, these are not supposed to
be taken from it, but on the contrary precisely secured for it by the
idea of creation. Tied to God's need in this fashion, the world would
lose all meaning of its own, all internal unequivocalness. Like the work
of an autobiographical poet, its essence would consist in being less an
"independent work of art" than a testimony to the stranger-than-
fiction inner life of the author. And with that it would cease to be
creation, cease to be the indigenous formation prophesied in the
metalogical world.

Here the concept of divine caprice comes to the rescue. But this
stone, which we expressly rejected in constructing the concept of
the creator, are we now by any chance to make it the cornerstone?
By no means the cornerstone, and not "make" it either, but rather to
recognize it, as foundation stone. For there is caprice, not *in* the
creator's act of creation, but prior to it in the self-configuration of
God which precedes his act of creation. The power of the Creator
is substantive attribute, but had its origin in caprice which, not attribute but occurrence, burned with ceaselessly renewed flame in God's

bosom before creation. Divine freedom first clearly emerged from unconditional caprice into activist power under the impact of the fated compulsion of the divine essence. The mysterious self-manifestation of this freedom prior to creation was the sealed prophecy which found manifest fulfillment in the substantive power of the creator. But the prophecy was pre-formed in the flaming caprice in which the creator vitalized himself, and this fact remains preserved in the miraculous power of the creator. The creative power of the manifest God manifests itself in serene vitality, and the caprice of the concealed God reposes at the base of this power. God's power expresses itself with pure necessity precisely because its interior is pure caprice, unconditional freedom. As a "created," self-contained, "concealed" God he could do without creating, assuming—which will hardly do—that as such he could emerge from himself altogether, and create. But as "manifest" God he cannot do otherwise than to create. Those who ascribed inner, substantive necessity to the divine creative act are right as against those who assert its capriciousness. But this inner necessity was based on the transformation of the concealed into the manifest. And as against those who exaggerated it into a passionate need, and reinterpreted power as love, those others who asserted the divine caprice were on the right track by pointing to the inner nucleus of boundless freedom in God. To be sure this nucleus, as it bursts forth, forfeits its inner boundlessness and manifests itself as serene, necessarily creative, omniscient omnipotence.

Islam: the Religion of Intellect

In Islam, world history furnished a proof of this problem. Mohammed came upon the idea of revelation and took it over as such a find is wont to be taken over, that is, without generating it out of its presuppositions. The Koran is a "Talmud" not based on a "Bible," a "New" Testament not based on an "Old" Testament. Islam has only revelation, not prophecy. In it, therefore, the miracle of revelation is not a "sign," it is not the revelation of divine providence, active in creation, as a "plan of salvation." Rather the Koran is a miracle in itself, and thus a magical miracle. It claims legitimacy as a miracle not for having been predicted but for being inexplicable. To this day, the proof of the divine character of the Koran is found in the claim that a book of such incomparably grand wisdom and beauty could not have sprung from a human brain. By contrast both Talmud and

New Testament certify their divine origin theoretically by means of their connection with the "Old Testament," the Talmud by asserting throughout the ability to be logically derived from it, the New Testament by asserting throughout the character of historical fulfillment with respect to it. Thus while Mohammed took over the concepts of revelation externally, he necessarily remained attached to heathendom in the basic concept of creation. For he did not recognize the interconnection which ties revelation to creation.

Thus it could not dawn on him that the concepts of creation—God world man—need an inner conversion to transform themselves from finished configurations into sources of power for revelation. These concepts too he took as he found them, in finished form. Only he took them from the pagan world and not, like the concepts of revelation, from the belief in revelation. And he cast them, just as he found them, into the movement which leads from creation via revelation to redemption. These recondite prophecies did not turn into emerging revelations. Their sealed eyes did not open radiantly; they retained their mute, introspective stare even while they trained it outwardly on each other. Here the Yea remained Yea and the Nay Nay. It was a belief in revelation derived directly from paganism, without God's will as it were, without the design of his providence, in "purely natural" causation. And thus we can—and continually will—picture to ourselves by means of this remarkable case of plagiarism in world history how such a belief would have to look. For it would be of the essence of such a purely natural derivation that it lack the inner reversal of the "notations," the transformation of prophecy into sign, of creation into revelation which first reveals creation as the basis of revelation, and revelation as renewal of creation. Thus Islam has neither creation nor revelation, although it struts about, full of pomp and dignity with both of them as it found them.

As we have already mentioned, Mohammed's creator is "wealthy without any world." He is really the creator who could as well have done without creating. He proves his power, like an Oriental despot, not by creating what is necessary, nor by authorizing the promulgation of the law, but in his freedom for the capricious act. Significantly enough, rabbinic theology by contrast formulates our concept of the divine power of creation in the question whether God created the world in righteousness or rather in love. The power which we have recognized as peculiarly the creator's is that which acts out of an inner necessity and which actualizes the necessary. And this power, after all, proves its mettle precisely in the generation and execution of justice. Caprice is the explicit antithesis of such power. It proves its mettle precisely in the absence of any inner compulsion, in the freedom to realize justice or injustice equally, to commit a deed or omit it. Caprice knows no necessity. It does not emanate its expressions with endless necessity as something equally necessary. Instead, every individual deed issues from the short-lived mood of the individual moment to which alone it is responsible. It denies the moment of the immediate past just as much as it resists the notion that the action of this moment somehow creates a binding precedent for that which immediately follows. Its endlessness is only authenticated in the notion that every future moment has the same freedom for each and everything as the present one. Never will caprice cap its work with a rainbow, vaulting the heavens as the token of its obligation not to let the laws of its existence cease "so long as the earth endures." For it, creating and destroying are all one. It boasts of both in one breath and demands of its believers equal veneration—nay better only: equal fear—of both. The God of revelation, however, never compares his future role of judge of the world directly with his role as creator. Yet the former too is already something other than caprice. Like the latter itself, it is suspended in the inner framework of necessity which revelation has constructed. Thus the individual deed of caprice issues from the individual moment in which, as the embodiment of all its other moments, it denies itself. The act of substantive power, however, is extracted from the essence and imparted to the infinite in sweeping necessity. In Islam, the act of creation is unconditionally responsible to the instant and only to the instant, like any capricious act, and therefore it is self-negation for the creator in the sense just clarified. According to the belief in revelation, the act of creation liberates something ever necessary from within itself outward, like any internally necessary expression of essence, and thus it is the world-affirmation of the creator. World-affirmation: creation is creation of the world. What about it?

The Creature

THE NOUGHT

We had accompanied the world in the process of forming itself up to the point at which it seemed complete in itself, a configuration wholly structured throughout, infused with spirit in itself. This result is a peak for it too; no path leads beyond this point unless the result here too become a beginning. But that means: becoming created. It is the idea of creation which first tears the world out of its elemental self-containedness and unmovedness into the current of the All, which opens outward its eyes hitherto turned inward, which renders its mystery manifest. To be sure, it appears at first sight paradoxical to assert that the world can still be created "after" its completion as configuration. At the very least we appear to be moving hopelessly far from the traditional concept of creation *ex nihilo*, from "nought." For us, the world has already originated as configuration out of "nought." Should the world-as-configuration have once more to become nought itself in order to represent the "Nought" from which the world was supposedly created?

Thus it is. Let us recall here how we previously threw light on the path of creation by declaring that the "metalogic" world would in reality only take form with the beginning of the age of belief, that is, after the passing of antiquity, though its image had been designed by antiquity. To the extent that that age has begun and not ended we formulated the world as Becoming, in contrast to the God who became before all beginning, and to the self which became in the past. Thus we classified the world in its "becoming out of nought" with the end of the world, and God in it with the dawning morning of the world, and the Self with the bright noon of the world. For the world, therefore, the world-morning of creation need not mean its becoming created. That God created the world is unlimited truth only for the subject, like any sentence consisting of subject, predicate, and object. Without involving the subject, no mere analysis of this sentence can elicit a true statement about the object alone. From a sentence like "The stork ate the frog" one could quite analytically derive the other unlimited truth, that the frog was eaten by the stork; the relationship between stork and frog and that between frog and stork is fixed unambiguously. But the destinies of the frog, apart from his relationship to the stork, are not. All kinds of other possibilities remain with respect to being eaten up, and only the stork's participation in the process is beyond question. Thus the sentence "God created the world" has unlimited validity only for the relationship between God and the world. The past tense of the sentence, its once-and-for-all form, is valid only for this relationship. The world, on the other hand, is not necesarily through being created with the act of creation performed once and for all by God. What is past for God, immemorial, really "in the beginning," may well yet be present for the world, even unto its end. The creation of the world need reach its conclusion only in its redemption. Only from that vantage point, or wherever such an end is to be posited, would the world be—and from there, it is true, it would absolutely have to be—retrospectively a *"creatio ex nihilo."* Vis-à-vis this created world—and now really—the configured world of the metalogic *Weltanschauung* would thus have to be really "Nought," that is, something utterly incomparable with the created world, unconnected to it, something vanished with its lust for it.

PROVIDENCE AND EXISTENCE

The world, however, did not have to "become" something created "complete" in the divine creation at the world's morning. Initially it need be no more than: creature. What is creation from God's point of view can only mean, from the world's, the bursting forth of the consciousness of its creatureliness, its being-created. In addition, the structured world would thus open its eyes to creatureliness. Seen from it own point of view, being created would mean for it manifesting itself as creature. This is creature-consciousness, the consciousness not of having once been created but of being everlastingly creature; as such, it is something thoroughly objective, an authentic revelation. It is by no means already an internal process in the world, but a process which emanates from the world itself onto the consciousness of the creator and first defines this completely. The creature consciousness of the world, the consciousness, that is, of being created, not of having been created, materializes in the idea of divine providence.

The process is as follows. For the world, its required relationship to the creator was, as we saw, not its having been created once and for all, but its continuing to manifest itself as creature. For the world, then, the relationship is not its self-creating but its self-revealing emergence. Thus it will emerge as conversion of the first, not the second act of the self-structuring of the world, as the conversion of what had been its enduring essence. The enduring essence of the structured world was the Universal, or more precisely the category which, although itself universal, yet contains the individual within itself, indeed steadily brings it forth from within itself. In the world which manifests itself as creature, this enduring essence is converted into a momentary essence "ever renewed" and yet universal. An unessential essence thus. What is meant by this? The world has embarked on the current of reality, and this its essence is not "always and everywhere." It is an essence which at every moment originates anew with the whole content of the Distinctive which it includes. It is an essence which includes all distinctiveness and yet is itself universal, which recognizes itself as a whole with every instant. It is: existence. Existence in contrast to Being means the universal which is full of the distinctive and which is not always and everywhere but, herein infected by the distinctive, must continually become new in order to maintain itself. The world is a firm configuration out of which existence emerges and which it denies in its constant need for renewal. In contrast, existence is in need, not merely of renewal of its existence, but also, as a whole of existence, in need of—Being. For what existence lacks is Being, unconditional and universal Being. In its universality, overflowing with all the phenomena of the instant, existence longs for Being in order to gain a stability and veracity which its own being cannot provide. It has such a Being of its own in back of it, or had it before it became creature, but that Being stayed behind in the "essenceless semblance" of the proto-cosmos. A Being "outside" itself, but within the circuit of reality, a Being which is not ramified in itself, must help it over its ramification. Its creatureliness presses under the wings of a Being such as would endow it with stability and veracity.

Thus the difficulty which we detected in the much-ramified system cast into the metalogical world may be solved here. We sought a simple Being of truth "somewhere" over that multiple Being of the Logos, without however being able to find such a "somewhere," either in the metalogical world or anywhere else, with any certainty. The multiple existence of the Logos and of the reality which has been poured into it rests on the "simple word of truth," and the need of the creature now shows us quite naturally in which direction we have to look for this word. But let us remain for the time being with the creature itself.

Its need is its existence as such, not the universal existence of the distinctive. In it constant momentariness, existence as such challenges the constant renewal of becoming created. And as such too it is seized by the power of the creator. We have now arrived at God's providence, and in the world this pertains directly only to the universal, to "concepts" and "kinds." It pertains to things only "each after its own kind," to the distinctive, therefore, only by means of its universal character and in the final analysis only by means of universal existence altogether. We concur with Maimonides in thus rejecting a "special providence" for the things of the world as distinguished from man. Only later will we find out to what extent God's dominion nevertheless seizes things as individuals too, without mediation. For the creator, however, things present themselves only in the universal framework of existence as a whole. His creation apprehends them only through existence, "each after its kind." But this universal is not essentially universal; it only fights its way to the fore momentarily in the

Nay. That is clear because this divine grasp of existence does not occur in creation, which took place once and for all. Rather it is a momentary grasp, a providence which, though universal, renews itself with every minimal distinctive instant for the whole of existence in such wise that God "renews day by day the work of creation." It is really this morning-by-morning providence which is alluded to in the idea of the creature.

Islam: The Religion of Necessity

Again Islam furnishes the proof of our problem. Here too it introduces the proto-cosmic concept, here that of Being, without inner conversion into the ideational ambit of revelation. Without more ado, it asserts as the Being of the creaturely world that Being of the worldly logos which, though abundantly ramified, is essentially at rest, as it collaborated at the structuring of the world. Its Being is accordingly not existence; it is not something universal and yet only momentary and thus as a whole daily in need of renewal. Rather the world externalizes its Being in essential affirmation and lays it at God's feet as its creatureliness. And now Allah can choose how to let his providence hold sway. On the one hand he can have it trained once and for all on the entirety of the world, and on everything individual within only by virtue of its being somehow included and posited in this entirety. That is the notion which we generally have of Kismet. But the other possibility is more remarkable still, because it comes closer to the authentic concept of providence as we have just developed this, and just for that reason is characteristically distinguished from it. For Allah can also wish to grasp the individual thing directly. It is, after all, posited within this universal too. As we recall, the universal as it penetrated the structured world is not simply universal but " concept," the universal of the distinctive, the embodiment of the universal in all distinctive things. But within this universal, which is essential where previously it had been momentary, the distinctive likewise can only be essential, not momentary. Essentially distinctive means, in a sense, universal in miniature; it means distinctive and yet, as far as it is up to itself, "always and everywhere." But what does this mean? It means that it can originate only by means of creative liberation, that is, by means of "affirmation," not by means of the self-negating renewal. Accordingly it is here expected of Allah that he create, with every instant, every individual thing, precisely as if it were the universal itself. Thus creation here consists of an infinite multitude of subdivided acts of creation, unrelated to one another, which each have the weight of an entire creation.

That was the doctrine of the dominant orthodox philosophy within Islam. Here the individual thing bears the whole brunt of the divine creative power with each instant. It is not "renewed" with every instant, but "created" from top to bottom with every instant. It cannot escape this awesome, infinitesimally subdivided providence of Allah. Precisely because it grasps the individual unit only in the whole, the idea of world-"renewal" preserves for it the relationship to the single creation and thereby to the unity of existence. Thus it bases providence on creation. On the other hand, this conception of providence as one of constant creative interference destroys any possibility of that very relationship. There providence, as eventful renewal of the act of creation, is the fulfillment of what was essentially devised in creation; here it is in every case again essential interference in creation in spite of its momentariness, a continuous competition between creative acts and the unity of creation. It is not a sign made by God the ruler of the world for God the creator, but it is magic directed by God the ruler of the world against God the creator. For all that it proceeds vigorously and arrogantly behind the idea of the unity of God, Islam thus slips into a monistic paganism, if one may use the expression. God himself competes with God himself at every moment, as if it were the colorful, warring heaven of the gods of polytheism.

To sum up, Islam asserts the "special providence" in immediate relationship to the creatureliness of the world. True belief, on the other hand, asserts only universal providence in connection with creatureliness. It directs the idea of a "special" providence to the detour via revelation which, by proceeding on to redemption, also eventually returns to the creature. Thereby man, and God's relationship to him which seems, for Islam, completely elucidated in the concept of creation, is lifted out of the realm of creation in the very concept of creation itself. Here too, the authentic concept of creation again points forward to its fulfillment in the miracle of revelation. True, man takes his place as a creature among creatures, and as such his distinctive existence is affected by providence—directed as that is toward all existence altogether, but this creaturely relationship to God is still likewise no more than "prophecy." Man as God's creature is the presage of man as God's child. Fulfillment is more than augury, sign is more than omen—child is more than creature. But let us not anticipate. We have studied God and the world, the two poles of the creative act, in their mutual interaction, both active and passive: God summoning the world into existence in the wisdom of his creative power, the world manifesting itself in its creatureliness vis-à-vis divine providence by means of its existence. Let us now turn to the result, to creation itself.

Grammar of the Logos
(The Language of Cognition)

LIMITS OF MATHEMATICS

The language of mathematical symbols in which we were previously able to demonstrate the evolution of the elements fails us here. Within the equations, it is no longer possible to elucidate with precision even the conversions, because the sense of the conversions only becomes clear when that which has previously merged in them radiates apart again. As it does so, the notation of the individual letters would have to alternate regularly, leading to impossible combinations. But above all there emerge from the completed configurations of the elements not the original pure forms of the Yea and Nay as these had originated in the Nought and which alone are represented in the symbols, but rather those forms which, on the way from the Nay to the Yea, have already transformed themselves on each other, have already experienced their reciprocal influence on each other. Such an influence already exists, say, in the fact that the distinctive is no longer the distinctive, pure and simple, but rather the individual as representative of its category; but it can simply no longer be represented in algebraic symbols. It would be different if geometric symbols could be used instead of the algebraic ones. Then one could represent both the conversion with its interchange of notations and, by measuring the relevant distances, the reciprocal influences in the relationship of the points in space which symbolize the various concepts. But we must dispense with the use of these symbols in the present Part; we will only adduce them subsequently. This is connected with the nature of geometry. It is true that geometry rests on the presuppositions of algebra and that it proves to be the fulfillment of what is adumbrated in algebra, thereby becoming, as analytic geometry, the mathematics of perceptual nature. But this objective sequence is not paralleled by the sequence of cognition. Subjectively, an understanding of geometry presupposes not only the algebraic concepts of equality and inequality but also, in contrast to the objectively valid sequence, a prior knowledge of the natural configuration. Although it establishes the objectivity of the configurations of nature, subjectively it is nevertheless only possible as an abstraction from them. Thus we would here have to represent the finite configuration of the symbol in advance if we wanted to employ its evolution already here to make the individual steps graphic. And that would distract the reader more than rally him. The same difficulty, after all, seems to confront the immediate exposition itself too. Here too it should thus be possible to describe the "path" subjectively only to those who already bring to it a view of the "configuration," and not only, like the reader of this book, a knowledge of the "elements." But in fact we may safely presuppose the presence of this view, as the exhibition of the "configuration" will prove later.

But not only these expository reasons make it undesirable to work with mathematical symbols here. There is also a deeper reason. In describing the elements and their birth out of the somber foundations of the Nought, we assigned a meaning to mathematics which we were entitled to give it because mathematics, in view of its essence, was in its place here. Mathematics—those mute signs of life which nevertheless contain the model of all this life for the initiate—mathematics is pre-eminently the language of that world which is prior to the world. And within mathematics, algebra is its most essential, one might say its most specific, most mathematical part. It is the part which operates directly with the basic concepts of all mathematics: the equal and the unequal. It is for that reason that algebra is in its place here. That is the place which belongs to mathematics altogether, in view of its essence. And within mathematics, its most essential discipline occupies the place. This role as speech of the speechless proto-cosmos it has to share with art as speech of the unspeakable, for in art too it is here that the basic concepts, the essence, find expression. But art is here subjective speech, the "speaking" of that speechless world, as it were. Mathematics is the objective language, the "sense" of that silence, as is already attested by its necessarily written form. This task of representing the sense, this organon's role of supplying symbols, is thus assumed by another bearer in the world which expresses and manifests itself. A science of living sounds must take the place of a science of speechless signs; mathematical science must be replaced by the morphology of words, by grammar.

LAW OF GRAMMAR

The speechless, merely implicit arch-words, rendered visible in the algebraic symbols, created the timbre of the three-part bass of our world symphony. Audible words must spring forth directly from them, root-words so to speak, which, still in close touch as definite words with the arch-words, yet are capable of propelling forth out of themselves the whole system of rules embracing the real of real language. After all, the grammatical categories, just like those of logic, are peculiarly unamenable to a genealogical type of presentation. Such presentations only become possible by virtue of these categories. They themselves already completely presuppose themselves wherever one may wish to begin. The concept of the noun, for example, already presupposes the concept of case, number, even person, and finally of subject and object, and yet all these in turn become explicable only on the supposition of the noun concept. Accordingly a genuine arrangement is necessary, an arrangement which is not internal but rather adduced for grammar, and in a certain sense for language altogether, from without, that is, from the role of language as against reality. In such an arrangement, the multiplicity of word formations can be integrated in continuously repeated surveys by means of root-words. Thus in place of the genealogical, only the tabular form of presentation would be considered here. The root-words generate classifications which intersect and thus cease to accord with the picture of the family tree. Consequently each of these classifications must be viewed individually in direct relation to the root-word, which the tabular form alone can do.

ROOT-WORD

Such root-words should be required to appear in a form which admits but one unambiguous use in the sentence. For it is not words that constitute language, but the sentence. Therefore the root-words have to coalesce with unambiguous necessity into a sentence which would be called a root-sentence. Thus the word "dog," for example, would certainly not be a root-word in our sense, because it can mean the actively barking as well as the passively thrashed dog, the dog as subject as well as object. We are seeking here to begin with the root-word which leads from the inaudible arch-yea into the audible reality of language—to begin with from the arch-yea, for we find ourselves here in the realm of creation. Creation, however, as a movement of God toward the world, is distinguished by the nature of divine activity, not of worldly passivity, in short by the Yea.

Affirmation places a Thus freely into the infinite. Such a free Thus is not rendered graphic by a noun which, after all, still needs to have its How defined; without this definition it lacks configuration, it is the "Ding an sich." The Thus means answering the question concerning the How. The How, however, requires an adjective, and that in a grammatical form in which it can only be adjectival, only predicative and nothing else. The word "beauty" can be used in the combination "a beauty spot" as well as "beauty is in the eye of the beholder," but "beautiful" can only be used adjectivally.[1] Thus the predicate adjective is the specific configuration of the adjective and, as we already indicated in passing in the first Part, it is the formation belonging to the arch-yea. Now which specific word in the form of such a predicate adjective will take it upon itself to make the arch-word audible as root-word? Which word of this form means affirmation pure and simple? All words referring to visual properties are here excluded as a matter of course. For visual properties affirm themselves only by simultaneously negating endlessly, that is, in the "and" of Thus-and-not-otherwise. It is different with properties which express a value judgment. In order to affirm yellow, one has to deny not only, say, blue, but all the colors of the rainbow, the whole rich diversity of perceived colors, and the infinity of colors that may yet be perceived. With an estimational property, on the other hand, "beautiful" for example, one need at most deny the contrary contrast which itself could in turn be defined only by a denial, specifically of beauty. We cut this circle by realizing that estimation occurs absolutely—naturally only positive estimation, for the negative kind is really only negation of the positive one, and indeed the word "esteem" in and of itself only means, in the final analysis, a positive evaluation. This positive evaluation is nothing more than the arch-yea become audible. Incidentally, this is shown by the possibility, in many languages, of saying "well!", "good!" or the like for "Yes."

ATTRIBUTE

Let us now proceed from the root-word to the schematic presentation of the word formations. From the root-word we come at once to the part of speech to which it belongs, the adjective, which substantially and initially posits a Thus. The "attributive" or rather the predicate adjective[2] is, in distinction from the noun and verb, properly the expression for freely being Thus. It grasps the Thus absolutely, initially without regard for any bearer, for relationships or origins, just

---

[1] R's examples have been altered; they make sense only in German, which distinguishes formally between nouns and attributive adjectives on the one hand and predicate adjectives on the other. (Tr.)

[2] See preceding note.

as the eye of the artist imbibes the blue of the sky or the green of the meadow without initially caring too much about sky or meadow. The world is all attribute, and it is that from the beginning.

Attribute is simple attribute. It is not compared. Every attribute is as it is. Equivalence, comparison, uniqueness—in other words, comparative and superlative degrees—do not grow directly out of the individually affirmed attribute; rather they presuppose that the attribute has become attribute of a thing. The things in themselves are many; *they* are compared, and the attributes with them, but the attribute in itself is individual and incomparable; it is simple affirmation —in short, it is "positive."

MATERIALITY

But here the thing enters, the bearer of the attributes. As such it is a pure abstraction vis-à-vis the reality of the attributes. The reference, the sign, lies on the way from this reality to that abstraction. Thus the pronoun is much more pre-noun than pro-noun. It designates not the thing already recognized, but the thing while it is still unrecognized and unnamed, only perceived in its attributes. The "this" merely points to the thing and in so doing expresses the fact that a "something" should be looked for here. The "Here," which is inherent in the "This," thus makes space the general prerequisite for looking for the thing, hitherto defined only as a something. "To look for" does not mean "already found." It is still a question "what" it is. The indefinite article first answers this "what"; we are dealing with "a" representative of this or that category. And the definite article first affixes its seal to this great process and designates it as completed, "the" thing as recognized. The definite article, however, or determination by whatever other means it may be expressed, is always fused with the substantive in immediate juxtaposition. In it, the thing is directly apprehended; it is now recognized as this individual thing.

INDIVIDUALITY

Really as this individual thing? It had, after all, been recognized only as a representative of a category, and was a dark abstraction vis-à-vis the reality of the attributes. How little it is in itself an individual becomes clear as soon as we consider the proper noun, the name. It is not an individuality. To become one in spite of the highly suspicious visit with the species observed on its way hither, it has to legitimate itself as member of a plurality. Multiplicity first gives all its members the right to feel themselves individuals, individualities. If they are not individuals in themselves, like the single individuality indicated in the proper name, yet they are individuals vis-à-vis the multiplicity.

SUBSTANTIALITY

Thus the individual thing fixed by the definite article can now finally be safely designated as substantive. It now "stands" on its own feet over against a possible creator, a definite, affirmed thing in the endless space of cognition or creation. That it comes to rest as object also becomes clear by the fact that it receives its place as such, as grammatical object, in the sentence. Nothing emanates from it, for that would require it to negate itself, in which event it would not be a thing at rest, standing there free and affirmed. Only as object does it traverse the "cases"; in the nominative of a passive sentence it is only a disguised accusative or—to be sure this may be more correct— a prediction of the subject still veiled in the form of an object. In the genitive, the case of possession, there merge two streams, one each from the nominative as well as the accusative. After joining, they then assume a name and direction of their own in the dative. The dative, however, lies beyond the bare object and the bare point of departure. It is the form of belonging, giving, thanking, of submission as well as of striving. In it object and subject come together.

REALITY

Thus the world, which at first seemed only attribute, a chaos of attributes, has now filled itself with things for us, and so has become object. Therewith we return to the beginning, to the attribute. So far we had developed its affirmedness further only in the direction of its How. But the Yea contains not merely the Thus, but also already the That. The "root"-affirmation "good!" for example, contains not only a How but also a Whether: "good!" means "it is good." The attribute "red" contains the sentence "red is." The copula "to be" is contained in every affirmed attribute. And it now also permits us to overcome what has hitherto been the rigid identification of object with thing. Things are, after all, in motion; motion too, and with it therefore its supra-objective presupposition, time, as well as the circumstances and form in which the motion occurs—all these are connected with attribute, originally the only thing affirmed, in the copula "to be." The connection occurs here in that form which is intermediate between adjective and verb, between thing and event therefore, and which, in certain late phases of linguistic development, and in modern German in the entire passive, virtually displaces the verb: the participle. Activity is here conceived as attribute, and fixed in its relationship to time, to definite things, and to reality altogether only by the copula, only, therefore, by the general designation as being. These fixations undertaken on the copula, it is true, nevertheless already presuppose the fully developed verb, which is also why they appear as simplifications only in late stages of development. But the fact that they are thoroughly possible makes graphic the close connection which binds the verb too to the root-word, the adjective.

PROCEDURE

For the verb itself, the simple affirmation—not, it is true, of its "that" but of its "what"—occurs in a different grammatical form, in the infinitive. In it there resides a really original possibility to come to terms with movement. Instead of "the stork swallowed the frog," many languages say: "there was swallowing on the part of the stork with respect to the frog." Within the verb there thus appears the impersonal construction such as we have, for example, in "it is raining"—the Greeks had a word for it: "Zeus is raining"—or in "it grieves me" by the side of the active form "I grieved."[1] It is the form in which movement is simply set forth in its factuality, in which it is defined only as to its specific presupposition, its time relationship, but without regard to its particular place among the things of the world. In "process," movement is itself still a Being, a thing among things, so to speak.

RELATIONSHIP

Thus substantiality has now to be further secured within the verb. This is done by bringing the individual movement calmly into that parallelism with the totality of occurrence which the indicative creates for it. By contrast, the lines of the imperative, subjunctive, and optative diverge from those of the rest of the occurrence.

OBJECTIVITY

Moreover, even when movement ceases to be mere process by the side of the stationary objects and becomes, as action, movement among

[1] The original example, based on dreaming, has been changed to illustrate English usage. (Tr.)

the things, it will of itself assume the form of the third person. After all, by virtue of their transit through the pronoun which establishes their substantiality, all things are by nature in the third person. And the verb, by virtue of its transit through the impersonal construction, as well as of its relationship to the particle—which itself has, after all, already covered part of the way from adjective to thing, namely the piece up to the indefinite article—the verb, likewise, then, presses of its own accord toward the third person as its most "objective" person.

PERFECTION

The noun, individually and apart from its position in the sentence, reaches the pinnacle of its objectness at that point where, in spite of its relation to the category, it is fixed to one single point in space by the definite article, for its plurality is but complementary hereto. And the verb does likewise by the fixation of its relationship in time. But here it is not enough to fix its relationship to time in general, for that fixation has already been achieved in the indicative label, which accomplishes what corresponds to the fixation of a point in space for the member of a plurality by means of the definite article. But space does not exhibit the same qualitative difference as do the various "dimensions" of time, which therefore demands a further fixation. Among the tenses, one must present itself as specifically objective. It is the past which "stands ever at rest," objective, object-like, in thing-like stillness. The perfect tense completes the objectiveness of occurrence, as that of being is completed by the definite article and its thing-like character. In spite of the specifically verbal garb, wholly its own, that it wears, the adjectival root-word of affirmation is yet visible under the past even of the active form; only after the work has been done can the craftsman say "Good!" to himself "as his due."

Logic of Creation

BEING AND BEING CREATED

Thus the concept of creation, which was our starting point, at the end emerges here into bright daylight. It is the idea of the being-from-the-beginning which is contained in the conception of being created "in the beginning." Here we learn that the world exists before all. It is simply there. This being of the world is its pre-existence: "What are you making of the world? It is already made." What we recognized as the configuration in which the world manifests itself as creature we now recognize as the decisive mark of creation altogether. For now we grasp existence as being-in-existence, as pre-existence, and not simply any longer as universal being that conveys everything individual within it. The creature is, after all, but one of two poles in the idea of creation. The world must have creatureliness, as God must have creative power, before creation can result as the real process between them. Both the existence of the world and the power of God merge in the new concept of being-in-existence. Both are "already in existence." The world is already made on the basis of its creatureliness, its capacity for ever being created anew, while God has already created it on the basis of his eternal creative power. And only for this reason it "exists" and is yet renewed with each morning.

THE SCIENTIFIC IMAGE OF THE WORLD

That is the reason why all concepts which comprehend reality generally seek to assume the form of the past tense. To be recognized, the world is projected every time into the past, beginning with the concept of "basis" and the "basic" concept itself, with "underlying" cause, "origin," "pre-supposition," "a priori." The idea of natural law itself is expressly thought of as a con-stitution, something constituted, a statute. Occurrence is not reduced to the changeable present. Rather, as in differential calculus, everything must be brought down to the at-rest form, that is, the past tense, even the present, the instant of movement, not to mention the future, which is accounted absolutely unsuited and "sterile" for cognition of the real. We are alluding to the famous dictum of Bacon which discredits the purposeful cause as one which "like a virgin consecrated" to God gives birth to nothing. In it there already lurks the image in which the created world becomes scientifically comprehensible if the idea of creation is to be circum-vented and if nevertheless the problem posed and even really solved in it—by relating creation to an overall context—is to be taken up. We refer to that frontispiece of the picture album of the idealistic world, the concept of generation.

THE CREATED WORLD

For the metalogical image of the world was not internally content in spite of its plastic self-containedness, and demanded supplementa-tion. In the case of the logos of the metalogical world, domiciled everywhere and thus too much at home in the world, we know only too well that it needs a unicum, a simplex beyond itself, beyond even the world, in order to be privileged to claim to be in truth logos. The same thing we had still found fully valid for that existence of the creature which stems from this logos too. This existence too had been no unity, albeit in its universality a whole, a unicum. But this time the "beyond" where we should have to seek the unity had been no mere "anywhere" for us; this time its direction had been clearly pointed out to us. That world-sense which had become only too "sensual" had to have its basis and origin in something supersensual. As "existence" it unlocked itself to the effects of such a supersensual basis. The idea of creation brought them together as the form of causality was stamped on existence, and existence became pre-existence. Precisely this temporalization, more specifically this being distinguished by the character of the past, this it was that the world-sense still lacked entirely within the metalogical world and this is why only a "somewhere" could be asserted there for the unity of the world-logos, a somewhere whose locus that wholly closed world itself never pointed out in a recognizable and unambiguous fashion.

The existence of the creature then pointed out the direction; the being-in-existence of creation has reached the desired point, which secures in objectivity at the same time the truth of the world and maintains the validity of the elemental metalogical view of the world. The world is neither shadow nor dream nor picture; its being is existence, real existence—created creation. The world is wholly objective, all activity in it, all "making," is, since it is within it, occurrence. The process is at least that basis of reality on which activity too is based. Thus even occurrence within it is thing-like, and adapts itself to the basic concept in which the objectivity of the world altogether realizes itself, in short to thing-likeness. The world consists of things. In spite of the unity of its objectivity it is no unitary object. It is a multiplicity of objects, in short: the things. The thing has no stability as long as it stands alone. It is certain of its individuality only in the multiplicity of the things. It can only be displayed in connection with other things. Its definiteness is a space-time relationship to other things in such a connection. Even as something defined, the thing has no essence of its own; it is not something in itself but only in its relationships. Such essence as it has is not within it but is the relationship which it has to its category. Its essentiality, its universality is contained not in but behind its definiteness. But before it can be "a representative" of its category, its deputy so to speak, it must be something, indeed "any-thing," something demonstrable in the first place.

In the first place it must be spatial, or at least related to space. This is its general precondition. The unity of objectiveness is the unity sought by the world. No one object corresponds to it except for this one, which is no object: space.

The world, however, is not originally space; space is not the first-born of creation. Before space can exist as the precondition of all definiteness given in the Here, the precondition of the Here itself must exist. It is the This that precedes the Here. Definition first origi-nates out of This and Here as "this here." Thus the deictic This still precedes space as the precondition of the Here. Quite originally the world is the fullness of the This. It is expressed only by the pure uninflected adjective such as "blue" or "cold" in its constantly bubbling-over novelty. This wealth, this chaos, is the first-born of creation, the perpetual renewal of its existence—once this existence has itself been summoned into existence, once the world is created. Exis-tence in its universality and all-embracing morphology remains the immediately created basis, the "beginning" from which the ever-new births of the fullness shoot forth. The world can be wealth because it exists; it is itself existence, and fullness is its manifestation, the first of all statements about existence. The root-word still precedes the plenitude of adjectives; chaos is within creation, not prior to it; the beginning is in the beginning.

Idealistic Logic

This metalogical image of the world loses its last obscurities through the idea of creation. But it is hardly a "proof" for this idea for all that. Creation makes the world utterly transparent, without depriving it of reality. For the world would also, it is true, be utterly trans-parent as "dream," for example, but at the cost of its reality; its sense would now abide only in the dreamer, instead of being at home within the world itself. But creation itself is not proved by the world, if only because God is more than only creator. If one wanted to conclude from the world image as we are presenting it, and the demand for the creator built into it, to the creativity of God—one would rightfully confront this conclusion with the question who God might be. To answer this question, it is necessary to demonstrate the creator, that is both to prove him and to point him out in his entirety. The creator is also the revealer. Creation is the prophecy which is confirmed only in the miraculous sign of revelation. It is not possible to believe creation because it provides an adequate explanation of the world riddle. He who has not yet been reached by the voice of revelation has no right to accept the idea of creation as if it were a scientific hypothesis. The questionable part of the metalogical image of the uncreated world had once been subjected to debate by the revealed idea of creation. Thus it is only right that reason, which was not permitted to appropriate the idea of creation, should now seek a substitute for it. The doctrine of emanation should be understood as an attempt in this direction by late antiquity, as we have already stated. But this tendency reached its completion, as has also been set forth already, only in idealistic philosophy.

GENERATION

Its basic concept, with which it seeks to circumvent as well as to replace the idea of creation, is the concept of generation. Generation is supposed to accomplish the same as creation. It is supposed to give the plastic world of objects, as antiquity saw it, what it lacks: the fixed point from which its multiplicity closes ranks and arranges itself as unity. Only thereby could the world be lifted inwardly out of the uncertainty of the Perhaps and gain outwardly the stability of what is attested as real. At the same time it was to retain its elemental character, precisely its "graphic" nature, its plastic self-containedness. The idea of creation meets this condition, because it locates the fixed point outside its borders and does not let the creator merge with the world. Indeed it posits no connection at all between him and the world except that the creator has created and that the world, as creature, presses forward toward being created. The question is how well the concept of generation does justice to this task.

The idea of generation also seeks the fixed point, the generator, outside the world which is to be generated. Between the point of unity and what is to be unified, however, it thinks itself required—and able—to erect a rationally conceivable connection. Something on the order of cause and effect, so to speak, is supposed to be present. Not equality but comparability, proportionality is supposed to rule between and over both. Neither equality nor proportionality rules between an apple and a pear, but between one apple and three apples there exists a proportion, albeit likewise not an equation. Generator and generated must be equal in one relationship. Precisely this is what recommends the image of generation. The creator can say to the creatures: "To whom then will you compare me, that I should be like him?" Although generator and generated are not the identical person, they are of a kind—comparable. But where outside the world is there such a "point" which could take over the role of the generator vis-à-vis the world? The recourse to God lay, of course, nearest to hand. The relationship of generation, it seemed, could rule between God and world just as well as that of creation. And in view of his concept of unconditionality, God seemed well suited to represent origin and condition of the existence of the world. For the generator had to be comprehended no less than the creator as unconditional condition, as origin without origin, as pure A equal only to itself, as $A = A$ if we may resume here the mathematical symbols whose re-emergence will be explained shortly.

EMANATION

If he was thus to be generator, this then had to take effect initially in an alteration of the mathematical world-symbol. To be rationally comparable to its origin, the world could no longer be comprehended as $B = A$, but rather as $A = B$. This inversion was foreign to the idea of creation, which rather accepted the world in its elemental configuration; it permitted an inversion, not of the whole, but only of the parts, to appear only where the world's content emerged from the stillness of completion into the movement of occurrence. Here, on the other hand, the whole, the world itself, has to be comprehended the other way round. The rationally conceivable effect of a God who "is" A is possible only with a world which "is" A and is only defined as B. There can be no proportion between an A and a B, between $A (= A)$ and $B (=A)$, only between $A (= A)$ and $A (= B)$, that is between two different A's. Only a world which is $A (=B)$ can have emanated from a God who is $A (= A)$. Emanation is the downpour of the world out of God and, within the world, of ever new out-pourings from whatever poured forth last. It is the conception which first tried to compete with revelation's idea of creation in the history of the world. For every new emanation, that from which it emanates is again an analogy to the divine origin of the whole, and it itself an analogy to the original emanation of the world. For each, its origin is again "$A (= A)$," and it itself "$A (= B)$." For each, precisely as for the created world, its existence altogether counts as what first and actually originated of it. But the wealth of what is distinctive in it is the predicate; it is the universality, the presupposition, into which this existence is created—for the predicate has always to be thought of "prior" to the subject of the predicate. The path of emanation is a "path downward," it is, to use a common analogy, an effulgence of a light into the darkness which thus is already presupposed everywhere beginning with the first origin of the emanation, and thus posited in advance. The doctrine of emanation cannot do without the idea of primordial chaos, of a primordial night older than the light, of a "darkness which at first was everything."

Beyond this, however, the idea of emanation also fails in other respects to satisfy that requirement of reason which had called it forth. The idea of creation was rightfully indigestible for it, but its reaction to it was too immediate. It replaced God the creator with God the generator, without asking itself whether the pure reason which it served could agree to this occupancy of the place of the generator. Was God not himself object of cognition? How could one then within reason assume him to be origin and thus withdraw him from cognition? No, God too had to be recognized, and thus turned from the origin into a content of the embodiment of everything recognized. Another origin of the world, including thus possibly God too, had to take God's place. But the world itself is not its own origin. This can no longer be overlooked since the emergence of revelation's concept of creation. Rather it demands an origin outside itself precisely for the sake of its self-containedness. Accordingly only one thing can still be considered for the place of this origin: the self. Not, to be sure, the self as we have come to know it: as objective, albeit blind factuality, but rather a self which, though equally immersed in itself, is purely subjective and as this pure subject can assume the role of the origin of cognition vis-à-vis everything objective: the "I" of Idealism.

THE "I" AND THE "THING"

"I," "subject," "transcendental apperception," "spirit," "idea"—all these are names which the self assumes, this sole element outside of world and God which is still available, after it has decided to take the place of the generating "$A = A$." It too can solve its problem only if the world adapts to it into the form of comparability; it too therefore demands of the world that it convert from $B = A$ into $A = B$. This world it can now "generate." It generates it out of itself. The world is of a piece with it, subject like itself, "A." But it generates it as non-I. The subjectivity of the things is fulfilled in the distinctiveness B into objectivity. As concepts, the things bear the traits of their generator, the I; but as things they are something in their own right, something which has taken its leave of the generating I: things. Each thing stands in the same relation to its concept as the world of things in general to the "I:" the concept is the generator of its thing. Even the concepts themselves, as far as they still have "content," are themselves things in their turn, and as such they have their concept in their turn, and so on ad infinitum. Thus a single current of generation passes from the I through the whole world of things. They all range themselves in one row, one "path downward" from the pure I to the pure non-I, from the I-in-itself to the thing-in-itself. For this is the consequence of the conversion of the world as it has occurred in idealism exactly as in the doctrine of emanation. Although the universal existence of the world, which originated first, is its conceptuality, this universal existence is fulfilled as "thing-likeness" in the distinctive. Thus the plenitude of the distinctive is in its turn the ungenerated, the womb into which existence is generated. For idealism, too, chaos is the presupposition of generation, and the presupposition of such a passive "datum" is already made likely by the image of "generation" here, in contrast to the "outpouring" of the doctrine of emanation. None of the great idealistic systems has been able to avoid this concept. As *Ding an sich*, "multiplicity of sensuality," "datum," "resistance," as "plain infinity"—again and again there emerges that chaos prior to creation without which the absolute subject would have no basis for "egress" out of itself and its absoluteness.

The Logic of Creation
VERSUS
The Logic of the Idea

At this point, incidentally, it becomes clear what the concept of *creatio ex nihilo*, which we could not properly use before, signifies. It contains the denial of chaos. We see how it is impossible to avoid asserting chaos in any "reasonable" theory of the origin of the world, that of generation as well as that of emanation. For these theories demand a concept of the world according to the symbol $A = B$, a concept, that is, which posits the distinctive as predicate, and the universal as subject of the predicate. The predicate sentence always becomes intelligible only if the predicate has been known "for longer already" than its subject. Thus the distinctive here becomes the presupposition of the generation of universal existence. If now we were to confront this concept of the world with our own, where the distinctive B is the subject of the predicate and the universal A, which is, after all, also in the creator, means the predicate, it would become clear at once that the chaotic plenitude of the distinctive is the first thing created in the creation, and that the universal consists of the "given" vessels placed there by the creator, into which the distinctive is funnelled as it bubbles forth freely in creation. In an authentic confrontation of the world-concepts, the concept of *creatio ex nihilo* would be completely in its place.

But we do not intend such a confrontation. We are not developing creation as the scientific concept of the world. How indeed could we let an occurrence count as such which interconnects but two of the "elements" of the world without even touching the third? If we did, then the confrontation would, to be sure, be necessary. But then we should not have assailed the applicability of algebraic symbols to creation, nor turned to the grammatical ones. For us, the concept of creation stands in a larger scientific framework. Thus it applies to only two elements of the world, and even these two not as wholes, but each only in one of its parts. Thus we had to leave the language of mathematical symbols with those proto-cosmic, "finished" elements, and to construct the concept of creation out of the elements as they emerged from themselves and dispersed into their individual parts. To put it less formulaically, we developed the idea of creation in the light of revelation. Thus the elements of the All may not join for creation just as they are before revelation. Rather they must open up out of their occlusion, and turn to face each other. In this rapprochement, however, it becomes clear that the entire content of the elements cannot join in a single concept such as the concept of creation is in and of itself. As they open up, both elements retain contents which can only go into effect in other directions, in God's case his revealing himself, in the world's case its being redeemed.

Idealism, then, has the feeling that it must solve the riddle of the world here, "on the spot" so to speak. For it cannot grant validity to anything outside of the world and of knowledge. It must at all costs place these elements—world and knowledge, subject and object—into a rational relationship. It is therefore compelled to hold on to the mathematical symbols. We, however, are free of these symbols. We can freely allow the concept of creation to count as a beginning of knowledge, without bringing everything to a conclusion in it. We put it in the larger context of revelation. Thus it need not let itself be comprehended in the rationality of mathematical symbols. It leaves these behind. Grammar, the structure of the living language, supplies us with the symbolism to elucidate its content. Science as we conceive it contains more than merely the concept of creation. Creation cannot therefore be simply placed alongside of the concept of generation, even if the originators of the latter concept have put it, as before that of emanation, alongside the concept of creation. Creation is at home in the land of revelation and we would only have to remove it from this its native ground if we were practicing "philosophy of religion," that is, presenting religion in the framework of philosophy and according to its yardsticks. Then we should construct creation parallel to this philosophic idea, but then, of course, we would have to counter the philosophic concept of chaos with that of the *creatio ex nihilo*. And indeed, this concept originated, historically, in the philosophy of religion, not in theology, the science which we are practicing here.

Idealistic Metaphysics

But let us here return to the pursuit of the course taken by idealism. It is not, after all, theology that believes it can develop the All of knowledge in the presentation of the "origin." For it, creation counts only as beginning and prophecy, not as middle or end. It is philosophy that thinks of this as its realm and that will not cease before it can delude itself with having comprehended "everything" here. We had followed the basic idealistic concept of generation on its descent from the *Ich an sich* to the *Ding an sich*. The entire world of things as the objects of cognition is stretched out between these two poles. The concept of generations permeates it at every point. In the previous Part we already demonstrated how it thereby differs from the metalogical world at every point. Here we should only add that Idealism therefore attempts to develop a logic of its own, independent of grammar, in contrast to us: we preserve the metalogical character of the world by means of creation. True, the image of the world which we presented in the symbol of grammar appears to coincide in detail with the idealistic image of the world. The entire attempt to trace the non-objectiveness (not to say subjectivity) of action—via the occurrence as the thing—back to the attribute as the purely objective itself appears, after all, to characterize equally the presentation of the idealistic image of the world. The latter too is subsumed under the grammatical categories of the preterite, the third person, the intransitive, the two articles, definite and indefinite, the pronouns, from the indefinite via the interrogative to the demonstrative, and finally the adjective. This appearance is no more than natural. Both images of the world desire to secure the objectiveness of the world, the metalogic one based on creation as well as the idealistic one based on generation, and it is just objectiveness which is described in this selection from the grammatical categories. Nevertheless, Idealism seeks to elevate itself over language with a logic of its own, hostile to language. The cause of this must therefore lie in the proof, not in the proven. It will thus become visible when the first proven originally emerges from that which proves.

THOUGHT VERSUS SPEECH

A grammatical connection which Idealism cannot accept really shows up here. We based the last proven, the symbol of the first created thing, the adjective, on a root-adjective, the affirming "(it is) good." This free affirmation was expounded, so to speak, without pain or struggle. Itself an adjective, it at the same time represents the first grammatical category. In the place of this adjectival Yea, Idealism places a pronominal "root-word." But it is not a veritable root-word here for, gramatically, it does not belong together with the adjective which Idealism too recognizes as the basic form of objectiveness. Rather the connection between the I and the attributes is "purely logical." Both thereby prove to be presuppositions. Both exist "prior" to generation, both the I and the chaos of the datum. This failure of language precisely at the first instant paralyzes the harmless self-confidence with which it thought of itself as the never-failing tool of the spirit in creation. The idealistic world is not created through the word but through thought. The transition from the I to the attribute which is basic for Idealism can be comprehended only in "pure thought," in a thought, that is, which, alienated from the natural soil of language, thinks up dialectic contradictions. And since this first transition is decisive for all later transitions, the mistrust of language and its apparent "harmony" with thought remains a permanent legacy of Idealism and drives it ever further on the tilted plane of its "pure" logic, a logic that is foreign to language and beyond man.

THE FLIGHT FROM THE THING

The *Ding an sich* is the other pole of the idealistic world, whose presence is actually demanded by the very concept of generation. One could designate it as $B = B$, so that $A = B$ would be enclosed between a begetting $A = A$ and a parturient $B = B$. But Idealism does not cherish this allusion to an underlying chaos of the distinctive, and it quickly seeks to get away from it. An opportunity to do this presents itself to it in a circumstance which we may already find indicated in

$B = B$, familiar to us as the symbol of the self. For a brief while, Idealism too noted the incomparability and absolute occlusion of the self at this point. The indissoluble sediment of the world and the mystery of character have a "common obscure root." This surmise was clearly enunciated by Kant, though to be sure he could not, as Idealist, surmise its actual meaning. The common factor is designated by the symbol $B = B$. Now Idealism prepares to take the "path upward" which alone permits it to close the circle and thus to attain what must hover before it as the final goal of its utter rationality (for reason feels secure only when it returns into itself). As it does so, Idealism leaves the realm of surmises as quickly as possible and seeks the way back, initially, to the real world, that mixture of the particular and the universal.

IDEALISTIC ETHICS

Initially this return route thus leads from "$B = B$" to "$B = A$," for this, not "$A = B$," is the world-formula rationally attainable from $B = B$. Since "$B = B$" means the self, $B = A$ means that the particular defines itself more narrowly by means of an overlapping universal. In this case it means that the self submits to a universal. The concept of submission is the counterpart of the concept of generation. The latter dominates the downward path from the universal to the particular, the former the path upward from the particular to the universal. Both together, generation and submission, close the idealistic world into a whole. The path upward begins with that original submission of the "maxim" of one's own will—and what is $B = B$ if not this!—to the principle of a universal legislation—and what else is $B = A!$ This goes on and on now. Each time the most recently attained "principle of a universal legislation" is again taken up into the "maxim of one's own will." Thus the strength of the idealistic submission has to pass the test of this principle by itself likewise becoming the principle of a universal legislation. Via this submission to ever higher communities, ever more inclusive generalities of life, the universal proves to be the presupposition, that which is posited in advance, just as does the particular via generation—both times, in fact, against the original tendency. In generation as in submission, this is directed toward "purity": generation will not be bound to a foreign substance, nor submission to a strange law. Both want to legislate for themselves; here as well as there "freedom is to be rescued."

IDEALISTIC RELIGION

Yet freedom is not rescued, neither here nor there. Rather, in the one case, in generation, it loses itself in the dark womb of the nethermost substance; in the other, in submission, it disappears in the blinding ray of the supreme law. For the way upward finally merges into this, this uppermost universality of the law, this ultimate form. Submission recurs each and every time only in order to recover, at the goal of the submission, what was "submitted" in the submission, for to yield oneself is supposed to yield profit. This submission, then, ever rediscovers the personality in each universal, ever rediscovers that the A to which it has submitted is in its own turn but the statement about a B and thus must in its own turn consider it profitable to yield to a higher A. True, the doctrine of emanation also knew of this dissolving of the personality in the mystic delight of apotheosis. But it remained for Idealism to interpolate the whole world and thus to develop this dissolution into a veritable counterpart to the world-generating descent of the cognitive subject. Only in Idealism does the ascent of the volitive subject give birth out of ever new submissions to a reconstruction of the world as a grand staircase of personality. For him who submits, each individual step of the ascent implies equation with and wholly valid representation of the highest stratum. Just so, for the subject, each individual step of the descent to the pure object possesses, at the instant of generation, all the validity of objectiveness. With every preceding link in the sequence, man already feels himself sharing in the blessed height of that voluntary submission to what is higher, purer, unknown which is implied in the word "piety." He feels it as soon as he stands before "it," and not only once he stands before God. Note also the indefinite continuation of the sequence which dawns on us in the comparatives "higher" and "purer."

The end point of the sequence remains an "unknown," as the end point of the descending sequence did likewise. It remains an unknown —invisible, that is to say, at each individual point of the sequence. Indeed, visibility is not even demanded of it, since each individual link is fully representative at its own place. Individual cognition did not need to concern itself with the profoundest objectiveness, but only with the objectiveness of whatever object just stood before it. So too individual volition need not concern itself with supreme personality, but only with the personality of the person or community before which it is just standing. Admittedly, however, philosophy attains this outermost point in the case of objectiveness as well as of personality. Again, the cognitive I and its inexhaustible capacity for generating things found its pre-condition—and hence its "so far and no further"—in the *Ding an sich*. So too the volitive I and its submission, ever newly giving birth to its personality, finds its goal in the supreme personality. In "$A = A$," volition no longer recovers itself; here it surrenders, as cognition disintegrates in the $B = B$ of the *Ding an sich*—without hope of resurrection.

GOD AS OBJECT

Who is this "$A = A$"? It is personality, but a personality in which human volition is no longer found, any more than cognition rouses itself again once it has arrived at the *Ding an sich*. Quite manifestly it is the personality of God, and Idealism has not shunned this consequence. Thus Idealism has accomplished what it had presumed to do from the very beginning when it made of the I the root of cognition: God has become object, absolute object not of cognition, it is true, but of volition—God, that is, as personality even if absolute personality. Actually, absolute personality is a contradiction. The formula of personality, $B = A$, characterizes it as one world-content among many. If God is called absolute personality, this can only mean that he is the brightness in which all personality pales, but also that he is no more than this border of all human-worldly personality. To address God, as he "originates" here, as absolute "I" would not do, nor did this take place in Idealism. The name which Idealism created for him is not absolute I but absolute spirit, not an I, therefore, but a He—nay, less than a He: an It. The object remains object even after becoming God. But at this point Idealism now regularly discovers what our symbolic language has already laid at our feet, what we have merely to pick up: God as spirit is none other than—"I," the subject of cognition. And now the ultimate sense of Idealism becomes clear: reason has triumphed, the end merges again with the beginning, the highest object of thought is thought itself; nothing is inaccessible to reason; the irrational itself is only its boundary, not a beyond.

COLLAPSE

This then is a triumph along the whole front, but at what a price! The great edifice of reality is destroyed. God and man are reduced to the marginal concept: subject of cognition; world and man on the other hand to the marginal concept of a mere object of this subject. And the world, whose cognition was Idealism's initial intent, has become pure bridge between these two marginal concepts. Idealism entered the lists against the idea of creation in order to substantiate the metalogic character of the world, its factuality. This is now wholly laid waste, along with the factuality of God, which is foreign to Idealism, and of the self, which is a matter of indifference to it, both being hurled into the general vortex of annihilation on this occasion.

In the end, only one fixed point is left standing in this chaos: the *Ding an sich* which Idealism had not itself "worked on," which it had shunted to the outermost edge of objectiveness. Idealism surmises a common root for the *Ding an sich* and for human character, and with this surmise alone, denying its own essence for one fateful moment, it opens the prospect on an All in which these three elements, world, man, God, live side by side in undisturbed factuality. Idealism itself cannot enter this land which it espies at the border of its existence. It forfeited its admission when, self-confidently incredulous of God, it would have forced the living water of the All from out of the rock of creation with its own rod of reason, rather than be confidently satisfied with the wellspring of language which God ordained to issue from this rock. In blind one-sidedness, Idealism compressed everything into the scheme of creation because it wanted to compete with this concept which it thought could be lifted out of the circuit of revelation and mastered scientifically as an isolated concept. This one-sidedness is the sin for which Idealism was punished.

Theory of Art

THE IDEALIST AND LANGUAGE
By thinking that it could take its stand outside of the current of revelation, Idealism had, as we have seen, rejected language as an organon, and we had to form algebraic symbolism for it in keeping with its own postulates. Idealism lacked straightforward confidence in language. It was not of a mind to listen and respond to this voice, which resounds in man without apparent reason but the more realistically for that. Idealism demanded reasons, accountability, calculability—everything that language was unable to offer it—and invented for itself logic, which offered all this. It offered all this, only not what language possessed, its self-evidentness: though language is rooted in the subterranean foundations of being with its arch-words, it already shoots upward into the light of terrestrial life in these root-words, and in this light it blossoms forth into colorful multiplicity. It is thus a growth amidst all growing life; it nourishes itself on life as life

nourishes itself on language. Yet it is distinguished from this life precisely because it does not move freely and capriciously over the surface, but rather sinks roots into the dark foundations beneath life. Idealistic logic, however, thinks it must remain entirely in these dark subterranean foundations. Without knowing it, it thus rather drags the life of the world above, into which it does not dare to grow, down into the nether world. It transforms the living into a realm of shadows.

IDEALISTIC ESTHETICS

At its zenith, Idealism thus gave itself over completely into the power of its own creature, logic. At the same time it could not help but sense how it was losing touch with that living existence which it had undertaken to substantiate and to comprehend. Submerged in the hypocosmic and protocosmic shadow realm of logic, it sought to keep an access to the world above open for itself. Philosophy was driven out of the paradise of confidence in language—here, too, its original sin was to have trusted more in its own wisdom than in the creative power of God which encompassed it visibly. And at the very moment when it lost that confidence in language which even its critical precursors in England still possessed to some degree, it cast about for a surrogate. In the divinely created Eden of language, philosophy had lived without the distrust and mental reservations of logic, and it had to leave it because of its own fault. In its place, it sought a human Eden, a human paradise. It had to be a garden planted by man himself, yet not consciously his work. For such a work could not have offered a surrogate for the lost garden that God himself had planted. Like that lost garden, it had to be one that surrounded man though he knew not whence. Man would have to have planted it, but he could not himself know this. It had to be his work, but unconsciously so. It had to bear all the marks of purposive labor, and yet have originated aimlessly. It had to be effected work and yet plant-like growth. Thus it came about that Idealism, at the moment when it rejected language, apotheosized art.

Never before had philosophy done this. True, in Plato, Plotinus, Augustine and, less consciously, in many another, it had recognized God's handiwork in the vibrantly beautiful; but from the first, Idealism acclaimed not living beauty as such but "fine arts." It taught that art alone was visibly real, that the shadows from the realm of ideals could imbibe life from it at the entrance to the netherworld, thus assuring themselves of their remnant of life as they recalled, while this blood of reality circulated within, their own life, long since submerged.

Idealism did not have to harbor any distrust against the work of art, for it was a product. And since it nevertheless stands there like a part of nature in its unconscious becoming and its unquestionable being, it could be addressed and venerated as the revelation of reality. For Idealism believed it could recognize here, without recourse to reasoning and invisible form, the reality of the All which was only guessed at in the "common root." Thus art became for Idealism the great justification of its procedure. If doubts haunted it about the admissibility of its method—that of the "panlogistically" pure generator—it had only to regard the work of art, produced by mind and yet nature-like reality, to clear its conscience. The work of art stuck roots in the same colorless, protocosmic night of pure spirit, and yet blossomed on the beautiful green pastures of existence. Thus art appeared to be an Ultimate, at once confirmation of the method of reasoning— "organon," that is—and visible manifestation of an "absolute": this step lay at hand and Kant already paved its way with his allusion to the "common root." Idealism was incapable of acknowledging the word of man as answer to the word of God, and refused to repose confidence in it. Yet it gave away this same confidence to a work of man. The speech of the soul, the manifestation of the inner man encompasses all other human self-expression, sustains it and completes it. Yet instead of believing this speech, Idealism threw the whole weight of its gullibility onto a single limb torn loose from the whole body of humanity.

ART AS SPEECH

For art is no more than one limb, a limb without which, it is true, man would be a cripple, but remain man withal. It is one limb among many. Man is more. The only visible witness to his soul, the one which he cannot lack without ceasing to be man, is the word. Art too reposes in the womb of the word. Art itself is only the language of the unspeakable, the language as long as there is no language, the language of the protocosmos. Not the word but art is the true language for the world prior to the miracle of revelation, the world which stands there for us as a historical analogy for that protocosmos. In the arrangement of its nature, it is the visible demonstration for the elements of the All which ascend out of the dark foundations of the Nought. But the reality of art, as work of art, is not speech but something itself spoken vis-à-vis the lifestream reality of real language. Were it still speech here too, then it would be a language beside speech, and while there may be many languages, there is but one speech. As something "spoken," however, art is inherent in every other living reality, inseparable from it, indispensable for its completeness, a limb among its limbs and recognizable as such. Recognizable as such but not, as Idealism would have it, in all its reality to be subsumed under the relationship between the world and its origin, or commensurable with this relationship. Rather we grasp only a part of the work of art, only its beginnings, in the concept of creation. Life is richer than the world and its becoming. So too language in its individual structuring, and now art as well, are too abundant to be wholly conceivable in the idea of creation. The epoch of creation is only the beginning—albeit the everlasting beginning—even as it is mirrored in the brief life span of the work of art.

The independent linguistic value which the universal nature of the work of art had assumed in the speechless protocosmos leaves no aftereffects in the merely "spoken" reality of the work of art except in one respect. Real language presupposes the inner conversions of the elements which came into being in the speechless protocosmos, and the emergence of their individual segments into the realm of the manifest. Its relationship to revelation is thus one of identity, just as is that of "reasoning" to "being" in the basic dogma of Idealism. In the same way art derives directly from its essential elements just as these emerged in the twilight of the protocosmos. The "mythical" is that self-contained entity which sets off being from everything else like a frame; the "plastic" is that interconnection of inner form which holds all the abundance of the details of the work of art together; the "tragic" is that human content which endows the beautiful with the power of speech. And directly above these three basic pillars there vault the arches which, joining them by twos and leading from one to the other, constitute the work of art. The individual emerges from the whole into the open; in effect, then, an esthetically opulent reality is created out of its pre-esthetic predecessor, and directly on this emergence, on this creation, there reposes the beginning of the life span of the work of art, the creation—sequence of the fundamental concepts of which the first ones may be briefly surveyed here.

GENIUS

The creation of a work of art takes place in the author. It is not as if the author created the work of art; that would contradict the unconscious becoming of the opus which was already expressed in Plato's *Ion* and rightly emphasized by Idealism. But the eruption of the work of art presupposes that the author has come into being.

Although the author is by no means the creator of the opus, his own having been created is that creation which precedes the emergence of the work of art, just as, on the other hand, the opus attains the perfection of its genuine vitality only in that event which transpires within the beholder. The author does not fall ready-made from heaven any more than any other maestro. Genius is by no means innate, as current liberal education would have it; on the contrary, it one day takes a person by surprise because it depends on the self and not merely on the personality. A child prodigy is not a genius and has no more prospect of becoming one than any other human being, whereas a genius, once he is a genius, never ceases to be a genius; in a genius, even depravity and insanity are still ingenious. Now the theory of art need know nothing of personality and self; for it, the evolution of the author presents itself thus: a pre-existing whole of man, prior, so to speak, to genius—precisely what we know as personality—externalizes from itself that complex of ingenious attributes which we know as the self and liberates it, frees it to originate the work of art.

POET AND ARTIST

The whole curriculum vitae is in its turn traversed in the author himself, that is within the "genius" and also, as is to be demonstrated in the following books, in the work of art and its beholder. Genius means very little if it is merely genius; it must augment itself from within and perfect itself. That man is a genius, that the capacity for originating a work of art has penetrated him, this is in itself only a beginning, the beginning of a new beginning. To break out of this closed circle of mere capacity to be originator, he must, as a first step, turn into a real creator, a *poiētēs* in the original sense of the word, a "poet" in the sense which this word, in contrast to the mere "artist," has assumed today to describe, say, a Balzac as against a Flaubert, or a Lagerlöf[1] as against a Huch,[2] though in truth there is no poet who is not at the same time an artist. The capacity to be creative must release an inner diversity, a world of creatures, insights, ideas which nevertheless are held together in an intrinsically harmonious juxtaposition by the personal style, the internal way of the artist. All the ideas, the inspirations, the creations of a Beethoven, a Goethe, a Rembrandt constitute, after all, a kind of "family" among themselves, a family likeness connects them regardless of the fact that they are not

---

[1] Selma Lagerlöf (1858–1940), Swedish woman novelist. (Tr.)
[2] Riccarda Huch (1864–1947), German woman novelist. (Tr.)

outwardly united into the unity of a single opus. This is the creativity of the genius, this being "inwardly full of form." It is the elemental basis of all his reality. He who is not a creator, who is never inspired, whose well of inspiration is not inexhaustible, and whose inspirations are not, for all their inexhaustibility, bound together by the bond of that family resemblance—he will never be more than a "frustrated" genius at best.

The Word of God

The work of art thus supplies us with an analogy to creation. To pursue this analogy to its conclusion here, and with it the first series of fundamental concepts of the theory of art, we would now have to anticipate concepts which we can only elucidate in the next book. For the theory of art—and here we suddenly see again, in the clearest form, its distinction from the theory of language as developed in this volume—is wholly systematic, on the analogy of a family tree. Precisely this clarifies why art cannot be organon, why it is here something spoken as contrasted with speech. Any one single concept, any one individual human trait—and art is none other than this—can only be further developed in genealogical fashion. The theory of language can at best be given tabular form and even this form introduces only a retrospective order which does not correspond to the original emergence of the categories. For the categories emerge, originally and immediately, in a manner wholly identical with the actual process which they categorize, that is to say, here, with creation. With each of the subsequent processes, the sequence of categories will always be quite different, corresponding—indeed, responding—to the individual character of each process; each category has its analogies within other processes, but not at the same place. Thus the tabulation can easily be derived from the material, but only by introducing a formal order into it which does not emerge here as the material of an independent subordinated science of language, but which appears as the original symbolism of reality itself and accordingly in the closest sense of "identity" with this reality. Language here is no independent content which would have to develop according to an inner system. Rather it describes the daily cosmic orbit of our planet along the zenith of world history, that orbit, in other words, whose elements originated for us in algebraic symbolism. We describe the orbit in which we believe with the words in which we trust. It is difficult to believe in the orbit, for at any given time we see only the individual point which we are experiencing. But language is truly that "higher" mathematics which, in the individual point of the miracle that we have ourselves experienced, reveals to us the entire course of the orbit of the believed miracle. And language is easily trusted, for it is within us and about us; as it reaches us from "without," it is no different from language as it echoes the "without" from our "within." The word as heard and as spoken is one and the same. The ways of God are different from the ways of man, but the word of God and the word of man are the same. What man hears in his heart as his own human speech is the very word which comes out of God's mouth. Beginning with the root-word which resounds upward directly from the speechlessness of the arch-word, and ending with the completely objectivizing narrative form of the past tense, that word of creation which reverberates within us and speaks from within us—all this is also the word which God has spoken and which we find inscribed in the Book of the Beginning, in Genesis.

GRAMMATICAL ANALYSIS OF GENESIS I

The entire chapter which reports on the work in the beginning is traversed by a phrase, a phrase which recurs six times, only a single word in length, introduced only by a colon. The phrase says: "good!" —it was and is and will be—"good." Creation consists of this divine affirmation of creaturely existence. This "good" is the sonorous finale of each day of creation, because it is none other than the mute arch-word of its beginning.

What is it that is "good"? What is it that this sixfold divine Yea affirms? It is the daily achievement of each day of creation, the thing not simply as thing but as labor, as elaborated, existence as pre-existence. Existence is affirmed by God's pronouncing his own work "good": he has made it and it is good. He created—this narrative form runs through the whole chapter: he created, he spoke, he divided, he saw and so forth. Past tense and third person mean double objectness. There is no subject apart from the single, always selfsame divine one. And this does not, like every other subject, merge as something distinctive into its predicate as something universal, thus subjectivizing the predicate, personalizing it and thus dis-objectivizing it; rather it remains in a pure untouchable beyond and emits the predicate, free of itself for serene objectness. If two do the same thing, it is not the same thing. But when the one who can only be one does the same thing it is always and ever the same: the divine subject is the only one which does not color its predicate personally. To secure this pure objectness of the "he created," it follows that the creator cannot have a name; he is only "God" pure and simple.

God created. And the world, that which was created? It "became." This word too resounds again and again. As the psalm summarized it, "He spoke and the world came to be."[1] Creation, which for God means having-made, is having-become for the world. What is it that became? The same as that which God created: things. God created the heavens and the earth. Since the place of the active subject in this chapter is occupied by God alone, its nouns are accusatives, objects created by God or else, as things that have become, they are the nominatives of passive constructions. Older Jewish exegetes translated the first sentence by "in the beginning when God created the heavens and the earth." "The" heavens and "the" earth—the other nouns appear with the indefinite article, but this first sentence anticipates creation as a whole. It gives to creativity in advance the clear, active form of the past tense and thereby to creation its reality as time. And at a stroke it endows the Created as a whole with its appropriate form, the definite form. Each individual thing gains definition only after a detour via its membership in a category as expressed by the indefinite article. The entirety of things—heaven and earth—is after all not subordinated to any other category; it possesses this definition without mediation. Here the definite article provides the substantiality of things in general with spatial form prior to any individual determination. So too the definite, personal, general "he created," which first fixes the temporal form of the substantiality of occurrence altogether, precedes the first "was." On the other hand, every individual, personalized occurrence, that is, every individual act, only becomes possible by that particular determination of time which only reaches the act by a detour via the pure occurrence in its connection with the copula. Thus it only *follows* the "was."

"The" heaven and "the" earth—the totality of creation is its sole unique feature, the only thing which does not first derive its individuality by way of the detour via multiplicity. Subsequently, created things appear in the plural, even things which impress man as unique in type and veritably offer themselves for individualization as divine persons. Thus sun and moon here become "luminaries" and, their individuality thus brought back to a pluralistic category, they are

---

[1] The ambiguity between "was" and "became" inherent both in the original Hebrew and in the archaic German translation (ward) is difficult to reproduce in English. (Tr.)

mercilessly and without regard to their person banished into creation's world of things.

"In the beginning, when God had created the heavens and the earth, the earth was waste and void, with darkness over the abyss, and the spirit of God brooding over the waters." A double "was." The first statement about the world of things appears in adjectival form as waste and void, connected to that copula of being and being-already-past which here, contrary to linguistic usage, appears as explicit word in the original text. Altogether adjectivally. It is a darkness in which all qualities show but the one gray color of the-waste-and-the-void until God intones his "let there be light" into it. Light is no more a thing than darkness. It is itself a quality. It is to cognition what the "good!" is to volition, the utterly affirming valuation. And now God "separates" the chaos of attributes, and when the separation is accomplished, and the beginning of creation is completed in the visibility of the individual attributes, then what had already become visible in the light rings for the first time as resounding sound, as word: the "good."

The individual objects of creation, however, emerge from the first mass of attributes, as yet waste and void, in the same sentence where the first individual act, too, is born: the action-word out of the event-word in its adjectival form of a participle. That his spirit is "brooding" —this is the beginning of the divine acts of creation. Nor is it God that is brooding, though that is already a depersonalization. Rather it is the still more impersonal "spirit of God." In the original text this involves an even stronger depersonalization, since God as "spirit" wears the garment of feminine gender in his train. And "brooding" is the dullest of all activities of which the intrahuman analogy to creation —the procreation of individuals within a category—is constituted, and an activity of the female part at that. Yonder the pitch darkness of the waste and the void, here the dullness of brooding. Both thing and act here emerge in the form of qualities, qualities, at that, which stand at the very lowest limits where thing and act each arise out of what is as yet respectively neither thing nor act at all.

This then is creation's thesaurus of word formations. But let us not forget "the" word on account of all these words. Does not creation itself take place in the word? God "said," did he not? Was it permissible simply to reckon this having-said of his, as we did, seriatim among his creative acts? It was not permissible. True, creation is, at least at first, inwardly broader than revelation. There is in it much which has not remotely been revealed as prophecy yet. No one knows how long it will be before all that was created will have finally opened its mouth and become audible as the prediction of miracle. Only a first glimmer of revelation already leaps up with the first moment of creation or at least with the second, for the first moment is, after all, that of the intransitive "it was," the dark and speechless attributedness of things as well as of action. But with the second moment, the "God said" bursts forth as the first action-word in creation on the heels of the creative word of the whole creation. And "light" burst forth as the first visible attribute word, albeit still mute. And in the sentence which God says, the present tense appears for the first time beneath all the past tense, under all the quiescent indicatives with the suddenness of the imperative: "let there be." And yet this presentness and this suddenness are still bound by the impersonal construction of pure occurrence. God speaks, but his word is still as if something inside of him, not he himself, were speaking. His word is like a prophecy of his own future speech, but so far he does not speak himself, not yet as self. The words of creation resolve themselves naturally out of his nature as an It from out of an It.

Until he opens his mouth for the final act of creation and says: "Let us make man." "Let us"—for the first time the magic circle of objectivity is breached, for the first time an "I" resounds out of the sole mouth which hitherto has discoursed in creation, instead of an "it." And more than an "I." Together with the I there resounds at the same time a Thou, a Thou which the I addresses to itself: "let" "us." Something new has dawned. Something new? Is not he who speaks the same as before? And is not what he speaks the same as what was reported of him before? Is it not a making that emerges personally from the self, just as it is asserted in "he created" and so forth? It was indeed asserted, but if it wanted to become explicit hitherto, it petered out into an "it." Now it *remains* personal, now it declares "I." Really "I?" Here we come up against the boundary which warns us that even on the sixth day we are still in creation, and not yet in revelation.

As long as he is engaged in creating, God does not say "I" but "we," and an absolute, all-inclusive we which implies no I beyond itself, the plural of absolute majesty. It is an I which, as the modern translation shows very nicely, contains the Thou immediately, an I which discourses only with itself and can discourse only with itself. It is, thus, an impersonal I, an I that still remains within itself, which does not step outside of itself in the Thou, does not reveal itself but, like the metaphysical God of the protocosmos, is alive only within itself. The creator reveals himself in the act of creation. The creative word, even that of the final creation, is not that of the revealer which reveals the revealer. In the last analysis it too is but another creative act of the creator.

And what of man, that last created among the creatures? Let us make man—one man:[1] the personal name Adam is audible in the original text at the same time. It becomes the first personal name among all the generic creatures, all the beings which are merely created "after their kind." And truly he is created "in the image of God" —and thus set apart from the other creatures and, with or without personal name, endowed with what the creator denied even to the heavenly luminaries: with resemblance to God, with a personality not mediated through the generalization of category nor necessitating multiplicity, with a self. Something new has dawned. But something more than self too—a soul? The breath of life has been breathed into man, but does he really exhale it too? Does he speak? He is created speech-less. And again we run up against that wall which separates portent from sign, prophecy from miracle.

THE PROPHECY OF MIRACLE

But prophecy is here. For the last time, God regards what he has created. And this time: lo!—"very good." The root-word of creation emerges from itself. It remains an adjective, remains within the framework of its own essence. But it ceases to designate the simple, individual, uncompared attribute. It becomes a comparative; it compares. Within the general Yea of creation, bearing everything individual on its broad back, an area is set apart which is affirmed differently, which is "very" affirmed. Unlike anything else in creation, it thus points beyond creation. This "very" heralds a supercreation within creation itself, something more than worldly within the worldly, something other than life which yet belongs to life and only to life, which was created with life as its ultimate, and which yet first lets life surmise a fulfillment beyond life: this "very" is death. The created death of the creature portends the revelation of a life which is above the creaturely level. For each created thing, death is the very consummator of its entire materiality. It removes creation imperceptibly into the past, and thus turns it into the tacit, permanent prediction of the miracle of its renewal. That is why, on the sixth day, it was not said that it was "good," but rather "behold, very good!" "Very," so our sages teach, "very"—that is death.

[1] In Hebrew: 'adam. (Tr.)

BOOK TWO

Revelation

or

The Ever-Renewed Birth of the Soul

Love is strong as death.[1] Strong in the same way as death? But against whom does death display its strength? Against him whom it seizes. And love, of course, seizes both, the lover as well as the beloved, but the beloved otherwise than the lover. It originates in the lover. The beloved is seized, her love is already a response to being seized: Anteros is the younger brother of Eros. Initially it is for the beloved that love is strong as death, even as nature has decreed that woman alone, not man, may die of love. What has been said of the twofold encounter of man and his self applies strictly and universally only to the male. As for woman, and precisely the most feminine woman above all, even Thanatos can approach her in the sweet guise of Eros. Her life is simpler than that of man by reason of this missing contradiction. Already in the tremors of love her heart has become firm. It no longer needs the tremor of death. A young woman can be as ready for eternity as a man only becomes when his threshold is crossed by Thanatos. No man would die the death of an Alcestis. Once touched by Eros, a woman is what man only becomes at the Faustian age of a hundred: ready for the final encounter—strong as death.

Like all earthly love, this is only an analogy. Death as the capstone of creation first stamps every created thing with the ineradicable stamp of creatureliness, the word "has been." Love which knows solely the present, which lives on the present, pines for the present—it challenges

[1] Song of Songs 8:6.

156

death. The keystone of the somber arch of creation becomes the cornerstone of the bright house of revelation. For the soul, revelation means the experience of a present which, while it rests on the presence of a past, nevertheless does not make its home in it but walks in the light of the divine countenance.

The Revealer

THE CONCEALED ONE

The living God to whom the heathen cry, insofar as he is not just "asleep or on a journey," had disclosed himself, in the mighty wisdom of his creative activity, as the God of life. With that there reappeared that limitless power which once had merged with God's mythical vitality. But from a caprice which was chained to the fleeting moment, it has turned into a wisdom enduring in its essence. That which had struggled to the surface out of God's "Nought" as self-negation of this Nought, re-emerged from its immersion into God's living "Aught," not any longer as self-negation, but rather as world-affirmation. God's vitality thus became to a certain extent again a Nought, a Nought on a higher level, Nought only with reference to that which emerged from it, but in its own right a Nought full of character, in short no Nought but an Aught. It was Nought only in this respect that, in disclosing itself, it at once broke up into new configurations one of which, essential power, we have already learned to recognize. For these new configurations have nothing designable behind them out of which they might have emerged. If one wanted to regard God's vitality as such a background, say, of the manifest creative power, it would justifiably have to be countered that this emergence could not have taken place out of the mythical vitality of the concealed God, but only out of its conversion into the revealed. This conversion, how-ever, lacks a name; it is no more than, as it were, the geometric point out of which the emergence takes place.

True, even "before" the conversion, God's vitality was but a geo-metric point of this sort, the convergence of the two segments of the divine Nought, the arch-yea and the arch-nay; and the conversion can only be comprehended as the reversal of the directions which, then, converged in the one case and diverged in the other. But the result of the conversion of two lines, albeit but a point, is yet as generated point something designable, defined, an Aught, like the point (x, y) within a system of co-ordinates. A point, on the other hand, which is defined only as the point of departure of directions, albeit fixed like the end point (o) of a system of co-ordinates, is not defined. It is only the origin of the determination taking place in the system of co-ordinates. This is why God has a highly vital, visible countenance in paganism, and is not in the least felt to be a concealed God, while belief senses quite clearly that it knows nothing at all of a God who might not become manifest, that God as such is rather a "concealed God" for him, this same God who before his conversion out of concealment into the manifest seemed not concealed at all to unbelief. Paganism's position, as we defined it throughout Part One, becomes recognizable precisely in this distinct relationship to revelation: on that side the original Nought is the fundamental source of the original Aught, on this the original Aught is the visible result of that original Nought for all that it is not manifest, that it is wrapped up in itself. Visible though not manifest means visible for him whose eyes, enwrapped by the same darkness in which that original Aught wraps itself, are thus attuned to this darkness.

THE MANIFEST ONE

Do we not, however, stand to lose the elemental "factuality" of God, which we believed we already held in our hands, if God—and we will later make the corresponding finding for the other two elements of the protocosmos—is an utterly concealed God except for revelation, whereas within revelation he at once becomes manifest, that is, breaks up into the configurations of his becoming-manifest? If God is but concealed origin of his becoming-manifest, what then remains in revelation of that veritably palpable reality which God already possessed in paganism? But did he then really possess it? Was it not shattered a hundred times over by the unbroken omnipotence of the Perhaps? True, factuality does not appear to be directly touched by the Perhaps. But in the final analysis, a factuality which refuses all inquiries into its How can hardly be very sure of itself. It may be surmised that a revelation which disclaims all ability to recognize the elemental factuality of God, and which disposes of this God as "concealed," would instead strive for a suitable factuality of its own, itself established not on the elements but on the one track of the one reality, a factuality elevated above every Perhaps onto the height of utter certainty.

And so it is. Just as the protocosmic God first became result out of his Nought, so too the concealed God—only as such does belief get to see this result of the protocosmos—is but the beginning of an occurrence whose first act we have already seen in the divine creation of the world. For God, creation is not merely creation of the world; it is also something which occurs within himself as the concealed one. In this sense we had to designate creation as already a becoming-manifest on the part of God. And at that he manifests himself in it as creator, that is to say, entirely in acts, acts which no longer grow, no longer increase, which are in the beginning *and* once and for all, which are thus, as far as God is concerned, not acts at all but attributes. If anything "outside" creation is to emerge from God's concealment and to supplement this limitless infinity of the divine creative power, liberated once and for all, in the direction of a coupling of that infinity with the factual unity, then it must be something which contains enough drive to traverse all the widespread infinity of divine power little by little. It has to be, that is, something inherently growing, inherently augmentable. Where and how it realizes this drive may be left open here, but it is essential, and must already become clear here, that it has it.

LOVE

Previously it was original freedom, the untrammeled passion of the mythical God, which burst forth from the concealed God into the light of the new day as divine creative power. So too the *moira* of God, that fateful divine essence, now seeks a path into the open. God's inner "nature," the infinite silence of the sea of his being had, it is true, coalesced and gravitated into fate under the impact of the divinely internalized freedom of action. But fate too had always been something enduring. *Moira* did not change her decree: though the decree might disclose itself only in the course of time, it is valid from the beginning. Fate is the primeval law; its heralds are the oldest in the race of the Gods, and it is no coincidence that they are mostly feminine. For the maternal is always that which is already there; the paternal is only added to it: the female is ever mother to the male. Fate is thus enduring and primeval, qualities which it must lose as it leaves the darkness of divine concealment to burst forth into brightness. Freedom of action had become manifest in creative power as essential, attributive being. Now, however, fated being must manifest itself in a corresponding reversal as occurrence sprung from the moment, as occurred event. Fate bursts forth eventfully with the whole force of the moment. It is not destined from of yore. On the contrary, it is precisely the negation of everything valid from of yore, the negation, indeed, of the very moment which immediately precedes this one.

It is the moment which, within its own constricted space, harbors all the weight of destiny, a destiny not "destined" but suddenly there and yet as inescapable in its suddenness as though it were destined from of yore. What is this fate? A glance at that creature which was created in God's image and analogy teaches us the only way we can, the way we must name this intra-divine fate-become-affect. Just as God's caprice, born of the moment, had converted itself into enduring power, so his eternal essence converted itself into—love, a love newly awake with every moment, ever young love, ever first love. For love alone is at once such fateful domination over the heart in which it stirs, and yet so newborn, initially so without a past, so wholly sprung from the moment which it fulfills, and only from that moment. It is wholly compulsion. In the words of that great lover who bore and was borne by his love through hell, purgatory, and heaven, it is wholly *"deus fortior me."* And yet, in the words that immediately follow, it is not supported in its domination by a fate created from of yore, by an everlasting long-ago of its pre-existence, but rather by the ever new just-now of its quality of having this moment arrived: *ecce deus fortior me "qui veniens dominabitur mihi."* It is none other than the decree of destiny on which the caprice of the mythical God broke up within him. And yet it is as different from this as the heavens from the earth. For it has transformed itself from that decree which emerges from the Nought as simple Yea, as simple "It is thus," "thus it was fated," into a compulsion. From the night of the concealed God, this compulsion bursts forth into the manifest as a Nay, as an ever new self-denial, unconcerned with whatever may have preceded or be yet to come, wholly offspring of the immediately present *coup d'oeil*, the lived-in moment of life.

Here begins that supplement to the divine self-manifestation which merely commenced in the acts of creation, and of which we spoke above. The "factuality" of God threatened to become lost in his concealment. To regain it, it is not enough that he become manifest a first time in an infinity full of creative acts. There God threatened to lose himself again behind the infinity of creation. He appeared to become mere "origin" of creation and therewith once more the concealed God after all, just what he ceased to be by virtue of creation. From out of the darkness of his concealment there must emerge something other than bare creative power, something in which the broad infinity of the acts of creative power is captured in visible form lest God should once more be able to retreat behind these acts into the Concealed. Thus to capture an extensive infinity can only mean that this expanse is traversed in its entirety. But as infinite expanse it

can only be traversed by the strength of an infinite breath, an indefatigable strength. And it goes without saying that this strength, likewise, must burst forth directly from the depth of the divine
concealment. For only thus can it achieve what we are here demanding: securing the revelation which takes place in creation against
retrogression into the night of mystery. Precisely for the sake of its
revelational character, the first revelation in creation thus demands the
emergence of a "second" revelation, a revelation which is nothing
more than revelation, a revelation in the narrower—nay in the narrowest—sense.

This must, then, be a revelation which does not "posit" anything,
which creates nothing from within itself into the void. For such a
manifestation, though it was also a case of becoming manifest, was
only incidentally this; in essence and above all it was creation. The
manifestation which we seek here must be such a one as is wholly
and essentially revelation, and nothing else. But this means that it may
be none other than the opening of something locked, none other than
the self-negation of a mere mute being by a sonorous word, of an
everlastingness, quietly at rest, by a moment in motion. The power to
change the color of created being, which is illuminated by such a
moment, from created "thing" into a testimonial to occurred manifestation resides in the effulgence of this *coup d'oeil*. Each thing is
such a testimonial, if only because it is a created thing and because
creation itself is already the first revelation. But precisely because it
is a created thing from of yore, therefore the fact that it is testimonial
to an occurred revelation remains behind it in the darkness of a first
beginning. Only when it is once, somewhere in time, irradiated by
the effulgence of a revelation taking place at that very moment—not
of one which has taken place once and for all—only then will the
circumstance that it owes its existence to a revelation become for it
more than a "circum-stance"—the inner nucleus of its factuality. Only
then—as the expression of a revelation occurring then and there, and
no longer as the testimonial to a revelation that has occurred altogether
—will the thing emerge from its substantive past into its vital present.

This "effulgence" flows, ever anew, from thing to thing in the
fullness of time. And in doing so, it frees the things from their state
of being merely created. At the same time, it liberates creation from a
fear constantly hanging over it: the fear that it sink back into its
origin from the Nought on the one hand, from divine concealment on
the other. Precisely as it is unconditionally product of the moment,
revelation is thus the means for confirming creation structurally. The
creator could still retreat behind creation into the darkness which is

itself without structure just because so rich in structures. There always remained to him, so to speak, the flight into the past of "origin," where he "could modestly hide behind eternal laws." But the revealer in his all-time presentness can at every moment transfix him in the Bright, the Manifest, the Unconcealed, in short in the present. And by doing so, he lets God's concealedness sink into the past once and for all. Now God is present, present like the moment, like every moment, and therewith he proceeds to become a "matter of fact"—something which as creator he had not yet truly been and which even now he only begins to become—like the gods of the heathen behind the ramparts of their mythology.

THE LOVER

It is love which meets all the demands here made on the concept of the revealer, the love of the lover, not that of the beloved. Only the love of a lover is such a continually renewed self-sacrifice; it is only he who gives himself away in love. The beloved accepts the gift. That she accepts it is her return-gift, but in her acceptance she remains within herself and becomes a contented soul at peace with herself. The lover, however, extorts his love from the very marrow of his self, as the tree extorts its branches from itself: every branch breaks out of the trunk and no longer knows anything of the tree, which it denies. Yet the tree stands there in the splendor of its branches, which belong to it for all that each of them denies it. The tree has not let them go; it has not let them fall to the ground like ripe fruits. Each branch is its branch and yet a branch to itself. Each has broken forth at a spot of its own, all its own, and is forever bound to this spot. So too the love of the lover is rooted in the moment of its origin, and for this reason it has to deny all other moments, deny the whole of life. It is faithless by nature, for its nature is the moment, and thus it must, to be true, renew itself with every moment; each moment must become for it the first sight of love. Only this completeness of each moment permits it to grasp the entirety of created life, but thereby it can really do so. It can do so by traversing this entirety with ever new meaning, illuminating and vitalizing now one, now another individuality within it. This is a route which begins anew with every new day; it need never end; it considers itself at every moment—because it *is* entirely in this moment—to be on that height beyond which lies nothing else; and yet it learns with each new day that it has never yet loved that piece of life which it loves as much as today: love loves the beloved each day a little more. This constant augmentation is the form which steadfastness takes in love, although—and because—it is instability itself; it is a faithfulness devoted only to the individual present moment. Out of abysmal faithlessness it can thus turn into steadfast faith, and only out of this. For it is only the instability of the moment that enables love to experience every moment in turn as a new one, and thus to bear the torch of love through the whole nocturnal realm and twilight zone of created life. It escalates because it ever wants to be new; it wants to be ever new so as to be capable of stability; it can be stable only by living wholly in the Unstable, in the moment; and it must be stable if the lover is to be vital soul and not merely the empty vehicle of a passing agitation. So God loves too.

THE PRESENT

But does he, then, love? Can we attribute love to him? Does not the concept of love imply want? And could God be in want. Did we not gainsay the Creator's creating from love so as not to have to attribute want to him? And should the Revealer now reveal himself, for all this, from love?

But what was our reason for gainsaying the Creator's want? It was because his creating is supposed to be attribute and enduring essence, not caprice, not the whim or necessity of the moment. And for God, want can hardly be attribute and enduring essence. But then that is not what love is either. It is not an attribute of the lover. The lover is not a man who loves; that he loves is not a descriptive modifier of a man. Rather, love is man's momentary self-transformation, his self-denial. When he loves, man is no longer anything but a lover. In love, the I which would otherwise bear the attributes disappears totally in the instant of love. Man dies his way into the lover and is resurrected in him. Want would be an attribute—and how could an attribute find room for itself in the narrow confines of an instant? Is it then altogether true that love means wanting? Perhaps want precedes love. But what does love know of that which precedes it? The instant that awakens love is its first instant. Seen from without, some want may, it is true, be at its base. But this means no more than that the point of created existence which love has not yet fixed with its glance remains in darkness, the darkness, precisely, of creation. This darkness is the Nought which, as created "basis," lies at its base. But there is no room for want within love itself, on the narrow plank of its momentariness.

Love is completely fulfilled in the moment in which it exists. The love of the lover is always "lucky." Who would want to tell him that he wants anything more than—to love?

Thus love is not an attribute, but an event, and no attribute has any place in it. "God loves" does not mean that love befits him like an attribute, as does, say, the power to create. Love is not the basic form of his countenance, fixed and immutable. It is not the rigid mask which the sculptor lifts from off the face of the dead. Rather it is the fleeting, indefatigable alternation of mien, the ever youthful radiance which plays on the eternal features. Love hesitates to make a likeness of the lover; the portrait would reduce the living countenance to rigor mortis. "God loves" is present, pure and simple: how should love itself know whether it will love, whether, indeed, it has loved? It is enough that it knows this one thing: it loves. Nor does it proceed into the breadth of infinity, like an attribute. Though wisdom and power be omniscience and omnipotence, love is no all-love. Revelation knows of no "all-loving" father; God's love is ever wholly of the moment and to the point at which it is directed, and only in the infinity of time does it reach one point after another, step by step, and inform the All. God's love loves where it loves and whom it loves. No question has the right to approach it, for each question will one day have its answer when God loves him too, even that questioner who feels himself abandoned by God's love. God always loves only whom and what he loves, but his love is distinguished from an "all-love" only by a Not-yet: apart from what he already loves, God loves everything, only not yet. His love roams the world with an ever-fresh drive. It is always and wholly of today, but all the dead past and future will one day be devoured in this victorious today. This love is the eternal victory over death. The creation which death crowns and concludes cannot stand up to it; it must submit to it at every instant and thereby in the final analysis also in the sum of all instants, in eternity.

Islam: The Religion of Mankind

As conceived by belief, then, divine love does not, like light, radiate in all directions as an essential attribute. Rather it transfixes individuals—men, nations, epochs, things—in an enigmatic transfixion. It is incalculable in its transfixion except for the one certainty that it will yet transfix also what has not yet been transfixed. This would seem to imply a constriction of the concept of divine love, yet this apparent narrow-mindedness first turns this love into veritable love. Only by hurling itself completely into every instant, even if it be at the cost of forgetting all else, only thereby can it really transfix all in the end. Were it to transfix all at one blow, how would it differ from creation? For creation too created all at one blow and thus became ever-lasting past. A love which had transfixed all from the first would likewise be simply a From-the-first, only a past. It would not be that which first makes love constitute love: the present; pure, unadulterated present.

It is this kind of a past which determines the concept of revelation in Islam. Like the concept of the Creator in the preceding Book, that of the Revealer here derives directly from the living God of mythology without that much-discussed reversal of Yea and Nay. In that case the creative caprice did not congeal into creative sagacity. So too in this case revelation remains divine attribute, a necessity of the divine nature. The moment does not befall it, it does not become self-denying passion. Thus revelation resembles creation, not creation according to the concept of Islam, which is the free, optional act of divine caprice, but creation according to the concept of belief. In Islam, revelation is externalized from God as necessarily, as essentially, as characteristically as is creation.

Allah's essence is that all-love which does not limitlessly give itself away in every moment of love, but which gives revelation to mankind from within itself like a material present. The gift is not capricious; everything momentary—and caprice would after all, be momentary—remains far from it. God is the Merciful One: every Sura of the Koran declares this. To be merciful is his attribute, which radiates substantially over all men and all nations. The Koran rejects the idea of partisan preference, say, for a nation, from the concept of God. Allah has sent a prophet to every nation, not alone to the Arabs. Each prophet taught his nation the entire truth of belief. Of course it remains to be explained why this truth is today nevertheless silenced or distorted among most of the nations. But the explanation lies at hand: these nations simply did not believe the prophets. It is their own fault if they did not hold fast to the revelation; Allah gave it to them as much as now to the nation of Mohammed. In order to erect this fiction, it is necessary freely to invent prophetic figures of the past and their fate. The fundamental outlook demands it: Allah must reveal himself. This is his nature, to be "merciful," and thus he has revealed himself. Presumably one has to translate that word of the first verses of the Sura's by "merciful." For it is here excised from the living corpus of the holy language, where it can be used between men and from man to God as well as from God to man, and confined to the last-named, specifically theological application. Thus it no longer implies love in general, but a love which can only proceed from God to man, in short only: mercy. And this revelation is complete from the beginning: God already enjoined "Islam" on Adam and thus on all subsequent prophets! The patriarchs, the prophets, Jesus—they are all "believers" in the full, the official theological sense of the word. Mohammed's advantage rests in his personal qualities, not in the fact that, say, the greatest wealth of divine love had poured over him. The ride through the seven heavens is no proof of divine grace, but a miraculous deed on the prophet's own part. The wealth of this love does not increase. It is simply directed toward the world once and for all; there is no augmenting it. Everything "momentary," every deluded "partisan" stance is foreign to it, but so too is all ever-blind strength such as informs authentic love. The God of belief may tell his believers to their face that he has elected them above all others in their sins and in order to call them to account for their sins; Allah could not. The idea that man's shortcomings are more powerful to arouse divine love than his merits—the conceptual nucleus of belief—is an inconceivable paradox for Islam. Allah has mercy on human weakness, but he does not love it more than strength; such divine humility is alien to the God of Mohammed.

Here in Islam, revelation is not a living event between God and man, an occurrence into which God himself enters even unto his own complete self-negation, his divine self-sacrifice. Rather it is a freely offered gift which God places into the hands of man. As if to signalize this, revelation in Islam is from the beginning that which, in belief, it only becomes gradually even for its own consciousness and then never completely: a book. The first word of the revelation to Mohammed says: Read! He is shown the page of a book; it is a book that the archangel brings down to him from heaven in the night of the revelation. For Judaism, the oral law counts as older and holier than the written law, and Jesus left no written word to his followers. Islam, however, is a religion of the book from its first moment on; the book is sent down from heaven. Can there be a more thorough renunciation of the concept that God himself "descends," himself gives himself, surrenders himself to man? He sits enthroned in his heaven of heavens and presents to man—a book.

The Soul

DEFIANCE

To man. He is the other pole of revelation. It is over him that divine love is poured out. How does he prepare himself to receive it? For he must prepare himself. What we have learned to know as "metaethical" man is unprepared. He hears not, neither does he see—how then should he receive the divine love? His enclosedness too must first open up if he is to learn to hear God's word, to see God's illumination. Defiance and character, hubris and *daimon* had merged in him and had turned him into a speechless, introverted self. Here, too, now that he emerges from himself, the forces that formed him are disclosed again. And again they emerge in the opposite order from their immersion. The defiant pride of free will had amalgamated the existing character into a self in its ever-renewed surges. It now becomes the first to emerge from the interior of the self to the exterior. And as a first, as the beginning of an emergence into the exterior, it necessarily emerges in serene diffusion, and no longer in the form of passionate surges each of which scales the highest height in its momentariness.

A serene pride instead of one that froths with defiance, a pride, that is, which simply exists instead of distorting man's countenance with convulsive might, which spreads out under and around man like the still waters and supports him instead of transforming him beyond recognition, which, in short, seems to contradict the pride of defiance —what kind of pride is that? A pride which emerges as an attribute borne constantly by man but possessed of no actual expressions of a particularly characteristic physiognomy, instead of seeming to create a particular kind of man at the instant of its expression—for the defiant man is a particular image of man—what kind of pride is that? It would have to be a pride which was not proud "of" this or that. For then it would indeed be attribute, but only one attribute among many, not the essential attribute in which the whole man is capable of reposing. Perhaps the word "pride" is loaded with too much of the other con-notation. Too much of arrogance is heard with it, an arrogance whose authentic expression is, precisely, only defiance. And yet pride stands exactly midway between defiance and that inversion of defiance which we are seeking. It can "express" itself; then it becomes, quite automatically, arrogant defiance, hubris. Wholly beyond any idea of expression, however, it can also simply—be; and nothing more. But a

pride which simply is, in which man is at rest and allows himself to be
borne, such a pride is, to be sure, the very opposite of ever-resurgent
defiance. It is humility.

HUMILITY

Humility too is, after all, a kind of pride. Only haughtiness and
humility are contradictory. That humility which is conscious of being
what it is by the grace of a Superior, however, is pride, so much so
that it was possible to consider this consciousness of the grace of God
as itself veritably a haughty consciousness. Humility rests secure in
the feeling of being sheltered. It knows that nothing can befall it. And
it knows that no power can rob it of this consciousness which
carries it wherever it may go and by which it is perpetually surrounded. Humility is the only kind of pride which is secure against
all surgings, which needs no expression, and which means an altogether essential attribute for him who has it, an attribute in which he
moves because he simply does not know differently any more. And
yet this humility in its proud-reverential matter-of-factness is nothing
more than defiance emerging from out of its speechless self-containedness. When defiance assumed visible form as the tragic hubris, it
aroused the specter of fear in the crowd of spectators without, however, feeling any itself. Just so now, after the conversion, it in turn
feels itself overcome by tremors of awe, and borne by them withal;
the term of the Greek theoretician of tragedy and the term
which revelation elected once it learned to speak Greek is one and the
same: *phobos*. Hero and spectator are separated in tragedy's world of
art and appearance; awe reunites them forcibly. The lifeless image
now becomes itself filled with the life which it hitherto only aroused
in the spectator, and thus it comes alive. Now it can open its mouth
and speak.

THE OBJECT OF LOVE

An awe compounded of humility and pride, together with a feeling
of dependence and of being securely sheltered, of taking refuge in the
arms of eternity—behold, is this not also love again? Only, to be sure,
it is not the lover who reposes in that consciousness but the object of
love. It is the love of the beloved that we are describing here. The
object of love, then, knows itself borne by the love of the lover, and
sheltered in it. The beloved knows as eternal, as ever and aye, that
which to the lover is a moment, ever to be renewed. The love of the
beloved has "ever" inscribed above it; it is never greater than at the

moment when it is kindled; it can never grow, but neither can it diminish. At most it can die: the beloved keeps faith. Being loved is the very air in which it lives. The love of the lover is a light which is ever kindled anew for him; the moment of its kindling provides it with presentness. The love of the beloved sits quietly at the feet of the love of the lover; its presentness is provided not by the individual, ever-new moment, but by serene duration. It knows itself loved at every moment only because it knows itself loved for "ever." Only the lover loves the beloved a little more with each passing day; the beloved senses no such increase in her being loved. Once overcome by the tremors of being-loved, she remains in them to the end. She is content to be loved: what does she care about heaven and earth? What does she care even about the love of the lover? Her requital is only that she allows herself to be loved. No gratitude of hers responds to the love of the lover. If the object of love gives thanks, its thanks cannot be directed toward the lover. Rather it must seek outlets in other directions, symbolic outlets so to speak. Love would bring thank-offerings because it feels it cannot give thanks. With respect to the lover: it can only allow itself to be loved, nothing more. And it is thus that the soul receives the love of God.

Indeed it is only to the soul and the love of God that all this applies in the strict sense. Between man and woman the roles of giver and receiver of love pass back and forth, the higher the blossoms which the plant of love generates between them, the more that it rises above itself and its subterranean roots like a veritable palm-tree, although the roots of sexuality ever restore the unambiguous relationship of nature. But the relationship between God and the soul ever remains the same. God never ceases to love, nor the soul to be loved. The peace of God is granted to the soul, not the peace of the soul to God. And God gives himself to the soul, not the soul, here, to God. Indeed, how could it? It is only, after all, in the love of God that the flower of the soul begins to grow out of the rock of the self. Previously man had been a senseless and speechless introvert; only now is he—beloved soul.

FAITHFULNESS

Beloved? Is the soul beloved? Can it be beloved? Is the love of God something from which nothing can any longer separate the soul? Can it no longer be expelled from this repose in God? Is it ever with him? Can he no longer turn his countenance away from it? Is its love-by-God a bond so secure that it simply cannot conceive of God ever being able to loosen it again? Being-loved is, after all, apparently a purely passive attribute. What really is it that gives this attribute the strength to be essential attribute once wholly of the soul and now forever inseparable from it? Normally something passive like this is, after all, not attribute; it depends on whether something active exercises its activity upon it, the more so now, where the activity is a momentary one. And yet its effect is supposed to endow the passive with an enduring attribute? Here too, our questions are again those which have vexed dogmatics in connection with this concept of the soul's divine belovedness from the beginning. Is it not setting an undeniable limit to the power of God if the soul beloved of God claims permanent divine belovedness for itself? Does not God have to have the freedom to be able to withdraw from the soul? True, it would be understandable if he had divested himself of such freedom in the face of a faithfulness which had held him. But how can the soul presume to wish to be faithful if it is nothing other than the object of love? Is faithfulness not something which only the lover can harbor, and even then not as attribute but only in the act of constantly renewing his love? Can faithfulness wish to be an enduring, serene attribute? Indeed may it? For it is as such that the object of love would possess it.

The secret prehistory of the soul in the self supplies us with the answer to all these doubts. If the soul were a thing, it could admittedly never be faithful. For while a thing too can be loved, and even be the beneficiary of the faithfulness of ever renewed love, it cannot itself be faithful. The soul, however, can. For it is not a thing, nor does it originate in the world of things. It derives from the self of man. Specifically it is defiance which emerges to the fore in the soul, that defiance which asserts the character in constant surges. *It* is the secret origin of the soul, *it* provides the soul with the strength to withstand, to stand fast. Without the storms of defiance in the self, the silence of the sea in the faithfulness of the soul would be impossible. Defiance is the arch-evil in man, bubbling up darkly; it is the subterranean root whence the juices of faithfulness rise into the soul beloved of God. There is no bright revelation without the somber occlusion of the self, no faithfulness without defiance. Not that there is still defiance in the beloved soul itself—this defiance has wholly turned to faithfulness within it—but the strength to hold fast, which the beloved soul maintains toward the love with which it is loved, this strength of trust is drawn by it from that defiance of the self which has integrated with it. And because the soul holds on to him, therefore God allows himself to be held by it. Thus the attribute of faithfulness endows the soul with the strength to live permanently in the love of God. And thus a kind of strength also emanates from the object of love, not the strength of constantly new impulses, but the serene glow of a great Yea in which that love of the lover which always belies itself finds that which it could not find in itself: affirmation and constancy. The trusting faith of the beloved affirms the momentary love of the lover and consolidates it too into something enduring. This is requited love: the faith of the beloved in the lover. By its trust, the faith of the soul attests the love of God and endows it with enduring being. If you testify to me, then I am God, and not otherwise—thus the master of the Kabbala lets the God of love declare. The lover who sacrifices himself in love is recreated anew in the trust of the beloved, and this time forever. When the soul is first overcome by the tremors of the love of the lover, it hears an "unto eternity" in itself which is no self-delusion. It does not remain in its interior but proves to be a vital, creative force by tearing the lover's own love away from the moment and "eternalizing" it once and for all. The soul is at peace in the love of God, like a child in the arms of its mother, and now it can reach beyond "the uttermost parts of the sea" and to the portals of the grave—and is yet ever with Him.

Islam, the Religion of the Deed

This serenity of the soul, in a faithfulness born of the night of defiance, is the great secret of belief. And again Islam proves to be outward acceptance of these concepts without inner comprehension. Again it has made them entirely its own—but for the inner conversion. And again, therefore, it does not have them at all. The very notion that "Islam" means being resigned to God, as Goethe thinks, is a misleading translation. Islam does not mean being resigned to God, but resigning oneself to God, acquiescing in God. In its unmodified baseform in the sacred (Hebrew) language, the word designates that serene peace of God which is in a state of being; in the word "Islam," however, it is transformed into a causative by virtue of the prefix, into a making, an effecting, a deed. Islam's "acquiesce!" does not merge in a "be still!"; it never gets beyond this acquiescing which, with every moment, has to be renewed. So too the humility of the man to whom revelation is directed retains in Islam that symptom of the self's defiance, the Nay which disowns itself at every moment. "Islam" is not a condition, a stance of the soul; rather it is an incessant sequence of obligatory acts. Nor is it the understanding that these obligations are carried out, so to speak, only symbolically, precisely as sign and visible expression of the pacified condition of the soul or as means to the attainment of this condition. Rather they are esteemed for themselves and indeed they are more or less rational to an extent that presumably justifies such an esteem. Thus Islam arrives at an explicit ethic of works. Each individual moral act provides its own yardstick for the measure of resignation to God required to accomplish it. The harder the deed, the more highly it is esteemed, for the greater is the resignation to God which is required.

For belief, on the other hand, the individual moral deed as such is really valueless. At most it can be esteemed as symbol of the entire condition of humble fear of God. Here the soul itself is weighed in the balance, the authenticity of its belief, the strength of its hope, not the individual deed. There are no difficult and easy obligations. All are equally difficult and equally easy since all are merely symbolic. In its estimate of the difficulty of the individual performance, Islam thus becomes the involuntary heir to Stoicism, the ethics of terminal paganism, as it becomes on the other hand likewise the harbinger of *virtu*, the neo-pagan ethics as this survives into our own days. Al-Ghazzali, the great reformer of Islam, provides a highly significant discussion in which this whole relationship immediately leaps into view, together with those historical points of comparison. He contrasts the chastity of Jesus with the sensuality of Mohammed, and extols his Prophet above the Nazarene, holding that Mohammed thereby proved himself the greater, since his ardor for God was sufficiently powerful to burn over and beyond the satisfaction of his drives, while the Prophet of the Nazarenes had to forego this satisfaction since his piety burned too low not to be extinguished in it. If it were feasible for man, every performance would thus have to be measured by piety itself, and piety, the innermost quality, is here subsumed under the viewpoint of performance and measured by inhibitions overcome.

This then is man as he confronts divine love in Islam, not quietly receptive in the least, but rather pressing forward in ever-new deeds. But God's love was, after all, not actual love here either, but a broad diffusion of revelation in all directions. Thus Islam knows of a loving God as little as of a beloved soul. God's revelation transpires in calm expansion, man's reception in stormy action, restlessly pressing forward. Were we to speak of love in this connection, then God would have to be the object of love, man the lover. Therewith, however, the sense of that revelation which proceeds from God to man would be nullified. And in Islam it is indeed man who, out of a need on which God "has mercy," actually extorts revelation for himself. The point is that mercy is not love. Islam fuses the beloved soul with the needful creature as it did the Revealer with the Creator. Here too it remains stuck to the untransformed figures which the pagan world pointed out to it, and supposes that it can set them in motion, just as they are, with the concept of revelation. Mohammed was proud of having made belief easy for his followers. He made it too easy. He thought he could save them and himself the need for inner conversion. He did not know that all revelation begins with a great Nay. All the concepts of the protocosmos undergo a conversion as they enter into the light of the real world, and this conversion is none other than that Nay. Revelation stands under the sign of the Nay as creation does under that of the Yea. Nay is the primeval word of revelation. Its first audible word, however, its "root-word," is I.

Grammar of Eros
(The Language of Love)

ROOT-WORD

"I" is always a Nay become audible. "I" always involves a contradiction, it is always underlined, always emphasized, always an "I, however." Even if it would remain unrecognized and wraps itself in the unpretentious cloak of self-evidence—as when Luther confesses his positiveness, his certainty, his confidence to the Diet, and all three not as "his"—even then the flashing eye gives away the king in disguise, and world history underlines threefold that triple I at the time of the unmasking. "I" is simple always willy-nilly subject in all sentences in which it occurs. It can never be passive, never object. Ask yourself once honestly: in the sentence "You are beating me," or "He beat me" —assuming, of course, that you are reciting the sentence, not reading it—is the "You" or the "He" really the subject? Is not the subject rather the "I"? Is this not already indicated by a noticeable stress in the accentuation which is absent with an ordinary object? But the primeval Nay is heard as primeval word, as "not otherwise" in every word. From this primeval word too, the path of incipient audibility leads straight to the "I." Indeed it here first becomes clear why we could not be satisfied with a sic et non based on the Scholastic model, why we had to assert a Thus and not-otherwise, thus replacing the non with the double negative of a not-otherwise.

PART TWO / BOOK TWO

DIALOGUE

The "not otherwise" is at once confronted by the question: "not otherwise than what, pray?" It has to answer: "not otherwise than everything." For when we designate something as "thus and not otherwise," we mean to delimit it as against "everything" pure and simple. And it is, in fact, "none other" than everything. It is already posited as otherwise than everything by the "thus"—the "not otherwise" coupled with the "thus" means precisely that, though otherwise, it is nevertheless not at the same time otherwise than everything, that is, capable of being related to everything. What then is it that is "not otherwise" in this sense, that is to say "otherwise" and at the same time "not otherwise" than everything? For "everything" implies "the All." It can only be that which is identical with the "Being" of the All and of each individual object, with the "thinking," that is, which is at once identical with Being and its opposite—in short, the I. In the previous Part we discovered the "good" to be the Thus become audible. Similarly we have here discovered the "I" as Nay become audible, not as a word within its species of words, however, but rather as individual response to individual question in the quiz-game of reasoning. And so too we will henceforth proceed from real word to real word, not from one species of word to another as we did in describing creation. This accords with the wholly real employment of language, the center-piece as it were of this entire book, at which we have here arrived. Only in retrospect can we recognize the actual word as a representative of its verbal species as well—and indeed we must do so. But we do not find it as such a representative of a species. Rather we find it directly as word and response.[1]

MONOLOGUE

To the I there responds in God's interior a Thou. It is the dual sound of I and Thou in the monologue of God at the creation of man. But the Thou is no authentic Thou, for it still remains in God's interior. And the I is just as far from already being an authentic I, for no Thou has yet confronted it. Only when the I acknowledges the Thou as something external to itself, that is, only when it makes the transition from monologue to authentic dialogue, only then does it become that I which we have just claimed for the primeval Nay become audible. The I of the monologue is not yet an "I, however." It is an unemphatic I, an I that is also self-understood precisely because

---

[1] German "Ant-wort," etymologically "counter-word." (Tr.)

it is only self-addressed. It is thus an I still concealed in the secret of the third person and not as yet a manifest I, as we already recognized in the "let us" of the narrative of creation. Only in the discovery of a Thou is it possible to hear an actual I, an I that is not self-evident but emphatic and underlined. But where is the Thou, independent and freely confronting the concealed God, in which he could discover himself as I? There is a material world, there is the self-contained self, but where is there a Thou? Yes—where is the Thou? So God asks too.

THE QUESTION

"Where art Thou?" This is none other than the quest for the Thou, and for the present only for the Where of it, not for its nature, for this is at this moment still far out of sight. Where is there a Thou altogether? This inquiry for the Thou is the only thing that is already known about it. But the question already suffices for the I to discover itself. By the very act of asking for the Thou, by the Where of this question, which testifies to its belief in the existence of the Thou even without the Thou's coming into its purview, the I addresses and expresses itself as I. The I discovers itself at the moment when it asserts the existence of the Thou by inquiring into its Where.

THE ADDRESS

The I discovers *itself*—not perchance the Thou. The quest for the Thou remains a mere quest. Man hides, he does not respond, he remains speechless, he remains the Self as we know it. The responses which God finally elicits from him are not responses. The divine quest for the Thou receives no "I" for an answer, no "I am," "I have done it." Instead of an I the responding mouth brings forth a He-She-It. The human being materializes as "man": it is the woman who did it, and specifically the woman wholly materialized as she was given to man. And she transfers the blame to the ultimate It: it was the serpent. The self demands to be conjured by a more powerful spell than the mere inquiry after the Thou before it will utter the I. The indefinite Thou was merely deictic, and so it was answered by man with a mere deictic: the woman, the serpent. Its place is taken by the vocative, the direct address, and man is cut off from every retreat into hypostatization. The general concept of man can take refuge behind the woman or the serpent. Instead of this the call goes out to what cannot flee, to the utterly particular, to the nonconceptual, to something that transcends the sphere of influence of both the definite and the indefinite articles—a sphere which embraces all things if only as objects of a universal, nondistinctive providence—to the proper name, the proper name which yet is not properly *his* name, not a name which the man gave himself arbitrarily, but the name which God himself created for the man and which is properly the man's only because it is the creation of the Creator. To God's "Where art Thou?" the man had still kept silence as defiant and blocked Self. Now, called by his name, twice, in a supreme definiteness that could not but be heard, now he answers, all unlocked, all spread apart, all ready, all-soul: "Here I am."

HEARING

Here is the I, the individual human I, as yet wholly receptive, as yet only unlocked, only empty, without content, without nature, pure readiness, pure obedience, all ears. The commandment is the first content to drop into this attentive hearing. The summons to hear, the address by the given name, the seal of the discoursing divine mouth— all these are but preface to every commandment. In fully explicit form, they preface only that one commandment which is not the highest, which is in truth the only commandment, the sum and substance of all commandments ever to leave God's mouth. What is this commandment of all commandments?

THE COMMANDMENT

The answer to this question is universally familiar. Millions of tongues testify to it evening and morning: "Thou shalt love the Lord thy God with all thy heart and with all thy soul and with all thy might." Thou shalt love—what a paradox this embraces! Can love then be commanded? Is love not rather a matter of fate and of seizure and of a bestowal which, if it is indeed free, it withal only free? And now it is commanded? Yes of course, love cannot be commanded. No third party can command it or extort it. No third party can, but the One can. The commandment to love can only proceed from the mouth of the lover. Only the lover can and does say: love me!—and he really does so. In his mouth the commandment to love is not a strange commandment; it is none other than the voice of love itself. The love of the lover has, in fact, no word to express itself other than the commandment. Everything else is no longer direct expression but already declaration—declaration of love. A declaration of love is a very poor thing; like every declaration it always comes behindhand and thus, since the love of the lover is present time, the declaration of love is in reality always too late. It would drop wholly into the void but for the fact that, in the eternal trust of her love, the beloved opens her arms wide to receive it. But the "Love me!" of the lover—that is wholly perfect expression, wholly pure language of love. It is the imperative commandment, immediate, born of the moment and, what is more, becoming audible at the instant of its birth, for emerging and finding voice are one and the same thing in the case of the imperative. The indicative has behind it the whole cumbersome rationalization of materiality, and at its purest therefore appears in the past tense. But the "Love me!" is wholly pure and unprepared-for present tense, and not unprepared-for alone, but also unpremeditated. The imperative of the commandment makes no provision for the future; it can only conceive the immediacy of obedience. If it were to think of a future or an Ever, it would be, not commandment nor order, but law. Law reckons with times, with a future, with duration. The commandment knows only the moment; it awaits the result in the very instant of its promulgation. And if it possesses the magic of the true voice of command, it will truly never be disappointed in this expectation.

THE PRESENT

Thus the commandment is purely the present. But while every other commandment could equally well have been law if one but viewed it from without and, so to speak, retroactively, the sole commandment of love is simply incapable of being law; it can only be commandment. All other commandments can pour their content into the mold of the law as well. This one alone resists such recasting; its content tolerates only the one form of the commandment, of the immediate presentness and unity of consciousness, expression, and expectation of fulfillment. For this reason, as the only pure commandment, it is the highest of all commandments, and where it takes the first place as such, there everything else too becomes commandment though otherwise, and viewed from without, it could as well be law. God's first word to the soul that unlocks itself to him is "Love me!" And everything which he may yet reveal to the soul in the form of law therefore without more ado turns into words which he commands it "today." It turns into execution of the one initial commandment to love him. All of revelation is subsumed under the great today. God commands "today," and "today" it is incumbent to obey his voice. It is in the today that the love of the lover lives, in this imperative today of the commandment.

REVELATION

This imperative can only proceed from out the mouth of the lover, and no imperative but this from out this mouth. So too the I of the speaker, the root-word of the entire dialogue of revelation, is the seal which, stamped upon each word, marks the individual commandment as a command to love. Revelation commences with "I the Lord" as the great Nay of the concealed God which negates his own concealment. This "I" accompanies revelation through all the individual commandments. In the prophet, this "I the Lord" creates a tool of its own and a style of its own for revelation. The prophet does not mediate between God and man, he does not receive revelation in order to pass it on; rather, the voice of God sounds forth directly from within him, God speaks as "I" directly from within him. The master of the great plagiarism of revelation lets God speak and passes the revelation which occurred to him in secret on to the dazed assemblage. Not so the true prophet. He does not let God speak at all. Rather, he no sooner opens his mouth than God already speaks. Hardly has he uttered his "Thus saith the Lord," or the even briefer, even more hurried "Oracle of the Lord"—which even dispenses with the verbal form—before God has already taken possession of his lips. God's "I" remains the keyword, traversing revelation like a single sustained organ note; it resists any translation into "he"; it is an "I" and an "I" it must remain. Only an "I," not a "he," can pronounce the imperative of love, which may never be anything other than "love me!"

RECEIVING

But what, then, of the soul, the ready, the opened, the all-speechlessly hearkening soul? What can it reply to the commandment of love? For there must be a reply. The obedience to the commandment cannot remain mute. It too must become audible, it too become word. For in the world of revelation everything becomes word, and what cannot become word is either prior or posterior to this world. What then does the soul respond to the demand to love?

SHAME

The beloved's admission of love responds to the lover's demand of love. The lover does not admit his love. How should he? He has no time at all to do so. His love would have vanished before he had admitted it; it would no longer be present. If he nevertheless makes the attempt, then the lie inherent in acknowledging the present is its own punishment. For what is once acknowledged is already knowledge; therewith it retreats into the past and is no longer the present that was intended in the admission. For this reason the acknowledgment of the lover soon turns into a lie. It is only right that even faith rejects the bare admission, and that the soul of the beloved, though already opened, closes up again; it is an indication of how deeply all this is anchored in the unconscious. The lover speaks the truth only in the form of the demand for love, not in that of the admission of love. It is otherwise with the beloved. For her acknowledgment does not turn into a lie. Her love, once born, is static, a constant. Thus she may stand by it, stand up for it. Her love too is of the present, but unlike that of the lover it is present only because it is enduring, because it is faithful. In the acknowledgment it is admitted as something present like this, something which has and seeks duration. For the acknowledgment the future appears bright and clear. The beloved is conscious of wanting nothing in the future but to remain what she is: beloved. But back in the past, there was a time before she was beloved, and this time of unbelovedness, of lovelessness, seems to her covered in deepest darkness. Indeed, since love to her becomes something enduring only as faithfulness, that is, only with reference to the future, therefore that darkness fills all of the past right up to the moment of the acknowledgment. Nothing short of the acknowledgment carries the soul off into the bliss of being loved. Previously, all is lovelessness, and even the readiness with which the self that was summoned by name opened itself to the soul still lies in that shadow. Hence it is not easy for the soul to admit. In the admission of love, the soul bares itself. To admit that one requites love and in the future wants nothing but to be loved —this is sweet. But it is hard to admit that one was without love in the past. And yet—love would not be the moving, the gripping, the searing experience that it is if the moved, gripped, seared soul were not conscious of the fact that up to this moment it had not been moved nor gripped. Thus a shock was necessary before the self could become beloved soul. And the soul is ashamed of its former self, and that it did not, under its own power, break this spell in which it was confined. This is the shame which blocks the beloved mouth that wishes to make acknowledgment. The mouth has to acknowledge its past and still present weakness by wishing to acknowledge its already present and future bliss. And thus the soul which God summons with the command to love is ashamed to acknowledge to him its love, for it can only acknowledge its love by acknowledging its weakness at the same time, and by responding to God's "Thou shalt love" with an "I have sinned."

ATONEMENT

"I have sinned." Thus speaks the soul and abolishes shame. By speaking thus, referring purely back into the past, it purifies the present from the weakness of the past. "I have sinned" means I was a sinner. With this acknowledgment of having sinned, however, the soul clears the way for the acknowledgment "I am a sinner." And this second acknowledgment is already the full admission of love. It throws the compulsion of shame far away and gives itself up entirely to love. That man has been a sinner is abolished in the acknowledgment. He had to overcome shame for this acknowledgment, but as long as he acknowledged, shame remained at his side. But now he acknowledges that he is still a sinner even though he had divested himself of the past shame, and now shame withdraws from him. Indeed, the very fact that his admission dares its way into the present is the sign that it has overcome shame. As long as it lingered in the past, it still lacked the courage to express itself fully and confidently; it could still harbor doubts about the answer that it had coming to it. For it must be admitted that only the summons by name and the commandment to love had so far reached the soul from God's mouth, and not as yet any "declaration," any "I love you." And as we know, none such was allowed to be forthcoming for the sake of love's tie to the moment on which the authenticity of the love of the lover rests. This authenticity would only be debased[1] by acknowledging, by continuously declaring it. It would really be debased, debased to its "bases," for the love of the lover is baseless, in contrast to the love of the beloved which, after all, has its base in that of the lover. Thus the soul which would like to make acknowledgment still harbors doubts as to whether its acknowledgment will find acceptance. It sheds its doubts only as it dares to emerge from the acknowledgment of the past into acknowledging the present. It becomes certain of the answer by acknowledging its sinfulness, not as transpired "sin," but as a sinfulness yet present, so certain that it no longer needs to hear this answer out loud. It perceives it in its interior. It is not God that need cleanse it of its sin. Rather it cleanses itself in the presence of his love. It is certain of God's love in the very moment that shame withdraws from it and it surrenders itself in free, present admission—as certain as if God had spoken into its ear that "I forgive" which it longed for earlier when it confessed to him its sins of the past. It no longer needs this formal absolution. It is freed of its burden at the very moment of daring to

[1] Literally: destroyed. (Tr.)

assume all of it on its shoulders. So too the beloved no longer needs the acknowledgment of the lover which she longed for before she admitted her love. At the very moment when she herself dares to admit to it, she is as certain of his love as if he were whispering his acknowledgment into her ear. Past sins are confessed altogether only for the sake of yet-present sinfulness, but to acknowledge the latter is no longer to acknowledge sin—this has passed like the acknowledgment itself—no longer to acknowledge the love-void of the past. Rather the soul says: even now, even in this most present of moments, I still do not love nearly as much as I—know myself loved. And this acknowledgment is already the highest bliss for it, for it encompasses the certainty that God loves it. This certainty comes to it, not from God's mouth, but from its own.

ACKNOWLEDGMENT

On this, the zenith of its self-acknowledgment, the soul thus spreads itself wholly before God, freed of all shame. In so doing, it is already acknowledging more than just itself, more than its own sinfulness. Its acknowledgment becomes, nay is already immediately, acknowledgment of—God. The soul renounces shame and dares to acknowledge its own presence and thus becomes certain of divine love: just so it can now attest and acknowledge this divine love of which it has gained knowledge. The acknowledgment of belief originates in the acknowledgment of sin. This relationship would be incomprehensible if we did not know that the acknowledgment of sin—beginning with the confession of the past and ending in the acknowledgment of present sinfulness—is none other than admission of love by the soul as it emerges from the fetters of shame into complete and confident submission. The soul which admits its being in love thereby attests most assuredly the "being" of the lover. Every acknowledgment of belief has but this one content: him whom I have recognized as the lover in experiencing my being loved—he "is." The God of my love is truly God.

Islam's acknowledgment that " God is God" is not an acknowledgment of belief, but an acknowledgment of disbelief. In its tautology, it makes acknowledgment, not of the God become manifest, but of the concealed God. Nicholas of Cusa can rightfully say that a pagan or an atheist could make acknowledgment in this form too. In the authentic acknowledgment of belief, there always occurs this unison of two names or natures. It always consists of this testimony that one's own experience of love must be more than an individual experience, that he whom the soul experiences in its love really lives, that he is not merely illusion and self-delusion of the beloved soul. When the beloved becomes conscious of her love in blissful admission, she cannot help herself: she must believe that her beloved is a veritable man; she cannot be satisfied with the notion that it simply is the one who loves her. Just so the soul becomes certain in its belovedness that the God who loves it is truly God, is the true God.

In this belief of the beloved in the lover, the lover first really becomes a human being. True, the soul awakes and begins to speak when it loves, but it attains being, a being visible to itself, only when it is loved. Just so God now also attains reality on his part only here, in the testimony of the believing soul, a reality that is palatable and visible, that is on this side of his concealment, a reality which, on the other side of his concealment, he previously possessed in paganism in another fashion. The soul makes acknowledgment before God's countenance and thereby acknowledges and attests God's being; therewith God too, the manifest God, first attains being: "If ye acknowledge me, then I am." What then is God's answer to this "I am thine" by which the beloved soul acknowledges him?

KNOWLEDGE

Within revelation, then, and on the basis of revelation, God attained being, a being, that is, which he only attained as manifest God, quite independent of any secret being. And now he too, for his part, can make himself known without danger to the immediacy and pure presentness of experience. For the being which he now makes known is no longer a being beyond experience, no being in the concealed, but rather one which gained stature entirely within this experience; it is wholly in the manifest. Not that he makes himself known before he has revealed himself, but on the contrary his having become manifest must precede so that he be able to make himself known. He cannot make himself known to the soul before the soul has acknowledged him. But now he must do so. For this it is by which revelation first reaches completion. In its groundless presentness, revelation must now permanently touch the ground. This ground lies beyond its presentness, that is, in the past, but revelation itself renders it visible only from out the presentness of experience. What we refer to here is, in the last analysis, that much debated derivation of revelation from creation. Not that revelation, to repeat, is explained by creation, for then creation would, after all, be something independent vis-à-vis revelation. Rather the past creation is demonstrated from out the living, present revelation—demonstrated, that is: pointed out. In the glow of the experienced miracle of revelation, a past that prepares and foresees this miracle becomes visible. The creation which becomes visible in revelation is creation of the revelation. At this point the experiential and presentive character of revelation is immovably fixed, and only here can revelation receive a past. But here it really must do so. God does not answer the soul's acknowledgment, its "I am thine," with an equally simple "Thou art mine." Rather he reaches back into the past and identifies himself as the one who originated and initiated this whole dialogue between himself and the soul: "I have called thee by name: thou art mine."[1]

THE GROUND

The "I am thine" of the beloved soul can be said groundlessly, indeed only groundlessly. The soul speaks it purely out of the living overflow of its blissful moment. But the answer, the "Thou art mine" of the lover, is a sentence which does not have "I" for a subject. As such it is more than just the word of his own heart. It posits a relationship into the world of things, even if only within the narrowest, most inward ambit. Thus this word may only be spoken if it adapts itself to the form of the world. A ground has to be premised for it, a past as a grounding for its presence. For this presence is no longer content to be merely inner immediate presence; it asserts itself as presence in the world. The lover who says "Thou art mine" to the beloved is aware of having begotten the beloved in his love and given birth to her in travail. He knows himself the creator of the beloved. And with this awareness he now enfolds her and envelops her with his love in the world—"thou art mine."

But with God's so doing, his revelation to the soul has now entered the world and become part of the world. Not that something strange is entering the world with it. Rather revelation remembers back to its past, while at the same time remaining wholly of the present; it recognizes its past as part of a world passed by. But thereby it also provides its presentness with the status of something real in the world. For that which is grounded in a past is, in its presentness too, a visible reality, and not merely internal. The presentness of the miracle of revelation is and remains its content; its historicity, however, is its ground and its warrant. Individually experienced belief had already found within itself the highest bliss destined for it. Now it also finds the highest certainty possible for it, but only in this its historicity, its "positivity." This certainty does not precede that bliss; it must, however, follow it,

[1] Isaiah 43:1.

Experienced belief only comes to rest in this certainty of having been long ago summoned, by name, to belief. True, even before this nothing could part it from God, but still—only because it saw nothing outside of itself in its immersion in the presentive. Now it can calmly open its eyes and look around itself at the world of things. There is no thing that could part it from God, for in the world of things it recognizes the substantive ground of its belief in the immovable factuality of a historical event. The soul can roam the world with eyes open and without dreaming. Now and forevermore it will remain in God's proximity. The "Thou art mine" which was said to it draws a protective circle about its steps. Now it knows: it need but stretch out its right hand in order to feel God's right hand coming to meet it. Now it can say: "my God, my God." Now it can pray.

THE PETITION

Prayer is the last thing achieved in revelation. It is an overflow of the highest and most perfect trust of the soul. There is no question here regarding the fulfillment of the prayer. The prayer is its own fulfillment. The soul prays in the words of the Psalms: let not my prayer and your love depart from me.[1] It prays to be able to pray—and this is already given to her to do in the assurance of the divine love. To be able to pray: that is the greatest gift presented to the soul in revelation. It is only an ability to pray. By being the highest gift, it already steps beyond the limits of this area. For the obligation to pray is imposed on the soul together with the gift of being able to pray. Its belief comes to rest in the divine proximity of unconditional trust, with whose strength God endowed it in that "Thou art mine" of his which is grounded in the past. But its life remains in unrest. For that which it possesses as the grounding of its belief in the world is not the whole world, but only a piece of the world. The soul is entirely filled by its experience, but the historical reality which is the foundation of the experience in the creation is not the whole of the world; it is only a part. Thus the soul's ability to pray becomes an obligation to pray. God's voice fills the innermost soul, but it fills its world only in smallest part—enough to enable the soul to be certain of its worldly reality in belief, but not enough to live by this belief. The basic miracle of revelation occurred once in the past; it demands its complement in a further miracle which has not yet happened. God once summoned the soul by name; that is a "constant" like everything past,

[1] Psalm 66:20.

and yet has not come to the attention of any third party. And God must do it "again" one day, but this time "in the eyes of everything that lives."

THE CRY

Thus the soul must pray for the coming of the kingdom. God once descended and founded his kingdom. The soul prays for the future repetition of this miracle, for the completion of the once-founded structure, and nothing more. The soul cries out: Oh that you would part the heavens and descend. In the usage of the original language of revelation, such an "Oh that you would" is expressed most profoundly by the interrogative form "who would grant that you . . ." Revelation climaxes in an unfulfilled wish, in the cry of an open question. That the soul has the courage to wish thus, to ask thus, to cry thus shows the completeness of the trust reposed in God; it is the achievement of revelation. But to fulfill the wish, to answer the question, to still the cry—that is beyond its power. What is present is its own; into the future it only casts the wish, the question, the cry. For the future does not appear in what is present except in these three forms, which are but one. And hence this ultimate, the prayer, although it is the soul's highest, nevertheless only half belongs to it, only as ability to pray and as obligation to pray, not as—actual praying. The prayer for the coming of the kingdom is ever but a crying and a sighing, ever but a plea. There is still another kind of praying. The completely pacified belief, the soul's acquiescence in God's "Thou art mine," the peace which it has found in his eyes—these remain, after all, the last thing which belongs entirely to the realm of revelation. The dialogue of love ends there. The cry which the soul utters at the moment of supreme, immediate fulfillment steps beyond the limits of this dialogue. It no longer derives from the blissful pacification of being loved. It rises in new unrest from a new depth of the soul which we have not yet recognized. It sobs beyond the proximity of the lover, unseen but felt, and into the gloom of infinity.

The Logic of Revelation

GRAMMATICAL APPENDIX

The language of revelation speaks. The language of creation de-lineates, re-counts, de-termines. At what point did the one take leave of the other? In the hurried back and forth of discourse, we could hardly indicate these points with sufficient clarity. Let us here make good this omission, summing up briefly and so to speak schematically. As act, creation was founded, and as result it climaxed, in the past. To this tense there here corresponds in dominant fashion the present. Revelation is of the present, indeed it is being-present itself. Revelation too looks back into the past at that moment in which it would like to give its presentness the form of a predicate. But the past only becomes visible to revelation when and as revelation shines into it with the light of the present. Only in this backward glance does the past prove to be the base and prediction of the present experience, domiciled in the I. In and of itself, however, the form of the predicate is not initially proper to experience at all, as it is to the occurrence of creation. Rather, the presentness of experience is only satisfied by the form of the command, originating, spoken, perceived, and carried out all at one blow. The imperative belongs to revelation as the indicative to creation; only it does not abandon the ambit of I and Thou. That which sounded in advance out of that all-embracing, lonely, monologic "let us" of God's at the creation of man reaches its fulfillment in the I and Thou of the imperative of revelation. The he-she-it of the third person has fallen silent. It was but the foundation, the soil from which the I and Thou sprang. The verb no longer serves to express occurrence; now it serves to express experience. Thereby the noun turns from object into subject. Its case is now the nominative instead of the accusative. As the object of experience, however, the noun ceases to be thing. It no longer exhibits the basic character of the thing, that of a thing among things. Now it is subject and hence something individual. On principle it occurs in the singular. It is something individual, or rather someone individual. Just this was anticipated, in its turn, in the creation of man, the first individual, the "image of God."

THE PROPER NAME

Seen thus in its substantiality the I or the Thou is an individual without more ado, without the mediation of any plurality. It is not a "the" for being an "a." Rather it is an individual without category. The place of the article is here taken by the immediate determination of the proper name. With the summons by the proper name, the word of revelation entered the real dialogue. With the proper name, the rigid wall of objectness has been breached. That which has a name of its own can no longer be a thing, no longer everyman's affair. It is incapable of utter absorption into the category for there can be no category for it to belong to; it is its own category. Nor does it still have its place in the world, its moment in occurrence. Rather it carries its here and now with it. Wherever it is, there is a midpoint and wherever it opens its mouth, there is a beginning.

In the intricate world of things there was no midpoint or beginning at all; the I, however, together with its proper name, introduces these concepts of midpoint and beginning into the world. In keeping with its creation as man and at the same time as "Adam," the I is midpoint and beginning within itself. For it demands a midpoint in the world for the midpoint, a beginning for the beginning of its own experience. The I longs for orientation, for a world which does not just lie there in any old arrangement, nor flow past in any old sequence, but a world which supports the inner order inherent in the I's experience on the solid base of an external order. One proper name demands others. Adam's first deed is to give names to the creatures of the world, and this too is but prologue. For Adam names the creatures, as they step before him in creation, by categories and not as individuals. And he names them himself, thus only expressing his demand for names. The demand still remains unfulfilled, for the names which he demands are not such as he himself might give; rather, they are names which are revealed to him like his own name, names to secure a firm basis for the individuality of the individual name. For this it is not yet necessary that the whole world be full of name; but at least it has to contain name enough in order to provide a base for his own name. One's own experience depends on one's own name; it therefore needs to be grounded in creation, that creation which we previously designated as the creation of revelation, as historical revelation. Thus grounded in the world, it must therefore be grounded in space and time precisely in order to provide a ground for experience's absolute certainty of possessing its own space and its own time. Thus both the midpoint and the beginning in the world must be provided to experience by this grounding, the midpoint in space, the beginning in time. These two, at least, have to be named, even if the rest of the world still lies in the darkness of anonymity. There must be a where in the world, a still visible spot whence revelation radiates, and a when, a yet echoing moment, where revelation first opened its mouth. Both must have been one and the same at one time, though no longer today, something as united in itself as my experience is today. For it is supposed to put my experience on a firm foundation. In their after-effect, the spatial taking-place of revelation and its temporal having-transpired live on today in separate media, the former in God's congregation, the latter in God's word: at one time, however, both must have been founded at a single blow. The ground of revelation is mid-point and beginning in one; it is the revelation of the divine name. The constituted congregation and the composed word live their lives from the revealed name of God up to the present day, up to the present moment, and into the personal experience. For name is in truth word and fire, and not sound and fury as unbelief would have it again and again in obstinate vacuity. It is incumbent to name the name and to acknowledge: I believe it.

Theory of Art (Continued)

THE NEW CATEGORIES

Thus revelation is just as essential as creation. For the name is just as essential as the thing and yet it cannot be "derived" from the thing even if, for its part, the thing is essential presupposition and mute prediction of its name. The monumental error of Idealism consisted in thinking that the All was really wholly contained in its "genera-tion" of the All. Our fragmentation of the All in the first Part should have disposed of this error. In the idea of creation we had then indi-cated and at the same time delimited the truth contained in Idealism. For us, Idealism had proven to be in competition, not with theology in general, but only with the theology of creation. For creation we had sought the way to revelation and had thus arrived in the bright-ness of a cosmic noon in which the idealistic shadow, cast by created things in the slanted rays of the sun of the cosmic morning, shrank to the point of total disappearance. These shadows had been able to acquire an illusion of vitality while sleeping in the realm of night; in the realm of created things, there was nothing to prevent them from entering, at least as the comparisons which distorted the plastic and variegated reality of things into shapeless imitations of a ghastly gray. But their admission into the realm of revealed names is barred; no Altogether passes through this portal, no If and Then, no On-the-one-hand and On-the-other, no Anywhere and Anytime. The "object" already sees its place in there occupied by names, the "statute" by the commandment. Thus they stagger back from the threshhold in confusion; here their power is at an end. But the power of revelation just begins here. It was already effective in the concept of creation too, but only here does it come into its own.

Thus the "categories" of theology demonstrate a greater extension than those of the idealistic philosophy. The idealistic categories can

at most cover the terrain of the first theological category of creation—
or try to do so. The attempt to extend their realm beyond this collapses before it begins. In the collapse of this attempt, the series
creation-revelation-redemption demonstrates its categorical character.
Might and nothing but might decides among concepts in their struggle
for—existence. If certain concepts prove to be powerless against
others, then they simply lose their character as categories to the latter.
For a concept to have the character of a category means, after all,
nothing more than that, as concept, it refers directly to existence, not
indirectly through the prior mediation of some kind of intervening
circumstance such as experience. The category is a "bill of particulars";
it asserts something that is already "in existence," not something which
has still to emerge in order to exist.

Of course we are already employing the language of Idealism when
we attribute the character of categories to the sequence creation-revelation-redemption, and deny it to the concepts of Idealism. In reality
creation, revelation, and redemption are not categories. Categories
never form a sequence among themselves. At most they can lay the
foundations on which a sequence can be formed in reality. As the
sequence creation-revelation-redemption, however, creation, revelation,
and redemption are themselves a reality, and it is a concession to the
idealistic mode of thinking if we place commas between them instead
of hyphens. But why, then, did we make this concession in the first
place? We assert that everything real is included in the three as in
reality, the real course of the cosmic day. If this is so, what can it still
matter to us whether this "real" is subject to them even in the event
that they should be mere concepts? To be injected is, after all,
infinitely more than to be subjected, by as much as freedom is more
than slavery. And injected into the reality of revelation, everything
gains that freedom which it had forfeited when subjected to the
slavery of the concepts. Wherefore, then, this concession?

ART AND ARTIST

Because everything real is, it is true, called to freedom, but not the
half-real, not the second-rate real, everything that effects, in other
words, but not the effect. The opus, the product—the opus-and-no-
more, mark you, for even man can be considered an opus in a certain
sense—the nothing-but-opus, that is, proves to be second-rate reality.
It does so precisely because the sequence in which all first-rate reality
is comprised and which is a real sequence, a succession of way stations, becomes, in its case, a mere plurality of categories. It is half-

real, it is real only as segment, as member. For it, the sequence creation-revelation-redemption is not domicile but only courthouse of its jurisdiction; it is summoned there only in order to be interrogated. Such questions as may be dealt with by philosophy in logic or ethics have their permanent residence in the sequence of reality, as we have already indicated in the case of the logical problems and those ethical ones assimilated to them by "intellectualization." Man, in short, is whole when he reasons and whole, too, when he acts, for it is simply incumbent on him, on every man, to reason and to act. But the artist is no man: he is a non-man. This is already clear from the fact that not every man is enjoined to be an artist. Artists are but a segment of mankind, albeit an essential one, and it is not incumbent on every man, as indeed it is on the artist, to create the work of art. By the same token, the artist who now creates it is not wholly a man. The artist's human failings are counted to his credit and he is conceded "poetic license" and "artistic morals." Thereby it is conceded that he is not recognized as a full-fledged human being. It is no coincidence that many great artists have sooner or later taken leave of the falsehood of artistic life, and cast their magic wand with Prospero into the sea in order to live out their lives humanly, as simple mortals, in some Stratford or other. For the thinker will one day place his thoughts before God's throne, and the doer his deeds, in order to be judged in their midst. But the artist knows that his works will not follow him, that he must leave them behind on that earth whence they sprang, like everything which does not belong to the whole human being.

Thus the stations of reality become mere categories for art as for everything empirical. Art is here, so to speak, the firstborn and representative of everything "empirical." What is valid for art is valid also for everything half-real and quarter-real—and, after all, that is what the ever isolated empirical is—except that the categorical character of the "concepts" creation, revelation, redemption can be demonstrated consistently only in art. For of everything empirical, everything that is real only as member, art alone is essential. If there were no cobblers, men would walk barefoot, but they would still walk. But if there were no artists, mankind would be a cripple. For then it would lack that language prior to revelation whose existence alone makes it possible for revelation one day to enter time as historical revelation and there to prove itself something that has already been from of aye. If man really were to learn to speak at that moment which we must recognize as the historical beginning of revelation, then revelation would be what it must not be: a miracle without the meaning of a sign. But in reality man possesses, in art, a language already then when he is yet unable to pronounce what is inside him; art, then, is the language of what is otherwise still unpronounceable. Accordingly, language exists eternally and thus from creation on, in its entirety. And thus revelation's miracle of language becomes the sign of the divine creation and thereby an authentic miracle. Thus artists are actually sacrificed on behalf of the humanity of the rest of mankind. Art remains piecework so that life might be and become a whole. And thus art is an essential episode, albeit only an episode, for us in all the books of this Part though not, be it added, in those of the other parts. In the previous book we expressed it thus: art is the Spoken, not speech. Now we must add: among everything Spoken, it is that which should not remain unspoken. In the previous book we began to describe its basic concepts; now we continue this description on the basis of revelation, the "category" which has been added in this book.

REVELATION AS ESTHETIC CATEGORY

Just as, in the previous book, the category of creation had to be determined, in its significance for art, by going back directly to those elements of its nature which we had uncovered in the protocosmos, so now too the category of revelation. The creation concepts of the doctrine of art originate in the effect of the "mythical" on the "plastic," in the emergence, that is, of the Individual out of the Whole, of an esthetically fulsome Real out of its pre-esthetic predecessor. Their relationship is that of creator to creature: he freely externalizes it out of himself into the exterior. Similarly, the revelation concepts of the doctrine of art originate in the effect of the "mythical" on the "tragic," that is, of the Whole on the spiritual content which is to be com-posed. The two effects are quite distinct. Inspiration is not created, not liberated; rather it wrenches itself loose from the wholeness. The pre-esthetic Whole must sacrifice itself for the sake of esthetic inspiritedness. Nor do the concepts of revelation originate in the concepts of creation; rather they are both equally original. The concepts of creation derive directly from that Whole which, in relation to them, is pre-esthetic.

THE OPUS

The highest relationship of concepts which we must consider here already teaches us as much: the opus is just as old as its originator. The originator himself only became originator by becoming originator of the opus. As we have demonstrated, a genius is not, after all, born. The pre-esthetic Whole of a man, his "individuality," his "personality," liberates the genius in him for the opus—and at that same moment, the opus too exists. For the self bursts in upon the personality simultaneously with the conception of the opus. There is simply no such thing as a "frustrated" genius; that could only be the case if the opus were younger than its originator. But they are coeval. When the genius awakens, the opus too begins to appear. Thus the opus does not appear in the genius and out of him even though, conceptually, it presupposes that the genius has come into being in the man. Rather the opus itself comes into being in the man. Genius comes into being as the liberation of a characteristic trait, namely of genius, which previously could not even have been detected, from the pregenial wholeness of the man. But the opus comes into being when that human wholeness foregoes itself in favor of a Something which it itself does not consider to have proceeded from within it, but which it appears to confront and to inspire with life and spirit by giving itself away to it. Human integrity pours its loving overabundance into the work without limitations or qualms; it becomes the originator of the work; it turns it from something pre-esthetic, from raw material and capacity, into something inspired. The *matériel* becomes *oeuvre*, the capacity, content. It is quite clear that this inspiration of the material, this conversion of the capacity into content proceeds, not from man as the originator, but from the integral man. Only in him can the originator himself originate. Not that the originator loses himself in his opus—not at all—but man as a multiple integer sacrifices his integrity and his occlusion and, unmindful of self, immerses in the dormant material until the marble comes to life. Genius is already far too constricted still to be able to love in the measure required by this process of inspiration. The opus comes to life in the very love of man. The inspiredness of the opus derives from the same depths as the geniality of the originator. The latter, however, emerges once and for all, overpowering and incomprehensible; the former opens the human breast and gives away its secret ever anew.

THE ARTIST

The attributes of the "poet" in the original sense of the word are creativity, his "inwardly full of form" the common character and the family resemblance, as it were, of his inspirations. We had recognized these as fundamental, in their turn, for the originator himself. It is that which emerges from the originator without his knowing how, the essential prerequisite of something greater. But again that which must join this essential prerequisite cannot be derived from it but emerges directly out of the character of being an originator. Talent, or artistry in the narrower sense, does not originate in the wealth of creative inspirations. It is not enough to have inspirations; "perspiration" also belongs here. Whoever relies solely on the former and expects everything from it is liable to experience what befell the youthful Spitteler, who did not dare to carry out the concept of his first opus for a full decade because he thought that had to come "by itself" just like the conception. True, genius does not equal diligence, but it must become diligence, must turn itself into diligence. This implies a self-sacrifice on the part of genius. Creativity does not alter his nature, for the figures emerge freely from him into the void. But artistry consumes his very marrow. As creator, genius towers in quiet power above the figures which it has externalized. But as artist it must sacrifice itself to them, passionately unmindful of self. It must renounce its integrity precisely for the sake of that which it is and which it seeks to become, namely: originator. It must immerse itself into whatever detail confronts it and fill it, as individual detail, with that life which it can only attain through the work of a diligence which, unmindful of self, surrounds it and fills it with love. Contrariwise, the detail thus come to life in turn rewards the originator for the diligence which he has invested in it, operating ever anew as if there were no other object, by bringing him to a consciousness of his own self. As creator, the genius knows neither what he does nor what he is; as artist he awakens to consciousness in labor that is without genius, that is so to speak craft. Not the wealth of his creatures but the individual figure vitalized by his love attests his existence for him. His creativity is his self-creation; in it he is already genius, but without knowing it. In artistry, however, his self-revelation takes place for him.

EPICAL

Let us proceed to the opus and subsume it too under the two categories hitherto familiar to us. There are, of course, wholly general "attributes" which every opus, regardless of its type, displays. These are not those wholly general attributes which characterize the opus as opus in the first place, but those which, once given the opus, describe its nature more closely. All are displayed in each work of art, though in varying measure, and the peculiarity of the work of art depends on the emergence of the one or the other. The opus is a whole, has details, and contains spirit: these three elements of the opus operate together in its attributes. The opus is originally conceived as an integrity and this integrity is realized in the exposition of the details.

There thus originates that which one is entitled to designate as the Epical of any opus, "epic" used here, that is, without specific reference to the poetic genre; in epic poetry, this "Epical" is itself but an attribute. A wealth of detail belongs to every work of art; the idea of the whole is nothing in and of itself, it is but a "concealed" opus: the opus becomes manifest only when and as the idea externalizes the details. Vis-à-vis these details, the idea ever remains that which hovers above them, immutable, the origin on which, in esthetic regard, their existence solely rests. On the other hand, however, the idea cannot help but realize itself in creatively bringing these details forth; it then remains to confront them as ground, origin, esthetic point of unification. The opus is free to be a plenitude sprung from the one idea of the whole, and we may well designate this its attribute as "epical." For we are dealing here with matters of content in their sweeping exposition, and it is not for nothing that one speaks of "epic scope." But content is not meant as something antedating the opus; on the contrary, it is only that which is all contained within the work itself. This or that phrase, this or that verse or whatever else just happens to be on the tip of my tongue—does it "occur" in this or that opus? This is an inquiry into the "content" of the opus in the sense in which we understand the word here.

LYRICAL

Content in the other sense is that which precedes the work of art, though esthetically inspired only in the work of art. This content we were able to designate as the "Lyrical" of the opus in contrast to its "Epical." For the self-sacrifice to the individual moment, the forgetting of one's own integrity and of the multiplicity of things—this is lyric. The integrity of the opus stands behind the wealth of details as common esthetic point of departure on the one hand. Yet on the other it must be capable of being forgotten over every detail, and this detail must be such that all other details can be forgotten over it. This detailing of the detail, this unique beauty originates in that self-sacrifice of the Whole by means of which whatever detail just happens to be affected becomes itself a small Whole. The whole depth of inspiredness can thus open up in this self-sacrifice. It is indeed the "lyric" beauty of the moment which becomes possible in the Whole of the work of art only as this Whole immerses itself wholly into moment, unto complete oblivion. But in the very act of self-immersion, it emerges in each individual case from its concealment. For confronting the wealth of details, it was no more than a "concealed" Whole.

But now, in the inspiriting of the detail, it becomes manifest to itself: the soul that attains the detail attains it only from out of the soul of the Whole which, manifesting itself precisely out of this, is still concealed vis-à-vis the wealth of the detail.

MUSIC AND ART

"Epical" and "Lyrical" attributes in this sense belong to every work of art though, as stated, in varying proportions. The different arts can be distinguished according as the one or the other of these basic attributes emerges respectively. The visual arts are predominantly epical if only for the simple reason that they place their works in space. For space is the form of juxtaposition and thus intrinsically that form in which the whole wealth of details can be directly viewed, esthetically, at one glance. For a corresponding reason, music is predominantly "lyrical," for it places its works into the current of time, and time is that form which never allows more than one individual moment to step into consciousness. Here, accordingly, the work of art must inevitably be perceived in lots of minimal particles. Nor does isolated beauty play the same role anywhere else that it does in music. The perception of music is much more truly felt as "enjoyment." It leads to an unmindfulness of self that is far more ardent, not to say more passionate than the perception of works of fine art. These on the contrary admit and justify a degree of objectivity, within enjoyment, which in its turn can be explained by the character of art, namely, as something which can be surveyed at one glance as an esthetic Whole, that is, as something really "objective." The "connoisseur" is as much at home with art as the "amateur" with music. All these distinctions are, of course, not rigid; they leave room for transitions.

FINE ARTS: THE CREATIVE VISION

For want of a fixed expression, we wish to designate as "vision" that fundamental ingredient of the individual work of art on which the opus is constructed as if on a skeleton, and which, precisely as skeleton, is nevertheless only the mere beginning, merely the first day of creation of the work. What then is the beginning of the work of fine art? What else if not this: that the Whole of the opus confronts the inner eye of the artist all at once as a whole completely formed in all details. What he there sees has no relationship whatever to "nature," even if this emergence of the Whole apparently occurred in the presence of nature. On the contrary, the "natural impression" has to be completely crowded out in this creative moment in order to make way for the vision to burst into flame. One may even say that the artist, and even the portraitist in the first session, contemplates his "theme" as intensively as he does only in order to get beyond the impression and the impressions. In effect, then, he regards it only in order to disregard it. The picture exists in the artist at the same moment that he ceases to see the subject and sees instead a Whole freed from any nature and made up of directions, proportions, intensities or, to use the jargon of the studio, of "forms" and "values." But now it exists wholly, and nature no longer contributes anything, objectively speaking. The whole execution of the opus is already anticipated in this nature-less, one would almost say purely ornamental, conception of the first moment. But it is only anticipated or, to put it more precisely, predicted. For the execution is now by no means a simple, mechanical execution of the picture created in the vision; it is, rather, just as original a process as that creative vision itself.

FINE ARTS: THE PROBLEM OF FORM

The execution occurs in view of nature, and must come to terms with nature. In this process, the vision is joined by the "form," form, that is, in the technical sense which Hildebrand introduced into the theory of art, meaning the transformation of the natural form into the artistic form. This form, then, presupposes the being-perceived of the "vision." Without this, indeed, there would be no need for the artist to come to terms with a natural form at all. He does not, however, come to terms on the basis of the vision. Rather the artist now confronts nature directly, as if he had forgotten the vision. The concealed integrity of the work of art had evolved into spatial multiplicity in the vision; now it plunges headlong into visible nature wherever that may happen to present itself. Detail is now evolved not as in the vision but in immediate contact with nature, indeed directly out of it. The will to work is poured anew and entire into each and every detail that may be occupying the artist at any given moment. This is what artists themselves express best when they describe some detail as done "with feeling." For with this they certainly do not imply a sentimental, extra-artistic feeling, nor even a feeling for the integrity of the creative work that may have been alive in the vision though precisely here it falls silent; rather the concern here is with that feeling which immerses itself into the individual natural form and transforms it, through the power of this immersion, from a natural form—in and of itself but dimly visible, ambiguously unclear, esthetically therefore invisible, and so to speak mute—into an artistic form which is determined, unambiguous, esthetically therefore visible and so to speak eloquent. This is the second act in the development of the graphic work of art. The loving vitalization of the natural subject emerges via the artistic form into nature-less, esthetically creative vision.

RHYTHM

Matters are different in music, if only because, as already noted, time rules here and it is thus impossible to survey the details at a glance. In the fine arts, the internally perceived vision of the finished work of art can be the positing of the details out of the Whole, but not in music. Here it is impossible thus to survey all at once, even internally. The vision which preceded the *oeuvre* was still mute only because of its natural-less-ness; for the rest it was already full of all the forms and colors of the eventual *oeuvre*. Here, however, it is the truly mute part of art that precedes. Hans von Bülow was completely correct when he observed: "In the beginning was rhythm." The whole musical opus exists, albeit still as mute music, in the rhythm—initially simply in the measure valid for the whole, but subsequently also in the evolution of this tempo, anticipating as it does only the roughest sort of outline, into the ever finer ramifications of the rhythmic phrasing. That vision which preceded the work of graphic art did not really have an optical shape, but rather seems an interrelationship of directions and weight-proportions—balance, imbalance, pressure, suspension, burden—in other words, a static interrelationship. Similarly, rhythm anticipates the work of art, not in musical but only in mute-dynamic form. One can "beat out" a work of music, that is, one can represent its outline soundlessly through a sequence of motions. Movement is in fact the only possible way to objectivize the temporal sequence which otherwise collapses irreparably into the time-point of the Presentive. Music rests on the possibility of this objectivization. The conception of the whole work as a unity is possible only through this possibility. The individual note has no rhythm, but even the smallest sequence of notes does. In rhythm, the creation of the work of music in all its scope truly takes place. But here too, although it has anticipated everything with its "in the beginning," the creation is still no more than the mute prediction of the miracle which reveals itself in sound.

HARMONY

This revelation must here too descend in blindly oblivious exclusiveness on the individual moment of the opus. It must inspire the opus, and initially only that, regardless of neighbors and heedless of risks. It must breathe sonant life into it. It cannot emerge until the whole of all moments has been created in the rhythm, but does not itself inquire into the rhythmic value of the individual moment. It makes this moment resound by itself—and does not care whether briefly or for long. This inspiring of the detail is the achievement of harmony. In rhythm, the individual moment forms but a mute link in the whole; harmony provides it with sound and life at the same time. It makes it sonant in the first place and inspires it, giving it pitch, and both at once, quite like revelation which endows the mute self with speech and soul at once. The individual point of the work of art must be "formed" but cannot be "viewed"; instead the vision previews the sum of all details creatively. Similarly the individual moment of the work of music is harmonically inspired with the whole depth of a pitch of its own which, as moment and for the moment, appears to make it wholly independent of the rhythmic whole.

This is as far as we can explain the world of art here. Here we are applying the basic concepts only as categories and consequently constructing them on the analogy of a family tree. Precisely for this reason our explanation cannot reach a conclusion before the next book even for the categories of creation and revelation. There it will also become clear that this whole doctrine of art is, in the final analysis, more after all than a mere episode as which, admittedly, it figures here. Let us now therefore revert from the episode to the main theme.

The Word of God

Under the love of God, the mute self came of age as eloquent soul. This occurrence we had recognized as revelation. If language is more than only an analogy, if it is truly analogue—and therefore more than analogue—then that which we hear as a living word in our I and which resounds toward us out of our Thou must also be "as it is written" in that great historical testament of revelation whose essentiality we recognized precisely from the presentness of our experience. Once more we seek the word of man in the word of God.

THE SONG OF SONGS

The analogue of love permeates as analogue all of revelation. It is the ever-recurring analogy of the prophets. But it is precisely meant to be more than analogy. And this it can be only when it appears without a "this means," without pointing, that is, to that of which it is supposed to be the analogy. Thus it is not enough that God's relationship to man is explained by the simile of the lover and the beloved. God's word must contain the relationship of lover to beloved directly, the significant, that is, without any pointing to the significate. And so we find it in the Song of Songs. Here it is no longer possible to see in that simile "only a simile." Here the reader seems to be confronted by the choice, either to accept the "purely human," purely sensual sense and then, admittedly, to ask himself what strange error allowed these pages to slip into God's word, or to acknowledge that the deeper meaning lodges here, precisely in the purely sensual sense, directly and not "merely" in simile.

Up to the threshhold of the nineteenth century, the latter alternative was chosen unanimously. The Song of Songs was recognized as a love lyric and precisely therewith simultaneously as "mystical" poem. One simply knew that the I and Thou of human discourse is without more ado also the I and Thou between God and man. One knew that the distinction between immanence and transcendence disappears in language. The Song of Songs was an "authentic," that is, a "worldly" love lyric; precisely for this reason, not in spite of it, it was a genuinely "spiritual" song of the love of God for man. Man loves because God loves and as God loves. His human soul is the soul awakened and loved by God.

This view of the relationship of the human to the divine, of the worldly to the spiritual, of the soul to revelation, was temperamentally lucid because rooted in revelation. It remained for the turn from the eighteenth to the nineteenth century to confuse and muddy this view. Herder and Goethe claimed the Song of Songs as a collection of "worldly" love lyrics. In this designation, "worldly" expresses no more and no less than that God does not love. And this was, after all, really the opinion. Even if man "loved" God as the symbol of perfection, he would never demand that God "requite" his love. Spinoza's denial of divine love for the individual soul was welcomed by the German Spinozists. If God had to love, he might at most be the "all-loving Father." The authentic love-relation of God to the individual soul was denied and the Song of Songs thereupon made out to be a "purely human" love lyric. For authentic love, which is precisely not all-love, existed only between men. God had ceased to speak the language of men. He withdrew again into his neopagan-Spinozan concealment beyond the heavenly vault of the "attributes" covered by the cloudbank of the "modi."

What this explanation of the language of the soul as "purely human" meant only became clear in the sequel. Unintentionally, Herder and Goethe had at least preserved this much of the traditional conception: they regarded the Song of Songs only as a collection of love lyrics, thus leaving it its subjective, lyrical, soul-revealing character. But thereafter the same road was followed further. Once the Song of Songs was understood as "purely human," the step from "purely human" to "purely worldly" was also possible. Thus it was de-lyricized with a will. From every side, the effort was made to read dramatic action and epic content into it. The peculiar obscurity with which a second lover, the "king," played a visible role by the side of the shepherd seemed to challenge everyone to such interpretations, and left the field free to them. Thus the nineteenth century is full of such interpretations, though not one equals another. Such comprehensive rearrangements or rather convulsions of the traditional text have been undertaken by biblical criticism on no other biblical book. The goal was always to transform the lyric I and Thou of the poem into an epic-graphic He and She. The language of the revelation of the soul seemed somehow uncanny for the spirit of the century which recreated everything in its image, as objective and worldly. The denial of the word of God occurred initially in unbounded joy over the word of man which had now become "pure." But presently it revenged itself on the word of man which, loosened from its direct and vitally confident unity with the former, now petrified into the dead objectivity of the third person.

Then science itself mounted a counterattack. The hopeless caprice and text-critical adventurousness of all those interpretations into the objective realm of the "musical drama" made the learned spirits receptive to a new view. After all, the actual crux of these interpreters had been the enigmatic relationship of the shepherd to the king and of Shulamith to both. Was she faithful?—or unfaithful?—to one?—or to both?—and so on into an infinity of such combinations as the curiosity of erudite eroticism is wont to excel in. The simple solution of the former "mystical" conception, according to which shepherd and king were one and the same person, to wit God, was of course long obsolete. And then it was suddenly discovered that among the peasants of Syria the wedding is celebrated on the analogy of a royal wedding to this day, with the groom as the king and the bride as the royal choice. And now the alternating juxtaposition of the two persons suddenly stood explained: it really is only one after all, the shepherd who, in the week of his wedding, is allowed to feel himself as King Solomon in all his glory. Therewith every incentive to a dramatic exegesis falls by the wayside. Now everything is once more enclosed in the lyrical duo-solitude of the lover and the beloved. And now, above all, the simile is brought back into the "most original" sense of the Songs; already there, a sensual sense is topped by a supersensual meaning, the shepherd who is bridegroom by the king whom he feels himself to be. This, however, is the point at which we are aiming. Love simply cannot be "purely human." It must speak, for there is simply no self-expression other than the speech of life. And by speaking, love already becomes superhuman, for the sensuality of the word is brimful with its divine supersense. Like speech itself, love is sensual—supersensual. To put it another way, simile is its very nature and not merely its decorative accessory. "All that is transitory" may be "but simile." But love is not "but simile"; it is simile in its entirety and its essence; it is only apparently transitory: in truth, it is eternal. The appearance is as essential as the truth here, for love could not be eternal as love if it did not appear to be transitory. But in the mirror of this appearance, truth is directly mirrored.

GRAMMATICAL ANALYSIS OF THE SONG OF SONGS

The transitory in its temporal form, that is, as present, as a moment gone like an arrow, is the veritable bearer, visible or invisible, of all the sentences of the Song of Songs in the root-word I. Comparatively speaking, the word "I" occurs this frequently in no other book of the Bible—and not merely the unemphatic I, but specifically also the accented I which is, after all, the actual root-word, the Nay become audible. Only Ecclesiastes, eroded as he is by the spirit of perpetual negation, shows anything like this predilection for the emphatic I. The force of this fundamental negation is also expressed by the fact that, alone among all biblical books, the Song of Songs begins with a comparative, "better than wine." The attribute here is a compared one; it is viewed, that is, from a "point of view" which negates all other points, in perspective; it is not a quality which exists purely in its substantiality, which has being where it is in being. This "better" takes up the thread directly at the point where the final "very good" of creation had dropped it. Thus the word I is now the keynote. Like a single sustained organ note, it runs under the whole melodic-harmonic texture of mezzo-sopranos and sopranos, now in one voice, now, switching to the Thou, in the other. There is just one short passage in the whole book where it falls silent. It is immensely conspicuous precisely through this momentary interruption of the deep bass which one otherwise almost fails to notice because of its ceaselessness, just as one becomes conscious of the ticking of a clock only when it suddenly stops. These are the words of the love which is strong as death. Not for nothing did we designate the transition from creation to revelation with them above. We have recognized the Song of Songs as the focal book of revelation; in it, these words constitute the sole objective moment, the sole rationalization, the sole passage which is only stated, not spoken. In these words, creation visibly extends upward into revelation and is visibly topped by revelation. Death is the Ultimate and Consummate of creation—and love is strong as death. This is the only thing that can be stated, pre-dicated, re-counted about love. Everything else can only be spoken by love itself, not stated "about" it. For love is—speech, wholly active, wholly personal, wholly living, wholly—speaking. All true statements about love must be words from its own mouth, borne by the I. The only exception is this one sentence, that it is strong as death. In it, love does not speak itself; in it, the whole world of creation is conquered and laid at the feet of love. Death, the conqueror of all, and the netherworld that zealously imprisons all the deceased, collapse before the strength of love and the hardness of its zeal. Its glowing embers, its divine flames warm the stone-cold past from its rigor mortis. The living soul, loved by God, triumphs over all that is mortal, and that is all that can be objectively stated about it. For nothing can be stated about the soul itself, only about its relationship to the world of creation. Only the soul itself can speak about itself, the world of created things excepted. The ground lies beneath her, not submerged but surmounted. She soars above it.

She soars along in the fleeting sounds of the I. No sooner does a note sound than it is absorbed in the next; soon it resounds again, enigmatic and profoundly unexpected, only to peter out again. The speech of love is all present: dream and reality, sleep of the limbs and awaking of the heart, intertwine indistinguishably. Everything is equally present, equally fleeting and equally alive—"like a gazelle or a young stag upon the mountains." A downpour of imperatives descends on this evergreen pasture of the present and vitalizes it. The imperatives sound different but always mean the same thing: "Draw me after you, open to me, arise, come away, hurry"—it is always one and the same imperative of love. Both the lover and the beloved here seem at times to be exchanging their roles, and then again they are clearly distinguished from each other. He immerses himself with ever new looks of love into her figure, while she embraces him wholly with the one look of belief in his being "distinguished among ten thousand." With infinite gentleness, the lover indicates the ground of their love in a protocosmos of creation which is lost to love itself with his quiet, ever-recurring address "my sister, my bride." Thus he lifts his love above the fleeting moment. For him, the beloved was once "in times gone by my sister or my wife." And yet again it is the beloved who belittles herself before him, not he before her. She admits full of shame that the sun has blackened her skin: "Do not gaze at me (because I am swarthy, because the sun has scorched me); my mother's sons were angry with me." But almost in the same breath she boasts of the same "darkness" as her beauty: "I am very dark, but comely . . . like the tents of Kedar, like the curtains of Solomon"—and has forgotten all shame. For she has found peace in his eyes. She is his and thus she knows of him: he is mine. In this blissful mine, this absolute singular, there is fulfilled that for whose sake she has constantly implored the companions with so much anxiety: "That you stir not up nor awaken love" until she herself awake. Her love is not to be a case of love, another case among many, a case that others could recognize and determine. It is to be her own love, unawakened from without, awaking solely from within herself. And so it happened. Now she is his.

Is she? Does not something ultimate still separate them at the pinnacle of love—beyond even that "Thou art mine" of the lover, beyond even that peace which the beloved found in his eyes, this last word of her overflowing heart? Does there not still remain one last separation? The lover has explained his love to her in the caritative name by alluding to the secret substrate of sibling feeling. But will this explanation do? Does not life demand more than explanation, more than calling by name? Does it not demand reality? And a sob escapes the blissfully overflowing heart of the beloved and forms into words, words which haltingly point to something unfulfilled, something which cannot be fulfilled in the immediate revelation of love: "O that you were like a brother to me!" Not enough that the beloved lover calls his bride by the name of sister in the flickering twilight of allusion. The name ought to be the truth. It should be heard in the bright light of "the street," not whispered into the beloved ear in the dusk of intimate duo-solitude, but in the eyes of the multitude, officially—"who would grant" that!

Yes, who would grant that? Love no longer grants it. In truth, this "who would grant" is no longer directed to the beloved lover. Love after all always remains between two people; it knows only of I and

Thou, not of the street. Thus this longing cannot be fulfilled in love, for love is directly present in experience and manifests itself only in experience. The sobs of the beloved penetrate beyond love, to a future beyond its present revelation. They yearn for a love eternal such as can never spring from the everlasting presentness of sensation. This eternity no longer grows in the I and Thou, but longs to be founded in the presence of all the world. The beloved pleads with the lover to sunder the heavens of his everlasting presentness which defies her yearning for love eternal, and to descend to her, so that she might set herself like an eternal seal upon his ever-beating heart and like a tightly fitting ring about his never resting arm. Matrimony is not love. Matrimony is infinitely more than love. Matrimony is the external fulfillment which love reaches out after from her internal blissfulness in a stupor of unquenchable longing—Oh that you were my brother . . .

THE PUBLICATION OF THE MIRACLE

This fulfillment can no longer come to the soul in its state of being loved. This cry is not answered from the mouth of the lover. In the love of the I for the Thou, the dark portents of the impersonal communal life of the natural kinship community had been beautifully fulfilled. But here the soul aspires beyond this love to the realm of brotherliness, the bond of a supernatural community, wholly personal in its experience yet wholly worldly in its existence. This realm can no longer be founded for her by the love of the lover from which she had previously always awaited the cue for her answer. If this longing is to be fulfilled, then the beloved soul must cross the magic circle of belovedness, forget the lover, and itself open its mouth, not for answer but for her own word. For in the world, being loved does not count, and the beloved must know itself, as it were, thrown solely upon its own resources, unloved, with all its love not being-loved but eternally-loving. And only in her heart of hearts may she hold fast to that dictum of the ancients which, on this her path from the miracle of divine love out into the earthly world, gives force and dignity to that which it behooves her to do through the recollection of what was experienced in that magic circle: "As he loves you, so shall you love."

BOOK THREE

Redemption
or
The Eternal Future
of the Kingdom

Love thy neighbor. That is, as Jew and Christian assure us, the embodiment of all commandments. With this commandment, the soul is declared of age, departs the paternal home of divine love, and sets forth into the world. A commandment to love like that arch-commandment of revelation, a commandment consonant in all individual commandments, one which first transforms them creatively from rigid laws into living commandments. That arch-commandment was able to command love because it proceeded from the mouth of the lover himself, of him whose love it commanded to requite—because it was a "love me." All commandments which derive from that primeval "love me!" ultimately merge in the all-inclusive "love thy neighbor!" Now if this too is a commandment to love, how is that to be reconciled with the fact that this "love me!" commands the only kind of love which can be commanded? The answer to this objection could easily be anticipated in one brief word. Let us rather devote the entire concluding book of this part to it instead. For this answer, simple as it is, contains within itself all that the two preceding books still had to leave open.

The Act of Love

THE SECLUDED ONE

The soul had prostrated herself before God in one endless Yea spoken once-and-for-all. Thus she had emerged from her seclusion within the self. Not that she denied the self. No, she had really only emerged from the self, emerged from the seclusion of the self into the open. Now she lay there, wide open. Opened, surrendered, trusting —but opened only in one single direction, surrendered only to a single One, trusting only in him. The soul has opened her eyes and ears, but only One figure meets her glance, only One voice reaches her ears. She has opened her mouth, but her words were intended for One alone. Though she no longer sleeps the rigid sleep of the self, she has been woken only by and for the One. And so even now she really remains as deaf and blind as the self, deaf and blind, that is, for whatever is not the One. Indeed it goes even further. For God had, as long as He appeared to be merely creator, really become more amorphous than he had previously been in paganism, had, moreover, been in constant danger of slipping back into the night of a concealed God. Just so the soul, too, as long as she is only beloved soul, is now likewise still invisible and amorphous, more amorphous than in its time the self. For although the self lacked every urge, every path to the exterior, although its only desire was, like that of Michelangelo's marbles, "not to see, not to hear"—nevertheless it at least became visible itself as tragic hero; it became audible in its perceptible silence. The soul, however, while opened to glance and word, is opened only toward God. In every other direction she remains just as secluded as previously the self, and on top of this has lost that visibility and audibility, that structured vitality, albeit tragically rigid, which the self had possessed. In its bliss at being loved by God, the merely surrendered self has become dead to the world, nay to everything except God altogether. As the mere creator is forever in danger of slipping back into the concealed, so the mere bliss of the soul, immersed in God's loving glance, is in danger of slipping back into the secluded. The secluded human being is the one who, like the concealed God, stands at the border of revelation and divides it from the protocosmos.

CLASSICAL TRAGEDY

For though pagan man, the self, was enclosed in himself, he was not secluded for all that. He was visible. Though he found no ingress to the world, still the world found its ingress to him. And though he was mute, yet he could be addressed. What is the chorus in classical tragedy, after all, if not this groundswell of the outside world toward the hero, this being-addressed of the mute-as-marble figure. This had to be presented on stage: it was not enough to leave it to the sensation of the spectator. For in and of itself it would be, admittedly, quite natural if the spectator were to feel himself become mute vis-à-vis the mute, blind vis-à-vis the blind hero. But this is precisely what is not to be. The hero is supposed to be a visible figure, to stand in the world, even if he himself neither knows nor wishes to know. And precisely the feeling that it is thus—this is forced on the spectator by the chorus which looks at, listens to, addresses the hero. Thus while the self was enclosed within itself, it was not closed off from the eyes of the world. For all his muteness, the mute hero stood in the world. That any kind of world was at all possible in paganism in spite of the hero's presence was because he stood in it, and only because of this. For though he did so like a block, he was not simply impervious to its effects: the cloak of invisibility and Gyges' ring are as uncanny and in the last analysis as disastrous as they are because they sunder every contact with the world.

THE MYSTIC

Magic cloak and Gyges' ring are, however, what the self appears to wear if one regards it solely as the devout recipient of revelation, just as the divinities of paganism, secure in their Olympus, but here fully alive and visible, fade into the concealed God if seen only from the viewpoint of creation. Loved only by God, man is closed off to all the world and closes himself off. What is uncanny for every natural feeling about all mysticism, as well as objectively disastrous is this: that it becomes such a cloak of invisibility for the mystic. His soul opens for God, but because it opens only for God, it is invisible to all the world and shut off from it. The mystic rotates the magic ring on his finger in arrogant confidence, and at once he is alone with "his" God, and incommunicado to the world. This becomes possible for him only by virtue of the fact that he wants wholly and solely to be God's favorite, and nothing else. To be this, to see, in other words, only the one track which connects him to God and God to him, he must deny the world, and since it will not be denied, he must in reality repudiate it. It is no coincidence, rather it is quite essential for him that he treat it—since for better or worse it *is* there—as if it did not truly "exist," as if it had no essence, no pre-existence. He must treat it as if it were not—created (for that, after all, is its essence), as if it were not God's creation, not set up for Him by the same God whose love he claims for himself. He is allowed, nay veritably compelled, to treat it as if it were created by the devil or rather, since the concept of "creating" seems inapplicable to an activity of the devil, one would have to say that he has to treat it as if it were not created (at all), but set up for him from one moment to the next, ready for use just for whatever requirements he may happen to have at the moment when he deigns to glance at it. This thoroughly immoral relationship to the world is thus utterly essential for the pure mystic if he wants, for the rest, to assert and preserve his pure mysticism. The world must close itself off against the arrogant seclusion of man. And instead of coming to life as discoursing figure, man, whom we already saw opening up, is swallowed back into seclusion.

DISCLOSURE

How now can this seclusion dis-close itself as configuration? For there must be such a disclosure if the profoundest base of that opening up of the soul is not to be denied. That base was, after all, the necessity for the secret protocosmos of creation to transform itself into the miracle of creation. The mute self had to become a discoursing self. As beloved soul it already seemed to have become this. But now the beloved soul suddenly sank back into nonfiguration for us, even before it had properly attained configuration. This is the grave offense of the mystic: that he detains the self on its way to configuration. The hero was a human being, if only in the protocosmos. The mystic, however, is not a human being, barely half of one. He is but the vessel of his experienced ecstasies. Though he speaks, what he speaks is only reaction, not action, his life only waiting not walking. But only he would be a real, a full human being whose reaction would grow up into action, whose waiting for God would grow up into a walking before God. Only he could be a match for the hero, for only he would be as visible, as much configuration, as the hero. As with God, so it is again here: out of the configuration "perfected" in paganism there does not at once, in the internal conversion, originate a new configuration; rather there initially originates from it something as yet only amorphous, a merely attributive act: the creative act of God, the opening up of the soul. This nonfiguration only attains configuration, henceforth, by being drawn into the cosmic orbit; this is, after all, the only way for all the forces which were joined together in that perfected configuration of the protocosmos to be reactivated. The secluded man is rounded out into a wholly disclosed man by waiting and walking, by the experience of the soul and by soulful act. Thereby he assumes a configuration which, to ancipate, is that of the saint. The saint is as far to this side of human seclusion as the hero is beyond it; it is the same relationship as that between the manifest God of love and that God of myth who is alive only in himself: between them stands as a partition the night of divine concealment.

MODERN TRAGEDY

By disclosing himself as a whole man, man has then become directly visible and audible. Now, after all, he can extort his being seen and heard. No longer is he a rigid marble statue like the tragic hero of antiquity—nay, he speaks. Accordingly, the chorus disappears as super-fluous in more recent drama. No longer is it necessary to direct the spectator's attention to the fact that the hero is visible in spite of his blindness, that he can be addressed in spite of being deaf and mute. It need no longer be brought to his attention: he sees it himself. The hero of the newer tragedy is no longer a "hero" at all in the old sense, he no longer "approaches" the spectator "rigid as antiquity." He is tossed with a will, wholly, receptive, into the to and fro of the world, wholly alive and full of undisguised fear of the open grave. This hero is every inch a human being. He quivers in every limb with mortality. His joys well forth from this earth, and this sun shines upon his sorrows. This hero awakens to full vitality in the dialogue under the eyes of the spectator. Here, in exact antithesis to the classical dialogue, everything is volition, everything action and reaction. No room is left for a consciousness which elevates itself above the moment. The spectator really has no alternative; he must recognize the hero, whom he sees willing and acting, as alive. In spirit he is himself drawn into the act. But it is not the self-awareness of the hero that is aroused in him, and thereby fear and sympathy, as in the spectator of classical tragedy; rather the human being on the stage forces the human being in the audience into a feeling of being one of his partners in dialogue. What transpires on the stage does not advance him to fear and sympathy but rather to contradiction and involvement. In the spectator too, it is volition that is aroused, not informed premonition.

This difference becomes most evident in those moments when the modern hero is alone with himself. The classical hero was really still able to live out his heroism in the monologue—better there than else-where. Here, alone with himself, he could be all willful defiance, wholly gathered within himself, wholly immersed in himself, wholly self. For the modern hero, the monologues are mere pauses, moments when he so to speak steps ashore out of that actual life, as agitated as it is active, which he leads in the dialogues; for a time he becomes observer. Observing oneself, integrating one's own existence into the world, clarifying decisions, eliminating doubts—this modern monologue always denotes a period of consciousness in the otherwise unconscious tragic existence which runs its course in action and passion. It is a consciousness, however, which remains ever limited, even though it is throughout a peculiar clarity hardly attainable in reality. It is never more than the view of the world and one's own position in it from one specific point of view, to wit, that of the individual, personal I.

And there are many of these I-viewpoints, as many as there are I's. For this is one of the most central differences between classical and modern tragedy, and one which has justifiably caused them to be contrasted as tragedy of action and tragedy of character respectively. The figures of modern tragedy are all different from one another, as different as every personality is from every other. For at bottom, each personality has, after all, a different "individuality," a different and indivisible portion of the world which quite automatically also implies a vantage point of its own for regarding the world. It was otherwise in classical tragedy. There only the actions differed, while the hero, as tragic hero, was always the same self defiantly buried within himself. The consciousness of the modern hero is necessarily limited, and the demand that he be essentially conscious, that is to say, when he is alone with himself, thus runs counter to this. Consciousness will always be clear; limited consciousness is imperfect. Thus he should really have a perfect consciousness of himself and the world. And so modern tragedy aims for a goal which is quite alien to classical tragedy: for a tragedy of the absolute man in his relationship to the absolute object. Those tragedies where the hero is to all intents and purposes a philosopher—for antiquity a perfectly fantastic idea—these philosophic dramas are unanimously regarded by us as the highpoints of modern tragedy altogether: Hamlet, Wallenstein, Faust.

But even these do not give us the sensation of having attained the essential. We are still disturbed by the fact that the hero is here merely —philosopher: a man, that is, who, though he confronts the "absolute," still and all only confronts it; absolute man would have to live *within* the Absolute. And so one goes on piling new Pelions upon this Ossa of a Faust in titanic conceptions intended to scale the heights of truly absolute tragedy. Every tragedian seeks to write a Faust of his own sooner or later. Basically they are all attempting to do what one of the first already attempted: to supplement Faust with Don Juan, to magnify the tragedy of *Weltanschauung* into a tragedy of life. In doing so, they are hardly conscious of their goal: to replace a multiplicity of characters which is beyond surveying with the one absolute character, a modern hero who is just as much one and the same, once and for all, as the classical hero. This hypothetical point of convergence for all tragic characters, this absolute human being who not only confronts the Absolute knowingly, but who has experienced the Absolute and who now, out of this experience, lives within the Absolute, this character whom the Faust-dramas can only strive for without attaining him because they remain, still and yet, stuck in the limited life—this is none other than the saint.

The tragedy of the saint is the secret longing of the tragedian. Perhaps it is a longing that cannot be fulfilled. For it could well be that this goal lies at a distance that tragedy cannot traverse, that this unity of the tragic character rules out the possibility of a tragedy which in essence is and remains a character-tragedy. If so, a saint could only become the hero of a tragedy by virtue of his earthly residue of profane ingredients. But it does not really matter whether this goal is still attainable for the tragic poet or not. Even if it is unattainable for tragedy as a work of art, for the modern consciousness it is, at any rate, the exact antithesis of the hero of classical consciousness. The saint is the perfect human being, the one, that is, who lives absolutely in the Absolute. He is thus disclosed to the Sublime and resolved on the Sublime. The hero, by contrast, is secluded in the darkness, ever one and the same, of the self. The place which in the protocosmos was occupied by the liege lord of his self is assumed in the renewed and ever renewing world by the servant of his God.

THE SERVANT OF GOD

The beloved soul vanished amorphously in the divine love. It threatened to dissolve in its mere prostration before God. To assume shape, it would need to be augmented by something more, something that would pull it together again. And specifically it must be a force capable at any moment of grasping the entire dedicated soul, entirely and at every moment, so that the soul has no more room to "vanish," no more time to "daydream piously." A new force, therefore, must arise out of the depths of the soul itself in order to lend it, in the perfervor of the saint, that firmness and structure which it had threatened to forfeit in the mystical fervor. But this can only happen if the hand of the world-clock moves forward from revelation to redemption now, while the soul is taking form, as it moved from creation to revelation previously, while God was taking form.

How then is that portal to break open which, even after he has heard the call of God and found bliss in His love, still excludes man from the world? We recall that defiance then emerged, in the form of trust, from the protocosmic darkness into the light of the world, but that it was not alone in merging into the self. There was something else. In contrast to seething defiance, this other was a still water: the static character, the peculiar nature of man. The rigid, circumscribed self originated in the constant reassertion by defiance of this peculiar nature. It was this character which made of the hero a tragic hero from the classical point of view regardless of the particular arrangement and mixture of the elements in him. For the consciousness of antiquity did not account him culpable for rising up in defiant surges and staking out a character as such, but rather for holding fast to a particular character which was unevenly blended and which lacked harmony, so that some one element in it predominated and disturbed the good proportions. Only this congenital defect was the *hamartema* which necessitated the tragic fall of the hero. In and of itself, it is the right and duty of every human being to be a self. To become tragic, therefore, is less moral delict than it is a misfortune conditioned by the disposition once it has overcome the man. It is for that reason that the spectator feels himself moved to tragic sympathy. Thus the character, the *daimon* by which man is possessed, now seeks a path into the open. Again it has to reverse itself internally. From being something "affirmed" once and for all, it has to become something struggling to the fore in ever-new self-denial of its origin, of the secluded self. But what kind of a character is it that is extinguished at every moment and with every moment shines forth anew? We had already seen something quite similar in the previous book in connection with the God who reveals himself. There it was the essence, the intradivine fate which, in manifesting itself, assumed the form of a passion renewed with every moment and yet ever fatefully powerful. Can it be, then, that we have here found a human counterpart to this divine love?

Yes and no! For it is not, admittedly, a counterpart. The love of the human, the earthly lover—that was a counterpart, nay more than counterpart, it was a direct likeness of divine love. But what we have found here resembles divine love only in being tied to the moment, in being ever newly present, in other words, only in what was already a function of its emergence under the sign of the Nay. But the fateful violence with which both divine and human love erupted and which made them directly equivalent—this is wholly inoperative in the eruption which we are now considering. Behind it there stands no fate, but a character, no essential compulsion in other words, but something equally essential, something demonic. What then was the *daimon*, the character as distinct from the personality? Personality was an innate disposition, character something which suddenly overcame a man. Character, then, was no disposition; vis-à-vis the broad diversity of dispositions it was, rather, a dividing line or, better, a direction. Once man is possessed by his *daimon*, he has received "direction" for his whole life. His will is now destined to run in this direction which directs him once and for all. By receiving direction he is in truth already corrected.[1] For that which is subject to correction in man, his essential will, is already fixed once and for all in its direction.

Fixed, that is, unless there occur the one thing that can interrupt this once-and-for-all again, and invalidate the correction along with the direction: the inner conversion. And precisely this happens to man, as it happens to God and the world by virtue of their ascending from their proto- and hypocosmic seclusion to the light of revelation. Now the volitional direction remains volitional direction, but it is no longer fixed once and for all; with every moment, rather, it dies and is renewed. This volition, ever capable of renewal and really renewing itself, knows nothing of short-lived caprice; in every one of its individual acts, rather, it applies the whole force of the firmly directed character which has merged in it. How are we to designate this volition? The force which we have seen erupting out of man in no wise corresponds to fateful divine love, to that divine inability to do other than to love at all, albeit with a love which, as authentic love, is wholly immersed in the moment and knows nothing directly of either past or future. For that force does not overpower man as if with fateful preponderance at all. Rather it appears new to him at every moment, appears at every moment to erupt entirely from out his own interior with all the thrust of directed volition. From out the depths of his own soul, it bursts ever anew upon the exterior. It is not fated but borne by volition. How then are we to designate it?

LOVE OF NEIGHBOR

The answer cannot be difficult if we recall that this force is to complement the dedication demanded in the commandment to love

---

[1] Literally "judged." The translation attempts to preserve the double meaning of the original *richten*. (Tr.)

God. It cannot be other than the love of neighbor. Love of neighbor is that which surmounts this mere dedication with every moment, while at the same time always presupposing it. For without this presupposition it could not be what, in keeping with its nature, it must be, namely essential in spite—yes, in spite—of renewing itself at every moment. Without it, this love would be mere "freedom," for its origin would then lie solely in volition. It is quite true that its origin lies solely in volition, but man can express himself in the act of love only after he has first become a soul awakened by God. It is only in being loved by God that the soul can make of its act of love more than a mere act, can make of it, that is, the fulfillment of a—commandment to love.

COMMANDMENT AND FREEDOM

We return here to the question raised at the beginning. Since love cannot be commanded except by the lover himself, therefore the love for man, in being commanded by God, is directly derived from the love for God. The love for God is to express itself in love for one's neighbor. It is for this reason that love of neighbor can and must be commanded. Love of neighbor originated in the mystery of the directed volition; it is distinguished from all ethical acts by the presupposition of being loved by God, a presupposition which becomes visible behind this origin only through the form of the commandment. Ethical laws are not content simply to be rooted in freedom—this is true of love of neighbor as well—but will recognize no presupposition at all other than freedom. That is the famous requirement of "autonomy." The natural consequence of this requirement is that the laws which are to determine this act lose all content, for any and every content would exercise a power disturbing the autonomy. It is impossible to will "something" and nevertheless only to will "in general." And the requirement of autonomy requires man to will only in general, only altogether. And since law thus does not come by any content, consequently the individual act does not come by any assurance either. In ethics everything is uncertain. Everything, after all, can be moral, but nothing is moral with certainty. The moral law is necessarily purely formal and therefore not only ambiguous, but open to an unlimited number of interpretations. By contrast, the commandment to love one's neighbor is clear and unambiguous in content. This love originates in the directed freedom of the character, and this commandment needs a presupposition beyond freedom. *Fac quod jubes et jube quod vis* means that God's "ordaining what he will" must, since the content of the present ordinance is to love, be preceded by God's "already having done" what he ordains. Only the soul beloved of God can receive the commandment to love its neighbor and fulfill it. Ere man can turn himself over to God's will, God must first have turned to man.

LOVE IN THE WORLD

Now this fulfillment of God's commandment in the world is not, after all, an isolated action but a whole sequence of actions. Love of neighbor always erupts anew. It is a matter of always starting over from the beginning. It cannot be diverted by any "disillusionments"— on the contrary: it needs disillusionments in order to spring forth again ever anew. Otherwise it would become rusty, it would harden into a schematic, an organized act. It may not have a past nor, within itself, the will for a future, the "purpose." It must be an act of love wholly lost in the (present) moment. Disillusionment can only help it to this end by ever and again dis-illusioning it against the natural expectation of a success such as it might expect on the analogy of past successes. Disillusionment keeps love in condition. If it were otherwise, if the act were the product of a given volitional orientation on the basis of which it were now, sure of its goal, to diffuse freely into the limitless material of reality; if, in short, it were to emerge as infinite affirmation, then it would be, not act of love, but purposive act. Then it would no longer emerge, fresh as the moment, from the volitional orientation of character. Rather, its relationship to its origin in this orientation would be one of subservience, conclusive and concluded once and for all. In other words: it would be, not the act of love of belief, but—the way of Allah.

Islam: The Religion of Obligation

The way of Allah is a concept quite distinct from the ways of God. The ways of God are a dominion of divine counsel high above human occurrence. But walking in the way of Allah means, in the strictest sense, the spread of Islam by means of the holy war. The piety of the Moslem finds its way into the world by obediently walking this way, by assuming its inherent dangers, by adhering to the laws prescribed for it. The way of Allah is not elevated above the way of man, high as the heavens above the earth: the way of Allah means very simply the way of his believers.

It is a way of subservience. This more than its content distinguishes it from the love of neighbor. The holy war can and should be conducted in a thoroughly "humane" fashion. In this respect Mohammed's prescriptions, as well as the rules of war and conquest developed on their basis, surpass by far the contemporary military usage, including Christian usage. In a certain sense, Islam demanded and practiced "tolerance" long before the concept was discovered by Christian Europe. And on the other hand love of neighbor could lead to consequences such as religious wars and trials of heretics—not aberrations but legitimate developments which will simply not fit into any superficial conception of this love. The difference, then, does not lie in the content, but solely in the inner form. In the way of Allah, this form is subservience by volition to the prescription established once and for all; in love of neighbor it is the ever-new disruption of the permanent mold of character by the ever-unexpected eruption of the act of love. Precisely for this reason one cannot predict what this act will consist of in any one instance. It must be unexpected. If it were possible to indicate it in advance, it would not be an act of love.

Islam is quite clear in its own mind how the world is to be transformed by following the way of Allah. Its world-act proves to be, precisely by this, pure obedience toward a law imposed on the will once and for all. The commandments of God, as far as they belong to that "second tablet" which specifices the love of neighbor, are throughout phrased in the form "Thou shalt not." They cannot assume the garb of laws except as prohibitions, as the delineation of the boundaries of that which can on no account be reconciled with love of neighbor. Their positive aspect, their "Thou shalt," can only be expressed in the form of the one-and-all commandment of love. The commandments in the garb of positive laws are for the most part ritual laws; they are the sign language of the love for God, amplifications, that is, of the "first tablet." The world act and precisely the highest act especially is therefore incalculable love, wholly free, while in Islam it is obedience to the law once promulgated. It follows that Islamic law everywhere strives to go back to direct pronouncements of the founder, thus veritably developing a strictly historical method, while both Talmudic and canon law seek to make their points by means, not of historical fact-finding, but of logical deduction. For deduction is subconsciously determined by the goal of the deduction, that is to say the present, and therefore it gives the contemporary power over the past. Investigation, on the other hand, makes the present dependent on the past. Even in this seemingly pure world of law, then, one can still recognize the difference between the commandment to love and the obedience to law.

Thus the world act in Islam means the practice of obedience. And therein its conception of man becomes quite clear. For here the pre-supposition of the obedient world act is "Islam" (in its original sense): the ever-anew, ever-brutally difficult surrender of the soul to the will of God. This surrender is an act of free will; it is, indeed, the only such act that Islam knows, and justifiably the act from which Islam took its name. This surrender contains—not the origin of the world act, for that is contained, here too, in the character, the character which has determined on obedience—not the origin of the world act, but its presupposition. The relationships to God and the world which make up the panorama of man have, then, in Islam, exactly the oppo-site notations as in true belief. And thus the result too is the opposite. In Islam the free surrender of the soul to God, ever newly to be fought for, is followed by the straightforward obedience of the act in the world. In the sphere of revelation, the soul's integration in the peace of divine love, once and for all, humbly proved, is followed by the ever sudden, ever unexpected act of love. In place of the saint and his form of piety—a paradoxical form which belies and exceeds every expectation, which makes all imitation ridiculous—Islam has the simple, exemplary life of the Faithful. Every saintly figure has its own traits: the figure of the saint is inseparable from the legend of the saint. In Islam nothing is related of the saint; his memory is honored, but the memory is without content: it is only the memory of a piety as such. This straightforward, obedient piety is based on a free self-denial ever laboriously regained. And it finds an exact counterpart, strangely enough, in the secular piety of more recent times which freely con-forms to universal law. The ethics of Kant and his followers, for instance, as well as the general consciousness, sought to evolve such a piety as against the uncannily incalculable rapture of the saint.

The Kingdom

THE NEIGHBOR

The act, then, is directed toward the world. The world is that other pole toward which love of neighbor is striving. The idea that God creates already contains an allusion to something else, something which he creates; the idea that he reveals himself, the allusion to something else, something to which he reveals himself. So here too there is the allusion to a something which man loves. In the commandment, this something is designated as the neighbor. More precisely the word designates, in the Hebrew original as well as in Greek, the *nearest* neighbor precisely at the moment of love, the one who is nighest to me, at least at this moment, regardless of what he may have been before or will be afterward. Thus the neighbor is only a representative. He is not loved for his own sake, nor for his beautiful eyes, but only because he just happens to be standing there, because he happens to be nighest to me. Another could as easily stand in his place—precisely at this place nearest me. The neighbor is the other, the *plesios* of the Septuagint, the *plesios allos* of Homer. Thus the neighbor, is as stated, only *locum tenens*. Love goes out to whatever is nighest to it as to a representative, in the fleeting moment of its presentness, and thereby in truth to the all-inclusive concept of all men and all things which could ever assume this place of being its nighest neighbor. In the final analysis it goes out to everything, to the world, though for the present we will leave aside how it does so. Let us turn first, rather, to that other pole, the world.

THE UNFINISHED WORLD

At this point we are confronted by a very conspicuous difficulty, a difficulty whose solution will, however, throw light on the entire path that we have so far traversed. For with God as well as with man, the emergence of the "Yea" preceded the emergence of the "Nay" in terms of world-time. Thus God "first" created and "then" he revealed himself; man "first" received the revelation and "thereupon" prepared himself for the world act. Each time, that is, the once-and-for-all occurrence preceded that which happens momentarily. For the world, on the other hand, this temporal relationship is reversed. The world first makes itself, that is to say in creation, into that which is renewed in its entirety with every moment; it makes itself into "creature," the creator into providence. Since revelation does not occur directly to it—it is an event between God and man—there remains to it for redemption only the "Yea." For God and man, redemption was preceded by the sweeping erection of their own being which their own act had then only to consolidate from within and to unify structurally. For the world, however, it was followed by this. Here the self-denying act comes first, manifesting its momentariness, its completeness at every moment. The fullness of its being, however, in the fullness of time, that is still to come. To put it paradoxically: the world manifests itself as creature in creation, but the substructure for this its self-"revealing" must await its being-"created" in redemption. Or perhaps more explicitly: while God and man are older in essence than as phenomena, the world is created as phenomenon long before it is redeemed for its essence.

THE WORLD BECOMING

In the transition from the first part to the second, we set forth the reason behind this exceptional situation of the world: man, as well as God, already are, the world becomes. The world is not yet finished. Laughter and weeping are still in it. The tears are not yet 'wiped from every countenance.' To grasp this condition of becoming, of being unfinished, it is necessary to reverse the objective temporal relationship. For the past is already finished; it lies there from its beginning to its end and can therefore be re-counted: all counting starts from the beginning of the sequence. The future, however, can be grasped as such only by means of anticipation. If one wanted to re-count the future as well, one would unavoidably be turning it into rigid past. That which is future demands to be predicted. The future is experienced solely in expectation. 'The last' must be here 'the first in thought.' In the normal sequence, identity is attained on the way from within to without, from essence to appearance, from creation to revelation. This sequence must be reversed for the world as becoming. For it, identification must begin with the self-denying appearance and end with the simple and wholly affirmed essence. God's soul and man's have a becoming which is from within to without, but the world's becoming is otherwise. The world is wholly self-revelation from the first, and yet it is still entirely without essence. Like its framework, like "nature," it is wholly of the broad daylight and withal mysterious in broad daylight—mysterious because it reveals itself before its essence exists. Thus it is every inch something which cometh—nay: it *is* a coming. It is that which is to come. It is the kingdom.

Only in the kingdom would the world be configuration as visible as had been the plastic world of paganism, the cosmos. It is the same contrast which we recognized, for God, in the mythical and the manifest God, for man in the hero and the saint. For the creature too is by no means already configuration, able to hold its own against the cosmos. With the mere creature it is much the same, if not exactly the same as previously with the divinely beloved soul, with God in his creative potential: it is in danger of vanishing—albeit, true to its distinctive notation, the Nay, in a different direction from those two. For the creative potential threatened to conceal itself again behind creation, "modestly" in the word of the great freethinker, Schiller. And the ardor of the divinely beloved soul was ever tempted to seclude itself again in proud isolation. The created world, however, is by no means in danger of sinking back again into the protocosmos which it left behind. All its dependence is concentrated into the moment of its existence, and looking backward from this dependence, that plastic cosmos appears as something enormously rigid, at rest in itself, wanting nothing. Looking backward from creation, God is concealed; looking backward from relevation, man is secluded. This cosmos is neither of these things, neither invisible like the concealed God, nor unapproachable like the secluded man. It is, however, incomprehensible: it is an enchanted world.

ENCHANTED WORLD

Previously that world had been, in itself, thoroughly comprehensible. It was thus so long as all life was contained in it. Now a new life has begun. The world has retreated into protocosmic and netherworldly shadows. As comprehensible as it was before, it now seems to withdraw from every reach and grasp of the new life. The ancient view of the world had not, after all, been magical in the least; it was thoroughly self-evident. For one was at home in this world, in it alone, and it felt thoroughly familiar. But once entered upon the world of revelation, this same formerly familiar view of the ancient world, this Platonic-Aristotelian cosmos, suddenly became an unfamiliar, an uncanny world. Now the plastic cosmos appeared to those who no longer lived in it as a world of enchantments, an enchanted world. In this enchanted world, then, magic first really became sorcery—and not before, as long as it was still a self-evident cosmos, no more than the mythic God had turned into a concealed God until viewed from creation's concept of revelation, or tragic man into the secluded man until viewed from revelation.

DISENCHANTMENT

For antiquity, the arts of magic and astrology were as far from uncanny as the arts of technology are for the modern world. This they became only when the ancient concept of the world began to be confronted by another, a new concept in which one began to live even while striving, at the same time, to keep alive the elements of a lost world—for such it now was. It is the concept of the world as created which first moved these arts into the sallow light of sin. For God's providence indeed tolerated no forcible magic interference, no artificially indirect investigation. Since the seventeenth century, the new science of the world has begun to turn away from ancient cosmology, and thereby the enchanted world has disappeared more and more from view. But at the same time the world was conceived one-sidedly as existence and as existence alone, as a momentary existence comprehended throughout all of space in the correlative formula—for correlation is the category which actually establishes the world view of the new science; substance and causality are but auxiliary categories for dealing with the material—and thereby the bare idea of the created world was moved into the place of the plastic, multistructured cosmos. This idea of existence, it is true, precluded a backsliding into the conception of the enchanted world. But it was far from providing the world with the support, the ability to stand by itself, which the ancient cosmos possessed. Existence was so thoroughly disenchanted that it constantly threatened to evaporate into mere imagination. Disenchantment implies a similar danger here as reconcealment for God or as reseclusion for man. It is dis-enchantment, not enchantment, and this is connected with the fact that the created world manifests itself under the sign of the Nay, the Creator as well as the beloved soul under that of the Yea. By itself, then, created being means quite properly "poor creature": as soon as it ventures outside the powerful shelter of divine providence, as in fact it does *qua* physical nature and in modern science's concept of the world generally, it always sinks away into the Nought, for it is in and of itself without essence or existence. For creature to become structure, to be of the kingdom and not merely apparent existence tied to the moment, it must acquire essence, it must acquire durability for its momentariness, and for its existence—well, what?

ESSENTIALIZATION

Spiritual being and phenomenal abundance are, in the last analysis, category and individual. Both had merged in the plastic protocosmos. As we have previously explained on the basis of the future-concept prevalent here, they re-emerged, not as might have been expected on the analogy of God and man, but in the opposite order, the order, that is, in which they had merged. This implies precisely a perversion. Category, that is to say the universal, had emerged in the created world, but under the sign of the Nay, in constant self-negation, therefore, from one moment to the next: each moment contains all the abundance of the created world, but only for this moment. The world is in existence—it exists where it is in existence but nowhere else. Now that other quality has to emerge: the content, the individual. And if it had already emerged into the plastic world in the tremendous shock of birth, it was as something momentary. Now, however, it must re-emerge as something enduring, constant. What then is this? An enduring content, an individuality which contains something imperishable, something which remains in existence once it exists? Individuality is normally such only by virtue of its delimitation from every other individuality. It is therefore fundamentally perishable, for its structural basis is not contained within itself but without. In other words, it does not, itself, delimit itself. Is there, then, an individuality which itself delimits itself, which determines its size and form from out itself, which can be constrained but not determined by others? There is such individuality in the midst of the world. It is scattered and cannot everywhere be strictly separated, but it is there, and its first beginnings are as old as creation itself. Its name is—life.

THE LIVING

Organic life in nature is this something, somehow present from the remotest beginning, certainly not to be derived from the bare existence of the bare substantiality—in terms of Idealism—of the world. It is but the visible symbol of a concept of life which extends its sphere of influence far beyond the boundaries of organic nature. Everything, yes indeed everything can be alive, not only living beings but also institutions, communities, feelings, things, works. What then does it mean to be alive as against merely being in existence? It really means only what we have just now already stated: a form of one's own, forming itself from within and therefore necessarily enduring. Plants and animals and similarly every "organism" in the metaphorically extended sense are not mere product or mere intersection of forces; once present they are, rather, a something which strives to assert itself in its form against all forces. Life offers resistance; it resists, that is, death. This distinguishes it from mere existence; which is mere subject, merely subjected, that is, to cognition. Here one can already see what life still adds to existence. By means of beings which are firm in themselves, stable and structured, life buttresses the creaturely weakness to which existence is subject, rich and all-encompassing though it is in and of itself. Compared to the "phenomena" of existence, living beings are truly "beings." Cognition of existence is the recognition of its transformations. Cognition of life, however, would be the recognition of its preservation.

But if life preserves its durability by resistance, it proves not to correspond entirely to what we are looking for here. After all, we were not looking for permanent points, foci of life, as it were, in an otherwise lifeless world. Rather, we were seeking the durability of the world itself, we sought an endless duration, able to take its place beneath the constantly momentary existence to form its basis. We sought, in short, a substance of the world beneath the phenomena of its existence. We sought an Infinite, standing by itself; we found all kinds of finites, indefinitely numerous. We found something finite which was finite in its very essence, for it attained its durability in resistance against something other.

This contradiction is resolved, like everything we have dealt with so far which appeared divergent, through the simple notion that that which we are seeking here is not something already present but something which is yet to come. We seek an infinite life, we find a finite one. The finite life that we find is thus simply the not-yet-infinite. The world must become wholly alive. It must become alive as a whole instead of becoming individual foci of life like so many raisins in a cake. Existence must be alive at all its points. That it is not yet thus means again no more than that the world is not yet finished, something which we first notice here, and not already in the concept of existence. That is because existence is always only momentary; it is, therefore, beyond "finished" and "unfinished." For the moment knows only itself. Its base and support existence has from what is enduring, once-and-for-all, in the search for which, as soon as it is instituted, it becomes apparent that the unknown is still not in existence. To be more precise, it exists as something as yet nonexistent. Life and existence do not coinside—as yet.

The profusion of the phenomenon which rained into the cosmos, the inexpressible wealth of individuality: this is what turns itself into something enduring, structured, fixed within the living. That profusion originated under the sign of the Nay, and thus was transient in and of itself. What is alive, however, emerged under the sign of affirmation and demands eternity. It wishes to persist in its structure. Without that overpowering profusion of the cosmos, there could not be the established depth of living abundance. If this profusion were mere rigid "datum," as Idealism would have it, then it would not be the protocosmic ground on which the vitality of the kingdom could grow. For all emergence into the manifest must be an inner conversion; therefore only that which is mobile, ever changeable, could grow out of the rigid. Vitality—calmly enduring, transmitting its form from past to future—grows only from out the ever renewed profusion. And only the plastic cosmos, in all its variegated factuality, can transform itself into the kingdom, not the generation of a lifeless existence out of a universal, intellectualized law. The steadfast defiance of the hero was the only possible root for the eruption of the faith of the saint who gives himself to God and faces the world. And the living God of mythology was the only possible soil for the loving God of revelation. Just so the kingdom of God could only begin to emerge into the world in the world-wide principate of the Emperor Augustus, the political realization of paganism's plastic image of the world.

GROWTH OF THE KINGDOM

From the very beginning, the world is destined for vitality. The beginnings of organic matter are lost in the dim past as if in token of this destiny; nor are they to be grasped, or even deduced. But only the foci of life are thus primordially vital. Vitality, therefore, must increase; of an inner necessity it must increase. And this Must is likewise primordial. The world is created in the beginning not, it is true, perfect, but destined to have to be perfected. Its future perfection is created, as future, simultaneously with the world. This obligatory perfection is not imposed on existence, which need not become perfected, but only renew itself constantly. Thus, to speak only of that portion of the world on which it is incumbent, the kingdom, the vivification of existence, comes from the beginning on, it is always a-coming. Thus its growth is essential. It is always yet to come—but to come it is always. It is always already in existence and at the same time still to come. It is not yet in existence once and for all. It is eternally coming. Eternity is not a very long time; it is a Tomorrow that could as well be Today. Eternity is a future which, without ceasing to be future, is nonetheless present. Eternity is a Today which is, however, conscious of being more than Today. If then the kingdom is eternally coming, this means that, while its growth is essential, the tempo of this growth is not fixed, nay, more exactly: the growth has no relationship at all to time. An existence which has once merged into the kingdom cannot drop out again; it has entered the once-and-for-all; it has become eternal.

IMMORTALITY

The inevitable growing of the kingdom is not, however, simply identical with the growth of life, and this becomes evident here. For while life too wants to endure, it wages a struggle uncertain of issue: that all life must die is a matter, if not of necessity, at least of ample experience. Thus the kingdom may build its growth on the growth of life. But in addition it is dependent on something else, something which first assures life of that immortality which life seeks for itself and which the kingdom must demand for life. Life is assured of citizenship in the kingdom only by becoming immortal. In order to become manifest form, the world thus requires an effect from without in addition to its own inner growth, the growth of life which is precarious because never certain of enduring. This effect affects its vitality in the act of redemption. In what manner, that we will see.

Islam: The Religion of Progress

Let us first take one last comparative look at Islam. Again the concept of life as the basis of the idea of the kingdom will thereby become still clearer for us. Islam too makes the world, in its individuality, the object of redemption. The way of Allah leads the faithful into real peoples of real epochs. How then are these peoples and epochs conceived of here? In the kingdom they emerge in a constant though incalculable growth in vitality. It cannot be said with certainty that a people or epoch, or an event, a person, a work, or an institution really attains immortality; nobody knows this. But the inherent form, even though it submerge again at the end, implies an increase in vitality, even if not eternal life. For the form endures in memory, as well as in after effects which in the end find their way, somewhere and sometime, into the kingdom after all.

In Islam, on the other hand, all worldly individuality remains under its protocosmic sign, the Nay. It is ever new, not gradually growing. Here every age is really immediate to God, and not alone every age, but also and in general everything individual. Thus it is that the soil of Islam nourished the first real historical interest since antiquity, a really and truly scientific interest in the modern sense, without any ulterior "philosophy of history." In the Christian world, by contrast, the interest in this philosophical background predominated. Its historical exposition was determined by the desire to make God's sway in history evident to human eyes on the basis of the growth of his kingdom. It is always thus determined, and will always continue to be, in spite of all the disillusionments by the course of events which again and again teaches that God's ways are beyond finding out. As against this growth of the kingdom which occurs out of inherent necessity, Islam develops a highly significant doctrine, the doctrine of the Imam's. Every age, every "century" since Mohammed, has its "Imam," its spiritual leader; he will lead the faith of his age on the right path. Thus the ages are not placed in any kind of mutual relationship by this means. There is no growth from one to the other, no (Hegelian) "spirit" permeating them all and connecting them into a unity and, barring a recourse to the inherited doctrine deriving from the Prophet himself, there remains to each age, wherever this doctrine is unequal to the needs of the age, only the resort to the consensus of the entire living community, the "Ijmāᶜ." "My congregation will never concur in error," Mohammed is supposed to have promised. This concurrence is thus again something wholly of the present. It simply cannot be compared to the ideas of the infallible Church, which is infallible only as living guardian of the received doctrine. It is, rather, the very antithesis of this, as it is, equally, the antithesis of the Rabbinic concept of the Oral Law, which ascribes to the contemporary decision, arrived at by pure logic, a direct origin in the revelation at Sinai itself. But the conspicuous analogy to the specifically "modern" concept of "progress" in history, and of the position of the "great man" within it, is clear here as well as in the doctrine of the Imam.

The inevitable growth of the kingdom is, thanks to the concomitant effect of the aforementioned "other," nonetheless incalculable. Now the substance of our analogy is that, as against that growth, the idea of the future is here poisoned in the root. For the future is first and foremost a matter of anticipating, that is, the end must be expected at every moment. Only thus does the future become the time of eternity. For just as the *tempora* in general are mutually distinguished by their relation to the present, so too the present moment obtains the gift of eternity only here: from the past it receives the gift of ever-lasting, of duration, from the present itself that of ever-being. Every moment can be the last. That is what makes it eternal and that, precisely, makes it the origin of the future as a sequence every member of which is anticipated by the first.

That the kingdom is "among you," that it is coming "today," is a notion of the future which eternalizes the moment. And it is this notion which expires in the concept of eras, the Islamic as well as the modern one. True, the ages form an endless sequence here, but endless is not eternal; it is only "evermore." The Islamic concept of time is concealed in the doctrine of the Imam and the concept of Ijmāᶜ. In it, the sequence of times is distended into the endless indifference of a sequence. Thus each individual member may be quite momentary but if one added them up, their sum would resemble a past rather than a future. For the pure historian who has faded into a mere tool for the discovery of things past, it is in fact an authentic notion that all eras are supposedly equally immediate to God. And indeed, at first sight at least, interconnection, growth, and inevitability seem just as alive in the idea of Progress as in the idea of the kingdom of God. But the former discloses its real nature soon enough through the concept of endlessness. Even if there is talk of "eternal" progress—in truth it is but "interminable" progress that is meant. It is a progress which progresses permanently on its way, where every moment has the guaranteed assurance that its turn will yet come, where it can thus be as certain of its coming into existence as a transpired moment of its already being-in-existence. Thus the real idea of progress resists nothing so strongly as the possibility that the "ideal goal" could and should be reached, perhaps in the next moment, or even this very moment. The believer in the kingdom uses the term "progress" only in order to employ the jargon of his time; in reality he means the kingdom. It is the veritable shibboleth for distinguishing him from the authentic devotee of progress whether he does not resist the prospect and duty of anticipating the "goal" at the very next moment. The future is no future without this anticipation and the inner compulsion for it, without this "wish to bring about the Messiah before his time" and the temptation to "coerce the kingdom of God into being"; without these, it is only a past distended endlessly and projected forward. For without such anticipation, the moment is not eternal; it is something that drags itself everlastingly along the long, long trail of time.

Grammar of Pathos
(The Language of Action)

GROWING AND DOING

From two sides there is thus a knocking on the locked door of the future. Life presses toward the world in a dark growth which defiies all calculation; the soul, sanctifying itself, seeks the way to the neighbor in the hot outpouring of the heart. World and soul—both knock at the locked gate, the former growing, the latter acting. All action too, after all, heads for the future, and the neighbor sought by the soul is always "ahead" of her and is only anti-cipated in the one who just happens, momentarily, to be ahead of her. Growing as well as acting become eternal by means of such anticipation. What, then, is it that they anticipate? None other than—each other. The soul's action, wholly turned toward the neighbor of the moment in deed and consciousness, wants to anticipate, in so doing, all the world. And the kingdom's growth in the world, hopefully anticipating the end already at the next moment—what is it waiting for at this next moment if not for the act of love? This waiting of the world is itself, after all, tantamount to the forcible eliciting of that act. Were the kingdom only to grow, with mute, insensate, compulsive propulsion, ever progressing, progressively further into the endlessness of time, with no end ahead of it outside of endlessness, then indeed the act would be lame. Then the ultimate would be endlessly far away, and therefore the proximate, and the neighbor, also inaccessible. In fact, however, the kingdom progresses in the world at an incalculable pace, and every moment must be prepared to assume the fullness of eternity. Accordingly the Ultimate is that which is expected with every next moment, while the Proximate is within reach at every moment, for it is but the *locum tenens* of the ultimate, the highest, the whole.

Here, then, man and world act and react upon each other in indissoluble reciprocity. Indeed, it is the insoluble element in all activity that freedom is tied to the object of its act, that the good would be possible only in a world already good, that the individual cannot be good until all are good, and on the other hand that, in the great words of a Prussian queen, no good can come of the world except through those who are good. The dilemma is insoluble; for man and the world cannot be resolved from each other. Action delivers the act out of man, but it also delivers the newly delivered act back into the world. And waiting delivers the kingdom out of the world—for were the world not to wait, it would progress progressively into endlessness and the kingdom would never come—but this waiting also delivers the delivered kingdom into the action of man. Thus they are themselves unable to deliver themselves from this reciprocal deliverance, for in delivering themselves, they only deliver themselves more and more firmly into and onto each other. They cannot deliver themselves by themselves from each other; they can only be delivered together with each other—delivered by a third one, delivering one on the other, one by means of the other. Besides man and the world, there is but One who is third; only One can become their deliverer.

METHODOLOGY

Together with one another—this applies only here. From God to the world, from God to man—that was, each time, a course unambiguous in direction. The world—God had to create it so that it could nestle under the wings of his providence as dis-enchanted creation. Man—God had to call him by name so that he might open his mouth as disclosed soul. Only here are both poles referred to each other from the first, and everything that transpires between them transpires in both at the same time. The discovery of the object occurred in the sequence of words from the root-word of objectivity all the way to the completed object. The soul, for its part, was awakened in the course of the dialogue which began with the awakening root-I of him who woke her up. But the redemption of the soul through the objects, of the objects by means of the soul occurs in one breath, in the duet of both, the sentence which resounds out of the voices of both words together. In redemption, the great And caps the arch of the All.

This And, by and of itself, was not an archetypal word; it was, itself, but the bridge of the two arch-words, the And between Yea and Nay. Accordingly no root-word erupts from the And. The And which is prior to language does not manifest itself in a root-word, but in the root-sentence, that is, in a sentence composed of the two root-words. As will be recalled on the basis of the role which it played, respectively, with each of the three elements of the protocosmos, the And is not original. No Aught originates in it; it is not, like Yea and Nay, immediate to the Nought; rather it is the sign of the process which permits the growth of the finished form between what originated in Yea and Nay. It is thus something entirely different from the "synthesis" of Idealism. One can observe this best in the latter's historical origin with Kant, where it is a truly creative synthesis of a lifeless "material" which is simply "given." In the course of the Idealistic movement, this synthesis finally reconstructs the thesis, finally becomes, that is, the actual creative principle of the dialectic. The antithesis is reduced to merely mediating between the construction and the reconstruction of the thesis. And in this constant recovery of the thesis, the course of knowledge proceeds to ever more profound cognition, thus endlessly practicing the fundamental Platonic idea of cognition as re-cognition, and at the same time transforming it absolutely à la Idealism. For Plato had still thought of this idea in wholly non-idealistic terms, as a re-creation in thought of the uncreated Being. Thus the (new) conception of synthesis necessarily implies the reduction of the antithesis to mediation; the antithesis becomes a mere transition from thesis to synthesis, and is not itself original. One need only think, for example, of Hegel's conception of the dogma of the trinity in order to visualize the relationship. For him, the essential thing is to recognize God as spirit; the God-man means to him only the How of this equation between God and spirit. Or again, in the basic three-tempo of his Encyclopaedia, nature is but the bridge between logic and spirit; all the emphasis rests on the juncture of these two.

With us, however, the Nay is at the very least equivalent to the Yea in originality, revelation is equivalent to creation in "factuality." This is our veritable starting point. Just so, our synthesis, the And, must accordingly assume an entirely different significance. Precisely because thesis and antithesis are both, of themselves, supposed to be "creative," our synthesis must not be creative. It may only draw the conclusion. It is indeed no more than the And, than the keystone of an arch which for the rest rests on its own pillars. Nor can it, thus, become thesis again. The keystone cannot, as with Hegel it must, transform itself back into a cornerstone. No dialectical process is arrived at. Insofar as this unique temporal sequence of the world-day assumes the signifi-cance of categories, these are only categories in the old sense. They are yardsticks by which to measure and subdivide a reality, not an inner force for its own propulsion. In a strict and direct sense, there is no universally conceptual sequence at all, only the one unique and dis-tinctive sequence of Creation-Revelation-Redemption. The end is really the end and as such has no privileged connection to either of the two processes at the beginning, only, at most, to the beginning itself. Redemption is not more intimately related to revelation than to cre-ation, or vice versa. It enjoys a closer relation only to him from whom both creation and revelation proceed: to God. God is the Redeemer in a much stronger sense than he is Creator or Revealer. For though he make himself Creator in creation, he there creates the creature; and though he make himself Revealer in revelation, he there reveals himself to the soul. In redemption, however, he is not only Redeemer but— since the work of creation and the act of revelation now lie, in a cer-tain sense, behind him and interact with each other as if he were not in existence—he redeems, as we are still to see, in the final analysis: himself.

ROOT-SENTENCE

But we are anticipating. Let us pause here first at the origin of the form which the netherworldly And assumes at its entrance into the upper world of language, the root-sentence. The root-sentence is sup-posed to unite the root-words of creation and revelation, that "good!" which is nothing but predicate with that divine I which is nothing but subject. And it must become a sentence which must be spoken simultaneously from both sides—really in two voices. Thus this I cannot remain I. Man and world must be able to sing it in one breath. Only God himself was able to pronounce the divine I. Its place must be taken by the divine name which man and the world too can carry in their heart. And of it it must be said: he is good.

CHORAL FORM

This is the root-sentence of redemption, the roof over the house of language. It is the sentence true in itself. It remains true regardless of how intended or by what mouth uttered. That two times two is four can become untrue, for example, if one has taught it to a parrot and he now "says" so; for what is mathematics to a parrot? But the sentence "God is good" cannot become an untruth even in this the most scurrilous of all possible vocalizations. For even the parrot was created by God, and even he is in the end reached by God's love. All other linguistic formations must be capable of connection with this sentence. From the root-words of creation these forms ensue in the sequence of an objective development like the individual sentences of a story, and the root-word of revelation opens a dialogue. Here, however, all linguistic formations must incorporate and explicate the meaning of the one sentence. They must all be formations which explain the connection between the two parts of the sentence and join them more securely. The basso profundo of the sentence must be audible in every formation and the formations themselves must elevate the sentence, ever more hymnically, in a constant crescendo. This time grammar emerges, not as a narrative striving to proceed from the narrator to the matter, nor as a dialogue oscillating between two partners, but as a chant which is enhanced with every stanza, and as an archetypal chant, which is always the chant of several parties. It is not a solo. The song supplements the recitativo of narration and antiphony, retroactively, only after it has originated as song of the many; only then does it become the ballad of a minstrel at the royal court, or the song of love. Originally, however, the chant is one of many voices which are identical in pitch and breath, and this common form dominates any and all content. Indeed the content itself is nothing more than the rationalization for this its form. Communal singing does not take place for the sake of a particular content; rather one looks for a common content for the sake of singing communally. If the root-sentence is to be the content of a communal chant, it can only appear as a rationalization of such a community. "He is good" must appear as "for he is good."

EXHORTATION

What then is first to be thus established? It can only be the community of the chant, and that not as accomplished fact, not as indicative, but only as a fact just now established. Thus the content of the chant must be preceded by the founding of the community, as an exhortation, that is, to communal singing, thanking, acknowledging "that He is good." This singing, thanking, acknowledging is paramount while that which is sung about, thanked for, acknowledged is only its rationalization. In view of this fact, one should rather translate: an exhortation to song, thanks, acknowledgment "because He is good." And this exhortation in its turn must not be an imperative, no exhortation from the exhorter to the exhorted, to fulfill the exhortation. Rather the exhortation itself must stand under the sign of the community. The one who exhorts must at the same time be one who is exhorted, he must include himself in the exhortation. The exhortation must be expressed as a cohortative, regardless of whether this distinction from the imperative is externally visible or not. Even the apparent exhortation, the "Thank ye!" must have no other meaning than "Let us thank." The one who exhorts joins in the thanks. Indeed he only exhorts in order to be himself able to join in the thanks. While calling upon his soul and all that is within him to praise, the one who exhorts immediately and simultaneously calls upon all the world, seas and rivers and all the heathen and God-fearing ones: Praise ye the Lord! Even what is within him is for him, because it "is," something external, something upon which he must first call. And on the other hand even the furtherest, all the world, is not something external for him, but something which harmonizes fraternally with him in praise and thanksgiving.

CONCENTRATION

Praise and thanksgiving, the voice of the soul, redeemed for harmony with all the world, and the voice of the world, redeemed for sensing and singing with the soul—how can these two voices blend as one? How could these two separate entities find each other except in the unity of him before whom they sing, whom they praise, whom they thank? What unites the one voice of him who exhorts with all the world? He is different from all the world; they are two different subjects, two different nominatives. And what he has and sees is also different from what all the world has and sees, two different objects, two different accusatives. Only he whom he thanks is the same whom all the world thanks; he is not object for him and thus tied to him; he is something "beyond" him and beyond anything that could become object for him. The voices of the hearts separated in this world find each other in the dative which is beyond all. The dative is what binds, what comprises. He who is given something such as, here, thanks, does not thereby become the property of that which he is given. He remains beyond the giver, and because he remains beyond the individual giver he can be the point at which all givers can unite. The dative is that which truly binds. As such it can be that which truly redeems all that is falsely, nonessentially bound. It can be the redemptive—"thank God."

ACKNOWLEDGMENT

All thanksgiving unites in the dative; thanksgiving gives thanks for the gift. By offering thanks to God, one acknowledges him as the giver and recognizes him as the fulfiller of prayer. The individual *qua* individual could not soar higher than the prayer of the individual, the individual lament. The fulfillment lay beyond except that, insofar as it occurred within the soul of the individual, the prayer was, as ability to pray, already its own fulfillment. All prayer, even the individual lament, subconsciously cries out for the coming of the kingdom, the visible representation of what is experienced only in the soul's holy of holies. But the kingdom does not come in revelation, and the prayer thus remains a sigh in the night. Now fulfillment is directly there. The kingdom of God is actually nothing other than the reciprocal union of the soul with all the world. This union of the soul with all the world occurs in thanksgiving, and the kingdom of God comes in this union and every conceivable prayer is fulfilled. Thanks for the fulfillment of each and every prayer precedes all prayer that is not an individual lament from out the dual solitude of the nearness of the soul to God. The community-wide acknowledgment of the paternal goodness of God is the basis on which all communal prayer builds. The individual lament out of the lonely depths of dire need is fulfilled by the very fact of wrestling its way out, by the soul's being able to pray. But the congregational prayer is fulfilled before ever it is prayed. Its fulfillment is anticipated in praise and thanksgiving. The congregational thanksgiving is already the fulfillment of all that for which it is possible to pray communally, and the coming of that for the sake of which alone all individual pleas can dare to approach God's countenance with the compelling power of community: namely of the kingdom. Communal confession and praise must precede all communal praying as its fulfillment.

But admittedly this fulfillment only precedes, it is only anticipated.

If it were possible to pray only for the coming of the kingdom and nothing else, then this fulfillment anticipated in the thanks would not be anticipation, then praise and thanks would not be simply the first sensation: they would be the only one. Then the kingdom would already be—in existence. Then the plea for its coming would not have to be prayed. The prayer would be finished with its first word, the praise. But it is not thus. It is not yet possible, for the community and for man in the community, to pray only for the coming of the kingdom. This prayer is still obscured and confused by numerous other pleas, for forgiving of sin, for ripening of the fruits of the earth, in short for all of what the Rabbis very profoundly designated as the needs of solitary man. These are indeed the needs of the solitary. If the individual were really united with all the world, as he anticipates in praise and thanks, then he would have shed all these needs. They are the sign that the deliverance from the bonds of need is only anticipated in the universal fusion of his soul with all the world in praise and thanks, that redemption is thus wholly and solely something yet to come, is—future.

ANTICIPATION

Thus the future has the same significance here as the present has for revelation and the past for creation. But the present is a fundamental concept for revelation and thus appeared at the very beginning of the "dialogue." And the past was the concluding concept for creation and thus the goal of the entire "narrative." The future, on the other hand, simply emerges for redemption in *medias res,* and almost incidentally. For the future it is, in short, decisive that it can and must be anticipated. This anticipation, this Today, this eternity of thanksgiving for God's love—for it "endureth forever"—an eternity as we explained, not "very long" but rather "even today": that is the actual melodic content of the opening cola[1] of the congregational chant, in which the future only entered like an accompaniment regularly surrounding the theme.

THE NEIGHBOR

If then a not-yet is inscribed over all redemptive unison, there can only ensue that the end is for the time being represented by the just present moment, the universal and highest by the approximately proximate. The bond of the consummate and redemptive bonding of man and

---

[1] Literally strophes, as contrasted with the antistrophes (or refrains). (Tr.)

the world is to begin with the neighbor and ever more only the neighbor, the well-nigh nighest. Thus the chant of all is here joined by a stanza sung by but two individual voices—mine and that of my neighbor's. The plural contains the things as individual representatives of their kind; and in the singular the soul experiences its birth. Instead of these, then, the dual rules here, that formation which is not durable in language, which is absorbed by the plural in the course of development, for admittedly it nowhere maintains itself securely except, at most, with the few things which *per se* appear in pairs. Otherwise it glides from one bearer on to the other, the next one, from one neighbor to the next neighbor. It is not satisfied until it has paced off the whole orbit of creation. But it only appears to have thus surrendered its dominion to the plural; in fact it leaves its traces everywhere in its migration by providing the plural of things everywhere with the sign of singularity. Where the dual has once applied, where someone or something has become neighbor to a soul, there a piece of world has become something which it was not previously: soul.

THE ACT

It is quite indefinite, however, which sequence this global migration will observe. The reveille is always answered by the nighest voice; but it is not for the bugler to choose which it will be. He never sees more than the next, the neighbor. Actually, he barely even sees the neighbor. He feels only the impulse to the act of love brimming over within him. But it is a matter of indifference to him which Aught presents itself to him from out of the fullness of Aught, or by which attributes it is characterized. Each Aught has its characteristics and its peculiarities, and it is enough for him to know that, for him, it will become unique, subjective, substantival through the power of the deed emanating from within himself. The verb, itself an indefinite copula, unites the sentence and thereby first provides the adjectival generality of the predicate with substantival fixity and uniqueness, while transforming the substantive into a subject. By the same token, once it has itself assumed definition as to content, the verb as word of action remains directed, by the subject, toward whatever object is placed before it, without choice in the matter yet withal delivering the object from passive rigidity to movement, the subject from self-seclusion to action.

REALIZATION

Indefiniteness is thus the sign under which the act of love creates a neighbor out of its object. In creation, the Definite was created on the background of its Indefinite through the collaboration of both the (definite and indefinite) articles. In revelation, the summons goes to the proper name of the individual, the wholly and solely definite substantive, unique in its way, a way peculiar to it and it alone. Now the Anyone appears, the Indefinite as such, without referring, as in creation, to a Definite coordinate to it, its Distinctive. Yet it too refers to a Definite. This Definite, however, is superior, not subordinate, to it. If the "Anyone" is completely indefinite, it is so with respect to something as completely definite as it is itself indefinite. But nothing individual can be completely definite; only the totality of everything definite, only the All can be completely definite. The effect of the love of "neighbor" is that "Anyone" and "all the world" thus belong together and, for the world of redemption, thereby generate a factuality which wholly corresponds to the reality effected, in creation, through the collaboration of that which is general in a limited sense with that which is distinctive in a limited sense. For the world of redemption, absolute factuality derives from the fact that whoever be momentarily my neighbor represents all the world for me in full validity; it now congeals in the concluding stanza of the chant. As its beginning, the individual voices had summoned one another, antiphonally, to thanksgiving. Now they unite in the mighty unison of a "we."

THE GOAL

This "we" always means "all of us," or at any rate "all those of us assembled here." In fact the word "we" can consequently be understood only when accompanied by a gesture. If someone says He, I know that one person is meant, and if I hear a voice say I or Thou, I know the same even in the dark. But if someone says We, I don't know whom he means even if I see him: himself and myself; himself, myself and any others; himself and others without me, or which others. The We per se embraces the widest conceivable circle; it takes an expressive gesture or an addition—we Germans, we philologists—to limit this maximum circle to a smaller segment as the case may be. "We" is no plural. The plural originates in the third person singular. It is no accident that this person displays the subdivision by gender, for with gender, albeit in mythopoeic oversimplification, the first conceptual order is introduced into the world of things. And thereby multiplicity as such is first made visible. "We," on the other hand, is the totality which develops out of the dual. It can only be narrowed down, not expanded, whereas the singularity of the I and its companion, the Thou, can only be expanded. Thus the concluding stanza of the chant of redemption begins with the We. It had begun, in the cohortative, with the summons to the individuals who emerged from the chorus, and the responses of the chorus thereto; it continued, in the dual, with a fugue for two voices, joined by more and more instruments; finally everything gathers, with the We, in the uniform choral tempo of the multivoiced finale. All voices have become independent here, each singing the words to the melody of its own soul; yet all these melodies adapt themselves to the same rhythm and unite in the single harmony.

THE BOUNDARY

Thus the voices of the animate world unite, but still only for words, for the word. The word they sing is We. As chant it would be something final, a full cadenza. But as word it can no more be final than any word. A word is never final, never merely spoken; it is always speaking as well. This its own life is, after all, the actual mystery of language: the word speaks. And thus from out the chanted We there speaks the spoken word and says: Ye. The We encompasses everything it can grasp and reach or at least sight. But what it can no longer reach nor sight, that it must eject from its bright, melodious circle into the dread cold of the Nought: for the sake of its own exclusive-inclusive unity, it must say to it: Ye.

THE VERDICT

Yes, the Ye is dreadful. It is the judgment. The We cannot avoid this sitting in judgment, for only with this judgment does it give a definite content to the totality of its We. This content nevertheless is not distinctive; it subtracts nothing from the totality of the We. For the judgment does not distinguish a distinct content as against the We, no other content, that is, than the Nought. As a result, the We acquires, as content, all that is not Nought, all that is real, all that is factual. Thus the We must say Ye, and the more its own volume increases, the louder the Ye resounds out of its mouth as well. The We must say it, though it can only say it by way of anticipation and must await the ultimate confirmation out of another, an ultimate mouth. This is the decisive anticipation, this incisive judgment in which the coming kingdom is really a-coming, and eternity thus a fact. The Lord's saint must anticipate the judgment of God; he must recognize his enemies as the enemies of God. It is terrible for himself, for by doing so he himself subjects himself to the judgment of God: "Lord, judge me, look on—Thou examinest me and knowest me—test me then and know what I think and see if there be falsehood in my soul."

THE END

God himself must speak the ultimate word which may no longer be a word. For it must be the end and no longer anticipation, while any word would still be anticipation of the next word. For God the We's are like the Ye's: They. But he does not say They: he consummates. He does it. He is the Redeemer. In his They, the We and the Ye sink back into one single blinding light. Each and every name vanishes. The ultimate judgment, anticipating in all eternity, erases the separation by and after confirming it, and quenches the fires of hell. In the last judgment which God himself passes in his own name, all All merges into His totality, the names of all into His nameless One. Redemption lets the day of the world end beyond creation and beyond revelation with the same stroke of midnight with which it began. But of this second midnight, it is true, as it is written, that 'the night is light with Him.' The day of the world manifests itself at its last moment as that which it was in its first: as day of God, as the day of the Lord.

The Logic of Redemption

THE ONE AND THE ALL

Thus redemption has, as its final result, something which lifts it above and beyond the comparison with creation and redemption, namely God himself. We have already said it: he is Redeemer in a much graver sense than he is Creator or Revealer. For he is not only the one who redeems, but also the one who is redeemed. In the redemption of the world by man, of man by means of the world, God redeems himself. Man and world disappear in the redemption, but God perfects himself. Only in redemption, God becomes the One and All which, from the first, human reason in its rashness has everywhere sought and everywhere asserted, and yet nowhere found because it simply was nowhere to be found yet, for it did not exist yet. We had intentionally broken up the All of the philosophers. Here in the blinding midnight sun of the consummated redemption it has at last, yea at the very last, coalesced into the One.

THE KINGDOM OF GOD AND THE KINGDOM OF THE WORLD

Belief's concept of creation competed with Idealism's concept of generation. Not so the kingdom of God and the kingdom of the world. This becomes clear here, notwithstanding that redemption, like creation, takes place with respect to the world in contrast to revelation, which is only for man. Redemption, however, takes place with respect to man too. And thus the kingdom is not a whit more worldly than human, no more external than internal. This in itself precludes a comparison between the two realms. They are never juxtaposed. The kingdom of God prevails in the world by being prevalent in the world. As if in token of this incomparability only a portion of the coming kingdom of God is perceivable from the world in any case, namely only the middle portion, the "dual" of love of neighbor. The attuned ear of the world is not opened for the "give ye thanks" of the opening portion, nor its provident eye for the conclusion, the "We." Thus the world sees only the act of love and compares it with its own act. And though it sees and hears here, it is with blind eyes and deaf ears. True it sees that something is happening here—as it did not in the case of the "Give ye thanks" and the "We"—but not what is happening: the animation of the growing life of the world. This occurrence is invisible from the vantage point of the world. Thus it only sees anarchy, disorder, interruption of its quietly growing life. For the starting point of this occurrence, of this animation, is the soul of man, and this the world would have to be able to espy in order to see what it was that was occurring. It cannot do this, for the soul awakens in man, and he does not belong to the world until it becomes animated with its own soul—in redemption.

THE NEIGHBOR AND THE SELF

Man's act of love is, after all, only apparently an act. He is not told by God to do unto his neighbor as he would be dealt with himself. This is the practical form of the commandment to love one's neighbor, for use as a rule of conduct. Actually it merely designates the lower negative limit; it forbids the transgression of this limit in conduct. For this reason even its external form is better phrased in the negative. Rather, man is to love his neighbor like himself. Like himself. Your neighbor is "like thee." Man is not to deny himself. Precisely here in the commandment to love one's neighbor, his self is definitely confirmed in its place. The world is not thrown in his face as an endless melee, nor is he told, while a finger points to the whole melee: that is you. That is you—therefore stop distinguishing yourself from it, penetrate it, dissolve in it, lose yourself in it. No, it is quite different. Out of the endless chaos of the world, one nighest thing, his neighbor, is placed before his soul, and concerning this one and well-nigh only concerning this one he is told: he is like you. "Like you," and thus not "you." You remain You and you are to remain just that. But he is not to remain a He for you, and thus a mere It for your You. Rather he is like You, like your You, a You like You, an I—a soul.

SOUL AND WORLD

Thus love turns the world into a world animated with a soul, not so much by what it does but because it does it from love. At the same time something does occur, something does get done even in the absence of any real Doing. This no longer accrues to man, but to the world, for the world moves toward the act of love. There is a law operative in the order in which things move toward man's act of love. This law is invisible only from the side of man. For him, everything nighest that occurs to him must be "any" thing, the representative of any other, of all others. He may neither ask nor discriminate: it is nighest him. But from the world's point of view, the unforeseen, the unhoped for, the great surprise is on the contrary precisely man's act of love. The world bears within itself the law of its growing life. This life accrues to it and claims duration in every new member that takes up its place. But how it is actually to achieve duration, whether it is to be endowed with immortality—that is not clear from the world's side. The world knows only that all that lives must die, or believes that it knows this. And if it claims eternity, it does so in the expectation of an outside influence endowing life with immortality. True to the law of growth, the world itself produces its branches, twigs, leaves, blossoms and fruits of life out of its age-old stem whose roots are daily watered anew out of the ever fresh wellspring of existence. Only when and where the animating breath of the love of neighbor wafts over the limits of this growing living being will these gain, in addition to their life, what life itself could not give them: animation, eternity.

The act of love thus appears to take effect only on the chaos of an "Any." In reality, without knowing it, it presupposes that the world, all the world with which it deals, is growing life. It is by no means enough for the act of love that the world have creaturely existence. It demands more of it: duration as a matter of law, interconnection, articulation, growth—in short, everything that it itself appears to deny in the anarchic freedom, immediacy, momentariness of its act. Just because it consciously denies it, it unconsciously presupposes it. The soul demands, as object animated with soul by it, an articulated life. It then exercises its freedom on this life, animating it in all its individual members, and everywhere inseminating this ground of the living structure with the seeds of name, of animated individuality, of immortality.

INSTITUTION AND REVOLUTION

Thus blood kinship, brotherhood, nationhood, marriage, in sum all human relationships are established in creation. Nothing exists but it is at bottom primeval. All have their prototypes in the animal kingdom, and through the rebirth of the soul in revelation, all are first animated with a soul in redemption. All are rooted in the community of blood which in its turn is nighest creation among them. Animated in redemption, they all strive to emulate the great simile of marriage which is nighest redemption among them: mystery of the soul become wholly and omni-visibly existing form visible to all, articulated life wholly infused with soul. It is for this reason that, on the pinnacle of love, the soul yearns across to the created community of love; she does not find her redemption except in the fateful, nay the God-given unification of love and blood-community, in marriage. And to look beyond the simultaneous mutual relationships of men: the kingdom of the world, articulated within itself, which grows in itself according to a law of its own; the course of history which pushes on within itself; the life of nations which is encased in a tough armor of law and public order—all this is creative basis which redemption needs for the kingdom of God. With apparently devastating effect, love reaches into this composite structure and detaches now here and now there a component for a life of its own which threatens to shatter the cohesion of the whole. In reality, however, it is not up to love which member it thus seizes with its power and delivers out of the context of life into its eternity. Not only is this not up to love; rather, the law of growth is instituted in the world by its Creator just as much as the overflowing drive of its love is instituted in love itself by the Revealer, and this law determines, without man himself being conscious of it, the way and object of love. The blossoming tree of love always reaches toward animating love only with the buds that have already opened. Thus redemption originates with God, and man knows neither the day nor the hour. He only knows that he is to love, and to love always the nighest and the neighbor. And as for the world, it grows in itself, apparently according to its own law. And whether world and man find each other today or tomorrow or whenever—the times are incalcuable; neither man nor world knows them. Only He knows the hour who at every moment redeems the Today unto eternity.

END AND BEGINNING

Thus redemption is an end before which all that has begun sinks back into its beginning. Only thereby is it consummation. Whatever is still attached directly to its beginning is not yet factual in the full sense, for the beginning whence it originated could reabsorb it. This is true for the matter which originated as Yea of the non-Nought as well as for the act which originated as Nay of the Nought. True durability is always duration into the future and with respect to the future. Not that is enduring which has always been: the world has always been; nor that which is always renewed: experience is always renewed; but only that which eternally cometh: the kingdom. Matter is not safe from sliding back into the Nought, nor is act, but only fact.

Theory of Art (Concluded)

This power of the And to establish form, to factualize, is well known to us from the significance which it had for the establishment of the "elements" in the first Part. Already there, so to speak proto- or hypocosmically, there occured an inner self-creation, self-revelation, self-redemption of each individual element, God, world, man, within itself. We could not have said that then, even if we had wanted to. Just as little do we still need to state it explicitly now. We now determine for redemption the same thing that we then observed of the And: that completion takes place only in redemption. This relationship becomes still clearer if we now, in this book too, return to that world in which our basic concepts are merely valid as categories, to art.

REDEMPTION AS ESTHETIC CATEGORY

In art too, the category of redemption includes completion. The categories of creation had throughout laid the broad foundation by spanning the arch from a somehow presupposed whole to a mass of details belonging to the world of art. The categories of revelation then described a new arch from the same presupposed whole to, this time, the individual detail which thereby became meaningful. The categories of redemption, now, span the third vault from this individual animated content to the broad whole of all individuality by virtue of the fact that an animated and significant interconnection comes into being, and thereby something complete and conclusive in the esthetic sense.

THE AUDIENCE IN ART

The work of art stands there unique, detached from its originator, uncanny in its vitality which is full of life and yet alien to life. Yes, it is truly uncanny.[1] It does not know the shelter of a category where it might nestle. It stands all by itself—a type to itself, a category to itself, not akin to any other thing, even to any other work of art. It can no longer find lodgings even with its own originator. He has already turned to other works for he is more than all his works: he is the whole dimension whence works can emerge. The individual work is his as long as he was occupied with it; it is quits for him when he has acquitted himself of it. He is barely capable of still enjoying his own work: he hardly ever warms himself at his own coals. Only a translation can provide the poet, for example, with the necessary detachment for enjoying his own work. Who then is to bridge the gap between the work and its originator? For the work is but a single work, the author but a potential author, circumstances which show that the world of art only begins in both. Who then will erect the bridge over which the work can move from its home-less isolation into a roomy, human home whence it can no longer be forcibly evicted, and where it meets many others of its own sort that permanently dwell together here in each other's company? This place where the works establish a broad, vital, enduring existence in beauty, and where the animation of the individual works themselves gradually animates an abundant whole of human life, this place is the spectator.

In the spectator, the empty humanity of the author has coalesced with the uncanniness of the work rich in content and full of animation. Without the spectator, the work would be mute, since it does not "speak" to the author: Pygmalion seeks in vain to breathe life into the marble that he has shaped himself. It would be merely spoken, not speech. It only "speaks" to the beholder. And without the beholder, it would be without any enduring effect on reality. Art does not after all truly penetrate into real life with the production of painted canvases or hewn stones or inscribed pages. "Vandals" have never yet killed anything but dead matter. Rather, in order to pass into reality,

[1] Literally: home-less. (Tr.)

art must re-create men. But the few wretches who live scattered and alone among the masses as artists are by no means re-created, if only because their authorship, like the creature existence of the world, is real only in the moment of creation of the individual work. For the same reason, the artisanry of the artists seems as if extinguished between the individual works, and until it shows that it is still there in a new work. Art manifests itself in artists, in the Bohemian quarters of the big cities or the artist-colonies of the country, as little as in the collections and recitals of the works. It only becomes reality by educating men as its beholders, and by creating a permanent "audience" for itself. The vitality of Wagner and his work is not proved by Bayreuth but by the fact that names like Elsa and Eva became fashionable, and that the idea of woman as redeemer colored the nature of masculine eroticism in Germany for decades. Once it has become public property, art can no longer be excluded from the world, but as long as it is merely work and merely artist it leads a highly precarious, day-to-day existence.

THE MAN IN THE ARTIST

Let us return once more to the author, whom we had recognized as creator and artist. Once more both are incapable of living without each other. The significance which the content of the individual moment attains in the conscious work of the "artist" must spread out over the entire realm of the creative imagination of the "poet." Only when the creator thus no longer resembles a volcano, blindly erupting in an indiscriminate emission of one picture after the other, only when all his contents are filled with symbolic gravity, only then is he more than conscious artist, more than blind creator. Only then is he—albeit within the limits which art happens to set men—a man. Let us add, but only for clarification, that Shakespeare, for example, would thus have been only creator in the form in which *Sturm und Drang* viewed him, only artist according to the conception of him in [Lessing's] *Hamburgische Dramaturgie*. But as [Georg] Brandes presented him—in a vital unity of imagination and conscious art, so that the former grew toward the latter in the development of the inner life—Shakespeare was a man.

THE "DRAMATIC" IN THE WORK

On principle we had set up the concepts of "Epic" and "Lyric" for each work. We understood by the former the material qualities of the work of art, circumscribed through the unity of form, by the latter its spiritual qualities, bursting the unity of form. This antithetical relationship to form already indicates that neither of them achieves stability until a third factor arises above them. In this, the "epic" fullness of the material unites with the "lyric" immediacy of an in-flammatory and volatile presence as all the points of the epic breadth are vitalized into such immediacy. If we call this third factor the "Dramatic," then this word, which may designate the "Dramatic" of a symphony as well as of a painting, a tragedy, or a song, will hardly require further explanation.

POETRY AMONG THE ARTS

By its very nature, of course, poetry stands in a closer relationship to this quality of the "Dramatic" than either art or music. This is because art, being at home in space, developed "in breadth," tended, that is, toward the "Epic" of its own accord, and music, because in time, tended toward "lyric" emphasis and sentient fulfillment of the individual moment. Poetry, on the other hand, is directly at home neither in space nor in time, but in the common inner source of both space and time, in conceptual thought. Not that poetry is the art of cogitation. But thought is its element just as space is art's or time music's. Space, the "epically" extensive breadth, is the world of ex-ternal observation; time, the "lyrically" intensive depth is that of inner observation. And poetry, proceeding from thought by means of con-cepts, at last also presses these worlds into its service. Thus it comes to be the truly vital art, and a certain human maturity is even more indispensable for the great poet than for the painter or musician. The very appreciation of poetry is conditioned on a certain wealth of experience. Art and music are still somewhat abstract; the former appears to some extent mute, the latter blind. As a result, oral revela-tion, beginning with Moses, has never confronted art, nor has struc-turally sated paganism, beginning with Plato, confronted music with-out some misgivings. No such misgivings apply to poetry; the author of Psalm 90[1] and that of the epigram on Aster meet in the exercise of the poetic art. For poetry supplies structure as well as discourse, by supplying what is more than both: conceptual thought. In this, both live as one. Therefore poetry is, because most alive, the most vital art. It is not necessary for every person to have a taste for music or painting, to be an amateur producer or reproducer in the one or the

[1] i.e., Moses. (Tr.)

other. But every complete human being must have a taste for poetry; indeed he really has to be an amateur poet himself. At the very least he must have once written poetry. Even if, at a pinch, one can be human without composing poetry, one cannot become human without having once done so for a time.

STRUCTURE IN ART

Clearly, in art, neither vision nor form suffice to create the work of art by themselves. Vision is merely the invisible background, in the mind of the artist, for the work which eventually becomes visible for the observer. Form is realization in its relationship to nature, directed to only one specific detail at a time, its feeling immersed in the detail, unable to attain law and direction except by means of mental imagery. And only when it has traversed this in its entire extent, lovingly, only then is the work of art a visible structure. Where there is a surplus of vision relative to the will for form, the structure threatens to remain mere ornament. Where, on the other hand, the vision is weak relative to the natural drive for formation of the detail, there the structure remains a mold: the work fails to "materialize."

Melos IN MUSIC

In music we have rhythm, whose mute motion permeates the whole, and harmony, which inspires the detail with sound. Here too, the line of the *melos* rises over both in motion as well as sound. Melody is the live part of music. To retain more than the "character and mood" of a musical piece—generally, that is, its rhythm and harmony—means to retain the course of its *melos*. Allusions to alien rhythms, or the assumption of alien harmonies in a composition are, quite rightly, felt not as inadmissible plagiarisms but simply as "relationships." But melody is so much the very essence of a composition that we are inclined to brand the slighest borrowing of it at once as theft.

THE TONE OF THE POEM

Poetry is based on what one might designate as meter if this term had a broader meaning. The theory of poetry lacks the distinction which music draws between rhythm and beat: where there is rhythm, there must be beat, but not vice versa. Thus meter is no more than a partial manifestation, externally measurable, of a whole which we would like to call tone. Tone is that on which the poetic work is based, the original conception embracing the whole in all its breadth. It is tone both as to rhythm and as to color. That is, it is the motion which permeates the whole, as well as the relationship between vocalic tones and consonantal sounds. We are dealing here with the really fundamental peculiarity of each individual work, one of which we are barely conscious, but which distinguishes it as a whole from all other works prior even to any further differentiation. A sensitive ear must be able to distinguish, simply on the basis of "tone," whether a sentence of perfectly indifferent content belongs in Schiller or Kleist, indeed whether it belongs in Schiller's *Don Carlos* or in his *Wallenstein*. To put it more plainly still: an accomplished actor would have to speak the sentence "the horses are saddled" quite differently depending on whether it occurred in [Kleist's] *Penthesilea* or in [Goethe's] *Die Natürliche Tochter*.[1]

THE POET'S DICTION

Thus tone determines the character of the whole. It is joined by immersion in detail which occurs in the choice of words. This is what is called the particular "diction" of the individual poet. Habituated as we are to literacy, we find this easier to grasp externally. It has, therefore, been observed much longer than the tone. This is equally individual, but heard only by him who takes to heart the poet's admonition "never read, ever sing!"

THE IDEA IN POETRY

By themselves, however, neither tone nor diction make the poem. Beauty of tone would be a mere feast for the ears, beauty of diction mere empty phrase. The "idea" first infuses the poem with life. And poetry really has an "idea." It is only its application to music and painting that has rightfully made this expression suspect. For indeed the only "idea" of the work of art would be its structure, of the piece of music its *melos*. For to us, the idea is not something concealed behind the work; on the contrary, it is the esthetically and sentiently perceptible component, the effective and affective reality of the work.

---

[1] In fact, however, the sentence occurs in Theodor Körner's *Hedwig*. It is usually cited as the type-case of an insignificant role since it represents the only words spoken by a servant in that drama (cf. Büchmann, Geflügelte Worte 200). (Tr.)

For thought has the same significance for poetry that the eye has for art or the ear for music. The idea is what "speaks" to the observer out of the poem, just as the melody does out of the piece of music or the pictorial structure out of the work of visual art. The idea is not somewhere behind the poem, but within it. Here too poetry is that one among the arts which emerges freely into the marketplace of life without having to guard its dignity anxiously. For the element in which it exists is the same as that in which life too spends most of its time: life too more often speaks the prosaic language of thought than the exalted language of song and pictorial gesture.

THE ARTISTIC CONTENT OF LIFE

Under the category of redemption, we have noticed everywhere in the doctrine of art this about-face into life, whose sense will not be fully disclosed to us until later. For art in general it took place in the audience, the spectator. In him all that had been poured into the work of art is once more stimulated and excited. And by being excited within him, it spills over into life. The basis of the soul of the spectator is filled to its full extent with the sum of the conceptions which art has aroused in him. The spectator, like the creative element in the author, is "inwardly full of form." Now when he turns toward the individual detail, he becomes a connoisseur of it, he gains consciousness. Here too something develops in the spectator which corresponds to the consciousness of artistry in the author. And as little as creator and artist could exist by themselves there, as little here imagination and consciousness. The unorganized breadth and wealth of artistic conceptions must be completely permeated by consciousness. Otherwise art will be, for the spectator, an indifferent or even disconcerting wealth of haphazardly acquired conceptions, when it should be the precious inner possession and treasure of the soul, collected and lovingly arranged in the course of a long life. Thus the door of the personal realm of art opens and discloses the way into life.

SUMMARY

And that is, after all, how it had always been. A somewhat naturalistic foundation always belonged to the category of creation; what was specifically "esthetic," professional, difficult, to be attained with might and main, always belonged to the category of revelation; the actual, the visible, the ultimate result, that for whose sake alone all else had to precede, always belonged to the category of redemption. The author, the genius, must be there. One cannot force him into existence. Nor is the creative imagination to be commandeered in the genius any more than the perceptive imagination in the spectator, about which, if it will not open up, there is simply nothing to be done. Within the work, for its part, the "Epic" of the material is the datum, and visual art is presumably the oldest among the arts both in the history of mankind and in the development of the individual. And the actual contents of the moment of conception are again vision, rhythm, tone; they are the given, once and for all, and nothing can be done about them. The work, on the other hand, is that by which the world of art at once becomes recognizable from without. It more than author or spectator is its distinctive mark, for genius and public also occur outside of art. And again, the consciousness of artistry and connoisseurship, respectively, is what author and spectator lack, what they must acquire. Of all the qualities of a work of art, the most profound is the "lyric" one; of all the arts, music has the reputation of being the most difficult because it possesses the most highly developed and assured theory, and thereby the one best able to be taught. And form, harmony, and diction are what, in the arts, only the "trained" artist knows how to master and to apply, while even the ordinary mortal may, nay really does sooner or later stumble upon the inner optical vision, the rhythmic motif, the tonal arch-inspiration of a poem. And finally: we have seen how all end up again in life at the very moment when they ful-fill themselves in full visibility, in authentic fulfillment—art in general within the spectator and his penetration of life; genius within his human kindness; the work of art in general within its "Dramatic"; the arts in poetry, the different kinds of art within structure, *melos*, idea.

PROSPECT

But here we leave this episode which, if only to identify it as mere episode, we have had to enter repeatedly in this volume. If we now encounter art again, it will not be as episode. For it was the final wisdom of the episode itself to realize that it must not remain episode. The shadow realm of art, which was supposed to deceive Idealism about the lifelessness of its own world—it longs for life itself. Pygmalion cannot by himself hammer life into his statue, try as he will. Only after laying aside his sculptor's chisel and falling to his knees, a poor mortal, only then does the goddess bend down toward him.

The Word of God

In this Part, creation was no longer protocosmos for us, but rather the content of revelation. Just so redemption too was not yet hyper-cosmos. Rather, we took it also only as the content of revelation. As content of revelation, creation turned, for us, from world to occur-rence, to a having-already-occurred, and redemption likewise from a hypercosmos to an occurence, a still-to-occur. Thus revelation gathers everything into its presentness; not only is it conscious of itself; nay: "everything is in it." Its own part, revelation considers to be an imme-diate lyrical monologue located between the two: in its mouth, cre-ation becomes narration, and redemption becomes—prophecy? No, prophecy is the bond which in its living factuality unites all these worlds: the syn-cosmos and amphi-cosmos of miracle, for such we took revelation to be, and with it creation and redemption as miracu-lous contents of revelation; and the protocosmos and hypocosmos of insensate, piecemeal factuality. Redemption too, to the extent that it is essential content of revelation, is tied to the protocosmos of creation, as interpretation of the portents concealed in this protocosmos. For redemption merely brings into the view of all the living that which had previously taken place in the actual revelation as invisible occur-rence in the individual soul.

THE LANGUAGE OF THE PSALMS

Thus prophecy is not the distinctive form in which redemption can be the content of revelation. Rather, this requires a form wholly peculiar to redemption. It must express the not-yet happened and the yet-to-happen. But this is the form of the congregational hymn. The congregation is not, or not yet, all. Its We is still limited, still tied to a simultaneous Ye. But it claims to be all—withal. This Withal is the word of the Psalms. It makes of the Psalms the congregational hymnal even though most of them speak in the first person singular. For the I of the Psalms, though quite truly an individual I and entangled in all the distresses of a lonely heart, fettered in all the straits of a poor soul, is withal, yea withal a member, nay more than a member of the congregation. "Withal God is good to Israel" is the motto of the Psalm which is considered the most individual of all. The I can be wholly I, can descend wholly into the depth of its solitary one—as the Psalmist calls his soul—only because, as the I that it is, it dares to speak with the mouth of the congregation. Its enemies are God's enemies, its distress is our distress, its rescue our salvation. This intensification of the individual soul into the soul of all is what first gives the individual soul the audacity to express its own distress—because it is, precisely, more than just its own individual distress. In revelation, the soul acquiesces; it surrenders its individuality so that it might be forgiven its individuality. He whom God's love has chosen hears God's command, takes the yoke of the mission upon his shoulders, and sets out for the land that God will show him, thus losing his own will, his friends, house and home. But in so doing he leaves the charmed circle of revelation for the realm of redemption and he enlarges the I, surrendered in revelation, to the all-encompassing We, and thus all that is his own returns to him—now, however, no longer as his property, no longer as his home, his friends, his relations, but as the property of the new congregation which God points out to him; its distress becomes his distress, its will his will, its We his I, its not-yet his—Withal.

Thus it is that within the Book of Psalms it is the group of pure We-psalms in which the profoundest meaning of the Psalms becomes wholly plain and clear. This is that group of Psalms from the 111th to the 118th, the Great Hallel, whose refrain we have already learned to recognize as the root-sentence of redemption. In the sacred tongue, indeed, the very word Psalm means none other than "song of praise," a word derived from the same root as "Hallel." And within this group, in turn, it is the middle one, Psalm 115.

GRAMMATICAL ANALYSIS OF PSALM 115

Alone among all the Psalms in general, it begins and ends with a mighty and emphatic We. And the first of these two We's is in the dative, in the basic dative, that is, which depends directly on the verb "to give." The prayer is for the advent of the kingdom, inasmuch as the We equate themselves, and that glory, that visible majesty which they entreat for themselves, with the glory of the divine name. They do so in the only admissible form: by simultaneously and expressly denying the equation: "not to us, oh Lord, not to us, but to thy name give glory!" In one breath they thus move the We into the fulfillment constituted by immediate proximity to the divine name, and from this conclusion withdraw it back into the not-yet of the present—"not to us but." This proximity, however, this being-with-God on the part of the We, is meant quite objectively, quite visibly. God is to fulfill the prayer not merely "for the sake of his steadfast love"—in the familiar duo-solitude of his love, such proximity is, after all, already furnished by revelation—but "for the sake of his truth." Truth is patent, visible to the eyes of all that lives. That the We are one day to receive glory is a demand upon divine truth.

But since they cannot yet be given glory at the time, since the We are not yet, in short, we all, they separate the Ye from themselves. And because the Psalm anticipates the being-with-God, it automatically regards the We with the eye of God, and they become a They. This is the only context in which the Psalms take up that recurrent prophetic theme: the ridicule of the idols, in which the life of divine love is said to petrify into inaction and speechlessness. The juxtaposition of the dead idols of a world dead "like them," and the living God of heaven and earth is initially governed by a fighting mood, but this mood disappears, together with the ridicule, in the mighty triumph of trust. Hopeful trust is the key word in which the anticipation of the future into the eternity of the moment occurs. The trust of the Ye was betrayed, but in three steps there rises up over against it the We's trust in a God who is "help and shield" on each of the three: the trust of Israel, that congregation of the We which rested under the heart of God's love as his first-born son; the trust of the house of Aaron, that congregation as it is constituted sacerdotally for the Ye's passage through world and time; and the trust of those "who fear the Lord," the fixed term for the proselytes, that messianic, yet-to-be congregation of mankind, of We-all. The triumph of trust anticipates the future fulfillment, and out of this triumph there now arises in exactly corresponding order the entreaty which prays for this fulfillment: again Israel, the house of Aaron, the Godfearing one and all, "both small and great."

And now the chorus intones the We of this fulfillment: the growth of the blessing, step by step, more and more, from one to the next, from one generation to the next. "May the Lord give you increase, you and your children!" For this living growth of the blessing is well established from the very first in the mystery of creation: "May you be blessed for the Lord, who made heaven and earth." But the human labor of love on earth remains free against this silent, spontaneous growth of creation. Man is to engage in it as if there were no creation, as if creation did not grow toward him: "The heavens are the heavens of the Lord, but the earth he gave to the sons of men." To the sons of men—not to the congregation of Israel, which knows that it is alone in being loved and in its trust, but in the act of love it knows itself only as sons of men in general, it knows only the Anyone, the Other in general—the neighbor.

And thus the act of love, free as the world, comes upon the created world and its living growth. But this life is, after all, completed by death and as such in the power of death from creation on. Or is it? Nevermore will the departed life join in the hymn of praise to redemption. The departed nevermore, but—and in this But the chorus swells to an immense vision of that We of all the voices which cohortatively drags all future eternity into the present Now of the moment: "Not the dead"—indeed not, "but we, we will praise God from this time forth and to eternity." The conquering But—"But we are eternal"—this our great master proclaimed as the final conclusion of his wisdom, when, for the last time before the many, he spoke of the relationship between his We and his world. The We are eternal; death plunges into the Nought in the face of this triumphal shout of eternity. Life becomes immortal in redemption's eternal hymn of praise.

THE MIRACLE ETERNALIZED

This is eternity within the moment, in the batting of an eye. It is that seeing of the light of which it is written: "by thy light we see light." It is the light which God separated in creation according to the Rabbis, who [thus] established a profound connection with creation and revelation within the concept of redemption. For it is written: "God separated the light," meaning that he set it apart at creation and put it away for safekeeping so that his pious ones might enjoy it in the world to come. For only thus did the Rabbis dare to describe the eternal bliss of the world to come, which differs from that ever renewed peace which the solitary soul found in divine love: the pious sit, with crowns on their heads, and behold the radiance of the manifest deity.

THRESHOLD

Recapitulation: The Order of the Route

THE NEW UNITY

The descent into the subterranean realm where the figures dwelled singly, strangers to each other, the fragments of a shattered All, had been followed by the ascent above the vault of the visible heaven. The pieces which had fallen apart in the descent were reassembled in this ascent, but not in the kind of unity which philosophy had previously sought and consequently presupposed, not in the unity of the sphere which everywhere returns unto itself. For philosophy wanted to recognize "Being" as a sphere, or at least a circle; so it had declared with naïve candor from its first beginnings, and by this it had been dominated till its conclusion in Hegel. Even Hegel's dialectic still believed itself able and compelled to justify itself by leading back into itself. The unity into which the fragments of the All now enter is a different one. The unity of returning unto oneself, unto one's own beginning, that infinity in the sense of a finish which immediately transforms itself into a new beginning and thus can never be grasped, physically or mentally, as finish—that unity lay only at the outer limits of our world for us, only at the stroke of both midnights. The ocean of infinity extended, as it were, only before the beginning and after the end. The beginning itself, the first hour, really was in the beginning, the end itself, the twelfth hour, really was at the end of days. Both of them, the first hour as well as the last, still really belonged to the day of life, just as much as the living noon of experience. Indeed, deviating from this analogy, the noon of life is not its most solemn hour but its last; it is really "high time." Just so the midnight of the beginning is dark, but that of the end is (all) light.

THE NEW TOTALITY

As it coalesces for us in our ascent, then, the world does not circle back in upon itself. Rather it erupts from the infinite and sinks back

into the infinite, each an infinite external to the world, in the face of
which the world is finite. The circle, on the other hand, or even the
sphere contained the infinite within itself, or indeed was itself the
Infinite, so that every apparent Finite in it proceeded from its own
infinity and merged in it again. This infinity is not curved back upon
itself; in [idealistic] philosophy's view it is thus "bad." Accordingly,
we had to shatter Idealism's infinity which is curved back upon itself
before we could make [ours] visible. What we did was to replace the
circumference, fully determined by the relationship of a single point
of one's own to a point of reference, with mutually isolated points
none of which could serve unambiguously as point of reference for
the others. Thereby we managed to construct a line through these
three points and only through these. And we did this without a theorem
of construction setting up an ideally and absolutely valid relationship
between "any given" point on the line and a common point of reference. Such a relationship, after all, turns the infinity which is of itself
"bad" into a "good" one, that is to say, the formula made possible
by the relationship turns the unclosed infinity of, say, a hyperbola,
into a closed one which can be expressed as a formula.

THE NEW RELATIONSHIP

We found the three points to be individual, mutually unconnected,
and could bring them together only arbitrarily, only subject to change,
only under the sign of the Perhaps. This very manner of finding them
already determined the impossibility of formulating the trajectory
which we are looking for here. If there was any connection here
between the individual points, it obviously cannot simply have been
of a geometric kind. And indeed, the three lines with which, in the
three books of this volume, we connected the points originating in
the first volume, were not lines in the geometric sense. They were
not the shortest distances between two points; rather they were lines
which issued out of the points in an act of conversion that, though
based on the historical origin of the points, was without foundation
in and of itself. Thus they were really not mathematical lines. But
how to characterize this reality, this factuality of the lines of connection?

THE NEW INTERCONNECTION

Precisely because they should have to be "lines" after all, it can
hardly be otherwise than by expressly and vividly upsetting the

mathematical concept of the line as the shortest distance between two points. If this is to happen with the same, as it were again mathematical, clarity, it would have to happen in such fashion that the line itself is designated by a further point of its own, even though already adequately determined, as mathematical line, by the two points. Moreover, if the first three points correspond to the elements God, world, man, then the three new points would have to stand for the trajectories creation, revelation, redemption, and the triangle which they formed would have to be so situated as not to end up within the first triangle. Otherwise the three new points would appear to acquire an unrelatedness, an autonomous status which is precisely what they do not have. On the contrary, the connection from one point to the other two must cross in its own turn the line of the original triangle so that the two triangles intersect. Thus, however, there now really originates a figure which, though geometrically constructed, is itself alien to geometry, in short is no "figure" at all but—a configuration. For this is what distinguishes configuration from figure, that though configuration may be assembled out of mathematical figures, its assembly has in truth not taken place according to mathematical rules, but on a hypermathematical basis. This basis was here provided by the idea of characterizing the connections of the elemental points as symbols of a real occurrence rather than as mere realizations of a mathematical notion.

THE NEW ORDER

Thus there arises a structure in the form of a star which now retroactively transforms the geometric elements of which it is constituted into configurations as well. But simple geometric structures such as points and lines can only acquire configuration by being lifted out of the life-element of mathematics, which is to say out of general relativity. Beyond its notion of limits, mathematics knows of no absolute quanta; the reality to which a particular number applies depends entirely on the size assigned to the unit to which the number refers, the direction of a line on the direction of a line of reference which was originally assumed arbitrarily, the locus of a point on the location of the point of departure of a system of coordinates originally fixed arbitrarily. If the angles and sides of the two triangles with which we are dealing here are to become demathematized configurations, they must acquire absolute location and absolute direction. It was just this which, in the transition from the first Part to the second, we had been unable to give them.

Just this we now can give them, indeed we really have now already given them. For we have recognized God as Creator and Revealer, the world for the first time as creature and man for the first time as beloved soul, thereby establishing beyond every Perhaps that God is above. And God is, moreover, both Creator and Revealer with equal originality; therefore it is established that the two points designating world and man must be accessible from the point which stands for God in the same manner, though in different directions. And furthermore, man and world are no further from each other than each is from God; on the contrary, vis-à-vis man's reception of revelation, his work in the world is only the other side of his emergence out of his Self, just as is the growth of the life of the world vis-à-vis its creatureliness. Therefore there remains for the three points only and solely the equilateral form of the triangle. And since the first, the protocosmic triangle is equilateral, it goes without saying that the second, or cosmic, triangle is equilateral too. For its angles are no more than symbols for the sides of the first. And if God was inevitably above in the protocosmic triangle, redemption must be at the bottom of the cosmic triangle with equal inevitability, and the lines issuing from creation and revelation must come together in it. For its very fixation in space, this concept of above and below which is mathematically quite senseless and precisely on that account productive of configuration, establishes each element of the protocosmos, as well as every segment of the trajectory, in its relationship to the other two: if it is above, it is origin; if below, it is result.

RELATIONSHIP TO THE PROTOCOSMOS

Those inner "secret" prehistories of the protocosmic elements, those theogonies, cosmogonies, psychogonies explained in the first Part only now, belatedly, become wholly intelligible to us in their progress. They were the inner histories of the self-creation, the self-revelation, the self-redemption of God, world and man. Already in themselves they followed the same path, from their origin in the Nought to their completion in the finished, closed configuration, which they followed later in their emergence with and to one another. The enigma of the obscure paths of the protocosmos is resolved: they are the portents of the manifest way of the World. The glowing tripod which in the first Part finally informed us, on our way to the Faustian Mothers, that we were at the nethermost depths, is the same that illuminates the way back to the hypercosmos which we followed in the second Part.

Prospect: Eternity's Day of God

THE ONE ETERNITY

We have already stated it: this way was a way to unity. Philosophy claimed unity on behalf of the All as a self-evident presupposition. For us, however, it is the ultimate result, indeed the result of the result. It is a point as far beyond the "route" as its divine origin lay beyond its beginning. Unity is, then, in truth but Becoming-unity; it is—only as it becomes. And it becomes—only as unity of God. Only God is—nay, precisely: only God becomes the unity which consummates everything.

THE ETERNAL GOD

But how about the world, how about man? Is there no unity of their own for them other than absorption in the world-day of the Lord? Do creation, revelation, and redemption mean the same for them as for God? For the times of that day are indeed experiences of his own for God; for him, the creation of the world means becoming the Creator, revelation means becoming the Revealer, redemption means becoming the Redeemer. Thus he is becoming to the very end. Whatever happens is, for him, a becoming. And everything that happens happens simultaneously, and in truth revelation is no more recent than creation and for this reason, if for no other, redemption too is no more recent than either. Accordingly, this Becoming of God is, for him, not a changing, growing, augmenting. Rather he is from the beginning, and he is at every moment, and he is ever a-coming. His Being is simultaneously everlasting, and at all times, and eternal, and only this is the reason that the whole has to be designated a Becoming. When, therefore, we say that God becomes eternally, we are saying only this: that God has not simply been once upon a time and now hides modestly behind eternal laws, or that God is not merely in the moments when someone is wholly blissful with the heavenly glow of feelings; we are certainly not saying that he "is still to become." What eternity does is to make the moment everlasting; it is eternalization. "God is eternal" thus means that, for him, eternity is his consummation. But to repeat: is it this for the world too, and for man?

Not at all. True, to attain eternal life they must merge into the world-day of the Lord. Immortality they can only acquire in God. But the foundation of their consummation is not first laid for them in the eternity of redemption. The plant of eternal life blooms for them there, but it was planted in a different soil.

Specifically, the plant of eternity is planted in the common ground whose firmness alone admits the discrete and even successive expression of the Yea and Nay expressions. The very fact that the elements take on the form of temporality nonetheless means, for them, the path to eternity. If so, then the possibility of a separation must be sustained on the certainty of a connection; then the world-day of the Lord must already bear within itself the predisposition to eternity's day of God. For God, redemption provides this assurance of eternity despite the temporality of self-revelation. Redemption connects creation with revelation; it is not only the assurance of eternity but also itself the fulfilling realization of eternity and thus, for God, his world-day becomes, without more ado, his own day. But this direct equivalence of assurance and fulfillment of eternity is not valid for the other "elements"; it is this, indeed, which makes them the "others" and God the One. It is, in fact, the real reason that, for us, God is "above" in the hierarchy, and world and man are eternally subordinated to him in rank.

THE ETERNAL IN MAN

Man's eternity is implanted in the soil of creation. Being loved and loving are the two moments of his life, separate before God, yet united in man, and creation would be the And between them. Being loved comes to man from God, loving turns toward the world. How else could they count as one for him? How else could he be conscious of loving God by loving his neighbor if he did not know from the first and the innermost that the neighbor is God's creature and that his love of neighbor is love of the creatures. And how could he be conscious of being loved by God other than as the equal of him whom he himself loves in the neighbor; how else than because God has created in his image that which is common to him and his neighbor, namely the fact that the latter is "like him" so that both "are men." He is the creature of God and the image of God, and this is the foundation, laid down from creation, on which he can build the house of his eternal life in the temporal cross-currents of love of God and love of neighbor.

THE ETERNALIZATION OF THE WORLD

For the world, mere existence and living growth are two very different things. It is world only in both combined, the former supplying it with the flesh of phenomena, the latter with the skeleton of duration. For the sake of the former, the created world confidently turns its face toward divine providence; for the sake of the other, life looks expectantly toward man, who alone is capable of "endowing it with duration." Thus the world appears to direct its glance now to this now to that side, now to seek refuge in the eternal arms of the Creator, now to expect everything from the earthy lord of creation. The world, that is—and together with it man himself insofar as he too is inhabitant and citizen of the world. Confidence in the divine Creator seems in eternal contradiction to the expectation of human action, as nature is to civilization. The world appears fated to remain in this eternal contradiction. But is it? We know that, for the world, the contradiction will vanish in the eternity of the day of the Lord, in the redemptive advent of the kingdom. Thus it is not an eternal contradiction. But how is this identification of human act and divine labor to take place unless the human act itself also derives, as act, from God, and unless God's creative labor augments and fulfills itself in awakening man? Thus God's revelation to man is the pawn given to the world for its redemption. It is the basis for the world's certainty that its doubts will one day be resolved—and all doubt is a hesitation between the confidence in creation and the expectation of action, and the dichotomy of this hesitation nourishes the world. For the world, revelation is the guarantee of its integration into eternity.

THE TENSES IN ETERNITY

Thus it would seem that, for the world, its Being-in-the-Light is embedded into the interval "between" revelation and redemption, that for man it occupies the entire interval between creation and redemption, and that only God himself lives alone in redemption in his pure light. Or in other words: God lives his pure life only in eternity, the world is at home in all time, but man was always the same. All history is but prehistory, and for man there is not prehistory: the sun of Homer shines for us too. The miraculous gift of speech was created for man and upon man at creation. Man did not make speech for himself, nor did it come to be for him gradually; at the instant of becoming man, man opened his mouth; at the instant of opening his mouth, he became a human being. For the world, however, and thus also for man as its citizen, there is history. While man was created to be a superman, the world only becomes superworld in the revelation of God to man. And before this revelation enters an orbit of the world, this orbit is subject to the law of development which lets it mature for superworldliness. Thus everything worldly has, at all times, its history: law and the state, art and science, all that is visible. The reveille sounds for God's revelation to man, its echo reverberates into such an It of the world, and only then does a segment of temporality die the resurrective death of eternity. Speech, however, is human, not worldly;

therefore it neither dies nor, admittedly, is it resurrected. In eternity there is silence. God himself, however, plants the sapling of his own eternity neither into the beginning of time nor into its middle, but utterly beyond time into eternity. For him there is nothing between broadcasting the seed and ripening of the fruit. In his eternity both are as one. His redeemedness transcends all worlds as completely as his createdness-from-of-yore preceded all time. Man's createdness-from-of-yore preceded only the fact that revelation became his, and thus it was still in the midst of time; the world's createdness-from-of-yore will only be wholly taken from it in the consummate redemption, that is on the outermost limit of time; but God's createdness-from-of-yore already existed before he resolved on his creative act. We have dealt with this arch-createdness of the three "elements" in the first Part. Similarly, the second Part dealt with their self-manifestation. That is why there was, in the book on creation, less talk of the Creator than of the world, sheltered in providence and renewed each morn within it, in the book on revelation more about God's love than man's being loved, in that on redemption more about man's act of love toward his neighbor than about the growing life of the world. We descended into the primordially created protocosmos, and ascended through the manifest world, and if we now seek the prospect on the redeemed hypercosmos, we know what view awaits us there. Man born of woman we will see there wholly redeemed out of his every peculiarity and selfishness into created image of God; the world, the world of flesh and blood and wood and stone, we will see wholly redeemed out of all materiality into pure soul; and God we will see redeemed from all the work of the six days' labor and from all loving distress about our miserable soul, as the Lord.

Such a view, however, would be more than miracle. It would
require no further prophecy, and wherever it may be
vouchsafed to us, there we ourselves walk in the
light. The mysteries of the protocosmos sink
back into the night, the symbols of the surrounding world lose their brilliance, the
rays of the hypercosmos absorb the
dark shadows of the mystery as well
as the colorful lights of the symbol into themselves. We step
upward across the threshhold
of the hypercosmos, the
threshold from miracle
to enlightenment.

PART

III

THE CONFIGURATION
or
THE ETERNAL
HYPER-COSMOS

INTRODUCTION

On the Possibility of Entreating the Kingdom

In tyrannos!

Concerning Temptation

That God could be tempted is perhaps the most absurd of all the many absurd assertations which belief has set in the world. Before God the Creator, on the authority of this same belief, whole nations are as a drop in a bucket, and yet man—again in the words of this belief— that maggot, and the son of man, that worm, is supposed to be able to tempt him! And even if it were not so much the almighty Creator who was thought of in this connection, but rather the Revealer—how could one conceive, even of him, if he is otherwise really the God of love, that man could tempt him. Would not this God then need to be constricted in his love, and bound to that which man does? Could he then, as belief itself again after all implies, be boundlessly free, following only the compulsion of his own love? Or is it, finally, the Redeemer whom man is supposedly able to tempt? Him, I daresay, if anyone. For vis-à-vis the Redeemer, man has, after all, really one freedom which, in the conception of belief, he does not possess as creature and child of God, namely the freedom to act, or at the very least the freedom to decide: the prayer. Precisely in prayer, however, Jew and Christian alike ceaselessly repeat: Lead us not into temptation! Thus on the contrary it is precisely God who is there accused of a twofold denial of his providence as well as his paternal love. He him- self is now supposed to be the one whom one believes capable of permitting himself the outrageous game of "tempting" his child and creature. If then prayer were really the opportunity to tempt God, then at best this opportunity would be considerably limited to the suppliant by the ever-present fear that, while he believes himself the tempter, he himself is perhaps already being tempted. Or did that possibility of tempting God perchance rest on the fact that God tempts man? Or again, is that possibility—*nota bene*: the possibility—a manifestation of the freedom which man has, at least vis-à-vis God the Redeemer if not the Creator and the Revealer? For though he is created without his will and revelation is his without his deserts, yet God will not redeem him "without him." If then this freedom of prayer shows itself in the possibility of tempting God, is man's temptation by God perchance the necessary presupposition of this his freedom?

It is. A rabbinic legend spins a tale of a river in a distant land, a river so pious that it supposedly halted its flow on the Sabbath. If but this river flowed through Frankfort instead of the Main River—no doubt all Jewry there would strictly observe the Sabbath. But God does not deal in such signs. Apparently he dreads the inevitable consequence: that in that case precisely those least free, those most fearful and miserable, would become the most "pious." Evidently God wants for his own only those who are free. But the mere invisibility of God's sway hardly suffices for thus distinguishing between the free and the enslaved spirits. For the fearful ones are fearful enough to take, in case of doubt, that side adherence to which can "in any case" do no harm and can possibly—with 50 per cent probability—even help. In order to segregate the spirits, God must not alone not help, he must actually harm. And so there remains nothing for him but to tempt man. Not only must he hide his sway from man: he must deceive him about it. He must make it difficult, yea impossible, for man to see it, so that the latter have the possibility of believing him and trusting him in truth, that is to say in freedom. And man, on the other hand, must reckon with the possibility that God is only "tempting" him, so as to have at least the impulse to preserve his trust against all temptations, and not to listen to the perpetual voice of Job's wife which urges him: "curse God and die!"

Thus man must know that he is tempted from time to time for the sake of his freedom. He must learn to believe in his freedom. He must believe that his freedom, limited though it may be everywhere else, is limitless vis-à-vis God. The very commandments of God, 'graven on stone tablets,' must be for him, as in an untranslatable rabbinic play on words, "freedom on tablets." Everything, it says in the same source, everything is in God's hands except for one thing: the fear of God. And how can this freedom show itself more audaciously than in the certainty of being able to tempt God? In prayer, then, the possibilities of temptation really do converge from both sides, from God's side as well as man's. Prayer is strung between these two possibilities; while fearing God's temptation, it nevertheless knows itself capable of itself tempting God.

The Coercion of the Kingdom

But what about this power of prayer? Does man really have God in his power? Can he, in prayer, restrain God's outstretched arm? Can he impose his law on the love of the Revealer? He can hardly do so directly. Otherwise the Creator would be no creator, the Revealer no revealer. But in another sense it could happen: insofar as the work of the Creator and the act of the Revealer find one another in redemption. There it is indeed conceivable that man intervene forcibly in the sway of divine might and love. For redemption is, in fact, not directly God's work or deed. Rather, God in his love freed the soul for the freedom of the act of love, just as he gave creation the power to grow vitally within itself.

ACT AND PRAYER

It is not, however, that freedom of the act of love itself which may intervene in God's sway, for that is itself willed by God; love of neighbor is divinely ordained. Rather, the possibility of tempting God is really first contained in the relationship of the act of love to that alternating life of the world, and nowhere else before this. And this relationship is produced by prayer, even the prayer of the lonely heart from out the need of the lonely moment. For the act of love as such is still blind; it does not know what it is doing, nor is it supposed to know. It is quicker than knowledge. It does the nighest, and what it does it takes to be the nighest. But prayer is not blind. Into the light of the divine countenance it puts the moment, including the act first performed and the will just resolved which constitute the nighest past and nighest future of this one lonely moment. It is an appeal for enlightenment. Enlighten my eyes—they are blind as long as the hands are at work. Not the searching eye locates neighbor and nighest; the groping hand discovers him as he stands directly in front of it. Love acts as though there were, at bottom, no God, nay not even a world. For love, the neighbor represents all the world and thus distorts the eye's view. Prayer, however, pleads for enlightenment and thereby, without overlooking the neighbor, sees beyond the neighbor, sees the

whole world to the extent that it is illuminated for it. Thus it frees
love from its bondage to the tactile sense of the hand. It teaches love
to seek its nighest with its eyes. What seemed to it hitherto inexorably
nighest, may now be removed far away from it; and what was quite
unknown appears suddenly nigh. Prayer establishes the human world
order.

HUMAN AND DIVINE WORLD ORDER

The human world order—but the divine one too? Apparently God
himself, by giving himself to many humans though creating but one
world, laid the basis for the fact that the two orders cannot simply
be one. Vis-à-vis the one order of growing life, there are many orders,
each one beginning from the 'Here-I-stand' of the individual, God-
awakened soul. The very fact that there are many human orders
means that they cannot simply be equated with the one divine order. To
that end, they would first have to be unified among themselves. And
this they are not as long as each of the many still goes back to the
solitary prayer of a single solitary soul. True, this prayer of the lonely
one is integrated into the prayer of the many for the advent of the
kingdom. But the solitary man remains no less in solitude for all that.
His own 'Here-I-stand' remains, for him, the basis of his 'Can-do-no-
other,' and he can only pray that God help him; he himself cannot
free himself from the individualness of his viewpoint, nor his prayer
from the compulsion to establish his own world order.

But what is so dangerous about this? Even if prayer, by opening
a window on the world for the suppliant, shows it to him in a distinctive system, does that then have any consequences whatever for
this one divine world-order itself? Can prayer possibly have the power
to intervene tyrannically in the course of the world as this proceeds
from its divine origin at creation? If prayer in essence is no more
than prayer for enlightenment, if enlightenment is, consequently, the
most that can accrue to the suppliant through the power of prayer,
how then is prayer to be able to intervene in the course of events?
Enlightenment, after all, appears to accrue only to the suppliant; his
are the eyes that are enlightened. Of what concern is that to the
world?

ACT OF LOVE AND PURPOSIVE ACT

True, enlightenment need be of no concern to the world. It has
no direct effect. What is absolutely effective is not enlightenment,

but love. Love cannot be other than effective. There is no act of neighborly love that falls into the void. Just because the act is performed blindly, it must appear somewhere as effect—somewhere, and there is no telling where. If it were performed with open eyes, like the purposive act, then indeed it would be possible for it to vanish without a trace. For the purposive act does not enter the world broad and open, off guard and unpremeditated. Rather it points toward a specific, sighted goal; it takes in as well the way to this goal and must, purposive as it is, take this way into account. Thereby it seeks, along with pointing for its goal, also to cover the long flanks left open by this pointing against all possible diversionary or disturbing influences which it must anticipate along the way. Thus it becomes a pointed act, guarded and premeditated. If it attains its goal at all, it merges with its success. Its further fate is therefore dependent on the fate of whatever it succeeded in. If that dies, the purposive act dies with it. The more purely and perfectly purposive the act, the more guardedly it pursued the way to its goal; thus it really remained itself unseen as act. And the more purely purposive, the more surely it reached its goal without having had any unintended effects along the way.

Quite different, then, is the act of love. It is very unlikely really to reach the object toward which it was running. It was, after all, blind. Only the sense of touching the nighest had provided it with knowledge of the object. It does not know where best to penetrate the object. It does not know the way. Seeking it thus blindly, unguarded, unpointed—what is more likely than that it should lose its way, than that it should never get to see the object for which it was originally intended? Granted that it arrives somewhere, indeed at more than a single Anywhere in consequence of its broadside diffusion.

Perhaps it is not too much to say that all the actual effects of love are side-effects. In any case, it never remains entirely without such, whereas the purposive act may be free of them; at least it always strives for such freedom. For every object is so completely interconnected with others and ultimately with the infinity of objects that it is quite impossible for an act, on its way to one object, not also to affect at least some other objects—unless, of course, it veritably prevents this by taking the shortest and most secret way, precisely like the purposive act. Some, most even of these objects which have been affected by it, may yet have to pay the toll of mortality because they were not yet ready for the inspiriting effect of love. Yet, because of the unbroken interconnection of all objects, the effect will somehow benefit even that object which is momentarily the "nighest," be that the one which the blindly groping sense had to take for its nighest, be it some other. And this object is then truly nighest ripe to receive soul. For this truly nighest one, everything depends on love really finding it, for in the growing life of the world he has been carried to just that point in time which is his time. And this nighest is really always found. Only in one case could he fail to be found: if love, instead of pouring blindly from man step by step, led only by feeling, were to seek to reach an object shown to it in sudden enlightenment with a single leap. For the leap leaps over. And if that whose time had just come happened to lie within the span leaped over, then indeed it would be a case of an act of love losing itself in the void. For the reckless act of love can never go back, as it can never look back, the way it came. And this is the danger inherent in prayer.

THE NIGHEST AND THE FARTHEST

For prayer, if it enlightens, shows the farthest goal to the eye. But the suppliant is fixed to the fixed point of his personality. Thus this farthest goal which is common to all appears behind the foreground of a wholly personal perspective, the perspective, that is, of this fixed point. The nearness of the nighest is sensed, the distance of the farthest is sighted, and the immediacy with which the latter is now experienced instead of the former—for it appears not to the eye torn open by the longing will of purpose, but to the eye enlightened in the receptivity of prayer—this immediacy, it is true, permits love to direct itself immediately toward that object, an object as near to its enlightened eye as the nighest is to the feeling heart. But at the same time the enlightenment illuminates the way which, in contrast to the universality of the goal, is its personal way. Thus love now directs itself in the first instance to the stations of this way. And these stations once sighted, it now hurries toward them, as quickly as possible, dreading every delay, indeed equating delay with every danger. It now leaps over the next-of-feeling, whose place is taken by the station which is recognized in the enlightenment as the first on the way to the farthest, and which love would like to leap toward. For love, the next is replaced by the next-but-one. The next-but-one displaces the next for love. Love shuts its eyes and ears to the one in order to attain the other in powerful-overpowering leaps and bounds, and it must succeed, since it is love and thus always effective.

THE MAGIC OF PRAYER

And thus prayer, though it has no magic powers as such, nevertheless, by lighting the way for love, arrives at possibilities of magic

effects. It can intervene in the divine system of the world. It can provide love with direction toward something not yet ready for love, not
yet ripe for endowment with soul. It conjures up what is distant, and
thereby it can be blamed for man's forgetting, yea denying his nighest,
at least insofar as it is his own nighest and no one else's, so that he, at
least, no longer finds his way back to his nighest. Since the prayer for
the advent of the kingdom is the prayer of the individual, it incurs the
danger of preferring the next-but-one to the next. But such preference
is in reality pre-ference, the ferrying forth of the fitfully ferreted out
forthcoming future, ere this future has become next-present moment
and as such ripe for eternalization. Thus the prayer of the individual,
precisely when it is fulfilled, when, therefore, it enlightens the suppliant, is always in danger of—tempting God.

TYRANTS OF THE KINGDOM OF HEAVEN
   Thus the possibility of tempting God does not contradict the divine
order. It would do so only if man really had the power, not only to
love his next-but-one, but thereby also to make him eternal. Such,
however, is not the case. True, the man enlightened in prayer would
like to adduce the kingdom of heaven forcibly, before its appointed
time. But the kingdom of heaven will not be coerced: it grows. And
thus the magic power of the individual suppliant falls into the void if
it strays beyond the nighest. The next-but-one to which it sought to
vault does not absorb it. Thus it finds neither a base in him nor a way
back from him, and therefore it is also denied the way forward. For
to spread further forward, it would first have to feel some ground
under its feet once more. This is the unfortunate aspect of love for
the next-but-one: although it effects an authentic act of love, it
nevertheless comes to nought in the attained goal just like the purposive act. The violence of its claim wreaks revenge on it itself. The
fanatic, the sectarian, in short all the tyrants of the kingdom of heaven,
far from hastening the advent of the kingdom, only delay it. They
leave their nighest unloved, and long for the next-but-one and thereby
exclude themselves from the host of those who advance along a broad
front, covering the face of the earth bit by bit, each of them conquering, occupying, inspiring his nighest. To anticipate, personally to
pre-fer the next-but-one is no pioneering service to those who follow
after, for it remains ineffectual. The ground prematurely cultivated by
the fanatic yields no fruit. It does that only when its time has come.
And its time too, will come. But then all the work of cultivation will
have to be undertaken afresh. The first seeding has by then rotted,

and to assert that these rotten remnants are "already" or "in reality" the same as that which later ripens into fruit is but the wilful foolishness of pedants. Time and the hour are the mightier the less man knows them.

The Appropriate Time

GOD'S TIME

Time and the hour—only before God they are powerless, since for him redemption is truly as old as creation and revelation. For him, moreover, redemption is self-redemption: he is not only Redeemer but also redeemed. For both these reasons, any conception of a development in time such as mystical impertinence or disbelieving arrogance may impute to him, bounces off his eternity. It is not for himself that he himself needs time, it is he as Redeemer of world and man, and not because he needs it but because world and man need it. For the future is not, for God, anticipation. He is eternal, he alone is eternal, he is the Eternal per se. In his mouth, "I am" is like "I shall be" and finds explanation in it.

EARTHLY TIME

For man and the world, however, life is not eternal by nature. They live in the mere moment or in the broad present. For them the future can be grasped only by being pre-ferred into the present as it comes forth, fitfully ferried forward. Thus permanence becomes of highest importance to them, for the future, by being anticipated into the moment, is constantly in friction with it. For prayer, accordingly, everything comes down to this in the final analysis: is the future of the kingdom accelerated by it or delayed? Let us put it more precisely. Both acceleration and delay count only in the eyes of man and the world, not for God. Man and the world do not measure time by a scale beyond or above them, but by each other. That is, man measures time by the growth of the world as this ripens toward him, the world measures time by the wealth of love poured into its lap. Into the darkness of the future, prayer casts a beam of light which reaches the farthest corners with its last offshoots, while it illuminates the nearest point for the suppliant at the place of its first impact. What matters for prayer is whether, at this point, that beam hurries ahead of love, stays behind it, or keeps pace with it. Prayer is fulfilled only in the last case; only then does it take place in the "desirable time," the "time of grace." Now we begin to understand this peculiar expression. In it, belief vitalizes an idea which pagan piety already possessed but only in lifeless recognition: the gods may be entreated only for what they are inclined to vouchsafe; in the event that one requests what is "improper," one must, of one's own accord, pray in advance for non-fulfillment.

THE SINNER'S PRAYER

Above this empty idea of the "proper" content of prayer, belief elevates the idea of the appropriate time. There is no improper content of prayer as such. The egotistical prayer on behalf of one's personal advantage appears to be crudely improper content; for the pious pagan it would be an abomination to pray it. Yet this is not improper by reason of its content. God wants man to have what is his own. He does not begrudge him that which he needs in order to live, or even that which he believes he needs in life, nay whatever he may be able to wish for. God begrudges him none of this, and therefore gives it all to him, nay he has already given it to him ere ever he could pray for it. There is no sinful plea on the basis of content. By creating the suppliant as individual, God has already fulfilled his prayer before it is uttered, even as criminal a prayer, say, as that for the death of another: it is after all true already without any prayer that the other must die. For only Others can die; man dies only as an Other, as a He. The I cannot conceive of itself as dead. Its fear of death is the horror of becoming the only thing which its eyes can see in the deceased Others: a deceased He, a deceased It. Man does not fear his own death. Awakened in revelation, bound as it is to conceptualize according to the forms of creation, the I can simply not conceive its own death; what it fears is its own corpse. As often as he sees a dead man, a breath of fear blows over the living, and this breath comes over the living man whenever he conceives of himself as a dead man, for strictly speaking one can never conceive of "oneself" as a dead man but only of "Another." Oneself thus out-lives the other, every other, regardless. For the other, every other, is dead simply by being another, from eternity on.[1] He was created as another, and as created being he becomes completed creature in death; as created being he is not destined, in the final analysis, to out-live any other. For life is not the apex of creation. Its destiny is to out-die itself. Not life but death

[1] Taking "world" in its biblical sense of "eternity." (Tr.)

perfects the created thing into individual solitary thing. Death endows it with the supreme solitude of which, as thing among things, it is capable. Thus the prayer for the death of another demands that the other remain into eternity what he already is by virtue of the world: created thing, Other. But oneself would like to be Self, awakened to a life of one's own, the survivor *par excellence*, the survivor of all that is eternally "Other." An eternal dividing wall is to remain in force between the I and all others. The bridge which leads from the I to the He, from revelation to creation, is inscribed: Love your Other, he is no Other, no He, he is an I like Thee, "he is like thee." The I that prays for the death of the other refuses to set foot on this bridge. It wants to remain wholly in revelation and leave creation to the "others," just like the mystic whose secret sin is freely spoken by the honest sinner, the criminal. Thus redemption is denied by the sinner, the patent criminal as well as the secretive mystic. For what is redemption other than that the I learns to say Thou to the He?

Thus the prayer for the death of the Other is fulfilled prior to any praying for, from eternity on, man is already on his own. Thus it is not the content of the request which is sinful, since as creation itself shows, it is not at all counter to God's will. What is sinful in the prayer is that man, rather than treating this content as already fulfilled and therefore thanking God for his own-being which is conditioned by the human, the creaturely otherwiseness of all the others, instead requests it and thus treats it as something as yet unfulfilled. For thereby he prays at the improper time. He should have requested it before his creation; once created, he can only thank for his Own. If nevertheless he requests it, he misses the period of grace for entreating that which he currently needs to pray for. If he requests the "own" which was already vouchsafed to him in creation and revelation, he misses the moment at which he should be requesting his "nighest." The beam of the searchlight struck its object too nearby, that is, still within the circumference of the Own, instead of hitting what is no longer Own for the self but only "like" its Own, "like" itself—the nighest.

THE FANATIC'S PRAYER

This is what happens when prayer falls behind love, when, in other words, the sinner within us prays. Thus the prayer of the sinner delays the advent of the kingdom. By remaining in the sphere of the Own, it excludes itself from the wealth of love which is awaited and needed by the moment of the desirable time. In the prayer of the fanatic, we see the opposite. He longs to accelerate the advent of the kingdom, to have it come before its time. He seeks to capture the kingdom forcibly at the point which the searchlight of his prayer shows him as the next one but which never is closer than next-but-one. His prayer and his love wither for him and so in the end he himself has also withdrawn from the moment, full of grace, which awaited his deed like everyone else's. He has delayed the advent of the kingdom which he wanted to accelerate. Thus only the prayer which is offered at the proper time will not delay the advent of the kingdom of heaven. But how is this prayer offered? And is there only a not-delaying? Is the fanatic entirely wrong? Is there only the possibility of not delaying, none of accelerating the advent of the kingdom? Is his prayer merely a tempting of divine impatience, to use the terms of the Kabbala, as the sinner's prayer tempts divine patience? When our lips pray, is there no one in our hearts other than the sinner and the fanatic? Are there no other voices praying within us?

The Life of Goethe

THE SUPPLIANT

"Labor of my hands that I/finish, grant, oh Fortune high!"[1] At first sight this prayer of the young Goethe hardly seems distinguishable from the 'prayer of Moses, the man of God': 'yea, prosper the work of our hands.' And yet it is different, as different as the last two forms of prayer that we will now find. The prayer of Goethe, the man of life, is directed to his own elation. He lays the work of his own hands at the feet of his good fortune and asks that he be permitted to complete it himself. This is the prayer which this great suppliant repeated in ever new formulations for years and decades until he attained a great and visible fulfillment. What of this prayer of man to his own fate? Who is this fate before whom he humbly bows his free head, before whom his heart bends the knee?

PERSONAL FATE

It would be an inadmissable reinterpretation to see in "fate" nothing more than a circumlocution for the divine "hearer of prayer" to whom all flesh comes. No, all flesh does not come to this fate and lay

[1] From "Hoffnung," by J. W. Goethe, p. 153, vol. I of *Goethes Säntliche Werke* in Tempel ed. (Tr.)

the work of its hands before it. Only one solitary individual steps before it, and it hears the prayer of only one solitary individual, only him and none other. It is a fate as personal as the suppliant himself, indeed it is precisely the personal fate of the suppliant. And is this prayer to be fulfilled? Could it be recited at the desirable time? Is it not akin to that prayer which prays for one's own and always comes too late, whose desirable time lies in the moment of the world's becoming and which is nevermore fulfilled because already fulfilled prior to every plea? But no—is it really prayer for its own? Is it not rather praying in its own? This suppliant little cares whether own or alien become the content of his life and love. He is concerned only that whatever comes should merge in his life, that he be privileged to offer up all in the sanctuary of his own fate, own as well as alien, alien as well as own, all. It is for this that he prays. To preserve his own is not at all what he desires. True, he is prepared to lose himself in the current of the outside, to expand his narrow existence here into eternity. And he does so. But in this desire he feels himself servant to his own destiny. And even if he is prepared to raze the fortifications of his own person, he does not believe himself able or permitted to leave the holy precinct of his own fate. Thus we ask once more: how is it with the personal fate?

MICROCOSM

Man is an impartible part of the multipartite world. The world grows throughout its ages. It has its own fate. Man's fate is a part in this fate. But it is not absorbed by it, nor dissolved in it. Though it is a part, it is impartible. Man is the microcosm. The fate of the world matures in the ages of its growth, and within it, man's fate therefore resembles a particular moment in the current of time; one cannot interchange it, relocate it, dissolve it in the totality of the current. It is a part of this totality, but an indissoluble, an indivisible one. It resembles a moment in the ages of the world or, more explicitly perhaps, an hour. For this fate is full of manifold content. The full hour, the hour which the clock has struck, is after all that time which man himself inserts into the sequence of the heavenly signs, like something stationary, as vessel of his own coherent experience. Its mimimal element, something not yet his own but still to be made his own, is no more than the moment. This hour of his own in the growing ages of the world, this hour which has tolled for him, that it is which is seized upon by the man who prays to his own fate. And, that being so, this prayer is always fulfilled. Even as it is prayed, it insinuates itself into the face of the world; it never misses its mark, is never too late nor too early. It is a prayer to the personal fate, not to an alien one; thus it occurs in the personal hour and simply cannot occur in an alien one. Accordingly it is ever in the desirable time, the 'time of grace,' and is fulfilled as fast as it is prayed. It is fulfilled from the side of the world;[1] in it, man enters his own fate, and thus it constitutes at the same time the confident entrance of man into that which has been from eternity, into creation.

THE ONLY CHRISTIAN

This is a great moment in human history: for the first time man thus lifts his hands in prayer to his own fate. The great moment erupted in the man Goethe; he confronted it not without feeling. He knew it, and he expressed it as an old man in an overly audacious dictum which nevertheless saw to the very bottom when he claimed to be, in his time, perhaps the only remaining Christian as Christ himself would have had a Christian be. What is the meaning of this dictum which borders on blasphemous madness? For by designating himself as "perhaps" the only one in his time, "though you may take me for a pagan," he gives himself a unique position in the history of Christianity, beyond all possibility of cognition and comprehension. After all, to be a Christian means, not to have adopted certain dogmas, but to have placed one's life under the dominion of another life, the life of Christ and, thereafter, to live one's own life only as an expression of the power derived thence. Thus if Goethe designates himself as perhaps the only Christian of his time, this can only mean that the entire power deriving from Christ is supposed to be gathered, "at present," in him, and that it is somehow bound to him and his apparent paganism in all its living flow. For the presupposition that the life of Christ is unique in the world, that its effects can derive only out of it and therefore from it, in one single uninterrupted flow, in all their unconscious vitality—apart from the unimportant conscious assurances of individuals—this presupposition is the only thing whereby submission under this life in a certain sense leads inexorably to dogmatic inferences after all. And in this sense the life of Christ would admittedly be a, or rather the, dogma of Christianity. And indeed, the life of Christ really constitutes the sole content of the dogma in its classical form, the doctrine of the trinity. It is conceptualized backward in its uniqueness in the created world, forward in its uninterrupted power

---

[1] *i.e.*, from eternity. (Tr.)

for continued effectiveness among a mankind that is to be redeemed. What then is it that, in the face of all this, the dictum of Goethe means to imply with its peculiar intertwining of his "paganism" and the imitation of Christ?

The Imitation of Christ

THE CLASSICAL WORLD

If the Christian wished to live his life equally unconditionally, equally tied to the fate of the whole world, then the imitation of Christ should have meant, to begin with, that he first create the external possibility for such a life. For while Christianity emerged into the world with a will to such a life, it discovered at once that the opposite law of life was enthroned in it. True, it did not emerge into a world fragmented into peoples, tribes, cities, a world whose parts, as parts, already led each its own life, self-conditioned and alienated from the world; that would have been the case a few centuries earlier and again a few centuries later. Instead the world was united under the scepter of Caesar, at least the Western world, and this was after all the only one to which the apostles of Christianity ventured forth. But in this unity it offered Christianity a soil that was only apparently and externally favorable. For its unity was not the unity of one world; the boundaries of the Imperium did not, for all its boastful self-deception, encompass the oecumene, the inhabited world. Nor was its failure to do so simply a matter of being unequal to its own intentions, stubbornly maintained. Rather, the idea of limitation to the existing possessions had been built into the cornerstone of this constitution by its architect, the Emperor Augustus. Only rounding off the borders for the sake of security was to be permitted. The Roman eagles were borne beyond the frontiers only to rob the surrounding peoples of their appetite for aggression. Like the great empire of the Far East which similarly equated itself naively with the world, this Mediterranean empire insured its existence versus the rest of the earth—which it forebore to conquer—by moat and rampart bisecting the continents.

Thus the empire as a whole shirked its responsibility for the fate of the world. And just so too, the fate of the individual within it was only very superficially tied to the fate of the whole. The history of its capital city is far from identical with that of the provinces, and just so too, the life of the individual is barely touched by the life of the totality. As end result of an imperial history of several centuries there remained the codification of civil law, and this is no coincidence: the Roman citizen suffered as little from the state as he affected it. The only thing that came to him from the whole was the delimitation and protection of his private legal sphere, a fence, as it were, which closed off each against every other as the great *limes* closed the empire off against the world. Into this mirror-image, this pseudo-portrait of a world empire, the Christians now placed its complete counterpart. Externally dependent on its structure, it survived the collapse occurring under the pressure of that world of peoples which moat and rampart had excluded in vain, and has survived it to this day: the Church of Rome.

THE PETRINE CHURCH

The envoys of the successors of Peter have crossed the *limes*: they have gone forth and taught all the nations. The Church no longer imposes any external limits on itself, as the Empire did; on principle it acquiesces in no border; it knows no forbearance. It draws its protective cloak about the fate of all the world on the outside, and just so too, none may remain isolated within its lap. It demands of each directly the sacrifice of his Self, but it generously deigns to restore it to each directly in its mothering love. Each and every one is a child precious and irreplaceable, an only child despite all the others. Through the Church then, the life of the individual depends directly on the life of all the world. The bond that ties him, as it does the mother Church itself, to the fate of the world is love. The expansion of the externally visible structure, the enlargement of the external borders takes place in the love of the missionary for those still dwelling in darkness. Inside the Church, too, it is love which unites man with it, and thereby with the whole, through the visible sacrifice of the pious work, through the visible offering of physical or spiritual charity. Thus the Petrine Church creates a visible body, initially for itself and for those who are its members and to the extent that they are its members, but beyond this also for the outside world. It penetrates this world structurally and administratively, step by step, in the unity of the empire above the kingdoms of the nations. In the superstructure of classes and professions above the individuals it eventually assimilates even the individual man to and thereby also into itself, to the extent that he still is and remains on the outside. Therewith it would seem that the condition for the possibility of a Christian life has been fulfilled. What more can be needed? Whatever he may do, man is [now] fused into the whole of the world, the fate of his act indissolubly tied up with the fate of all the world. Yea, the fate of his act—not, however, the fate of his thought.

THE MEDIEVAL WORLD OF DUAL TRUTH

True, the Church of Rome had been able to penetrate the physical world of the living peoples and to assert itself in successful counter-attack against the aggressive paganism of the Crescent; here it really created a new world of its own. Nevertheless it remained limited to defensive action against inner paganism, more precisely the internalized paganism, the pagan idea in the form of memory. Taking the offensive, the Church had overpowered the pagan idea, but only at the very beginning, up to the end of Patristics, just so long, that is, as the idea was still a living expression and not yet solely a memory. Augustine, audacious as only a victor can be, played fast and loose with the wisdom of the Hellenes, but no medieval Scholastic dared to do this. Love had the power to wrestle with pagan philosophers, but its weapons were useless against pagan philosophy. When the authorities became Christian, and closed the philosophers' schools in Athens, it meant the end of ecclesiastical antiquity and the beginning of the ecclesiastical Middle Ages or, to put in another way, the end of Patristics and the beginning of Scholasticism. For henceforth pagan antiquity became, for the Church, an adversary at once uncannily elusive and most color-fully visible, almost like a mural; the power of action—and that is what the power of love is—does not suffice to fight this adversary success-fully. How indeed is a picture to be converted by love—lifeless as it is! If it is to be converted, it must first be perceived by a wholly fascinated eye, comprehended by a wholly disconcerted soul. Only the Soul which has thus become a heretic can then be converted to faith. Medieval Scholasticism had draped a veil over the mural, to open or shut at will. For this idea was none other than such a veil—that most questionable of ideas, precisely in the Christian sense, because it interfered with missionary work, the idea of a dual truth, a truth of reason vis-à-vis the truth of faith. The painted figures had first to descend from the wall and to mingle in the Christian populace as living memories of paganism; then and only then could the forces of love grow again for the church as against these memories.

MODERN MAN

But these neo-pagans were, after all, only new pagans, pagans in a world already Christian, internalized memories, that is, in a Christian exterior, pagan souls in a world whose body had been converted to Christianity. Therefore the force that took it upon itself to convert them could no longer be one which, like love, operated only out of the soul and into a corporeal exterior. It had to be a force which acted within the soul itself and upon the soul, an inner action, that is, of the soul upon itself. It had to be a self-conversion of man which disregarded the world in order to gain, instead, the soul and only the soul, the solitary soul, the soul of the individual *sans* all the world.

THE PAULINE CENTURIES

This force overtook the world in the form of the Pauline centuries, a form which, as Church, was invisible by its very principles, being visible only as time, as an epoch of universal history, as *saeculum*. Where the Petrine Church had established a world-wide unity, these centuries saw that unity apparently sundered at every point, saw the pagan figures come back to life everywhere, saw the attempt by the nations to partition Christianity, by the states to divide the Empire, by the individuals to break down classes, by the personalities to burst the profession. In these three centuries—or four with its aftereffects—the Christian world-body seemed to disintegrate again. This was the price paid for the successful Christianization of the soul, for the belated conversion of a pagan spirit never wholly deceased and now reawakened. When the time was up, there was no longer any question of dual truth. Faith had succeeded where love had failed: it had baptized a soul without world, invisible, internalizing its memories. In the Petrine Church the soul had brought its whole presence, the whole outside world of its activity, before God. Even so the soul now brought its whole memory, its entire content before God as an invisible offering, and received it back from him in the invisible gift of faith. Thus the soul too was now freed from all fences and walls and lived in the Unconditional.

MODERN LIFE IN THE SPLIT REALITY

But it was "faith alone" that had led it into this life. It was the soul alone which led this life. The Petrine Church had unmasked the weak point in its all-too corporeal nature through the evil idea of the dual truth. Just so the German Idealistic Movement which followed those three centuries disclosed the weakness of a faith whose nature was far too much merely sentimental or rather: merely spiritual. Spirit deemed itself so completely "alone" as to be able to generate everything out of

itself alone, and out of itself alone everything. Faith had simply forgotten the body in its concern with the spirit. The world had escaped
it. True, it had done away with the doctrine of the dual truth. But
instead it dealt in a dual reality, specifically in the purely inner reality
of faith and in the purely external reality of a world which had become
ever more worldly. The greater the tension between the two, the more
at ease was this Protestantism; in the end it elevated this reciprocal
protest by faith against the world and by the world against faith into
its prize exhibit. In other words, the new Church dispensed with proselytizing. This had once, in point of fact, been the supreme activity of
the old Church, and so it became again now, precisely in reaction to
the new Church. When at last the work of converting the heathens
was taken up by a sect that had sprung from Lutheranism, namely by
Pietism, it was a sign that something new was dawning. It tolled the
death-knell of the old Protestantism.

FUTURE CHRISTIANITY

Still body and soul were separate. Each remained indebted to the
other, the body to the soul for its truth, the soul to the body for its
reality. The whole man was both and more than both. And as long as
the whole man was not converted but only a part of him, just so long
Christendom remained in a preparatory stage; it had not arrived at the
work itself. Man is a microcosm: what is within is also without. Above
body and soul, higher than both and supported by both, there vaults
life, life not as life of the body nor as life of the soul, but as something
in its own right, something that absorbs body and soul into itself, into
its fate. Life is the *curriculum vitae*. The real nature of man is not
exhausted in his corporeal or in his spiritual being; it is complete only
in the whole course of his life. Nor "is" it, in fact, at all; it becomes.
Precisely his fate is that which is most personally man's own. Both
body and soul he somehow still has in common with others: his fate
is all his own. His personal fate is body and soul in one; it is that which
he "experiences in life and limb." And yet, by uniting man in himself,
it at the same time unites him with the world. True, he does not have
it in common with the world, in the way that his body is part of the
created world or his soul co-heir of the divine revelation. But he has
his fate wholly in the world; he is in the world by having it. He grows
into the world by growing into himself. The individual days of his
life acquire meaning by being fused into the whole course of his own
life. His Today completes itself into a Tomorrow and a day after
tomorrow which could just as well be already today. For life can,

after all, end at any moment, but as personal fate it completes itself and is perfected at the moment of an end which, seen from without, is a coincidence. If this relationship of the part to the whole were merely that between the individual hour and the course of life, confined, that is, to life, then this life would as yet be no different from the self of pagan man. But this inner interconnection is the same as that which interconnects human life as a whole with the Whole of world life. It is, in short, fate. And by being experienced as fate, by the recognition of personal fate as something not merely to be undergone but something to which one can pray, there already exists the novel thing which lies beyond mere-body and mere-soul and their indebtedness, one to the other. And therewith a new age has commenced, the final and finite age of Christendom.

Goethe and the Future

THE PRAYER OF UNBELIEF

In the two preparatory ages, pagan man confronts Christianity in person, first as physical, external pagan, later as spiritually remembered, internalized pagan. This time it is otherwise, for now converter and convert are one and the same. Goethe is truly the great heathen and the great Christian at one and the same time. He is the one by being the other. In the prayer to his own fate, man is at one and the same time wholly domiciled within his Self and—by virtue of that very fact —also entirely at home in the world. Henceforth every Christian prays his prayer of unbelief, which nonetheless is at the same time a wholly believing prayer, namely believing in creaturely fashion—even if, as distinguished from Goethe, not as his sole prayer. And henceforth the peoples and all the worldly orders of Christendom also pray this prayer. All of them now realize that their lives must be their own and, precisely as such, integrated into the course of the world; all of them find the justification of their existence in the vitality of their fate. Only now can one speak of Christian peoples, whereas in the Pauline epoch there were only secular authorities and, in the Petrine one, nations subservient to the Holy Empire. Both states and tribes needed to supplement their lives, the former with the faith of the individual and the administration of the word, the latter with the kingdom and the visible Church. Only thus were they able to be fertile soil for the seed of Christianity. Only now the peoples contain within themselves a vitality whole and completing itself, now that every people knows

and believes that it has "its day in history." And should they need,
beyond this, an earthly completion, then they are provided with this
by the earthly, yea all-too-earthly, concept of society.

HOPE

By completing itself, life now remains in itself, nay in its uncom-
pletedness, that is to say in its growth. And so too, now, its sacrifice
and its deserts are no longer distinct for it. The external pagan used to
offer his body and receive love in return; the internalized pagan offered
his spirit in return for faith. But the living pagan, the great pagan sacrifices his life and receives in return none other than this: to be allowed
and able to sacrifice it. But from God's point of view, to be allowed
and able to offer one's life is the gift of trust. For him who trusts and
hopes, there is no sacrifice that would mean a sacrifice to him. For him
it is completely natural to sacrifice; he knows no other way. If love
was quite feminine, and faith very masculine, it is only hope that is
ever childlike; in Christianity the commandment to "be as the children"
begins to be fulfilled only in it. And thus Goethe is "always childlike."
He trusts his fate. He hopes for his own future. He cannot conceive
that "the gods" would not grant him to complete the work of his hands.
As Augustine loves, and Luther believes, so Goethe hopes. And thus
the whole world enters under this new sign. 'The greatest of these'
now becomes hope. Faith and love, the old forces, are integrated into
hope. From the child's sense of hope they derive new strength, so as
to renew their youth 'like the eagles.' It is like the dawn of a new
world day, like a great new beginning, as if nothing had gone before.
Faith which is proved in love, love which carries faith in its lap—both
are now borne aloft on the pinions of hope. For a thousand thousand
years, faith now hopes to have proved itself in love, and love to have
brought true faith into the one-and-universal light of the world. Man
speaks: I hope to believe.

THE JOHANNINE COMPLETION

Hope is given to man only if he has it. While love is presented precisely to the hard heart, and faith to the heretic, God presents hope
only to him who hopes. Consequently hope does not found a new
church. For here it is not a question of a new pagan but only of the
living one who unites for himself the little paganisms of body and soul
into the great paganism of life. And this union, the mere fact of the
pagan's appearance, already implies his conversion. The Johannine

completion has no form of its own; it is, in short, not a bit more but simply the completion of what was hitherto bits and pieces. Thus it will have to live within the old structures. For in this period, a third Christian church with its people entered the orbit of Christendom, the Eastern Church. It is as age-old as the other two; they are only seemingly successive, in fact all are equally old. But it did not come to life for Christianity as a new church. Rather a renewal of the forces of faith and love accrued to the old churches from the Russia of Alyosha Karamazov. And the Russian Church proved to be the soil which nourished a limitless force of hope only for its own people, and even for that only after emerging out of its dusky interior. The integration of the Russians into the Christian orbit was one of the great events of ecclesiastical history. The other was the liberation of the Jews and their admission into the Christian world. And this event, too, did not take the form of a new ecclesiastical structure, but again only a revitalization of the old churches. Here hope, however, the elemental force of the new world of completion, flows directly from the eternal people of hope, divinely childlike by nature, toward the Christian peoples more experienced in love and faith than in hope. And this time, instead of having to convert the heathen, the Christian must directly convert himself, the heathen within himself. Accordingly in this incipient fulfillment of the ages it is rather the Jew, accepted into the Christian world, who must convert the heathen within the Christian. For hope, which love would like to forget and faith believes it can dispense with, lives as a matter of blood-inheritance only in Jewish blood. Even this type of conversion, however, takes place within the existing churches. The Johannine Church itself does not assume a visible form of its own. It is not built: it can only grow. Wherever one attempts to build it nevertheless, as in Freemasonry and all that is related to this, there the entrance is barred to those forces of faith and love which, though they continue to operate vitally within it, can find their daily bread of life only before the altars and pulpits of the old churches. Only hope, which can nourish itself by itself, may enter into the Freemason's new structure dedicated, by a significant confusion, not to the Apostle John but to his pre-Christian namesake. But when it has no other content than itself, hope pales into a limitless, empty self-reflection of a barren and powerless "I hope—even to continue hoping" and, even if it knows that truth lies in God's right hand, it falls humbly into his left hand.

This Johannine church is amorphous and necessarily unestablished and thus always dependent on the established Church. Goethe is the first of its fathers, even though he had to be reckoned—and indeed was—a pagan. All the world now prays after him the prayer to his own fate. In it there is consummated that revival of the dead which is the indispensable precondition of their becoming eternal. The body prays for love: God have mercy upon me, the sinner; the soul prays for faith; how can I find a merciful God? In these prayers, the parts which, in their conjunction, make the 'Part' impartible, each have become alive in their own right.[1] Out of body and soul there is thus created a Whole: man has become an "individuality," and in his prayer for what he already possesses, his own fate, this wholly individual aspect is now also vitalized as such; it incorporates itself in All and yet does not cease to be individual. Where this prayer is recited, there commences that vitality of creaturely life which renders this life directly ripe for the irruption of eternal divine life.

GOETHE AND NIETZSCHE

For by being recited, this prayer renders a piece of life ripe for eternity. It does not already make it eternal itself; it only makes it alive. Goethe in particular remained a pagan all his life. This marks his position as a historical watershed. So he himself expressed it quite ingenuously in that quotation with which we began. No one can imitate him in this except at the risk of his own neck. Goethe's life is truly a hike along the precipice between two abysses; he managed never for a moment of his life to lose the ground of the well-founded, enduring earth from under his feet. Everyone else, unless caught by the arms of divine love and granted flight into eternity, would of necessity have to tumble into one of the two abysses which yawn on each side of that ridge which everyone must nonetheless ascend sooner or later for the sake of the vitality of life. The piety of the prayer to the personal fate borders directly on [that of] the prayer of the sinner, who presumes himself free to entreat everything, and of the fanatic, who thinks that, for the sake of the distant One which the moment of the prayer indicates as essential to him, everything other than this One, everything nighest, must be forbidden to him. Goethe slipped into neither of these two abysses. He made it—"let someone match it if he can!" A votive tablet is erected on the precipice. It illustrates, through the example of Zoroaster's decline and fall, how one can become a sinner and a fanatic in one person, an immoralist who smashes all the old tablets, and a tyrant who overpowers his neighbor as well as himself for the sake of the next-but-one, his friend for the sake of new friends. The tablet furthermore warns every traveller who has as-

---

[1] An allusion to Mephistopheles' "*Ich bin ein Teil des Teils, der einstmal alles war.*" Cf. also above, p. 276. (Tr.)

cended the ridge not to try to retrace Goethe's steps on Goethe's path, like him alone hopefully trusting the tread of his own feet, without the wings of faith or love, a pure son of this earth.

REVOLUTION

Goethe's prayer, the prayer of the nonbeliever, cannot itself protect itself from thus stumbling into the dual falsifications of time, in the too-late of the sinner and the too-soon of the fanatic. True, it grasps the precise moment of the right time, the favorable time, the time of grace. And time begins to be truly fulfilled only since the praying of this prayer. Only now does the kingdom of God really have its advent within time. After all, it is no coincidence that the demands of the kingdom of God begin only now to be genuinely transformed into temporal demands. The great deeds of liberation, as little as they constitute in themselves the kingdom of God, nevertheless are the indispensable preconditions of its advent, and only now are they undertaken. Liberty, equality, and fraternity, the canons of faith, now become the slogans of the age; in blood and tears, in hatred and zeal they fight their way into the apathetic world in unending battles.

MISSIONARY ACTIVITY

As long as the Petrine Church stood by itself, it grew only in space —"unto all the world." The hour of the age could be read only in the growth of the space. Dante found only a few seats still vacant in the assembly of the saints in Paradise, and thought he could conclude from this that the end of the world was nigh. It never occurred to him that it might take longer to fill the few remaining places than all the many that had gone before. Just so the Church was accustomed to measure the growth of the kingdom, as it were, by the map of its missionary activity. As against this projection of time into space, the Pauline Age represents the immersion of time in time itself. Time now, as it were, stood still in every man who believed. Indeed, the Pauline Church simply forgot the spatial expansion of faith which alone could serve as a measure of time: a clock requires a dial for a face. It remained for the Johannine world to create, in the prayer to fate, a truly living time, a self-contained current which, far from being swallowed up by the individual moment, hoists that moment on its back and carries it out to sea, a current which, far from diffusing and disappearing in the expanse of space, rather permeates and irrigates this expanse in a thousand ramifications.

GOETHE'S LIMITATIONS

The temporality of life is consummated in this river of living time. Were life wholly absorbed by its temporality, if, that is, the prayer to fate were its supreme and entire prayer, then the advent of the kingdom would be veritably laid to rest by this prayer which, after all, always hits the right moment and can thus always be certain of fulfillment—would, that is, if it were possible to pray this prayer and this prayer alone; it would neither hasten nor delay that advent. The life of Goethe, this most blissful of human lives, was the brief inimitable moment where it really might have seemed as if creaturely prayer could be prayed all by itself. Seen from this moment, time really appears to stand still. Only a muted echo of bells tolled long ago rises to the surface of life out of the city of God as if from a submerged Atlantis. But temporality is not eternity. Goethe was the most alive of men, but even his life was only temporarily alive, and in this its pure temporality no more than a single moment, to be imitated only at the risk of one's life. That which is temporal requires the eternal for support. True, life must first become wholly temporal or, in other words, time must first become wholly alive, wholly a real current flowing through the broad expanse of space and out beyond the precipice of the moment. Till then, eternity cannot go beyond time. Life, and all life, must first become wholly temporal, wholly alive, before it can become eternal life. The precise temporality of pure life is always at the right point of time; it always comes right on time, not too soon nor too late. An accelerating force must be added to it.

TODAY

In short, eternity must be accelerated. It must always be capable of already coming "today." Only thereby is it eternity. If there is no such force, no such prayer as can accelerate the coming of the kingdom, then it does not come in eternity; rather—it eternally does not come. What prayer is it then which hastens the coming of the kingdom in truth and not just in the feeble prayer of the fanatic which, though tyrannical and coercive, only achieves the opposite of its desire? How, where and when is that prayer prayed which, though the gods may remain silent toward it, yet God must answer: the prayer of him who supplements the nonbeliever's devotion to pure life into a plea for eternal life—the prayer of the believer?

The Proper Prayer

THE PROPER TIME

With all that we now know, this positive acceleration can only occur in one way: the kingdom must be anticipated, and this not alone in the personal enlightenment in which eternity becomes visible but without coming within reach. Some station or other, nigh, next, as nighest, was illuminated in the enlightenment of the fanatic on his personal way to the eternal; he applied all his magic powers of love to the attainment of this apparently nighest though in reality next-but-one; thereby he squandered his powers and instead of mightily accelerating the future he caused its delay. What we are here seeking directly resists such personal coercion of the kingdom of heaven. The prayer of the believer cannot possibly remain stuck in good intentions. If it is the supplement to the prayer of the nonbeliever which it already presupposes and which always comes on time because always at the favorable time of the Creator, and if it is effective only as such a supplementation, then the least that must be demanded of it is that it come neither too soon nor too late.

THE ETERNAL MOMENT

But more is to be demanded of it. It must really attain that which the prayer of the nonbeliever will not and the prayer of the fanatic cannot attain. It must hasten the future, must turn eternity into the nighest, the Today. Such anticipation of the future into the moment would have to be a true conversion of eternity into a Today. What would such a Today look like? Above all it could not perish. For even if we know nothing else about eternity, this much is sure: it is the Imperishable. A Today re-created into eternity must therefore in the first place correspond to this determination by an infinite Now. But an imperishable Today—is it not gone with the wind like every moment? Is it now to be imperishable? There remains but one solution: the moment which we seek must begin again at the very moment that it vanishes; it must recommence in its own disappearance; its perishing must at the same time be a reissuing.

THE HOUR

For this purpose it is not enough that it come ever anew. It must not come anew, it must come back. It really must be the same moment.

The mere inexhaustibility of birth does not make the world the less perishable; on the contrary. Thus this moment must have more of a content than the mere moment. The moment reveals something new to the eye with every batting of an eye. The novelty that we seek must be a *nunc stans*, not a vanishing moment thus, but a "stationary" one. Such a stationary Now is called, in contrast to the moment, hour.[1] Because it is stationary, the hour can already contain within itself the multiplicity of old and new, the fullness of moments. Its end can merge back into its beginning because it has a middle, indeed many middle moments between its beginning and its end. With beginning, middle, and end it can become that which the mere sequence of individual and ever new moments never can: a circle returning in upon itself. In itself it can now be full of moments and yet ever equal to itself again. When an hour is up, there begins not only "a new" hour, much as a new moment relieves the old one. Rather, there begins "again an" hour. This re-commencement, however, would not be possible for the hour if it were merely a sequence of moments—such as it indeed is in its middle. It is possible only because the hour has beginning and end. Only the stroke of the bells establishes the hour, not the ticking of the pendulum. For the hour is wholly a human institution. Creation knows nothing of it and the bells begin to ring the hour only in the world of redemption. Only there does the word for hour[2] begin to free itself from those for time or period of time with which it was previously identical.

THE ORBIT OF THE TIMES

In the hour, then, one moment is recreated, whenever and if ever it were to perish, into something newly issued and thus imperishable, into a *nunc stans*, into eternity. In the hour, instituted by himself, man frees himself from the transitoriness of the moment, and in the image of this hour he now re-creates those times which creation imposed on his life. From being solar and lunar periods, day and year, week and month too now become hours of human life. They too now receive their beginning and their end, and an end at that which immediately becomes a beginning again. The two luminaries, the greater and the lesser, mark time for man not because of the orbits

---

[1] In German: "*Stunde*," etymologically related to "*stehend*," standing, stationary. (Tr.)

[2] German "*Stunde*." Note however that English "hour" preserves the derivative of the generalized word for season (Latin, Greek *hōra*), whence "year" and "yore" also derive. (Tr.)

which they describe in the heavens for, without the fastened point of beginning and end, the orbit alone would be no more than the mere sequence of moments; the repetition which occurs in circling the orbit becomes perceptible only as this point, this feast, is fastened. These times are turned into hours, into guarantors of eternity within time, not by the celestial orbit but by the terrestial repetition. When God laid the first and most universal basis for his covenant with the new generation of mankind, he promised the father of that generation that the alternation of 'seedtime and harvest, cold and heat, summer and winter, day and night' would never cease. This ever new repetition, this is what first makes "hours" of the celestial periods, from the smallest which we can read off from the heavens between waking and sleeping, to the biggest through seedtime and harvest. What is bigger still than the solar year are no longer times which perceptibly determine the constantly repeated alterations of earthly work and human life. In the service of the earth, constantly repeated day in day out and year in year out, man senses his earthly eternity within the human community. In the community—and not as individual, for as individual he senses them rather in the changes of age and in the circuit of conception and birth.

THE WEEK

Between day and year there is placed the week. It is based in heaven through the orbit of the moon, but long since freed from it even where the phases of the moon still determine the calculation of time. It has become a purely human time of its own. The day had its prototype in the alternation of waking and sleeping, the year in that of seedtime and harvest. The week has no such basis in the created world; it is wholly human and consequently Scripture explains it as only an analogy of the work of creation itself. The alternation which makes of the week a *nunc stans* for man is posited as an alternation of workday and restday, of labor and contemplation. Thus the week with its day of rest is the proper symbol of human freedom, and is explained as such in Scripture where it deals, not with its reason, but with its purpose. It is the true "hour" among the times of common human life, established for man alone, freed from the cosmic orbit of the earth, and withal wholly law for the earth and for the changing times of its service. It is meant to regulate the service of the earth, the work of "culture," rhythmically, and thus to mirror, in miniature, the eternal, in which beginning and end come together, by means of the ever repeated present, the imperishable by means of the Today. The week is a law for the cultivation of the earth freely laid down by man and for man; in it the eternal is merely mirrored, merely as earthly eternity. But it is not for nothing that the words for cultivation and cult, for the service of earth and the service of God, for agri-culture and the cultivation of the kingdom are one and the same in the sacred tongue. As law of cultivation laid down by man the week is the earthly analogy of the eternal, but it is more than this: as law of the cult laid down by God it attracts the eternal into the Today, not just by analogy but in reality. It can be the kernel of the cult because it is the first ripe fruit of cultivation. It is the fixation of the fleeting moment, purely human and terrestial, and therefore all eternalization of the moment, divine and super-terrestrial, proceeds from it. By virtue of the week, the day too, and the year too, become human hours, temporal abodes into which the eternal is invited. The cycles of the cultic prayer are repeated every day, every week, every year, and in this repetition faith turns the moment into an "hour," it prepares time to accept eternity, and eternity, by finding acceptance in time, itself becomes—like time.

THE CULT

But does prayer really have the power to force eternity to accept this invitation? Is the cult really more than just the preparation of food and drink, the setting of the table, the dispatch of messengers to bid the guests? Admittedly we realize that eternity can become time in the cult, but how are we to understand that it *must* become time, constrained with the power of magic? The cult too appears merely to build the house in which God may take up residence, but can it really force the exalted guest to move in? Yes it can. For the time which the cult prepares for the visit of eternity is not the time of an individual; it is not mine, nor thine, nor his secret time. It is the time of All. Day, week, and year are the common property of all. They are based on the cosmic orbit of an earth which patiently bears them all, and in the law of the earthly work which is common to all. The bell tolls the hour for every ear. The times which the cult prepares are owned by none to the exclusion of all others. The prayer of the believer takes place in midst of the believing congregation. 'In assemblages' he praises the Lord. The enlightenment which befalls the individual can here be none other than that which can befall all others too. And in this enlightenment, since it is supposed to be common to all, the same thing should be enlightened for all. It is common to all, beyond all individual points of view and beyond differences of perspective conditioned by the differences of these points of view, and so it can be but one thing: the end of all things, the ultimate things. Whatever lies along the way would appear differently to each person according to the place where he was standing; every day has a different content for each person according to the day that he is living. Only the end of days is common to all. The searchlight of prayer illuminates for each only that which it illuminates for all, only the farthest: the kingdom.

THE NIGHNESS OF THE KINGDOM

Everything prior remains in darkness; the kingdom of God is the nighest. The star which otherwise gleams in the distance of eternity here appears as the nighest, and therewith the whole power of love turns toward it and with magical force draws its light through the night of the future into the Today of the praying congregation. The cultic prayer stakes everything on the one plea for the advent of the kingdom; all other pleas, though otherwise nearer at hand, are only incidentally prayed together with and for the sake of this one plea. It shows love that the eternal is the nighest and thus releases the irresistable force of the love of neighbor upon it; thereby it compels the redemptive advent of the eternal into time. God can do no other; he must accept the invitation. The prayer of the believer, because it occurs in the congregation of the believers, complements the prayer of the nonbeliever, which must needs remain the prayer of an individual.

THE UNITED PRAYER

The nonbeliever could at most pray for the favor of his personal fate, for permission to complete the labor of his hands. To his love, his prayer illuminated only what was more-than-nighest, what was personal. The searchlight threw its beam into the orbit of the personal, whose borders, however, expanded from a constricted Here to eternity while in the case of the sinner they remained narrow and rigid. The suppliant learned, in prayer that is, to love the more-than-nighest, his self, not as a secluded, rigid self, but as a personality woven into the fate of the world by its own fate. Were he not to pray for this permission to complete his daily handiwork, his request would, it is true, be granted, for he is only requesting what is ready to be granted to him, and likewise everyone else would be granted his due, but all these individual fulfillments would not add up to eternal fulfillment, nor all this individual life, to eternal life; for all its growth through time, care has been taken lest the tree of life grow into heaven. But the prayer of the congregation is addressed not to the personal fate but directly to the Eternal, that he might prosper the work, not of my hands or thine or his, but of "our" hands, so that He, not "I complete it." This prayer looks beyond everything individual to the Universal and to it alone. With a mighty grip it snatches the eternal into the moment, and endows the individual piece of life, which at this moment has become wholly alive in the nonbelieving prayer, with the spark of eternal life, brought down from on high, which remains within it as the seed of eternal life.

Liturgy and Gesture

Thus the prayer for the advent of the kingdom mediates between revelation and redemption or, more correctly, between creation and revelation on the one hand, and redemption on the other, much as the sign of the miracle mediated between creation and revelation. This relationship within the world of revelation described at the same time also the relationship between the primordially created protocosmos and the manifest world. So too now it describes the relationship between this manifest world, including the protocosmos which was absorbed in it precisely by means of miracle, on the one hand, and the redeemed hypercosmos on the other. Prayer is the force which lifts over the "threshold." From out the mutely created mystery of the self-growth of life and the speech-endowed miracle of love, it leads to the silent enlightenment of the completely fulfilling end. In this third Part, therefore, liturgy will assume a paradigmatic role similar to that of mathematics in the first and grammar in the second. To be sure, the relationship between the paradigm and the Essence to be delineated with its help will have to be different here from what it was in the case of mathematics and grammar. But these two themselves already stood in different relationships to their respective essences.

The mathematical symbols were really nothing but symbols; they were the mystery in the enigma, mute keys which were themselves entrusted for safekeeping to a secret compartment inside this shrine of the primordial world. They were hidden inside and behind the objects, and for this primordially created world they themselves represented something past, the a priori heirlooms of a prior creation. The forms of grammar, on the other hand, express miracle directly. No longer are they relegated to some mysterious background of the world belonging to them. Rather they are wholly at one with this world. Within miracle they are themselves again miracle; they are manifest signs of a manifest world. They are exactly simultaneous with their world. Where there is world, there speech is also. The world is never without the word. Indeed it only exists in the word, and without the word there would be no world. But the structures of liturgy do not possess this same simultaneity with that which is to be recognized in them. Rather, they anticipate. They take something future, and turn it into a Today. Thus they are neither key nor mouthpiece for their world, but representatives. For cognition they respresent the redeemed hyper-cosmos. Cognition takes cognizance only of them. It does not look beyond them. What is eternal, hides behind them. They are the light, by which we see light. They are the silent anticipation of a world gleaming in the silence of the future.

The protocosmos contained only the mute elements of which the course of the Star was built. The course itself was a reality but at no moment to be seen by the eyes. For the Star which runs this course never stands still even for the batting of an eye. Only what endures more than one batting can be seen by the eyes, and only that moment which has been arrested by its eternalization permits the eyes to per-ceive the structure in it. Structure is thus more than elemental, more than real; it is directly subject to perception. Our eyes have not yet seen the Star as long as we know only the elements and law of its course; it remains merely a material point which moves in space. Only after telescope and spectroscope have brought it to us do we know it as we know a tool of our daily use or a painting in our chambers: in familiar perceptions. Factuality is completed only in contemplation; now no more is heard of object or act.

That which can be perceived is superior to speech and exalted above it. Light does not discourse, it shines. It does not by any means seclude itself in itself, for it shines outward, not inward. But in shining out-ward, it does not give itself up, as does speech. Light does not sell itself, it does not give itself away, like speech, when it expresses itself. Rather it is visible by remaining wholly in itself. It does not really shine outward, it only shines forth. It shines, not like a fountain, but like a face, like an eye which is eloquent without the lips having to move. Unlike the muteness of the protocosmos, which had no words yet, here is a silence which no longer has any need of the word. It is the silence of consummate understanding. One glance says everything here. Nothing shows so clearly that the world is unredeemed as the diversity of languages. Between men who speak a common language, a glance would suffice for reaching an understanding; just because they speak a common language, they are elevated above speech. Between different languages, however, only the stammering word mediates, and gesture ceases to be immediately intelligible as it had been in the mute glance of the eye. It is reduced to a halting sign language, that miserable surrogate for communication. As a result, the supreme component in liturgy is not the common word but the common gesture. Liturgy frees gesture from the fetters of helpless servitude to speech, and makes of it Something more than speech. Only the liturgical gesture anticipates that "purified lip" which is promised for "that day" to the peoples ever divided as to language. In it, the impoverished muteness of the disbelieving members becomes eloquent, the voluble loquacity of the believing heart becomes silent. Disbelief and belief unite their prayer.

TRUTH

They unite it in the silence of the liturgical gesture—and never in the secular word? Is there no living work—even if it be but a single one, a mere token of cohesion—in which the two prayers, that of the man of life and that of the man of God, join into one? Let us recall what we said about theology and philosophy in the introduction to the previous Part. They appeared to us to be in reciprocal dependence, one on the other. That was an interdependence of two sciences. Or is it more? The scientist is, after all, more than his science. The philosopher must be more than philosophy. We learned that he must be a man of flesh and blood. But that is not enough for him. Flesh and blood that he is, he must pray the prayer of the creatures, the prayer to the personal fate, in which the creature unwittingly confesses that it is creature. The wisdom which inhabits him, his flesh and blood—God created it in him and as ripe fruit it now hangs on the tree of life. The theologian, too, must be more than theology. We learned that he must be truthful, must love God. And it is not enough that he does so for himself in the privacy of his quarters. Solitary lover that he is, he must speak the prayer of the children of God, the prayer of the God-fearing congregation, in which he acknowledges himself consciously as member of their immortal body. The wisdom which inhabits him, his reverent heart—God awakened it in him in the revelation of his love. As an igniting spark from the eternal light, it now leaves his mouth which is ready to 'praise God in assemblages.'

God's truth conceals itself from those who reach for it with one hand only, regardless of whether the reaching hand is that of the objectivity of philosophers which preserves itself free of preconceptions, soaring above the objects, or that of the blindness of the theologians, proud of its experience and secluding itself from the world. God's truth wants to be entreated with both hands. It will not deny itself to him who calls upon it with the double prayer of the believer and the disbeliever. God gives of his wisdom to the one as to the other, to belief as well as to disbelief, but he gives to both only if their prayer comes before him united. It is the same man, disbelieving child of the world and believing child of God in one, who comes with dual plea and must stand with dual thanks before Him who gives of his wisdom to flesh and blood even as to those who fear him.

BOOK ONE

The Fire

or

The Eternal Life

The Promise of Eternity

"Blessed art Thou . . . who hast planted eternal life in our midst." The
fire burns at the core of the star. The rays go forth only from this fire;
and flow unresisted to the outside. The fire of the core must burn
incessantly. Its flame must eternally feed upon itself. It requires no
fuel from without. Time has no power over it and must roll past. It
must produce its own time and reproduce itself forever. It must make
its life everlasting in the succession of generations, each producing the
generation to come, and bearing witness to those gone by. Bearing
witness takes place in bearing—two meanings but one act, in which
eternal life is realized. Elsewhere, past and future are divorced, the one
sinking back, the other coming on; here they grow into one. The
bearing of the future is a direct bearing witness to the past. The son
is born so that he may bear witness to his father's father. The grandson
renews the name of the forebear. The patriarchs of old call upon their
last descendant by his name—which is theirs. Above the darkness of
the future burns the star-strewn heaven of the promise: "So shall thy
seed be."

The Eternal People: Jewish Fate

BLOOD AND SPIRIT
There is only one community in which such a linked sequence of
everlasting life goes from grandfather to grandson, only one which
cannot utter the "we" of its unity without hearing deep within a voice

that adds: "are eternal." It must be a blood-community, because only blood gives present warrant to the hope for a future. If some other community, one that does not propagate itself from its own blood, desires to claim eternity for its "we," the only way open to it is to secure a place in the future. All eternity not based on blood must be based on the will and on hope. Only a community based on common blood feels the warrant of eternity warm in its veins even now. For such a community only, time is not a foe that must be tamed, a foe it may or may not defeat—though it hopes it may!—but its child and the child of its child. It alone regards as the present what, for other communities, is the future, or, at any rate, something outside the present. For it alone the future is not something alien but something of its own, something it carries in its womb and which might be born any day. While every other community that lays claim to eternity must take measures to pass the torch of the present on to the future, the blood-community does not have to resort to such measures. It does not have to hire the services of the spirit; the natural propagation of the body guarantees it eternity.

THE PEOPLES AND THEIR NATIVE SOIL

What holds generally for peoples as groups united through blood relationship over against communities of the spirit, holds for our people in particular. Among the peoples of the earth, the Jewish people is "the one people," as it calls itself on the high rung of its life, which it ascends Sabbath after Sabbath. The peoples of the world are not content with the bonds of blood. They sink their roots into the night of earth, lifeless in itself but the spender of life, and from the lastingness of earth they conclude that they themselves will last. Their will to eternity clings to the soil and to the reign over the soil, to the land. The earth of their homeland is watered by the blood of their sons, for they do not trust in the life of a community of blood, in a community that can dispense with anchorage in solid earth. We were the only ones who trusted in blood and abandoned the land; and so we preserved the priceless sap of life which pledged us that it would be eternal. Among the peoples of the world, we were the only ones who separated what lived within us from all community with what is dead. For while the earth nourishes, it also binds. Whenever a people loves the soil of its native land more than its own life, it is in danger—as all the peoples of the world are—that, though nine times out of ten this love will save the native soil from the foe and, along with it, the life of the people, in the end the soil will persist as that which was loved more strongly, and the people will leave their lifeblood upon it. In the final analysis, the people belong to him who conquers the land. It cannot be otherwise, because people cling to the soil more than to their life as a people. Thus the earth betrays a people that entrusted its permanence to earth. The soil endures, the peoples who live on it pass.

THE HOLY LAND

And so, in contrast to the history of other peoples, the earliest legends about the tribe of the eternal people are not based on indigenousness. Only the father of mankind sprang from the earth itself, and even he only in a physical sense. But the father of Israel came from the outside. His story, as it is told in the holy books, begins with God's command to leave the land of his birth and go to a land God will point out to him. Thus in the dawn of its earliest beginnings, as well as later in the bright light of history, this people is a people in exile, in the Egyptian exile and subsequently in that of Babylonia. To the eternal people, home never is home in the sense of land, as it is to the peoples of the world who plough the land and live and thrive on it, until they have all but forgotten that being a people means something besides being rooted in a land. The eternal people has not been permitted to while away time in any home. It never loses the untrammeled freedom of a wanderer who is more faithful a knight to his country when he roams abroad, craving adventure and yearning for the land he has left behind, than when he lives in that land. In the most profound sense possible, this people has a land of its own only in that it has a land it yearns for—a holy land. And so even when it has a home, this people, in recurrent contrast to all other peoples on earth, is not allowed full possession of that home. It is only "a stranger and a sojourner." God tells it: "The land is mine." The holiness of the land removed it from the people's spontaneous reach while it could still reach out for it. This holiness increases the longing for what is lost, to infinity, and so the people can never be entirely at home in any other land. This longing compels it to concentrate the full force of its will on a thing which, for other peoples, is only one among others yet which to it is essential and vital: the community of blood. In doing this, the will to be a people dares not cling to any mechanical means; the will can realize its end only through the people itself.

THE PEOPLES AND THEIR LANGUAGES

But is a native land the only thing aside from blood on which a people's community can rest? Does not a people have a living sign of solidarity, no matter where its children may go? Has not every people its own language? It would seem that the language of the peoples of the world is not bound to something lifeless, something external. It lives together with man, with the whole of man, with the unity of his bodily and spiritual life, which cannot be broken as long as he lives. So language is not bound to anything external. But is it really less transitory because of this? If it is closely bound up with the life of the people, what happens to it when that life dies? The same that happens to it so long as that life lives: the language participates in the ultimate experience of this life: it also dies. Down to the most subtle detail, the languages of the peoples follow the live changes in their destinies, but this very dependence forces them to share the fate of all things alive: the fate of dying. Language is alive because it too can die. Eternity would be an unwelcome gift to it. Only because it is not eternal, only because it is a faithful reflection of the destiny of a people among other peoples, of a people passing through the various phases of its life, does it deserve to be called the most vital possession of a people, yes, its very life. And so every people of the world is doubtless right in fighting for its own language. But the peoples should know that it is not their eternity they are fighting for, that whatever is gained in the struggle is something quite other than eternity; it is time.

THE HOLY LANGUAGE

That is why the eternal people has lost its own language and, all over the world, speaks a language dictated by external destiny, the language of the nation whose guest it happens to be. And if it is not claiming hospitality but living in a settlement of its own, it speaks the language of the people from whose country it emigrated, of the people that gave it the strength to found a new settlement. In foreign lands it never draws this strength from itself alone, from its own community of blood, but always from something that was added elsewhere; the "Spaniol" in the Balkan countries, the Yiddish in Eastern Europe, are the best-known instances of this. While every other people is one with its own language, while that language withers in its mouth the moment it ceases to be a people, the Jewish people never quite grows one with the languages it speaks. Even when it speaks the language of its host, a special vocabulary, or, at least, a special selection from the general vocabulary, a special word order, its own feeling for what is beautiful or ugly in the language, betray that it is not its own.

Since time immemorial, the Jewish people's own language has ceased to be the language of daily life and yet—as its constant influence on the language of daily life shows—it is anything but a dead language. It is not dead but, as the people themselves call it, a holy language. The holiness of the people's own language has an effect similar to that of the holiness of its own land: it does not allow all their feeling to be lavished on everyday life. It prevents the eternal people from ever being quite in harmony with the times. By encompassing prayer, the ultimate, loftiest region of life, with a holy region of that language, it even prevents this people from ever living in complete freedom and spontaneity. For the freedom and spontaneity of life rest on the fact that man can express in words all he thinks, and that he feels he can do this. When he loses this ability, when he thinks he must be silent in his anguish because it is given only to the "poet to say what he suffers," not alone is the strength of a people's language broken, but its spontaneity too is hopelessly destroyed.

Precisely this ultimate and most fundamental spontaneity is denied the Jew because he addresses God in a language different from the one he uses to speak to his brother. As a result he cannot speak to his brother at all. He communicates with him by a glance rather than in words, and nothing is more essentially Jewish in the deepest sense than a profound distrust of the power of the word and a fervent belief in the power of silence. The holiness of the holy language which the Jew employs only for prayer does not permit his life to put out roots into the soil of a language of its own. So far as his language is concerned, the Jew feels always he is in a foreign land, and knows that the home of his language is in the region of the holy language, a region everyday speech can never invade. The proof of this lies in the peculiar circumstance that, at least in the silent symbols of writing, the language of everyday tries to maintain contact with the old holy language which everyday speech lost long ago. This is altogether different from the situation of the peoples of the world; for with them, the case is that the spoken language survives a written language that is lost, rather than that the written language survives a language no longer spoken on everyday occasions. In his very silence, and in the silent symbols of speech, the Jew feels a connection between his everyday language and the holy language of his holiday.

THE PEOPLES AND THEIR LAW

For the peoples of the world, language is the carrier and messenger of time-bound, flowing, changing, and, therefore, transitory life. But the language of the eternal people drives it back to its own life which is beyond external life, which courses through the veins of its living body and is, therefore, eternal. And if the Jew is thus barred from his own soil and his own language, how much more is he deprived of the outwardly visible life the nations live in accordance with their own customs and laws. For a people lives out its day in these two: in custom and law, in what has been handed down from yesterday through force of habit, and in what has been laid down for the morrow. Every day stands between a yesterday and a tomorrow, and all that lives proves it is alive by not standing still one certain day but making of that day a yesterday, and setting in its place a tomorrow. Peoples, too, stay alive by constantly transforming their today into new customs, into new eternal yesterdays, while at the same time they lay down new laws structured out of their today, for the service of their tomorrow. Thus, in the life of the nations, today is a moment which passes fleet as an arrow. And so long as this arrow is in flight, so long as new custom is added to the old, new law outstrips the old, the river of a people's life is in flux, alive. For so long do peoples live within time; for so long is time their heritage and their acre. In addition to their own soil and their own language, the increase in custom and the renewal of law give them the final and strongest guarantee of their own life: a time of their own. So long as a people computes a time of its own—and it computes this time according to its still living store of customs and memories, and the continuous renewal of its lawgiving powers, its leaders and kings—just so long has it power over time, just so long is it not dead.

THE HOLY LAW

And here again the eternal people buys its eternity at the cost of its temporal life. Time is not its time, nor its acre and heritage. For this people, the moment petrifies and stands between unincreased past and immovable future, and so the moment is not fleeting. Custom and law, past and future, become two changeless masses; in this process they cease to be past and future and, in their very rigidity, they too are transmuted into a changeless present. Custom and law, not to be increased or changed, flow into the common basin of what is valid now and forever. A single form of life welding custom and law into one fills the moment and renders it eternal. But because of this, the moment is lifted out of the flux of time; and life, sanctified, no longer has the quality of temporal life. While the myth of peoples changes incessantly—parts of the past are continually being forgotten while others are remembered as myth—here the myth becomes eternal and is not subject to change. And while the peoples of the world live in a cycle of revolutions in which their law sheds its old skin over and over, here the Law is supreme, a law that can be forsaken but never changed.

The holy teaching of the Law—for the name Torah designates both teaching and law as one—raises the people from the temporality and historicity of life, and deprives it of the power over time. The Jewish people does not count years according to a system of its own. For it neither the memory of its history nor the years of office of its law-givers can become a measure of time. That is because the memory of its history does not form a point fixed in the past, a point which, year after year, becomes increasingly past. It is a memory which is really not past at all, but eternally present. Every single member of this com-munity is bound to regard the exodus from Egypt as if he himself had been one of those to go. Here there are no lawgivers who renew the law according to the living flux of time. Even what might, for all practical purposes, be considered as innovation must be presented as if it were part of the everlasting Law and had been revealed in the revelation of that Law. And so the chronology of this people cannot be a reckoning of its own time, for the people is timeless; it has no time of its own. It must count years according to the years the world exists. And so again, and for the third time, we see here, in the relation to its own history, what we saw before in its relation to language and land, that this people is denied a life in time for the sake of life in eternity. It cannot experience the history of the nations creatively and fully. Its position is always somewhere between the temporal and the holy, always separated from the one by the other. And so, in the final analysis, it is not alive in the sense the nations are alive: in a national life manifest on this earth, in a national territory, solidly based and staked out on the soil. It is alive only in that which guarantees it will endure beyond time, in that which pledges it ever-lastingness, in drawing its own eternity from the sources of the blood.

FATE AND ETERNITY

But just because this people trusts only in the eternity it creates and in nothing else in the world, it really believes in its eternity, while all the peoples of the world believe in common with individual man that death, even although it be at a very distant juncture, must come even-tually. The love they bear their own group is grave and sweet with this premonition of death. Love is wholly sweet only when it is love for what is mortal. The secret of ultimate sweetness is bound up with the bitterness of death. The peoples of the world, then, foresee a time when their land with its mountains and rivers will lie beneath the sky even as now, but be inhabited by others, a time when their language will be buried in books and their customs and laws stripped of living force. We alone cannot imagine such a time. For we have long ago been robbed of all the things in which the peoples of the world are rooted. For us, land and language, custom and law, have long left the circle of the living and have been raised to the rung of holiness. But we are still living, and live in eternity. Our life is no longer meshed with anything outside ourselves. We have struck root in ourselves. We do not root in earth and so we are eternal wanderers, but deeply rooted in our own body and blood. And it is this rooting in ourselves, and in nothing but ourselves, that vouchsafes eternity.

The One People: Jewish Essence

INDIVIDUALITY AND UNIVERSALITY

What does this mean: to root in one's self? What does it mean that here one individual people does not seek the warrant of its existence in the external, and reaches out for eternity in its very lack of relations with the outside world? It means no more and no less than that one people, though it is only one people, claims to constitute All. For whatever is individual is not eternal because the Whole is outside it. It can maintain its individuality only by becoming somehow a part of that All. An individual entity which, in spite of its individuality, strove for eternity, would have to take the All into itself. With reference to the Jewish people this means that it would have to collect within itself the elements of God, world, and man, of which the All consists. God, man, and world of a people are the God, man, and world of that people only because they are just as different and differentiated from other gods, men, and worlds as the people itself from other peoples. The very difference of an individual people from other peoples establishes its connection with them. There are two sides to every boundary. By setting separating borders for ourselves, we border on something else. By being an individual people, a nation becomes a people among others. To close oneself off is to come close to another. But this does not hold when a people refuses to be merely an individual people and wants to be "the one people." Under these circumstances it must not close itself off within borders, but include within itself such borders as would, through their double function, tend to make it one individual people among others. And the same is true of its God, man, and world. These three must likewise not be distinguished from those of others; their distinction must be included within its own borders. Since this people wants to be the one people, the God, man, and world must contain the distinguishing character-istics that make them God, man, and world of the one people. In order that each be something very definite and particular, one God, one man, one world, and yet at the same time All: God, man, and world, they must contain opposite poles within themselves.

POLARITY

God within himself separates into the God who creates and the God who reveals, the God of omnipotent justice, and the God of love and mercy. Man within himself separates into the soul beloved by God and the lover who loves his neighbor. The world separates into the exis-tence of the creature that longs for God's creation, and life that grows toward and into the kingdom of God. Up to now, we regarded all these separations not as separations but as a sequence of voices taking up the theme in the great fugue of God's day. Up to now, we re-garded as essential not separation but union, the union into one har-mony. Now, for the first time, now that we are preparing to see eternity as something present at every hour instead of as the twelfth stroke of the world clock, these synthesizing voices appear as anti-theses. For in the sheer present which renews itself hour by hour, it is no longer possible for them to pass one another, to interweave in contrapuntal motion; they oppose one another with inflexible rigidity.

THE JEWISH GOD

To his people, God the Lord is simultaneously the God of retribu-tion and the God of love. In the same breath, they call on him as "our God" and as "King of the universe," or—to indicate the same contrast in a more intimate sphere—as "our Father" and "our King." He wants to be served with "trembling" and yet rejoices when his children over-come their fear at his wondrous signs. Whenever the Scriptures men-tion his majesty the next verses are sure to speak of his meekness. He demands the visible signs of offering and prayer brought to his name, and of "the affliction of our soul" in his sight. And almost in the same breath he scorns both and wants to be honored only with the secret fervor of the heart, in the love of one's neighbor, and in anonymous works of justice which no one may recognize as having been done for the sake of his name. He has elected his people, but elected it to visit upon them all their iniquities. He wants every knee to bend to him and yet he is enthroned above Israel's songs of praise. Israel inter-

cedes with him in behalf of the sinning peoples of the world and he
afflicts Israel with disease so that those other peoples may be healed.
Both stand before God: Israel, his servant, and the kings of the
peoples; and the strands of suffering and guilt, of love and judgment,
of sin and atonement, are so inextricably twined that human hands
cannot untangle them.

THE JEWISH MAN

And man, who is created in the image of God, Jewish man as he
faces his God, is a veritable repository of contradictions. As the beloved of God, as Israel, he knows that God has elected him and may
well forget that he is not alone with God, that God knows others
whom he himself may or may not know, that to Egypt and Assyria
too, God says: "my people." He knows he is loved—so why concern himself with the world! In his blissful togetherness-alone with
God, he may consider himself man, and man alone, and look up
in surprise when the world tries to remind him that not every man
harbors the same certainty of being God's child as he himself. Yet no
one knows better than he that being dear to God is only a beginning,
and that man remains unredeemed so long as nothing but this beginning has been realized. Over against Israel, eternally loved by God
and faithful and perfect in eternity, stands he who is eternally to
come, he who waits, and wanders, and grows eternally—the Messiah.
Over against the man of earliest beginnings, against Adam the son of
man, stands the man of endings, the son of David the king. Over
against him who was created from the stuff of earth and the breath
of the mouth of God, is the descendant from the stem of anointed
kings; over against the patriarch, the latest offspring; over against the
first, who draws about him the mantle of divine love, the last, from
whom salvation issues forth to the ends of the earth; over against the
first miracles, the last, which—so it is said—will be greater than the
first.

THE JEWISH WORLD

Finally, the Jewish world: it has been dematerialized and permeated with spirit through the power of blessings which are said over
everything and branch everywhere. But this world, also, is twofold
and teeming with contradictions in every single thing. Everything
that happens in it is ambivalent since it is related both to this and the
coming world. The fact that the two worlds, this world and the com-

ing, stand side by side, is all-important. Even the object that receives a soul by a benediction spoken over it has a twofold function: in "this" world it serves everyday purposes, almost as though it had never been blessed, but at the same time it has been rendered one of the stones of which the "coming" world will be built. Benediction splits this world in order to make it whole and one again for what is to come, but for the present all that is visible is the split. As the contrast between holy and profane, Sabbath and workaday, "Torah and the way of earth," spiritual life and the earning of a livelihood, this split goes through all of life. As it divides the life of Israel into holy and profane, so it divides the whole earth into Israel and the peoples. But the division is not simple in the sense that the holy shuts out the profane. The contrast penetrates to the innermost core, and just as the benediction touches everything that is profane and makes it holy, so, quite suddenly, the devout and the wise among all the peoples will participate in the eternal life of the coming world, which but a short time ago seemed reserved for Israel alone. Those who were blessed will themselves become a blessing.

THE INQUIRY INTO THE ESSENCE

This maze of paradoxes appears when one tries to consider the elements of Jewish life as static elements. The question as to what is the essence can only be answered by exposing paradoxes, and thus cannot really be answered at all. But life that is alive does not ask about essence. It just lives, and insofar as it lives, it answers all questions even before it asks them. What in the investigation of essence seemed a maze of paradoxes falls into an orderly pattern in the yearly rings of life. The orbit of man's life, returning in upon itself, meets the eye as a visible illustration of that which the ear, listening to the music of the spheres, hears: the voices successively entering the course of the day of God on the heaven of the All, once and for all, not to be repeated, exceeding all visual estimates.

The Holy People: The Jewish Year

In eternity the spoken word fades away into the silence of perfect togetherness—for union occurs in silence only; the word unites, but those who are united fall silent. And so liturgy, the reflector which focuses the sunbeams of eternity in the small circle of the year, must introduce man to this silence. But even in liturgy, shared silence can come only at the end, and all that goes before is a preparation for this end. In the stage of preparation the word still dominates the theme. The word itself must take man to the point of learning how to share silence. His preparation begins with learning to hear.

SOCIOLOGY OF THE MULTITUDE: THE LISTENING

Nothing would seem easier than this. But here we are concerned with a kind of hearing quite different from that required in dialogue. For in the course of a dialogue he who happens to be listening also speaks, and he does not speak merely when he is actually uttering words, not even mainly when he is uttering words, but just as much when through his eager attention, through the assent or dissent expressed in his glances, he conjures words to the lips of the current speaker. Here it is not this hearing of the eye which is meant, but the true hearing of the ear. What must be learned here is not the kind of hearing that stimulates the speaker to speak but hearing that has nothing to do with a possible reply. Many shall hear. And so the one who speaks must not be the speaker of his own words, for from where could he take his "own" words save from the eloquent glances of his hearers? Provided he is a true speaker, even he who speaks before many is actually carrying on a conversation. The listening crowd, this many-headed monster, is constantly giving the public orator his cue by agreement and displeasure, by interjections and general restlessness, and by the conflicting moods it forces him to parry at every moment. If the orator wants to make himself independent of his audience, he must "deliver" a speech he has memorized instead of speaking impromptu, and so run the risk of having his listeners fall asleep. The more impromptu the impromptu speech is, the more certainly it will give rise to two factions in the audience, and so to something diametrically opposed to unanimous attention on the part of all the hearers. The very essence of the "programmatic speech" is that it is "delivered" and not given. Its purpose is to create an atmosphere of complete unanimity in a gathering—at any cost whatsoever—and so the speaker must necessarily recite a well-prepared program. The unanimity in hearing that is nothing but hearing, the hearing in which a multitude is "all ears," is not due to the person of the speaker, but to the fact that the living, speaking person recedes behind the reader of words, and not even behind the reader, but behind the words he reads. This is why a sermon must be on a "text." It is only this connection with a text that secures it fervent attention on the part of the entire audience. Spontaneous words from the lips of the preacher would not even be spoken with the aim of arousing fervor. Such words would serve only to dissolve the common attention of the hearers. But the text that the assembled congregation values as the word of its God secures him who reads it the unanimous attention of all who have come together to hear it. And insofar as everything he says professes to be an interpretation of that text, he holds this unanimous attention throughout his sermon. For a sermon that evoked interjections, or made it hard for the audience to refrain from them, a sermon in which the silence of the hearers could be discharged otherwise than by singing in unison, would be a poor sermon though it might be a good political speech. A political speech, on the other hand, would be a failure if it were not interrupted by "hear, hear" and applause, if the audience were not gay and excited. The sermon as well as the reading of the text is supposed to beget unanimous silence on the part of the assembled congregation. And the nature of the sermon is determined by the fact that it is not a speech but exegesis; the most important part of it is the reading of the text from the Scriptures, for in that reading the unanimity of hearing, and hence the firm foundation for entire unanimity among the congregation, is established.

THE SABBATH

Only established, only founded. But as such a foundation, the reading of the Torah becomes the liturgical focus of the holiday on which the spiritual year is founded, of the Sabbath. In the circle of weekly portions which, in the course of one year, cover all of the Torah, the spiritual year is paced out, and the paces of this course are the Sabbaths. By and large, every Sabbath is just like any other, but the difference in the portions from the Scriptures distinguishes each from each, and this difference shows that they are not final in themselves but only parts of a higher order, of the year. For only in the year do the differentiating elements of the individual parts again fuse into a whole. The Sabbath lends reality to the year. This reality must be re-created week by week. One might say that the spiritual year knows only what is dealt with in the portion, but it becomes a year because every week is nothing but a fleeting moment. It is only in the sequence of Sabbaths that year rounds to a garland. The very regularity in the sequence of Sabbaths, the very fact that, aside from the variation in the Scripture portions, one Sabbath is just like the other, makes them the cornerstones of the year. The year as a spiritual year is created only through them. They precede everything that may still come, and imperturbably go side by side with all else, following their even course amid the splendors of feast days. Through all the surge of joy and sorrow, of anguish and bliss that the feasts bring with them, the even flow of the Sabbaths goes on, the even flow which makes possible those whirlpools of the soul. In the Sabbath the year is created, and thus the main significance of the Sabbath lies in the symbolic meaning of its liturgy: it is a holiday that commemorates creation.

THE FEAST OF CREATION

For God created heaven and earth in six days, and on the seventh he rested. And so the seventh day became the "day of rest," the "Sabbath," to celebrate the "memorial of the work of creation," or, more accurately, the completion of that work—"and the heaven and the earth were finished, and all the host of them." The Sabbath reflects the creation of the world in the year. Just as the world is always there, and wholly there before anything at all happens in it, so the order of the Sabbaths precedes all the festivals which commemorate events, and completes its course in the year, undisturbed by other feasts. And just as creation is not contained in the fact that the world was created once, but requires for its fulfillment renewal at every dawn, so the Sabbath, as the festival of creation, must not be one that is celebrated only once a year, but one that is renewed throughout the year, week after week the same, and yet week after week different, because of the difference in the weekly portions. And just as creation is wholly complete, for revelation adds to it nothing that was not already latent in it as presage, so the festival of creation must also contain the entire content of the festivals of revelation; in its own inner course from evening to evening it must be all presage.

FRIDAY EVENING

On the Sabbath—in contrast to weekdays—the great prayer of benedictions, repeated thrice daily, is enriched by inserts of poetry which convert the simple repetition into an organized and rounded whole. The addition to the prayer on the eve of the Sabbath refers to the institution of the Sabbath in the creation of the world. Here the words that conclude the story of creation occur: ". . . and the heaven and the earth were finished." On returning from the service in the House of Prayer, this is repeated in the home, by the holy light of the candles, before—in the blessing over bread and wine as the divine gifts of the earth—the divine nature of what is earthly is attested in the glow of the Sabbath lights and the entire day thus consecrated as a festival commemorating creation. For bread and wine are the most perfect works of man, works that cannot be surpassed. They cannot, however, be compared to his other works in which his inventive mind artfully combines the gifts of nature, and in the act of combining goads itself on to greater and greater artfulness. Bread and wine are nothing but the ennobled gifts of earth; one is the basis of all the strength of life, the other of all its joy. Both were perfected in the youth of the world and of the people thereon, and neither can ever grow old. Every mouthful of bread and every sip of wine tastes just as wonderful as the first we ever savored, and certainly no less wonderful than in time immemorial they tasted to those who for the first time harvested the grain for bread and gathered the fruits of the vine.

SABBATH MORNING

While the eve of the Sabbath is primarily a festival in honor of creation, the morning celebrates revelation. Here the poetic insert in the great prayer of benediction proclaims the joy of Moses at God's gift of the Sabbath. And the joy of the great receiver of revelation, to whom God "spoke face to face as a man speaketh unto his friend," and to whom he gave greater recognition than to any later prophet of Israel, is followed, in the order of the day, with the reading of the weekly portion to the congregation by its representatives. On the eve of the Sabbath, expression is given to the knowledge that the earth is a creation; in the morning, we find utterance of the people's awareness of being elect through the gift of the Torah which signifies that eternal life has been planted in their midst. The man called forth to the Torah from the congregation approaches the book of revelation in the knowledge of being elect. When he leaves the book and again merges with the congregation, he does so in the knowledge of eternal life. But within the Sabbath, too, this knowledge of eternal life carries him over the threshold separating both revelation and creation from redemption. The Afternoon Prayer becomes the prayer of redemption.

SABBATH AFTERNOON

In the insert in this prayer, Israel is more than the chosen people, it is the "one and only" people, the people of the One and Only God. Here all the fervor which the praying Jew breathes into the holy word "One," the fervor which compels the coming of the Kingdom, is at its greatest intensity. Twice daily, in the morning and in the evening profession, after the community of Israel has been created through the injunction to "hear," and the immediate presence of God has been acknowledged by the invocation of God as "our God," God's "unity" is proclaimed as his eternal name beyond all name, beyond all presence. And we know that this proclamation is more than a fleeting word; we know that within it the eternal union of God with his people and of his people with mankind occurs through every individual "taking upon himself the yoke of the kingdom of God." All this vibrates in the Afternoon Prayer of the Sabbath, in the hymn on the one people of the One and Only God. And the songs of the "third meal," at which old men and children gather around the long table in the light of the waning day, reel with the transport of certainty that the Messiah will come and will come soon.

THE CLOSE OF THE SABBATH

But this entire course of the day of God is included in the circuit of the individual Sabbath like a preview that can only be realized to the full in other festivals yet to come. The realization does not occur in the Sabbath itself. The Sabbath is and remains a festival of rest, of reflection. It is the static foundation of the year which—aside from the sequence of weekly portions—is informed with motion only by the cycle of other festivals. As ornaments carved on a frame are the hints of the contents of revelation that make the actual pictures to be set within that frame, each at its own given time. The Sabbath itself is not merely a festival, but also just another day in the week, and very much so. It does not stand out in the year like the actual festivals, even though the structure of the year is based upon it; it stands out in the week. And so it also merges with the week again. When the congregation enters the House of God it acclaims the Sabbath with joy, as the bridegroom does the bride, but later the Sabbath vanishes into quotidian life like a dream. The smallest circuit set for man, the workaday week, begins again. A child holds the light that an older man lit while, with closed eyes, he drinks a cup of wine, waking from the dream of perfection spun by the festival of the seventh day. A way must be found from the sanctuary back into the workaday world. The year, all of life, is built up on the shift from the holy to the profane, from the seventh to the first day, from perfection to outset, from old age to early youth. The Sabbath is the dream of perfection, but it is only a dream. Only in its being both does it become the cornerstone of life; only as the festival of perfection does it become the constant renewal of creation.

REST

For this is the ultimate significance of the Sabbath: it was instituted primarily to commemorate the work of the beginning and thus forms the solid and lasting basis of the spiritual year. On the other hand, its institution was the first sign of revelation within the act of creation itself; though veiled, the revealed name of God appears in the Scriptures for the first time in the words instituting the Sabbath. So, through being at once the sign of creation and the first revelation, it is also, and even mainly, the anticipation of redemption. For what is redemption if not the concord between revelation and creation? And what is the first ineluctable premise for such concord, save man's rest after he has done the work of this earth! Six days he has worked and attended to all his affairs; now, on the seventh, he rests. Six days he has uttered the many useful and useless words the workday demanded of him, but on the seventh he obeys the command of the prophet: he lets his tongue rest from the talk of everyday, and learns to be silent, to listen. And this sanctifying of the day of rest by listening to God's voice in silence must be shared by all members of his house. It must not be fretted by the noise of giving orders. The man-servant and the maid-servant must also rest; and it is even said that just for the sake of their rest the day of rest was instituted, for when rest has penetrated to them, then all the house is, indeed, freed from the noise and chatter of the weekday, and redeemed to rest.

CONSUMMATION

The rest is intended to signify redemption and not a period of collecting oneself for more work. Work is an ever new beginning. The first day of work is the first day of the week, but the day of rest is the seventh. The feast of creation is the feast of consummation. In celebrating it we go, in the midst of creation, beyond creation and revelation. The great Sabbath prayer of benedictions involves none of those requests that are concerned with the needs of the individual. There are not merely none of the weekday requests for creature comforts, such as a good year, a good harvest, health, intelligence, and good management, but also none of the requests of every child of God for forgiveness of sins, and ultimate redemption. Besides the requests for peace and the coming of the kingdom—individual as well as community requests—there is only praise and thanks. For on the Sabbath the congregation feels as if it were already redeemed—to the degree such a feeling is at all possible in anticipation. The Sabbath is the feast of creation, but of a creation wrought for the sake of redemption. This feast instituted at the close of creation is creation's meaning and goal. That is why we do not celebrate the festival of the primordial work of creation on the first day of creation, but on its last, on the seventh day.

Sociology of the Community: The Meal

Silent listening was only the beginning of community. It instituted community; and, as always, here too there had to be continual return to the original institution, so that by this summoning to concentration new strength could again and again be drawn from the depths of the beginning. But the inner life of the community does not begin and end with this initial silent listening. This life is born only in an act which is essentially a renewal. Not in a mere repetition of a beginning once created, but in the re-creating of what has grown effete. The re-creating of bodily life, the transforming of matter grown old, occurs in the course of a meal. Even for the individual, eating and drinking constitute re-birth for the body. For the community, the meal taken in common is the action through which it is reborn to conscious life.

The silent community of hearing and heeding already establishes the smallest community, that of the household. The household is based on the circumstance that the word of the father of the family is heard and heeded. Still, the common life of the household does not become manifest in the common heeding but in the meal at which all the members of the house gather round the table. Here each is the equal of every other; each lives for himself and yet is joined with all the others. It is not table talk that establishes this community, for in many rural districts it is not customary to speak during the meal, it is even contrary to custom. Talking at table does not, at any rate, establish community; at most it expresses it. One can talk in the street and in the square wherever people meet haphazardly. The common meal with its silent community represents actual community alive in the midst of life.

Wherever a meal is held in common, there is such community, whether it be in the house, in monasteries, lodges, clubs, or in fraternities. And wherever such community is absent, as, for instance, in schoolrooms or at lectures, or even at the meetings of seminars, it is lacking even though the basis of community, listening in common, is most certainly in evidence. It takes social occasions, such as school excursions, or informal evenings for the members of the seminar, to achieve true community life on that basis which, in itself, is nothing but a basis. The shame of primitive peoples at the mere thought of eating together, and the opprobrious practice—in restaurants—of eating alone and especially of reading one's paper while eating, are signs of a civilization that is either unripe and sour, or overripe and touched with rot. The sweet, fully ripened fruit of humanity craves the community of man with man in the very act of renewing the life of the body. Even without this community the discipline of common obedience may, of course, persist. The suspicious savage, for instance, who takes his meal in solitude, is not trying to make himself independent of the laws of his tribe any more than the confirmed bachelor dining alone in his restaurant is deliberately falling short of the requirements of his particular duties. Common obedience may persist, but what is missing is the feeling of freedom which alone can conjure up the life of the community against the unfailing background of a common discipline. The common life as represented by the common meal is, of course, not the ultimate experience; it is no more ultimate than the common listening. But on the road of education to the ultimate experience of common silence this is the second station, just as common listening is the first. The common meal is an integral part of the Sabbath as well as of all other feasts. But as the actual focus of the feast we find it in the first of those festivals which together, in their sequence within the solid frame of the year, reflect the people's eternal course in changing images.

THE FEASTS OF REVELATION

The three pilgrimage festivals, that of the deliverance from Egypt, that of the revelation of the Ten Commandments, and the Feast of Booths in the wilderness, feasts on which everyone in the land once journeyed to the common sanctuary, give an image of the people as the carrier of revelation. Creation and redemption, too, are revealed in revelation, creation because it was done for the sake of redemption and thus, in a narrower sense, is actually the creation of revelation; redemption because revelation bids us wait for it. And so, in the course of the destiny of the people chosen for revelation, the periods of the feasts in which this people grows aware of its vocation to be the recipient of revelation are grouped around the day and the moment on which revelation is actually received. This vocation is shown in three stages: the people are created into a people; this people is endowed with the words of revelation; and, with the Torah it has received, this people wanders through the wilderness of the world. The eight-day periods of the Passover and of the Feast of Booths are grouped around the two-day Feast of Weeks. In these three festivals, the steps of eternal history pace the ground of the year with its cycle of Sabbaths, a ground which is, as it were, eternal in nature. For these feasts only seem to be feasts of commemoration. In reality, the historical element in them is living and present, and what is said to every participant at the first festival holds for them all: that he must cele-́ brate the feast as though he himself had been delivered from Egypt. The beginning, the middle, and the end of this national history, the founding, the zenith, and the eternity of the people, are reborn with every new generation.

THE FEAST OF DELIVERANCE

The welding of people into a people takes place in its deliverance. And so the feast that comes at the beginning of its national history is a feast of deliverance. Because of this, the Sabbath can legitimately be interpreted as a reminder of the exodus from Egypt. For the freedom of the man-servant and the maid-servant which it proclaims is conditioned by the deliverance of the people as a people from the servitude of Egypt. And in every command to respect the freedom of even the servant, of even the alien among the people, the law of God renews the awareness of the connection holding between the freedom within the people, a freedom decreed by God, and the freeing of the people from Egyptian servitude, a liberation enacted by God. Like the creation of the world, the creation of the people contains the final goal, the final purpose for which it was effected. So it is that the people have come to feel this feast as the most vivid of the three, including the meaning of the two others.

Among the many meals of the spiritual year, the evening meal of the Passover at which the father of the household gathers together all his family is the meal of meals. It is the only one that from first to last has the character of worship; hence the Seder ("Order") is, from first to last, liturgically regulated. From the very start the word "freedom" sheds its light upon it. The freedom of this meal at which all are equally free is expressed in a number of rites which "distinguish this night from all nights," among them the reclining of the participants on cushions. And even more vividly than in this reminiscence of the reclining of the guests in the symposia of antiquity, this particular freedom expresses itself in the fact that the youngest child is the one to speak, and that what the father says at table is adapted to this child's personality and his degree of maturity. In contrast to all instruction, which is necessarily autocratic and never on a basis of equality, the sign of a true and free social intercourse is this, that the one who stands—relatively speaking—nearest the periphery of the circle, gives the cue for the level on which the conversation is to be conducted. For this conversation must include him. No one who is there in the flesh shall be excluded in the spirit. The freedom of a society is always the freedom of everyone who belongs to it. Thus this meal is a symbol of the people's vocation for freedom. That this vocation is only a beginning, only the initial creation of the people, is shown in another aspect of this prominence of the youngest child. Since this youngest was permitted to speak for himself, the entire ceremony has, after all, to assume the form of instruction. The father of the family speaks, the household listens, and only in the further course of the evening is there more and more common independence until, in the songs of praise and the table songs of the second part of the meal, songs which float between divine mystery and the jesting mood begot by wine, the last shred of autocracy in the order of the meal dissolves into community.

The founding of the people affords a glimpse of its future destinies, but no more than a glimpse. All its further destinies are prefigured in its origin. It is not only today that enemies rise to destroy us; they rose to destroy us in every generation, back to the first which went out of Egypt, and in every generation God saved us! And we should have been content with what he did for us when he delivered us from the servitude of Egypt, but he to whom he alone suffices did not consider it sufficient. He led us to Mount Sinai and on to the place of rest in his sanctuary. The texts read from the Scriptures on the last days of the feast give a survey from the origin on to what is latent in this origin, in this creation of the people: on to revelation and ultimate redemption. The reading of the Song of Songs points to revelation. A distant view of redemption is afforded by Isaiah's prophecy of the shoot that shall come forth out of the stock of Jesse and smite the land with the rod of his mouth, of the day when the wolf shall dwell with the lamb and the world shall be as full of the knowledge of the Lord as the sea is of water. But the stock shall stand, an ensign for the peoples, and the heathen shall seek it. And this is the deepest meaning of the farewell which those who participate in the evening meal bid one another: Next year in Jerusalem! In every house where the meal is celebrated a cup filled with wine stands ready for the prophet Elijah, the precursor of the shoot from the stock of Jesse, who is forever "turning the hearts of the fathers to their children and the hearts of the children to their fathers," so that the river of consanguinity may not cease during the long night of time, and stream on toward a morning to come.

THE FEAST OF REVELATION

Among the three feasts of the people of the revelation, the feast of the revelation in a narrower sense lasts only two brief days. As a momentary present, revelation stands between the long, the everlasting has-been of the past and the eternal to-come of the future. And just as revelation is intimately linked with creation, so that it is contained within it, while creation in turn points to revelation, presaging revelation as a fulfillment of creation, so the feast of revelation to the people is closely connected with that which commemorates the founding of the people. From the second day of the feast of deliverance on, a counting of days to the feast of the revelation begins both in the House of God and in the home. The festival itself is concentrated exclusively on the twofold miracle of Sinai: God's descent to his people and the proclaiming of the Ten Commandments. In contrast to the feast in memory of the origin of the people, which contains everything else in the germ, this feast knows of nothing save of Him. The before and after of revelation remain in shadow. The people is wholly immersed in its togetherness with God. Even the passages read from the Prophets do not open backward or forward vistas, but guide the eye already turned inward still more wholly inward: Ezekiel's enigmatic vision of the celestial chariot which carries the throne of God, and Habakkuk's stormy song of God's tempestuous entry into the world, the first pointing to the secrets of God's essence, the second a picturing of his almighty manifestation, but both within the scope of the greatest moment of revelation. Neither do the festival hymns composed at a later date ever tire of inventing new poetic paraphrases for the one great content of revelation, for the Ten Commandments.

THE FEAST OF BOOTHS

But the people is not allowed to linger in the sheltering shade of Sinai, in which God sheathed it so that it might be alone with him. It must leave the hidden togetherness with God and issue forth into the world. It must start upon its wanderings through the wilderness, the wanderings whose end the generation that stood under Sinai shall not live to see. It will be a later-born generation that will find rest in the divine sanctuary of home, when the wanderings through the wilderness are over. The Feast of Booths is the feast of both wanderings and rest. In memory of those long wanderings of the past which finally led to rest, the members of the family do not have their merry meal in the familiar rooms of the house but under a roof which is quickly constructed, a makeshift roof with heaven shining through the gaps. This serves to remind the people that no matter how solid the house of today may seem, no matter how temptingly it beckons to rest and unimperiled living, it is but a tent which permits only a pause in the long wanderings through the wilderness of centuries. For rest, the rest of which the builder of the first Temple spoke, does not come until all these wanderings are at an end, and his words are read at this feast: "Blessed be He that has given rest unto his people."

The passages from the Prophets read on the occasion of this festival again prove—if there is still need of such proof—that this double meaning is the meaning of the feast, that it is a feast of redemption only within the circle of the three festivals of revelation. Because of this, redemption is celebrated here only as the hope and certainty of future redemption; and while this feast is celebrated in the same month as the Days of Awe, which are the feasts of a redemption present and eternal, and borders on these Days in neighborly fashion, it does not coincide with them. On the first day of the Feast of Booths the majestic closing chapter from Zechariah is read, the chapter concerning the day of the Lord with the prediction that concludes the daily service: "And the Lord shall be King over all the earth; in that day shall the Lord be One, and His name: One."

This ultimate word of hope concludes the daily service of the assembled congregation and also comes at the conclusion of the spiritual year. On the other days of the festival, these words are paralleled by the ones Solomon spoke at the dedication of the Temple, when the wandering ark at last found the rest the people had already found under Joshua. Solomon's concluding words wonderfully connect the hope for future recognition "that all the peoples of the earth may know that the Lord, He is God; there is none else," with a warning to the one people: "Let your heart, therefore, be whole with the Lord." And in the chapter from Ezekiel read at this festival, classical expression is given to this merging into each other of unity of the heart, unity of God, and unity of peoples which, in the concept of the sanctification of God's name through the people for all the peoples, forms the inmost basis of Judaism. This chapter is also the biblical source of the prayer which is primarily the prayer of this threefold sanctification, the Kaddish: "Thus will I magnify Myself and sanctify Myself, and I will make Myself known in the eyes of many nations; and they shall know that I am the Lord."

Thus the Feast of Booths is not only a festival of rest for the people, but also the festival of the ultimate hope. It is a festival of rest only in that it breathes hope. In this festival of redemption there is no present redemption. Redemption is only a hope, only something expected in the source of wanderings. And so this feast cannot be the last word, since it does not include redemption in its own domains but only glimpses it and lets it be glimpsed from the mountain of revelation. As the Sabbath flows back into the weekday, so this close of the spiritual year is not permitted to be an actual close but must flow back into the beginning. On the festival of Rejoicing in the Law, the last word in the Torah gives rise to the first. And the old man who, in the name of the congregation, is in charge of this transition, is not called "husband of the Torah," but through all time goes by the name of "bridegroom of the Torah." It is not without good cause that the book full of corroding doubt, Ecclesiastes, is assigned to be read at the Feast of Booths. The disenchantment which follows upon the Sabbath the moment its fragrance has been breathed for the last time and the weekday asserts itself in all its old unbroken strength is, as it were, included in the festival itself through the reading of Ecclesiastes. Although the Feast of Booths celebrates redemption and rest, it is nevertheless the festival of wandering through the wilderness. Neither in the feasts that unite people at a common meal, nor in those that unite them in common listening, does man have the experience of community begot by ultimate silence. Beyond the mere founding of the community in the common word, beyond the expression of the community in a common life, there must be something higher, even if this something lies at the farthest border of community life and constitutes community beyond common life.

Sociology of the Whole: The Greeting

The institution of listening in common became the premise of living in common. The community was called by a common name and as it responded, it began to exist. Now they could sit down at the table of life together. But the common meal united the community only at the hours in which the meal was eaten. And this meal constituted a community only of those whom it actually united. Only invited guests come to a meal. But anyone at all who hears the word can obey it. Only he who is invited can come to the meal, and that means he who has heard the word. Before he comes to the meal, he does not know the other guests. He himself did indeed hear the invitation, but then each one heard only himself being invited. Not before the meal does he become acquainted with the others. The common silence of those who heard the word is still a silence of the individual. Only at table do the guests become acquainted, in the talk which springs from sitting at table together. And so, when the guests leave, they are no longer strangers to one another. They greet one another when they meet again. Such greeting is the loftiest symbol of silence. They are silent because they know one another. If all men, all contemporaries, all the dead and all the still unborn, were to greet one another, they would have to eat a pound of salt with one another—as the saying goes. But this premise cannot be established. And yet it is only this greeting, of all to all that would constitute the utmost community, the silence that can never again be broken. The voices of all who have not heard the call disturb the devoutness of listening. The quiet of the family table is not respected by the noise of those who have not been invited and pass unsuspectingly beneath the lit window. The silence would be perfect, and the community common to all, only if there were no one who was not silent. The precondition for the greeting of all to all, wherein this common silence expresses itself, would have to be listening in common, just as every ordinary greeting has for its premise at least an introduction and the exchange of a few words. But how is this greeting of all to all to take place?

How can it take place? How is it brought about where it does take place—say in the army? Certainly not in the salute of two soldiers who meet! If this greeting, this salute, is from a private to an officer, it is only a token of listening in common, and by no means of listening on the part of one alone. If it is given to a comrade, it constitutes a reminder of working and suffering together, being hungry and being on guard together, of the common march and the dangers common to both. The stiff salute is intended for the discipline reigning everywhere and at every instant which is the basis of the whole structure; the comradely greeting is given for the sake of common life, which is not by any means always and everywhere but exists at certain moments while remaining in abeyance at others. Both together, unrelenting discipline and the easily awakened sense of comradeship, the first lasting, the second transitory, support and renew the morale of the army. Both are the sources of this common spirit, but not all of this spirit becomes visible in these two forms of greeting. This greeting is never anything more than one of the elements constituting the whole.

The whole, and the knowledge that one belongs to it, can only be experienced in a parade, in saluting a flag, in review before the commander-in-chief. Here, where the salute is directed to one who need salute no one at all, or who, like the flag, is not even in a position to salute, it does not merely express obedience common to soldier and officer alike, but the spirit common to all the members of this army, always. For the soldier feels that the flag and dynasty are older than anything living and will survive it. And what is meant here is not community of living, for neither flag nor king can die, but destiny, insofar as it is common to all those who salute here, now, and forever. Thus we know the sole way in which this greeting of all to all can take place, independent of how many of the living are prepared for such greeting by a common word and a common meal that has gone before; independent of the obvious fact that such a community of all through all can never be realized. The greeting takes place in this, that those who are prepared by such twofold community prostrate themselves in common before the Lord of all time. Kneeling in common before the Lord of all in the world, and "of the spirits in all flesh," opens the way for the community, and only for this community and the individual within it, the way to the all-embracing common unity where everyone knows everyone else and greets him wordlessly—face-to-face.

THE FEASTS OF REDEMPTION

The Days of Awe are festivals of a special character, celebrated in the month of that feast which, among the feasts of the community, has as its content: arriving at rest. What distinguishes the Days of Awe from all other festivals is that here and only here does the Jew kneel. Here he does what he refused to do before the king of Persia, and no power on earth can compel him to do, and what he need not do before God on any other day of the year, or in any other situation he may face during his lifetime. And he does not kneel to confess a fault or to pray for forgiveness of sins, acts to which this festival is primarily dedicated. He kneels only in beholding the immediate nearness of God, hence on an occasion which transcends the earthly needs of today. For the same reason, the Prayer of Benedictions said on every Sabbath omits the requests for forgiveness of sins. The Day of Atonement, which climaxes the ten-day period of redemption, is quite properly called the Sabbath of Sabbaths. The congregation now rises to the feeling of God's nearness as it sees in memory the Temple service of old, and visualizes especially the moment when the priest, this once in all the year, pronounced the ineffable name of God that was expressed by a circumlocution on all other occasions, and the assembled people fell on their knees. And the congregation participates directly in the feeling of God's nearness when it says the prayer that is bound up with the promise of a future time, "when every knee shall bow before God, when the idols will be utterly cut off, when the world will be perfected under the kingdom of the Almighty, and all the children of flesh will call upon his name, when he will turn unto himself all the wicked of the earth, and all will accept the yoke of his kingdom." On the Days of Awe, this prayer mounts beyond the version of the Concluding Prayer of the everyday service. On these Days of Awe the plea for bringing about such a future is already part of the Central Prayer, which—in solemn words—calls for the day when all creatures will prostrate themselves that "they may all form a single band to do God's will with a whole heart." But the Concluding Prayer, which utters this cry day after day, silences it on the Days of Awe, and, in complete awareness that this congregation is not yet the "single band" of all that is created, anticipates the moment of eternal redemption by seizing on it now, in the present. And what the congregation merely expresses in words in the course of the year, it here expresses in action: it prostrates itself before the King of Kings.

THE JUDGMENT

Thus the Days of Awe, New Year's Day and the Day of Atonement, place the eternity of redemption into time. The horn blown on New Year's Day at the peak of the festival stamps the day as a "day of judgment." The judgment usually thought of as at the end of time is here placed in the immediate present. And so it cannot be the world that is being judged—for where could the world be at this very present! It is the individual who faces judgment. Every individual is meted out his destiny according to his actions. The verdict for the past and the coming year is written on New Year's Day, and it is sealed on the Day of Atonement, when the last reprieve constituted by these ten days of penitence and turning to God is over. The year becomes representative of eternity, in complete representation. In the annual return of this judgment, eternity is stripped of every trace of the beyond, of every vestige of remoteness; it is actually there, within the grasp of every individual and holding every individual close in its strong grasp. He is no longer part of the eternal history of the eternal people, nor is he part of the eternally changing history of the world.

There is no more waiting, no more hiding behind history. The individual confronts judgment without any intermediary factor. He stands in the congregation. He says "We." But the "We" of this day are not the "We" of the people in history; the sin for which we crave forgiveness is not the sin of transgression of laws which separates this people from the other peoples of the world. On these days, the individual in all his naked individuality stands immediately before God. Only his human sin is named in the moving recital of the sins "which we have sinned," a recital which is far more than mere recital. It shines into the most hidden corners of being and calls forth the confession of the one sin in the unchanging human heart.

SIN

And so "We" in whose community the individual recognizes his sin, can be nothing less than the congregation of mankind itself. Just as the year, on these days, represents eternity, so Israel represents mankind. Israel is aware of praying "with the sinners." And—no matter what the origin of the obscure phrase may be—this means praying, in the capacity of all of mankind, "with" everyone. For everyone is a sinner. Though the soul is pure when God gives it to man, it is immediately snatched into the struggle between the two urges of this heart divided against itself. And though he may concentrate his will over and over, though he renew his purpose and vow and begin the work of unifying and purifying his divided heart over and over, still at that boundary between two years which signifies eternity, all purposes becomes vain, and all consecration desecration; every vow toward God breaks down, and what God's children undertook with assurance, is forgiven to them now that they are no longer sure.

DEATH AND LIFE

Throughout these days, a wholly visible sign expresses the underlying motif, namely, that for the individual, eternity is here shifted into time. For on these days the worshiper wears his shroud. It is true that even on ordinary days, the moment when the prayer shawl—chlamys and toga of antiquity—is donned, that moment directs the mind to the shroud, and to eternal life when God will sheathe the soul in his mantle. Thus the weekday and the weekly Sabbath, as well as creation itself, illumine death as the crown and goal of creation. But the entire shroud, comprising not only the shawl but also the under-robe—chiton and tunic of antiquity—is not the costume of every day. Death is the ultimate, the boundary of creation. Creation cannot encompass death as such. Only revelation has the knowledge— and it is the primary knowledge of revelation—that love is as strong as death. And so a man wears, already once in his life, on his wedding day under the bridal canopy, his complete shroud which he has received from the hands of the bride. Not until he is married does he become a true member of his people. It is significant that at a boy's birth the father prays that it may be vouchsafed him to bring up his son to the Torah, to the bridal canopy, and to good works. To learn the Torah and to keep the commandments is the omnipresent basis of Jewish life. Marriage brings with it the full realization of this life, for only then do the "good works" become possible. Only the man needs to be aware that the Torah is the basis of life. When a daughter is born, the father simply prays that he may lead her to the bridal canopy and to good works. For a woman has this basis of Jewish life for her own without having to learn it deliberately over and over, as the man who is less securely rooted in the depths of nature is compelled to do. According to ancient law, it is the woman who propagates Jewish blood. The child of a Jewish mother is Jewish by birth, just as the child of parents who are both Jewish.

Thus, in the individual life, it is marriage that fills mere Jewish existence with soul. The household is the chamber of the Jewish heart. Revelation wakens something in creation that is as strong as death and sets it up against death and against all of creation. The new creation of revelation is the soul, which is the unearthly in earthly life. Similarly, the bridegroom wears his death attire as his wedding attire, and at the very moment he becomes a true member of the eternal people he challenges death and becomes as strong as death. But that which is a moment in the life of the individual is also a moment, but an eternal moment, in the spiritual year. Here too, the father of the family wears his shroud, not as the attire of death but as wedding attire, on one single occasion: at the first of the feasts of revelation, at the Passover Seder, the evening meal of the summons of the people to freedom. Here too, the garments worn in death indicate the transition from mere creation to revelation. The shroud is worn at the first of the three feasts, and here too in drinking and eating, in gay, childlike jests and merry songs, it is a challenge to death.

ATONEMENT

But on the Days of Awe it is worn in a very different spirit. Here it is not a wedding attire but the true attire of death. Man is utterly

alone on the day of his death, when he is clothed in his shroud, and
in the prayers of these days he is also alone. They too set him, lonely
and naked, straight before the throne of God. In time to come, God
will judge him solely by his own deeds and the thoughts of his own
heart. God will not ask about those around him and what they have
done to help him or to corrupt him. He will be judged solely according to what he himself has done and thought. On the Days of Awe
too, he confronts the eyes of his judge in utter loneliness, as if he
were dead in the midst of life, a member of the community of man
which, like himself, has placed itself beyond the grave in the very
fullness of living. Everything lies behind him. At the commencement
of the last day, the Day of Atonement, for which the preceding nine
Days of Awe were only a preparation, he had prayed that all his vows,
his self-consecration, and his good resolves might be annulled, and
in that prayer he had attained to that pure humility which asks to be
nothing but the erring child of Him and before Him, whom he im-
plores to forgive him just as He forgave "all the congregation of the
children of Israel, and the stranger that sojourneth among them, for
in respect of all that people it was done in error." Now he is ready
to confess, and to repeat the confession of his own sin in the sight
of God. He is no longer guilty before man. If he were oppressed by
guilt against man, he would have to have it remitted in confessing it,
man to man. The Day of Atonement does not remit such guilt and
has nothing to do with it. On the Day of Atonement, all sins, even
those committed against and pardoned by man, are sins before God,
the sins of the solitary individual, the sins of the soul for it is the soul
that sins. And God lifts up his countenance to this united and lonely
pleading of men in their shrouds, men beyond the grave, of a community of souls, God who loves man both before and after he has
sinned, God whom man, in his need, may challenge, asking why he
has forsaken him, God who is "merciful and gracious, long-suffering
and abundant in goodness and truth, who keeps his mercy unto the
thousandth generation, who forgives iniquity and transgression and
sin, and has mercy on him who returns." And so man to whom the
divine countenance is lifted bursts out into the exultant profession:
"The Lord is God:" this God of love, he alone is God!

THE WAY BACK INTO THE YEAR

Everything earthly lies so far behind the transport of eternity in
this confession, that it is difficult to imagine that a way can lead back
from here into the circuit of the year. That is why it is most significant for the structure of the spiritual year that the festivals of immedi-

ate redemption do not conclude the feast month of redemption which closes the annual cycle of Sabbaths. For after them comes the Feast of Booths, which is a feast of redemption founded on the base of an unredeemed era and of a people yet within the pale of history. In the common unity of man, the soul was alone with God. To neutralize this foretaste of eternity, the Feast of Booths reinstates the reality of time. Thus the circuit of the year can recommence, for only within this circuit are we allowed to conjure eternity up into time.

The Peoples of the World: Messianic Politics

THE PEOPLE AT THE GOAL

It was the circuit of a people. In it, a people was at its goal and knew it was at the goal. The people had suspended for itself the contradiction between creation and revelation. It lives in its own redemption. It has anticipated eternity. The future is the driving power in the circuit of its year. Its rotation originates, so to speak, not in a thrust but in a pull. Its rotation originates, so to speak, not in a thrust but in a pull. The present passes not because the past prods it on but because the future snatches it toward itself. Somehow, even the festivals of creation and revelation flow into redemption. What gives the year strength to begin anew and link its ring, which is without beginning and end, into the chain of time, is this, that the feeling that redemption is still unattained breaks through again, and thereby the thought of eternity, which seemed contained in the cup of the moment, brims up and surges over the rim. But the people remains the eternal people. The meaning of its life in time is that the years come and go, one after the other as a sequence of waiting, or perhaps wandering, but not of growth. For growth would imply that consummation in time is still unattained, and so it would be a denial of the people's eternity. Eternity is just this: that time no longer has a right to a place between the present moment and consummation and that the whole future is to be grasped today.

THE PEOPLES AND THE WORLD

And so the eternal people must forget the world's growth, must cease to think thereon. It must look upon the world, its own world, as complete, though the soul may yet be on the way: the soul can indeed overtake the final goal in one single leap. And if not, it must needs wait and wander on—to quote the wise Spanish proverb,

"Patience, and a new shuffle of the cards." Waiting and wandering is the business of the soul, growth that of the world. It is this very growth that the eternal people denies itself. As nationality, it has reached the point to which the nations of the world still aspire. Its world has reached the goal. The Jew finds in his people the perfect fusion with a world of his own, and to achieve this fusion himself, he need not sacrifice an iota of his peculiar existence. The nations have been in a state of inner conflict ever since Christianity with its super-national power came upon them. Ever since then, and everywhere, a Siegfried is at strife with that stranger, the man of the cross, in his very appearance so suspect a character. A Siegfried who, depending on the nation he comes from may be blond and blue-eyed, or dark and small-boned, or brown and dark-eyed, wrestles again and again with this stranger who resists the continued attempts to assimilate him to that nation's own idealization. The Jew alone suffers no conflict between the supreme vision which is placed before his soul and the people among whom his life has placed him. He alone possesses the unity of myth which the nations lost through the influx of Christianity, which they were bound to lose, for their own myth was pagan myth which, by leading them into itself, led them away from God and their neighbor. The Jew's myth, leading him into his people, brings him face to face with God who is also the God of all nations. The Jewish people feels no conflict between what is its very own and what is supreme; the love it has for itself inevitably becomes love for its neighbor.

THE PEOPLES AND WAR

Because the Jewish people is beyond the contradiction that constitutes the vital drive in the life of the nations—the contradiction between national characteristics and world history, home and faith, earth and heaven—it knows nothing of war. For the peoples of antiquity, war was after all only one among other natural expressions of life: it held no fundamental contradictions. To the nations war means staking life in order to live. A nation that fares forth to war accepts the possibility of dying. This is not significant so long as nations regard themselves as mortal. While this conviction lasts, it is of no importance that of the two legitimate reasons for waging war as given by the great Roman orator—that of *salus* and that of *fides*, self-preservation and the keeping of the pledged word—the second may sometimes be in contradiction to the first. There is, after all, no good reason why Saguntum and its people shall not perish from the earth. But what it means becomes clear when Augustine, who is responsible for the clever refutation of Cicero, declares: the Church cannot fall into such conflict between its own welfare and the faith pledged to a higher being; for the Church, *salus* and *fides* are one and the same thing. What Augustine here says of the Church holds in a narrower sense also for worldly communities, for nations and states which have begun to regard their own existence from the highest point of view.

CHOSEN PEOPLES

Such notions of election, more or less, occurred to the individual peoples just by means of Christianity, and together with these notions also, of necessity, a claim to eternity. Not that such a claim really did determine the entire life of these peoples—that is out of the question; they are conscious even of the idea of election, which alone can establish such a claim, only in certain exalted moments; it is almost more of a festal garb in which they like to dress up than a robe of office without which they seriously believe themselves incapable of operating. At the bottom of the love for one's own people, the premonition that at some distant future date it will no longer exist yet ever rests and adds a bittersweet heaviness to the love. But at least the idea of the essential eternity of the people is there and, strong or weak, serious or half serious, it somehow has a concomitant effect. And now, to be sure, it gives the conduct of war a very different aspect. The life of the people which is at stake is something which in all seriousness should not be staked. How is the world to recover if the essence of this people is eradicated from it? And the more seriously a people has consummated in itself the identification of *salus* and *fides*, of its own existence, its own sense of the world, the more enigmatic appears to it the possibility which war discloses to it: the possibility of eclipse. Thus war begins to occupy the central place in its life. The states of antiquity centered their political existence around the public cult, the sacrifices, festivals and the like; while war kept the enemy at bay and certainly protected the native altars, it was not itself a sacrifice, itself a cultic act, itself an altar. The "Holy War," war as religious act, was reserved to the Christian Era after the Jewish people discovered it.

HOLY WAR

One of the most significant sections of our ancient law is the distinction between an ordinary war against a "very distant" people, conducted according to the general rules of the laws of war which regard war as an ordinary expression of the life of comparable states, and the holy war against the "seven nations" of Canaan, by means of which God's people conquers the area necessary for its existence. This

distinction contains within it a new view of war as an action necessary for God's sake. The peoples of the Christian Era can no longer
maintain this distinction. In keeping with the spirit of Christianity,
which admits of no boundaries, there are for it no "very distant"
peoples. Holy War and political war, which in Jewish law were con-
stitutionally distinguished, are here blended into one. Precisely because
they are not really God's people, because they are still only in process
of so becoming, therefore they cannot draw this fine distinction; they
simply cannot know in how far a war is holy war, and in how far
merely a secular war. But in any case they know that God's will
somehow realizes itself in the martial fortunes of their state. Somehow—it remains enigmatic how. The people must become familiar
with the idea of its possible eclipse. Whether it is to be used, as a
people, for a stone in the construction of the kingdom—about this the
consciousness of the individual has nothing to say. Only war, which
speeds on above the consciousness of the individual, decides this.

WORLD PEACE

As against the life of the nations of the world, constantly involved
in a holy war, the Jewish people has left its holy war behind in
its mythical antiquity. Hence, whatever wars it experiences are purely
political wars. But since the concept of a holy war is ingrained in
it, it cannot take these wars as seriously as the peoples of antiquity to
whom such a concept was alien. In the whole Christian world, the Jew
is practically the only human being who cannot take war seriously,
and this makes him the only genuine pacifist. For that reason, and
because he experiences perfect community in his spiritual year, he
remains remote from the chronology of the rest of the world, even
though this has long ceased to be a chronology peculiar to individual
peoples and, as Christian chronology, is accepted as a principle common to the world at large. He does not have to wait for world history
to unroll its long course to let him gain what he feels he already
possesses in the circuit of every year: the experience of the immediacy
of each single individual to God, realized in the perfect community
of all with God.

PEOPLE AND STATE

The Jewish people has already reached the goal toward which the
nations are still moving. It has that inner unity of faith and life which,
while Augustine may ascribe it to the Church in the form of the unity
between *fides* and *salus*, is still no more than a dream to the nations

within the Church. But just because it has that unity, the Jewish people is bound to be outside the world that does not yet have it. Though living in a state of eternal peace, it is outside of time agitated by wars. Insofar as it has reached the goal which it anticipates in hope, it cannot belong to the procession of those who approach this goal through the work of centuries. Its soul, replete with the vistas afforded by hope, grows numb to the concerns, the doing, and the struggling of the world. The consecration poured over it as over a priestly people renders its life "unproductive." Its holiness hinders it from devoting its soul to a still unhallowed world, no matter how much the body may be bound up with it. This people must deny itself active and full participation in the life of this world with its daily, apparently conclusive, solving of all contradictions. It is not permitted to recognize this daily solving of contradictions, for that would render it disloyal to the hope of a final solution. In order to keep unharmed the vision of the ultimate community it must deny itself the satisfaction the peoples of the world constantly enjoy in the functioning of their state. For the state is the ever changing guise under which time moves step by step toward eternity. So far as God's people is concerned, eternity has already come—even in the midst of time! For the nations of the world there is only the current era. But the state symbolizes the attempt to give nations eternity within the confines of time, an attempt which must of necessity be repeated again and again. The very fact that the state does try it, and must try it, makes it the imitator and rival of the people which is in itself eternal, a people which would cease to have a claim to its own eternity if the state were able to attain what it is striving for.

LAW IN THE STATE

An orbit, the orbit of the years assures the eternal people of its eternity. The world's peoples as such are without orbits; their life cascades downhill in a broad stream. If the state is to provide them with eternity, this stream must be halted and dammed up to form a lake. The state must seek to turn into an orbit that pure sequence of time to which the peoples as such are committed. It must transform the constant alternation of their life into preservation and renewal and thus introduce an orbit capable, in itself, of being eternal. Life seems to put an irreconcilable conflict between preservation and renewal. It only wants alternation. The law of change enjoins whatever endures from changing and whatever changes from enduring. Life can either be all rest or all motion. And since time cannot be denied, motion triumphs. "You cannot step twice into the same river." History seems to fade away in unobstructed alternation and transformation. But the state steps in and imposes its law on the change. Now of a sudden there exists something which endures. Indeed at first sight it now seems as if everything is decreed, everything enduring. But soon enough boisterous life again overflows the tablet of hard and fast rules. The law is conserved only as long as it is observed by the people. Law and life, duration and change, seem to part company. But the state reveals its true face. Law was only its first word. It cannot assert itself against the alternations of life. Now, however, the state speaks its second word: the word of coercion.

COERCION IN THE STATE

Coercion provides life with legal redress against law. By being coercive itself, and not just legal, the state remains hard on the heels of life. The point of all coercion is to institute new law. It is not the denial of law as one might think under the spell of its cataclysmic behavior; on the contrary, it lays the basis for law. But a paradox lurks in the idea of new law. Law is essentially old law. And now it is clear that coercion is: the renewer of old law. In the coercive act, the law constantly becomes new law. And the state is thus equally both lawful and coercive, refuge of the old law and source of the new. And in this dual form of refuge and source of law, the state rises above the mere runoff of the people's life, in which customs multiply and statutes change without ceasing and without coercion. The living people allows the living moment to transpire naturally, as the multiplication of customs and the alternations of law show, while the state opposes to this its mighty assertion of the moment. But it does so, not in the manner of the eternal people, not by eternalizing the moment into custom concluded once and for all and into unalterable law, but rather by newly and masterfully grasping the moment, and every subsequent moment, and shaping it according to its desires and capacities. At every moment the state is forcibly deciding the contradiction between conservation and renovation, between old law and new. It thus constantly resolves the contradiction, while the course of the people's life only delays the solution perpetually through the onward flow of time. The state attacks the problem, indeed the state is itself nothing but the constantly undertaken resolution of this contradiction.

WAR AND REVOLUTION

Thus war and revolution is the only reality known to the state; it would cease to be a state at the moment where neither the one nor

the other were to take place—even if it be only in the form of a thought
of war or revolution. The state can at no moment lay down the
sword. It must brandish it again at every moment in order to cut the
Gordian knot of the people's life, that contradiction between the
past and future which the people fails to resolve in its natural life
and which it only pushes aside. But in cutting the knot, the state
removes the contradiction from the world at every moment, though
admittedly each time only for this individual moment. The river of
the world's life which, until it finally merges in the ocean of eternity,
ever and for all time denies itself is thus dammed up at every moment
and turned into stagnant water. Thus the state turns every moment
into eternity. In each it forms a circle out of the contradiction between
old and new by forcibly renovating the old and lending the new
the legal force of the old. The new does not follow the old; rather
it coalesces with it in audacious integration, forming a "new law"
which is indissoluble for the moment. The moment remains entirely
moment: it perishes. But as long as it has not perished, just so long it
is a little eternity of its own, just so long there is nothing in it which
seeks to get beyond it; for the new, which otherwise always gets
beyond the old, is momentarily confined in its sphere of influence. It
takes the new moment to break the power of the old and to threaten
to let life flow on once more as a free river. But at once the state
raises its sword again and again condemns the river to a standstill, the
onward motion to a circle. These moments rooted to the spot by the
state are thus properly "hours" of the people's life, which knows no
hours on its own; it is the state which first introduces standstills, stations, epochs into the ceaseless sweep of this life. Epochs are the
hours of universal history, and only the state introduces them through
its martial spell which makes the sun of time stand still until on any
given day "the people shall have prevailed over its enemies." Thus
there is no universal history without the state. Only the state drops
into the current of time those reflections of true eternity which, as
epochs, form the building blocks of universal history.

The Eternity of the Promise

Therefore the true eternity of the eternal people must always be
alien and vexing to the state, and to the history of the world. In the
epochs of world history the state wields its sharp sword and carves
hours of eternity in the bark of the growing tree of life, while the

eternal people, untroubled and untouched, year after year adds ring upon ring to the stem of its eternal life. The power of world history breaks against this quiet life which looks neither right nor left. Again and again world history may claim that its newest eternity is the true eternity. Over and against all such claims we see the calm and silent image of our existence, which forces both him who wants to see and him who does not, to realize that eternity is nothing of the startlingly newest. Force may coerce the "newest" into an identification with the "final," to make it appear the very newest eternity indeed. But that is not like the bond which obtains between the latest grandson and the earliest forebear. Over and over, our existence sets before the eyes of the nations this true eternity of life, this turning of the hearts of the fathers to their children: wordless evidence which gives the lie to the worldly and all-too-worldly sham eternity of the historical moments of the nations, moments expressed in the destiny of their states. So long as the kingdom of God is still to come, the course of world history will always only reconcile creation within itself, only the moment which is about to come with that which has just passed. Only the eternal people, which is not encompassed by world history, can—at every moment—bind creation as a whole to redemption while redemption is still to come. The life of this people, alone, burns with a fire that feeds on itself, and hence needs no sword to supply the flame with fuel from the forests of the world. The fire burns through and in itself, and sends forth rays which shine out into the world and illumine it; the fire is not aware of the rays, nor does it have need of their light for itself. It burns silently and eternally. The seed of eternal life has been planted, and can wait for the budding. The seed knows nothing of the tree that grows from it, not even when it flings its shadow over the whole world. In time to come, a seed that is like the first will fall from the fruits of that tree. "Blessed art Thou . . . who hast planted eternal life in our midst."

BOOK TWO

The Rays

or

the Eternal Way

The Eternity of Realization

No man has the power to grasp the thought of the Creator for 'his ways are not our ways and his thoughts are not our thoughts.' This description of God's ways concludes the great survey of the entire contents of oral and written law which Maimonides has presented to us as the "Repetition of the Law." It introduces the subsequent sentences about the way of the true Messiah and about the great error of worshiping another besides God into which the world was led, according to the prophecy of the Book of Daniel, "by apostate sons of your people, who presume to fulfill the vision—and shall stumble." And our greater teacher continues thus.[1] All these matters only served to clear the way for King Messiah, to prepare the whole world to worship God with one accord, as it is written, 'Yea, at that time I will change the speech of the peoples to a pure speech, that all of them may call on the name of the Lord and serve him with one accord.' Thus the Messianic hope, the Torah and the commandments have become familiar topics, topics of conversation among the inhabitants of the far isles and many peoples, uncircumcised of heart and flesh. They are discussing these matters and the commandments of the Torah. Some say, "Those commandments were true, but have lost their validity and are no longer binding"; others declare that they had an esoteric meaning and were not intended to be taken literally, that

---

[1] After A. M. Herschman, *The Code of Maimonides Book Fourteen* (Yale Judaica Series III) pp. xxiiif. The passage is usually expunged from the censored editions. (Tr.)

the Messiah has already come and revealed their occult significance. But when the true King Messiah will appear and succeed, be exalted and lifted up, they will forthwith recant and realize that they have inherited naught but lies from their fathers.

The Way Through Time:
Christian History

The rays shoot forth from the fiery nucleus of the Star. They seek out a way through the long night of the times. It must be an eternal way, not a temporary one, even though it leads through time. Not that it may deny time—after all, it is meant to conduct through time—but time must not gain power over it. On the other hand, it must not create its own time, and thus liberate itself from time, after the fashion of the eternal people, continually reproducing itself in itself. Thus there remains for it only one thing: it must master time. But how could that happen? How could a way which traverses time partition time instead of being itself partitioned by time?

EPOCH

The question already embraces the answer. The tempo of time determines everything occurring in it only, after all, because time is older and younger than everything that occurs. Were an occurrence with a beginning and an end outside it to confront it, then the pulse of this occurrence could regulate the hours of the world clock. Such an occurrence would have to originate beyond time and run its course in a temporal beyond. True it would be within time in any present, but knowing itself independent of time in its past and in its future, it feels itself strong against time. Its present stands between past and future. The moment, however, does not stand. Rather it vanishes with the speed of an arrow. As a result it is never "between" its past and its future: it has vanished before it could be between anything. The course of the world knows a between only in the past. Only the point in past time is a point-in-time, an epoch, a stop. Living time knows of no points: as fast as it begins to be traversed with the speed of a flying arrow by the moment, every point is already traversed. But in the past the hours stand in that motionless juxtaposition. Here there are epochs, stations in time. They may be recognized by the fact that time precedes them and time follows them. They are between time and time.

Time, however, attains gravity only as such a between. Now it can no longer vanish like an arrow. The epoch no longer passes before I become aware of it, nor transforms itself before I notice it. Rather it signifies something. Something: in other words it has substantiality, is like a substance. In the past the course of the world assumes the form of immovable "substances," of eras, epochs, great moments. And this it can do only because in the past the vanishing moments are captured as stops, held between a before and an after. As a between they can no longer escape, as a between they have stability, they stand still like hours. Time has lost its power over the past, which consists entirely of betweens. It can still add to the past, but it can no longer change the past except, at the most, through what it adds. It can no longer take a hand in the inner structure of the past, for that is fixed, point by inte-grated point. The synchronized cadence of the years may appear to dominate the present so thoroughly that the impatience of a world reformer, the plaint of one haplessly aware of his turn of faith, bridle against it in vain. In the past, however, this cadence loses its power. In the past, events dominate time, and not vice versa. An epoch is that which stands—stands still—between its before and after. It little cares how many years it is assigned by the chronicle; every epoch weighs the same whether it lasts centuries or decades or only years. Here events rule time by marking it with their notches. Yet the event exists only within the epoch; the event stands between before and after. And a stationary between exists only in the past. If then the present too were to be elevated to the mastery of time, it too would have to be a between. The present—every present—would have to be-come "epoch-making." And time as a whole would have to become the hour, this temporality. As such it would have to be yoked into eternity, with eternity its beginning, eternity its end, and all of time but the between between that beginning and that end.

CHRISTIAN CHRONOLOGY

Thus it is Christianity that has made an epoch out of the present. Only the time before Christ's birth is now still past. All the time that succeeds, from Christ's earthly sojourn to his second coming, is now that sole great present, that epoch, that standstill, that suspension of the times, that interim over which time has lost its power. Time is now mere temporality. As such it can be surveyed in its entirety from any one of its points, for beginning and end are equidistant from each of its points. Time has become a single way, but a way whose beginning and end lie beyond time, and thus an eternal way. On ways which lead from within time to within time, by contrast, only the next segment can ever be surveyed. Every point on the eternal way is, moreover, a midpoint, since beginning and end are, after all, equidistant, no matter how time advances. It is a midpoint not because it is at the precise moment, the present point—not at all, for then it would be midpoint for one moment and already in the next instant no longer midpoint. That would amount to the kind of vitality with which time rewards a life that submits to it: a purely temporal vitality. It is the vitality of a life in the moment to be life in time, to let itself be carried off by the past, to summon up the future. Men and nations live thus. God withdrew the Jew from this life by arching the bridge of his law high above the current of time which henceforth and to all eternity rushes powerlessly along under its arches.

The Christian, however, takes up the contest with the current. He lays the track of his eternal way alongside of it. He who travels this road gauges the spot of the river which he is just looking at only by its distance from the points of departure and destination. He himself is ever and only en route. His real concern is only that he is still and yet on the way, still and yet between departure and goal. As often as he glances out the window, the current of time, ever yet passing by outside, tells him this, and nothing more. He who travels the current itself can only see from one bend to the next. For him who travels the iron tracks, the current as a whole is but a sign he is still en route, only a sign of the between. Beholding the current, he can never forget that the place whence he comes as well as the place whither he travels lie beyond the current's territory. If he asks himself where he may be now, at this moment, the current gives him no answer, while the answer which he gives himself is never anything but: en route. As long as the current of this temporality still runs at all, just so long he is himself with every moment midway between beginning and end of his course. Beginning and end are both equally near to him at every moment, for both are in the eternal, and it is only thereby that he knows himself as midpoint at every moment—as midpoint, not of a horizon which he surveys, but of a stretch which consists entirely of midpoint, which is, indeed, all middle, all Between, all path. He can and must sense every point along this path as a midpoint only *because* his path is all middle and because he knows this. The entire stretch, by consisting entirely of midpoints, is in short but a single midpoint. "Were Christ born a thousand times in Bethlehem and is not also born within you—you would still be lost"—this dictum of *The Cherubic*

Wanderer[1] is for the Christian a paradox only in the bold pithiness of its expression, not in its spirit. For the Christian the moment becomes the representative of eternity not as moment but as midpoint of the Christian world-time. And since it stays and does not perish, this world-time consists of such "midpoints." Every event stands midway between beginning and end of the eternal path and, by virtue of this central position in the temporal middle realm of eternity, every event is itself eternal.

Thus Christianity gains mastery over time by making of the moment an epoch-making epoch. From Christ's birth on, there is henceforth only present. Time does not bounce off Christianity as it does off the Jewish people, but fugitive time has been arrested and must henceforth serve as a captive servant. Past, present, and future—once perpetually interpenetrating each other, perpetually transforming themselves—are now become figures at rest, paintings on the walls and vaults of the chapel. Henceforth all that preceded the birth of Christ, prophets and Sibylline oracles included, is past history, arrested once and for all. And the future, impending hesitantly yet inescapably attracted, is the Last Judgment. The Christian world-time stands in between this past and this future as a single hour, a single day; in it all is middle, all equally bright as day. Thus the three periods of time have separated into eternal beginning, eternal middle, and eternal end of the eternal path through this temporality. Temporality itself is disabused of its self-confidence and allows this form to be forced on it in the Christian chronology. It ceases to believe that it is older than Christianity and counts its years from the birthday of Christianity. It suffers all that preceded this to appear as negated time, as unreal time so to speak. Hitherto it had re-counted the past by counting the years; now this counting becomes the prerogative of the present, of the ever present path. And Christianity treads this path, treads it deliberately, certain of its own eternal presence, ever in the middle of occurring world, ever in the event, ever *au courant*, ever with the imperious glance of the consciousness that it is the eternal way which it treads, and on which time now follows it as its obedient pedometer.

CHRISTENDOM

But what is Christendom if not people, successive generations, nations, states, persons differing in age, condition, sex, in color, educa-

[1] A popular collection of poems by Angelus Silesius (1674). (Tr.)

tion, breadth of vision, in endowments and capacities? And are these nevertheless to be henceforth at every moment one, gathered into a single midpoint and this midpoint in its turn the midpoint of all other midpoints of this one great middle? This question touches on the formative element in this community of Christianity. In the preceding book we raised the question of the formative element in the communion of Judaism, which Jewish dogma might have answered with "the Torah." But we were not entitled to be satisfied with that answer, and the dogmatic answer "Christ" would avail us no more here. Rather, it is precisely the manner in which a communion founded on dogma gives itself reality which we wish to fathom. More exactly still —for we know it has to be an eternal communion—we asked again, as in the preceding book, how a communion can found itself for eternity. We fathomed this for the communion of the eternal life; now we ask it concerning the communion of the eternal way.

The difference cannot simply be found in the fact that at every point of the way there is a midpoint. After all, at every moment in the life of the [Jewish] people there was the whole life. God led every individual out of Egypt: "I make this covenant . . . not with you alone but both with those who are not standing here with us this day . . . and with those who are with us here this day." Both the eternal life and the eternal way have this in common: they are eternal. Eternity is after all just this: that everything is at every point and at every moment. Thus the difference does not lie here. In the final analysis it must lie in that which is eternal, not in its eternal character. And so it is. Eternal life and eternal way are as different as the infinity of a point and the infinity of a line. The infinity of a point can only consist of the fact that it is never erased; thus it preserves itself in the eternal self-preservation of procreative blood. The infinity of a line, however, ceases where it would be impossible to extend it, it consists of the very possibility of unrestricted extension. Christianity, as the eternal way, has to spread ever further. Merely to preserve its status would mean for it renouncing its eternity and therewith death. Christianity must proselytize. This is just as essential to it as self-preservation through shutting the pure spring of blood off from foreign admixture is to the eternal people. Indeed proselytizing is the veritable form of its self-preservation for Christianity. It propagates by spreading. Eternity becomes eternity of the way by making all the points of the way, one by one, into midpoints. In the eternal people, procreation bears witness to eternity; on the eternal way this witness must really be attested to as witness. Every point of the way must once bear witness that it knows itself as midpoint of the eternal way. There the physical onward flow of the one blood bears witness to the ancestor in the engendered grandson. Here the outpouring of the spirit must establish the communion of testimony in the uninterrupted stream of baptismal water coursing on from each to another. Every point which this outpouring of the spirit reaches must be able to survey the whole path as an eternal communion of testimony. But the way can be surveyed only if it is itself the content of the testimony. In the witness of the communion the way must be attested at the same time. Tht communion becomes a single one through the attested belief. The belief is a belief in the path. Everyone in the communion knows that there is no eternal way other than the way which he is going. Only he belongs to Christianity who knows his own life to be on the way which leads from Christ come to Christ coming.

BELIEF

This knowledge is belief. It is belief as the content of a testimony. It is belief in something. That is exactly the opposite of the belief of the Jew. His belief is not the content of a testimony, but rather the product of a reproduction.[1] The Jew, engendered a Jew, attests his belief by continuing to procreate the Jewish people. His belief is not in something: he is himself the belief. He is believing with an immediacy which no Christian dogmatist can ever attain for himself. This belief cares little for its dogmatic fixation: it has existence and that is worth more than words. But the world is entitled to words. A belief which seeks to win the world must be belief in something. Even the tiniest union of units united to win a piece of the world requires a common faith, a watchword by which those united can recognize themselves. Anyone who wants to create a piece of way of his own in the world must believe in something. Merely to believe would never allow him to attain to something in the world. Only he who believes in something can conquer something—namely, what he believes in. And it is exactly so with Christian belief. It is dogmatic in the highest sense, and must be so. It may not dispense with words. On the contrary: it simply cannot have enough of words, it cannot make enough words. It really ought to have a thousand tongues. It ought to speak all languages. For it has to wish that everything would become its own. And so the something in which it believes must be—not a something but everything. For this very reason it is the belief in

---

[1] The original play on words involves the homophonous roots zeugen = testify and zeugen = (re)produce, and cannot be translated in its entirety. (Tr.)

the way. By believing in the way, Christian belief paves the way for
the way into the world. Bearing witness, it first generates the eternal
way in the world. Jewish belief, on the other hand, follows after the
eternal life of the people as a product.

THE CHURCH

Thus Christian belief, the witness to the eternal way, is creative in
the world. It unites those who bear witness into a union in the world.
It unites them as individuals, for bearing witness is always an individual matter. Moreover the individual is here supposed to bear
witness concerning his attitude to an individual, for the testimony,
after all, concerns Christ. Christ is the common content of all the testi-
monies of belief. But though they were united as individuals, belief
now directs them toward common action in the world. For the paving
of the way is the common labor of all the individuals. Each individual
can, after all, set foot on only one point of the eternal way—his point—
and make of it what the whole way must become in order to be the
eternal way: middle. And thus belief establishes that union of individuals, *as* individuals, for common labor which rightfully bears the
name of *ecclesia*. For this original name of the church is taken from
the life of the ancient city-states, and designates the citizens assembled
for common deliberation. God's People designated its festivals as
"sacred convocations" with what was essentially a similar term. But
for itself it used words, like people or congregation, which once designated the people-in-arms, that entity, in other words, in which the
people appears as the self-contained whole into which the individuals
have dissolved. In the *ecclesia*, however, the individual is and remains
an individual, and only its resolve is common and becomes—*res publica*.

CHRIST

Now Christianity gives itself precisely this name of *ecclesia*, the
name of an assembly of individuals for common labor. Still, this labor
only comes to pass by virtue of each one acting in his place as individual. In the assembly, similarly, the common resolve emerges only
by virtue of the fact that each expresses his opinion and votes entirely
as an individual. Thus, too, the community of the church presupposes
the personality and integrity—we may safely say: the soul—of its members. Paul's analogy of the congregation as the body of Christ does
not imply some kind of division of labor like, say, the famous parable
of stomach and limbs by Menenius Agrippa. Rather it alludes precisely

to this perfect freedom of each individual in the Church. It is illuminated by the great "For though everything belongs to you . . . yet
you belong to Christ."[1] Everything is subservient to Christianity because Christianity, and every individual Christian within it, proceeds
from the crucified one. Every Christian is privileged to know himself
on the way, not merely at any arbitrary point, but rather at the absolute middle of the way which, after all, is itself wholly middle, wholly
between. But inasmuch as Christianity and the individual [Christian]
still await the second coming, those who have just been manumitted as
lords of all things at once know themselves again as everyone's slave.
For what they do to the least of His brothers, that they do to him who
will return to judge the world.[2]

How then will the *ecclesia* constitute itself on the basis of that freedom and integrity of the individuals which must be preserved? How
is the bond which connects each to each within it to look? It must,
after all, leave the individuals free while it binds them; indeed, in truth,
it must first make them free. It must leave everyone as it finds him,
man as man, woman as woman, the aged old, the youths young, the
master as master, the slave as slave, the wealthy rich, the paupers poor,
the sage wise and the fool foolish, the Roman a Roman and the barbarian a barbarian. The bond must not place anyone in the status of
another, and yet it must bridge the chasm between man and wife, between parents and child, between master and slave, between rich and
poor, sage and fool, Roman and barbarian. It must free each one as
he is, in all his natural and God-given dependencies with which he
stands in the world of creation. It must set him in the middle of that
way which leads from eternity to eternity.

It is the bond of brotherliness which thus takes men as it finds them
and yet binds them together across differences of sex, age, class, and
race. Brotherliness connects people in all given circumstances—independently of these circumstances, which simply continue to exist—as
equals, as brothers "in the Lord." From being men they become brothers,
and the common belief in the common way is the content for this. In
this Christian covenant of brotherhood, Christ is both beginning and
end of the way, and thereby content and goal, founder and master of the
covenant, as well as the middle of the way, and therefore present wherever two have met together in his name.[3] Wherever two have met
together in his name, there is the middle of the way. There the whole
way may be surveyed. There beginning and end are equidistant because

---

[1] I Corinthians 3:21-23.
[2] Cf. Matthew 25:40.
[3] Cf. Matthew 18:20.

he who is beginning and end abides in midst of those assembled here. Thus in the middle of the way Christ is neither founder nor master of his Church, but rather a member of it, himself a brother of his covenant. As such he can also be with the individual in brotherliness: even the individual—and not only two who have met together—already knows himself as Christian. Though seemingly alone with himself, he yet knows himself as member of the church because this solitude is togetherness with Christ.

Christ is near to this individual in that form to which his brotherly feelings can most readily direct themselves. The individual is, after all, to remain what he is: the man a man, the woman a woman, the child a child. Thus Christ is a friend to the man, a spiritual bridegroom to the woman, a holy infant to the child. Tied to the historical Jesus, Christ may forego this identification with the familiar figure of the neighbor, the object of brotherly love; but there the saints substitute for Christ himself. At least they do so in the Petrine Church of love, the Church which holds its believers most ardently to the way and allows them to remember less of its beginning and end. There man is privileged to love Mary as the pure virgin, and woman to love her as the divine sister, and each to love the saint of his class and nation from within his class and nation. Indeed, everyone is there privileged to love his saintly namesake as a brother from within the narrowest confines of the Self as it is contained within his Christian name. This Church of love is even more intrinsically a Church of the way than the others. And in it the figure of the living world-wanderer pushes itself ahead even of the deceased God on the cross; in it—more than in the sister churches—this wanderer becomes an example to be followed like an exemplary human brother; in it, at the same time, the whole crowd of saints interceding for their frail brothers and sisters, surges before the judge of the last judgment, where the way reaches its goal.

THE CHRISTIAN ACT

Thus brotherliness weaves its bond among men of whom none equal each other. Nor is this brotherliness by any means identity of everything with human countenance, but rather the harmony precisely of men of the most diverse countenances. One thing is necessary, of course, but only one: that men have a countenance at all, that they see each other. The church is the communion of all those who see each other. It joins men as coevals, as contemporaries at disparate loci of the ample space. Contemporaneity is something which in temporality does not even exist. In temporality there is only before and after. The moment in which one catches sight of oneself can only precede or follow the moment where one catches sight of another. Simultaneously to catch sight of oneself and of another at the same moment is impossible. That is the profoundest reason for the impossibility of loving one's neighbor as oneself in the heathen world which is, after all, precisely temporality. In eternity, however, there is also contemporaneity. It goes without saying that, seen from its shore, all time is simultaneous. But that time too which, as eternal way, leads from eternity to eternity admits of simultaneity. For only insofar as it is middle between eternity and eternity is it possible for people to meet on it. Thus he who catches sight of himself on the way is on the same point—that is, on the exact midpoint—of time. It is brotherliness which transports men into this midpoint. Time, already overcome, is placed at its feet; it is left for love only to traverse the separating space. And thus it traverses in its flight the hostility of nations as well as the cruelty of gender, the jealousy of class as well as the barrier of age. Thus it permits all the hostile, cruel, jealous, limited ones to catch sight of each other as brothers in one and the same central moment of time.

THE JEWISH ACT

The contemporaries catch sight of one another in the middle of time. At the boundaries of time, similarly, those had encountered each other for whom the differences of space did not mean a separation that first had to be overcome. For there these differences had already been overcome, from the start, in the innate communion of the people. There the labor of love—both of divine love for men and of human love for each other—had to be directed solely toward the preservation of this communion through time, toward the creation of contemporaneity of the sequences of generations separated in temporality. That is the covenant between scion and ancestor. By virtue of this covenant the people becomes an eternal people. For in catching sight of each other, scion and ancestor catch sight in each other at the same moment of the last descendant and the first ancestor. Descendant and ancestor are thus the true incarnation of the eternal people, both of them for each other, and both together for him who stands between them, just as the fellow-man become brother is the Church incarnate for the Christian. We experience our Judaism with immediacy in elders and children. The Christian experiences his Christianity in the sensation of that moment which leads the brother to him at the height of the eternal way. For him, all of Christianity seems to crowd together there. It stands where he stands,

he stands where it stands: at the middle of time between eternity and
eternity. We too are shown eternity by the moment, but differently:
not in the brother who stands closest to us, but rather in those who stand
furthest from us in time, in the oldest and the youngest, in the elder who
admonishes, in the lad who asks, in the ancestor who blesses and in the
grandson who receives the blessing. It is thus that the bridge of eternity
does its spanning for us: from the starry heaven of the promise which
arches over that moment of revelation whence sprang the river of our
eternal life, unto the limitless sands of the promise washed by the sea into
which that river empties, the sea out of which will rise the Star of
Redemption when once the earth froths over, like its flood tides, with
the knowledge of the Lord.

CROSS AND STAR

In the final analysis, then, that tension of beginning and end withal
strives mightily toward the end. Though as tension it originates
only in both, it finally gathers nevertheless at one point, namely, at the
end. The child with its questions is in the final analysis still and all a
more powerful admonisher than the elder. No matter how we may
perpetually draw nourishment from the inexhaustible treasure of the
elder's inspired life, no matter how we may maintain and fortify ourselves on the merit of the fathers: the elder turns into a memory, the
child alone compels. God establishes his kingdom only "out of the
mouths of babes and sucklings." In the final analysis the tension after
all concentrates itself entirely at the end, on the latest sprout at last,
on the Messiah whom we await. So too the Christian agglomeration
at the midpoint at long last does not remain glued to that spot after all.
Let the Christian discern Christ in his brother: in the final analysis
he is after all driven beyond the brother to Christ himself, without
mediation. Let the middle be but middle between beginning and end:
it gravitates, for all that, toward the beginning. Let man discern cross
and last judgment alike from the middle of the way in eternal proximity: he cannot let that satisfy him. He steps directly under the cross,
and will not rest till the image of the crucified one cover all the world
for him. In this turning to the cross alone, he may forget the judgment: he remains on the way for all that. For though it still belongs
to the eternal beginning of the way, the cross is after all no longer the
first beginning; it is itself already on the way and whoever steps under
it thus stands at its middle and beginning at the same time. Thus Christian consciousness, all steeped in belief, presses toward the beginning
of the way, to the first Christian, the crucified one, just as Jewish

consciousness, all gathered up in hope, presses toward the man of the end of time, to David's royal sprout. Belief can renew itself eternally at its beginning, just as the arms of the cross can be extended to infinity. Hope, however, eternally unites itself out of all the multiplicity of time in the one near and far moment-in-space of the end, just as the Star on the shield of David gathers all into the fiery nucleus. Rootedness in the profoundest self—that had been the secret of the eternity of the [eternal] people. Diffusion throughout all that is outside—this is the secret of the eternity of the [eternal] way.

The Two Roads: The Essence of Christianity

Expansion to the exterior, and not: as far as possible but rather—whether possible or not—expansion into each and everything that is outside, and that, in each respective present, can only at most be a still-outside—if this expansion is all that unconditional, all that limitless, then what was true of the Jewish rootedness in its own interior is manifestly valid also for it, namely, that nothing may remain outside as something contradictory. Here too all contradictions must somehow be drawn into its own boundaries. But such boundaries as may have been possessed by the personal self, rooting itself in itself, are alien, nay they are unthinkable for this expansion into the exterior. Where is the boundless to have boundaries? It bursts all bounds every time! Admittedly, the expansion itself cannot have boundaries, but that exterior into which the expansion takes place, can have them: the boundaries of the All. But these boundaries are not reached in the present nor in any future present, for eternity can erupt today or tomorrow but not the day after tomorrow, and the future is always mere day after tomorrow.

Thus the manner in which the contradictions are alive must also be different here from what it was in the absorption in the self. There the contradictions were at once harnessed into the internal structures of God, world, man; the three contradictions were alive as if in constantly alternating currents between those three poles. Here, on the other hand, the contradictions must already inhere in the nature of the expansion if they are to be effective wholly and at every moment. The expansion must take place along each of two discrete and even opposite ways. Beneath Christianity's footsteps into each of the countries God, man, and world there must bloom respectively two different sorts of flowers. Indeed, these steps themselves must diverge in time, and two forms of Christianity must traverse those three countries, each along its own path, hopeful of reuniting again one day, but not within time. Within time they march their separate ways and only by marching separately are they certain of traversing the entire All without losing themselves in it. Judaism was able to be the one people, the eternal people, only because it already bore all the great contradictions within itself; for the peoples of the world, on the other hand, these contradictions emerge only where they part company one from another. Just so Christianity too, to be really all-embracing, must harbor within itself the contradictions with which other associations each delimit themselves against all others already in name and purpose. Only thus can Christianity distinguish itself as the all-embracing association and withal the only one of its kind. God, world, and man can become Christian God, Christian world, Christian man only if they disgorge the contradictions in which life moves out of themselves and work each one out individually. Otherwise Christendom would be no more than a club, entitled perhaps to its particular purpose and its special area, but without a claim to expansion to the ends of the world. And again, if Christianity were to try to expand beyond these contradictions, then its way, though it would not need to bifurcate, would not be the way through the world, the way along the current of time; it would rather be a way leading to the trackless ocean of the winds where the All is without content even if it be also without limits or contradictions. And the way of Christianity must lead elsewhere, into the living All that surrounds us, the All of life, the All composed of God, man, and world.

SON AND FATHER

The way of Christianity into the country labelled God thus divides into two ways. It is a duality which is simply incomprehensible to the Jew, albeit Christian life rests precisely on it. It is incomprehensible to us for though we too know a contradiction in God, a juxtaposition of justice and mercy, of creation and revelation, this contradiction is within him, it is in ceaseless connection precisely with itself. There is an alternating current oscillating between God's attributes; one cannot equate him with the one or the other; he is, rather, One precisely in the constant equalization of apparently opposite "attributes." For the Christian, however, the division into "Father" and "Son" signifies much more than merely a separation into divine sternness and divine love. The Son is, after all, also the judge of the world, the Father "so loved" the world that he gave his own son. Thus sternness and love are not really divided between the two persons of the deity at all. And no more can they be divided according to creation and revelation. For the Son is not without participation in creation, nor the Father in revelation. Rather it is Christian piety which follows different paths according as it is with the Father or with the Son. The Christian approaches only the Son with that familiarity which seems so natural to us in our relationship to God that we for our part can barely conceive of the existence of persons who mistrust this trust. The Christian dares to enter the presence of the Father only by means of the Son; he believes he can reach the Father only through the Son. If the Son were not a man he would avail nothing to the Christian. He cannot imagine that God himself, the holy God, could so condescend to him as he demands, except by becoming human himself. The inextinguishable segment of paganism which is innermost in every Christian bursts forth here. The pagan wants to be surrounded by human deities; he is not satisfied with being human himself: God too must be human. The vitality which the true God too shares with the gods of the heathen becomes credible to the Christian only if it becomes flesh in a human-divine person of its own. Once this God has become man, the Christian proceeds through life as confidently as we and—unlike us—full of conquering power. For flesh and blood will only be subdued by flesh and blood, and precisely the indicated "paganism" of the Christian qualifies him to convert the pagans.

But at the same time he is also proceeding along another path, the one which is immediate to the Father. In the Son, the Christian drew God immediately into the brotherly nighness of his own I: before the Father he may once more divest himself of everything personal. In his nighness he ceases to be I. Here he knows himself in the orbit of a truth which makes a mockery of everything that is I. He satisfies his need for the nighness of God by means of the Son, but the Father provides him with divine truth. Here he attains that pure remoteness and objectivity of cognition and action which, in apparent contradiction to the heartfeltness of love, designates Christianity's other way through the world. For knowledge as for action life is systematized into fixed orders under the sign of God the Father. On this path too, the Christian feels the glance of God directed toward him, of God the Father, that is, not the Son. It is un-Christian to confuse these two ways to God. It is a matter of "tact" to distinguish them and to know when it is proper to walk the one and when the other. The Christian does not know those unexpected reversals out of the consciousness of divine love into that of divine righteousness and vice versa which, quick as lightning, are of the essence of Jewish life. His approach to

God remains twofold and, if the compulsion of this twofold path should tear him apart, he is permitted to decide clearly for one of them and to devote himself entirely to it rather than to waver back and forth in the twilight between the two. The world, his fellow-Christians, will no doubt see to it that the balance is restored. For that which, in God, is here revealed as a separation of the divine persons corresponds, in the Christian world, to a twofold order, and in the Christian man to a dual form of life.

PRIEST AND SAINT

In Jewish man, man was one, and a living one at that, for all his contradictions, for all the ineradicable conflicts between his love by God and his love for God, between his Judaism and his humanism, between patriarch and messiah. But in Christianity, this man separates into two figures, not necessarily two mutually exclusive and antagonistic figures, but two figures going their separate ways, separate even when they meet in a single person as is always possible. And these separate ways again lead through all that broad country of humanity in whose districts form and freedom appear to be in perpetual conflict. Precisely this contradiction is given free rein in Christianity in the two figures of the priest and the saint. And again it is not simply a case of the priest being merely the human vessel of revelation, or of the saint's love merely supplying the warmth to ripen the fruit of redemption. For the priest is not simply the man in whom the word of the divine mouth awakens the slumbering soul with a kiss. Rather he is the man redeemed to his destiny as image of God, prepared to become the vessel of revelation. And the saint can redeem the world in love only on the basis of a revelation which has just, and always just, come to him, only in the nearness of his Lord which always anew becomes something he can taste and see. He cannot just act as though there were no God to put into his heart what to do, any more than the priest could wear his priestly garment if he were not able to acquire redemption in the visible forms of the Church, and with that the feeling that he discharges his office in the image of God. A bit of heretical caprice is concealed in that consciousness of divine inspiration which is borne by the saint; a bit of the self-apotheosis of the Grand Inquisitor is donned with the priestly garb as this implies the claim to be in the image of God. The outer limits of form and freedom are ceremonial and super-personal self-apotheosis on the one hand and momentary, personal caprice on the other—on the one hand the emperor of Byzantium, exalted above everything mundane and incidental by the greatest pomp and strictest etiquette, and on the other the revolutionary, hurling the torch of his momentary demand into millennial buildings. The broad realm of the soul stretches between these outer limits, and the bifurcated path of Christianity traverses it all.

STATE AND CHURCH

For the Jew, the world is full of smooth transitions from "this world" to the "world to come" and back; for the Christian, it is organized into the great dualism of state and Church. Not without justification it has been said of the pagan world that it knew neither the one nor the other. The *polis* was both state and Church for its citizens, as yet without any contradiction. But in the Christian world, these two separated from the beginning. The history of the Christian world thereafter consists of the attempt to maintain this separation. It is not as if only the Church were Christian and not the state. "Render unto Caesar that which is Caesar's" weighed no less heavily in the course of the centuries than the second half of this dictum. For the law to which the peoples submit proceeds from Caesar. And creation, the work of divine omnipotence, is consummated in the universal rule of law on earth. The very Caesar to whom one was to render what was his had already commanded a world which was a single constituency. The Church itself transmitted to a later age the memory of this state of affairs together with the longing for its restoration. It was the Pope who placed the diadem of the Caesars on the brows of the Frankish Charlemagne. It rested on the heads of his successors for a millennium, bitterly disputed by the Church itself, which postulated its own preeminent domain and title and defended it against the very claim to universal imperial jurisdiction which she herself had nurtured. While these two equally universal jurisdictions battled for the world there grew up new structures, "states" which presumed to fight for jurisdiction not, like the empire, over the world, but only over themselves. These states thus emerged as rebels against a world created by a single creative power and whose jurisdictional unity had been turned over to the emperor for safekeeping. And when these states were free to believe that they had found a firm foundation in creation, when they had found their niche in the natural nation, at that very moment the crown was removed from the head of the Roman emperor once and for all, and the neo-Frankish national emperor crowed himself with it. Others imitated him as representatives of their nations, but the imperial drive seemed now to have transferred to the peoples together with the title of emperor: now the peoples themselves became bearers of supra-national, world-oriented volition. And by the time this imperial drive has been eroded in the mutual friction of the peoples, it will assume a new form. For it is doubly anchored, once in the divine Creator of the world whose power it reflects, and again in the world's longing for redemption, which it serves. Thus it opens up one of the two essential paths of Christianity, leading into that part of the All which is the World.

The other path leads through the Church. The Church too is in the world. It must therefore come into conflict with the state. It cannot dispense with a legal constitution of its own. On the contrary, it is a visible sysem and of a sort which the state cannot tolerate—say because it were to limit itself to a particular sphere—but rather a system which claims to be not a whit less universal than the state. Church law, no less than Caesar's, sooner or later applies to everyone. The Church drafts man for the labor of redemption and assigns to this labor a place in the created world. Stones must be brought from the mountains and trees felled in the forest if there is to be a house in which man will serve God. The Church is in the world, visible and with a universal law of its own, and thus not a whit more than Caesar's empire itself the kingdom of God. It grows toward the latter in its history which is secular both in the sense of worldly and of centuries-long; it remains a segment of the world and of life, and it becomes eternal only through its animation by the human act of love. Ecclesiastical history is no more the history of the kingdom of God than is imperial history. In the strict sense there is in fact no history of the kingdom of God. The eternal can have no history, at most a prehistory. The centuries and millennia of ecclesiastical history are no more than the earthly form, changing with time, around which the ecclesiastical year spins the halo of eternity.

Sanctification of the Soul: The Clerical Year

Once more we must run the circuit of the clerical year. In the preceding book, we had learned to regard it as a curriculum of communal silence proceeding from communal listening via the communal meal to the communal prayer. This process remains the same here also. There, to be sure, a people and its eternity were meant to be reflected in the ambit of the year. Thus the stress was on the communal factor, whether in listening, in eating or in kneeling, and the theory of the forms of communal life as such was a prerequisite for the exposition of the liturgy. Here, on the other hand, we are dealing with a common way and its eternity, a common going, doing, becoming, rather than a common structure, result, or existence. If, then, the stations of the communal silence are to reappear here, it would have to take place in the individual soul's preparation for commonplaces. Each of these communal acts, after all, demands a specific directedness of the soul without which the soul will not set forth on its way. Eternal life is something transcendent into which the individual is born and with which he coexists. The decision and preparation to participate in the eternal way must be his own as individual.

But where is the solitary soul thus to prepare for community? Where in general is the soul to undergo a metamorphosis which, unbeknown to itself in the still cell of its solitude, would endow it with that form in which it could accord with others? Where indeed is the individual soul to be tuned to that note which would allow it to harmonize with others in true symphony? Such harmony, unconscious and yet conducting the soul on the path of supreme consciousness, of silent accord with others, can reach the soul from but one single force: from art. Nor do we mean an art which by preference detaches itself together with its creator and its consumer from all the world into an ultimate aside, but solely an art which has found its way out of that peculiar realm back into life, really found, that is, what this art, exiled into its esoteric realm, had already sought out everywhere by way of deliverance from itself. Only those arts designated as applied arts in what was meant to denigrate but in fact ennobles them, only they lead man wholly back into the life which he had left behind as long as he indulged in the "pure" enjoyment of art, and they do this without sacrificing so much as a spark of their grandeur. Indeed they are the only arts which can wholly cure him of that disease of alienation from the world which plunged the art lover into the misleading delusion of supreme health just as he exposed himself defenselessly to the disease. Thus art is its own anti-toxin. It decontaminates itself, and man, from its own purity. From demanding sweetheart it turns into good wife, strengthening him for the marketplace and the important hours of public life with a thousand small everyday kindnesses and domestic duties, and thereby first flowering into the full, mature beauty as lady of the house.

SOCIOLOGY OF THE FINE ARTS: CHURCH ARCHITECTURE

Among the arts it was the fine arts which, as the arts of space, re-created creation as it were. But their products are locked up in galleries, museums, and collections, between artificial frames, on individual pedestals, in folders—each separated from the others but none so thoroughly separate but that each work disturbs every other in these morgues of art. Then architecture comes along, frees the prisoners, and conducts them in festive procession into the solemn space of the Church. Now ceilings and walls and the rich shrine of the altar are being decorated by the painter, pillars and pediments, columns and cornices by the sculptor, and the holy book by the draughtsman. Yet these are more than mere ornament; the arts have not become handmaidens subservient to a foreign purpose. Rather they first awake here from the seeming death of those morgues into their true life. For though they were spatial arts and each work created a space of its own for itself, yet this space was only a space of its own, meaning an "ideal" space. As such it collided painfully with real space, and accordingly longed for the aforementioned artificial partitions, such as frames, pedestals, folders, so as to serve as barriers against the contact with real space. Thus the work of art appeared condemned to solitude even from its own kind, for the "ideal" quality of its space consisted of the fact that it was a space peculiar to this work of art alone. Indeed all "idealism," though ostensibly too good for reality, is in fact most often but a flight from the all-too-common reality into the dream world of selfishness. Thus the ideal spaces of several works of art do not emerge from themselves to converge with each other.

To become fully real, to cease to be mere art, the works of art must first be removed from the magic circle of their ideal space and deposited into a real space. But there is only one sort of fully real space in the world, for the space in which the world itself dwells is "ideal"—in "transcendentalist" if not in esthetic terms; its reality is real only in relation to its being-thought, not to createdness. Only the world is created, and space only as a portion of it, like everything logical. But the space in which the world would be, the mathematician's space, that is not created. As a result those who, like mathematicians and physicists, regard the created world under the aspect of space, necessarily strip it of its utter factuality which, exalted above all possibilities, it enjoys as creation, and relativize it into a football of possibilities. Architecture creates a space on the basis of the revealed spatial directions and spatial relations of heaven and earth, Zion and all the world, Bethlehem-Ephrathah and the 'thousands of Judah'; only this space is fully real. The architect, the master-builder, fixes points on the surface of the earth and measurements and directions on the inside of the structure; only from these there radiates a fixed, immovable, created space, where small and large, middle and end, above and below, east and west are meaningful. It radiates even into the world which, though spacious, was hitherto itself created nonspatially, and spatializes it.

And among buildings in turn, there is only one kind which is room pure and simple, that is to say which does not comprise separate rooms serving separate purposes like all residential, commercial, and official buildings, as well as assembly halls, theatres, and inns. For in all of these, man stops for a particular purpose, which is different for each one and requires the division of the available room into rooms. Even halls, if they constitute a single room, do so by accident. In itself there is nothing wrong with "housing" several meeting rooms or concert halls in a single building, and generally this is done. For since people are supposed to meet there for only one particular purpose at a time, there can be no objection to other groups of people meeting at the same time and under the same roof for other purposes. Man just does not tarry anywhere merely in order to tarry together with others in one space. For him only the house of God is this kind of space pure and simple. It is the only kind of house with a fixed orientation which is everywhere the same, and comprising of necessity a single room. For here it would, to be sure, be an offensive and unthinkable thought to have several spatially separate churches of the same community meeting under a single roof. Where this does happen—and it does so particularly with us [Jews]—there, and in *ecclesia pressa* generally, architecture has no business being. It needs freedom, spaciousness into which to create its space. Characteristically for its essential unicellular character, the Church is the only structure whose floor plan is immediately and constantly recognized and experienced by every visitor, not as floor plan of the spatial segment in which he just happens to find himself, as is the case elsewhere, but as floor plan of the [whole] building. Churches are the only edifices which really can, nay must be built from the inside out in the spirit of the architect as demanded by the highest challenge.

Thus architecture here creates one single space, beautiful of form and yet for a purpose, and an essential purpose at that, indeed the most universal purpose of human life. This is applied art in the truest sense of the word. And now all the works of "pure" art thereby also participate in the reality of the architectonic space, which presently incorporates all those "ideal" spaces into its one great spatial reality, reddening the sickly pallor of those pseudo-spaces with its powerful heartbeat. Everybody sojourning in this space is now attracted into it and into its essentiality. Here alone objects achieve essentiality as objects. At the very least the essentiality which may surround objects elsewhere too generally takes its origin from here. Only cultic objects, once formed, resist every change in their form. They are just not objects any more like other objects; they have become living things, as daring as this expression may sound. Torah and Scroll of Esther are the only ancient books preserved to the present day in precisely their ancient form, but by virtue of this strictly preserved form, the Torah-scroll has ceased to be an ordinary object. One might say that the feelings attached to such a parchment scroll are more personal than those for what is written on it, and at least equally alive. So too there is no garment that preserves itself as strictly as the cultic one. Again one should recall here the preservation of the ancient garb in the Jewish ritual. The case is similar with the priestly robes of the Catholic and Eastern Churches. Indeed, dress itself must derive from here. Armor is laid aside when no longer needed, and every piece of clothing likewise is in the first instance only a utilitarian object, not what dress is today. For today clothes truly make the man; clothes belong to the man and he is incomplete if he is not dressed appropriately for the occasion. Dress integrates man into human society. But this animation of dress first happens to the priest; it first becomes essential for him, and again under the compulsion, creating space and integrating everything into space, of the house of God. The priestly function is the first which can only be performed in a particular costume. In a real space, then, waves of realization flood through everything which enters that space. Everything corporeal comes alive; its form achieves stability and the capacity to reproduce itself through time, while man surrenders the freedom of appearing as the circumstance may happen to have it, and adjusts to the place. His body dispenses with the expression of his personality and dresses according to the rule of the space which unites him with others. The corporeality of man learns to keep silent about its peculiarities—a first step only for what is yet to come.

THE SACRAMENT OF THE WORD

For the purpose of the single room, that which turns architecture into an applied art is quite simply this: to generate the feeling of unification in every individual even before this unification itself has been established. For it is established only in the hearing of the common word; with that it already exists, while a crowd could be together in one room without a feeling of belonging together. But the common room nonetheless arouses in every individual at least the wish for community, or better: its presentiment. It forces the soul of every individual onto the path which leads into the communal silence of the hearers of the word. It attunes the soul. Further than this man is not accompanied by the muse, not even where she is not the muse of "pure" art, untainted by purpose, but the muse of applied art who has entered life's circle of duties. Here too another power must assume the lead, none other than: the word.

In Jewish worship, the word already signifies the common flag more than the power which first establishes the community. Scripture is read to the conspicuous lack of attention of those not immediately involved, and the sermon has been forced into the background for centuries. This shows that the community [in Judaism] is not first established in the act of listening. The reading of Scripture retains its central position in the service, but it is rather a symbol only of that community which has already been established, that "eternal life" which has already been planted. It is different with Christianity. Here the word truly takes the individual by the hand and guides him on the way which leads to the community. The preparations which were inaugurated by the building of the Church are completed in the word. With good reason, therefore, Augustine designated it as foundation of the sacraments, and subsequently the Church of Luther ranked it as the most important sacrament, the one which first turns the others into sacrament. For the sacraments serve "to complete the individual in what pertains to worship." And the word is the preparation for this preparation of the individual. With good reason, on the other hand, it was not included in the heptad of its sacraments by the Catholic Church, precisely because it is only preparation. The Catholic too cannot do without it, nor wishes to, and lets it co-operate in all the sacraments. But in Protestantism, the sermon has grown into the veritable centerpiece of the service, in keeping with its strong appeal to the individual, a tendency which quite naturally had and has to lay chief stress on the means which originally attracted the individual.

SUNDAY, THE FESTIVAL OF CREATION

Here too the weekly festival of creation established the clerical year. But the Church committed an act of deeper significance than it realized when it moved the festival from the seventh day of the week to the first in order to make a clean break with the Synagogue. On the Sabbath, the preview of the six ensuing working days permeates at most the prayers of its concluding service. But here this mood prevails throughout. Sunday is the day when the Christian accumulates that treasure of spiritual nourishment which he will consume during

the course of the week. The Sabbath is the festival of redemption, in
a double sense in fact, in both its bases: as remembrance of the work
of creation, for it celebrates the divine rest of the seventh day, and
also as memorial day for the liberation from the Egyptian house of
bondage, for its purpose is to let man-servant and maid-servant rest like
their master; Creation and revelation merge on the Sabbath in the rest of
redemption. Sunday, which has never taken the prescription to rest very
seriously, even in periods which were otherwise legalistic in orientation, has turned entirely into the festival of the beginning. Under the
symbol of the beginning of the world, it celebrates primarily the beginning of the week. We recognized the strength with which Christian consciousness strove from the middle of the path on which it
stands toward the beginning. The cross is ever beginning, ever the
point of departure for the co-ordinates of the world. Just as the
Christian Era begins there, so too Christian belief repeatedly begins
its course there. The Christian is the eternal beginner; completion is
not for him: all's well that's well begun. That is the eternal youth of the
Christian; every Christian lives his Christianity every day as though it
were the first.

And thus Sunday, with the power of its blessing irradiating the
workaday week, is the proper image of the power of Christianity,
radiant over the world ever anew, ever youthful, ever novel. The beginning of the Jewish year follows, significantly enough, immediately
upon the close of the festival of eternal redemption; in a certain sense
it grows out of this close again as a new beginning, for all that the
time for this eternity has not yet arrived. Just so the Church year, and
this is equally significant, begins with the first Sunday of Advent as
the prelude to that festival with which Christian revelation begins.
It is as if the cycle of Sabbaths were to begin before the festival
of national liberation. For us Jews, the highest of all the festivals of
redemption, the Day of Atonement, bears in even greater measure the
character of a Sabbath without regularly falling on a Sabbath. Just so
for the Christian, the splendor of a Sunday rests in still greater measure
over the festival of the incipient revelation which likewise is not externally fixed to Sunday, and that in conspicuous contrast to its sister-
festivals of Easter and Pentecost.

SOCIOLOGY OF THE MUSICAL ARTS: CHURCH MUSIC

Here, too, in the Church year as in ours, an annually recurring
celebration of revelation is erected over the substructure of creation
founded on the Sundays, and here too in the form of a sequence of

three festival seasons. And among the arts it is music that is coordinate with revelation. For in revelation, the ray of time bursts through the aperture of the moment into the broad basin of created space, and music is that art which spins a time period out of the moment. Every musical opus generates a time of its own. Compared to the reality of inner life it is an ideal time. To its admirers, music thus becomes an escape from the excitements, respectively the stultifying boredom, of their daily lives, very much as the fine arts provided *their* friends with a way out of the ugliness or the pettiness of the world about them. Thus the arts spare man the hard labor of implanting freedom and form in the world, discipline and life in the soul. Whatever he may desire he can, after all, find in museums and concert halls. He can find satisfaction here and delude himself for as long as he likes about the fact that the reality about him and within him is—so completely different. Indeed, he is liable to blame life for this contradiction between ideal and life; returning home from the concert, he holds the Creator responsible for having created world and soul so discordantly, instead of pinning the responsibility squarely on him who is charged with the task of making things different, on himself, on man.

The danger of self-satisfaction is almost greater still in the case of the "musical" arts than in that of the fine arts. For in his enjoyment, the devotee of the fine arts forgets, in the end, only the world. But the musical enthusiast forgets himself in his music. The former only excludes himself from productive life, and eventually can find his way back again; but the latter spoils himself, he debilitates his own soul and is thus by one whole step at a further remove from the possibility of being able to return into life. The musical person can arouse any given feeling in himself at will; worse still, he can cause the feeling within to discharge within himself. By generating its own "ideal" time, the musical opus disavows real time. It makes its listener forget the year in which he is living. It makes him forget his age. It transports him, wide awake, to those dreamers of whom each is said to have a world of his own. Even though he be rudely awakened, crying "it were better to have never dreamed," nevertheless, at the next opportunity he again reaches for the bottle and quaffs his potion of oblivion. Thus he leads a strange life, and, not just one strange life; nay, he lives hundreds of lives, from one piece of music to the next, and none is his own. Surely the dog who grieved inconsolably because his mistress played the piano is more truly alive, nay if the expression may be permitted, more "humanly" alive than the "musical" devotee.

The heinous aspect of music is that it disintegrates real time with ideal times in its desire to be pure. To be absolved from this crime, it would have to allow itself to be conducted out of its Beyond into the here and now of time; it would have to integrate its ideal time into real time. This would, however, imply the transition of music from concert hall to church. For the time in which the events of the world ensue is exactly like the space into which the world is created; it too is merely "ideal," merely "cognitive" and thus without beginning, middle, end: the present as marker of the standpoint of cognition is perpetually shifting. Only revelation fixes its marker in the middle of time, and now there is a Prior and a Posterior which will not be shifted; now there is a time-telling for all the places of the world independent of the teller or the place of the telling. This real world era gradually embraces all occurrence and permeates it. It is reflected with maximum clarity and can best be grasped by short-lived mankind in the Church year, and here again in the festivals of revelation in particular. These festivals, pointing backward toward the creation of revelation and forward toward revealed redemption, incorporate the immeasurable eternity of the day of God into the annual cycle of the Church year. By integrating itself in these festivals and in the Church year as a whole, the individual piece of music alights from the artificial frame of its ideal time and becomes wholly alive, for it is grafted onto the rich-sapped tree trunk of real time. He who joins in singing a chorale, or who listens to the mass, the Christmas oratorio, the [Easter] passion, he knows very exactly in what time he is. He does not forget himself and does not wish to forget himself. He does not wish to escape time; on the contrary, he wants to make his soul stand with both feet in time, in the most real time of all, in the time of the one day of the world of which all individual world days are but a part. Music is supposed to escort him there. Again it can do so only up to the gate. Again the sacrament must take over from music here and guide man to his destination. But in music, the preparation for this preparation of the individual who sets forth on the eternal way found itself in the proper hands.

For it is music which now elevates that initial togetherness, founded on the common space and the common hearing of the word, into a conscious and active togetherness of all those assembled together. Architecture only created the space; now it is truly fulfilled with the sounds of music. The chorale fills the space, sung by all together in a mighty unison; it is the real basis for the ecclesiastical employment of music. It still survives in Bach's Oratorios, and the Catholic Church has also continued to foster it albeit the musical mass leads in another direction. In the chorale, silence descends over speech, which otherwise has its own particular word to say in every individual mouth.

But it is not that silence which simply listens mutely to the recited word, but the silence of one's particularity in the unanimity of the chorus. So too the community of life is witnessed and becomes conscious in the common meal; all do the same thing in conscious community, that is to say they eat, and yet each one is doing it quite literally by and "for himself." Now music attunes the souls in preparation for this community of life, as it is then realized in the sacrament. At their entrance into the common space, the souls had only been pretuned for community in general, for potential community; in the common singing of the chorale they are pretuned for real community. Even the musical mass, although it is only heard and not sung in common, is at bottom a pretuning of all individuals for community just as much as is the chorale. For listening to music is a different kind of listening altogether from listening to a recited text or to a sermon; it does not establish a community but it arouses the assembled ones, each for himself, to the same feelings—each for himself as the sight of the audience in a concert will show at once. Thus to hear a musical mass is fully equivalent to singing a chorale in this respect. The common space absorbs the individual bodily; thereupon he is seized as discoursing individual in his soul; and as discourse is disciplined by rhythm and melody, the personality of the personal word of the individual learns to fall silent. He speaks, but what he says are not his words but the words set to music which are common to all.

Words and feelings, in short, man's inmost properties, thus ascend to that level of necessity which the objects had reached by their entrance into the space of the Church. The word which has become the text of the chant ceases to be an arbitrary one. Melodies preserve words. All transmission of words occurred in former times to the fixed notes of a song, and does likewise today wherever the word is still transmitted as spoken word. And all transmission is originally cultic. Cult raises even the word that is merely thought to the level of necessity: the breviary of the Catholic cleric or the silent prayer among us [Jews] is quite different from reading or reflection in general; it clothes the thought in a festive garb which leaves it less comfortable and free to move than ordinarily, but the words thus thought by man have a necessity and a validity which is entirely free of purpose and even of thought. Clothes make the man, make him fully valid in society, precisely because they are not as "personal" as the bare body but in accordance with one or another custom. In much the same way, as long as man thinks and speaks freely whatever he wants and means, he is not really at home with himself. He is that only when he hums or whistles a song to himself in complete unconcern, or when he applies a proverb to himself. This is also the case with breviary and silent prayer. Man only seems to be concentrating less here than when he is reading or thinking freely; in reality it is here that the words are elevated to the level of a universally valid feeling which they never attain outside. There they always remain the personal words of an individual. Words are already alive; they need not enter the church in order to become alive, as in the case of objects; but their vitality is perishable. They become durable because the music absorbs them. And if the music is Church music, then they enter the cycle of the year together with this music and, by being integrated into the eternal day of the Lord, become themselves eternal.

THE SACRAMENT OF THE MEAL

The guidance of the soul onto the common path, prepared by music, is now consummated by the sacrament, specifically by the highest sacrament, the Lord's Supper. It originated in the Jewish evening meal of the festival of liberation, but as celebration of the way it is distinguished from that meal as clearly as can be. For there the community of the meal becomes visible as real, as communal life; here, however, the community does not sit, united for the meal, around the table of the Lord. Rather, each one approaches individually, each one leaves, and the common element is only the community of the chalice, the equality of the food, of the benediction, of the belief. As man's personal I falls silent, a community of feeling comes alive which centers his consciousness only halfway in the music but which now, in the partaking of the sacrament, becomes fully conscious. Thus the sacrament of communion is really and truly sign and vehicle of revelation. And in the mass, by becoming the nucleus of every service, even of the daily service, it moves revelation into the center of the service altogether. Indeed, his belief being directed to the middle and the beginning of the way, the presence of Christ as it is experienced and partaken of in the sacrament means to the Christian something akin to our confident trust in the imminent advent of the Messiah and his kingdom, any and all delays notwithstanding. As our whole worship is entirely permeated by hoping and waiting for redemption, even where it is devoted to the remembrance of creation and revelation, even so Christian worship is permeated by the idea and the present feeling of revelation.

THE FESTIVALS OF REVELATION:

CHRISTMAS, EASTER, PENTECOST

There are three festival seasons, during which revelation enters the church year for the Christian too. They begin with Christmas time which, placed at the beginning of the church year, is a festival of the beginning like the Jewish festival of liberation. Here this beginning, this creation of revelation, must be the birth in the flesh, as it is the liberation in the case of the [Jewish] people. As the "firstborn of God," it becomes free to become a people, while the "only-begotten" one becomes flesh to become a person, and these events correspond to each other as exactly as people and individual, world and man can correspond. Both festivals celebrate the beginning of revelation's visible course across the earth. The scriptural reading is central to the whole celebration in none of the Christian festivals as much as here in the narrative of Christmas Eve. It is, in fine, the eu-angelion, the glad tidings in the gospel. Here too exactly the same is the case with our festival of liberation. The narrative which lies at the basis of the festival is itself treated in extenso and focally nowhere in the cult as much as here. Here we devote to the festival a booklet of its own, that booklet which we read at the evening meal in the home and which for us is the "story" pure and simple—"the" Haggada among all the countless haggada's. The recital of the story has the same central position in the celebration of Christmas Eve, which thus is shown to be, among the festivals of revelation, the recurrent festival of communal hearing, of the hearing of the glad tidings.

But at the same time the appearance of the festival also acquires already now the purely presentive features of revelation, by becoming midpoint of a festival season of many weeks. The preceding season of Advent renews the recollection of the prophecy of the "old" covenant and thus establishes its own basis in creation for the miracle of Christmas. But, still within the Christmas season, New Year's Day and Epiphany already herald redemption, the rapprochement of faith and life. New Year's Day is the festival of that circumcision which, in the Jewish view, publicly attests that the infant belongs to the people—an adherence resting first and last on the mystery of birth alone—in the initial execution of a commandment. Correspondingly, this festival conducts the course of the Church year out of its own superior beginning into the cycle of the civil year, while the devotion of the three kings of the East is a prelude to the future devotion of the kings and peoples of all lands. Both festivals together thus foreshadow the double event of Constantine's reign: the integration of the Church into the state and the conversion of the state to Christianity. Thus situated midway between its own basis in creation and its own anticipation of redemption, the miracle of Christmas already becomes, accordingly, a whole revelation of its own.

But within the three festivals of revelation, the real festal season of revelation is, in the last analysis, Easter. Not the manger of Bethlehem, but Golgotha and the empty tomb count as the beginning of the way for Christianity. In any case it is the Cross, and nothing previous from the "life of Jesus," which remains ever and equally near and visible from every one of the countless midpoints of its eternal way. Just so we regard as the revelation which evermore accompanies us in the present, not already the exodus from Egypt, but only the miracle of Sinai, the giving of the Torah. The Exodus we must first remember, albeit as vividly as if we had taken part in it ourselves; but the Torah we do not have to remember at all: it is present. So too it is the cross, not the manger, that is always present for the Christian; it is this not that which he always sees before him. One could well say to him concerning the Cross what is said to us concerning the Torah, that if it but be "in his heart, his steps will not slip."

This quality of presentness, moreover, turns Easter into the real festival of the Sacrament. The Eucharist was inserted into the context of the events of Easter, and it is here above all that it is received. And beyond this presentness, the Church now seeks to place man in spirit directly under the Cross, be it through the music of the mass, or of the oratorio of the Passion. Man must confront the head full of blood and wounds, face to face, directly. The great central event of Christian life thus undergoes one single re-presentation in the entire festival season, from Lent through Good Friday, to the day of the resurrection itself. The fastdays represent the long preparation. Good Friday, which the Catholic Church allows to recede while the Protestant Church, lacking Lent, celebrates it the more, represents the event itself. Easter, finally, represents the mighty finale or, within this festival of revelation, the day of redemption.

As to redemption itself, Pentecost, the third of the three festival seasons, is dedicated to it. The festival, of course, remains within revelation, and therefore can only anticipate redemption. It must exhibit redemption as a last act of the earthly sojourn of Christ, just as the Feast of Tabernacles could recall the ultimate rest only in the provisional rest of the desert wanderings. Thus the pentecostal season can of necessity call to mind only the beginning of redemption, not its subsequent course, let alone its conclusion. It has to designate the point at which the way of Christianity turns from the narrow path of the Lord and his disciples into the broad highway of the Church. Ultimate redemption is not celebrated yet, at least not here, only its prelude in revelation; accordingly this festival cannot itself represent that supreme communion of humanity in silent devotion. Rather it must content itself with exhortings thereto, and withal in universal exhortation intelligible to all mankind. But this universal intelligibility cannot be attained in silence. It requires the intervention of speech. Through the miracle of language, speech overcomes the resistance of the Today that once was, and, though separated by language, still is as of today. It is the first effect of the spirit to translate, to erect a bridge between man and man, between tongue and tongue. The Bible must surely be the first book to be translated and then held equal to the original translation. God speaks everywhere with the words of men. And spirit means precisely that the translator, the one who hears and transmits, knows himself equal to the One who first spoke and received the word. Spirit thus leads man and gives him the confidence to stand on his own two feet. It is man's own spirit precisely as the spirit of transmission and translation. That is the story of the pentecostal season: the Lord leaves his charges, ascending to Heaven, while they remain behind on earth. He leaves them behind, but he leaves them the spirit. Now they must learn to believe without seeing him with their own eyes; they must learn to behave as though they had no Lord at all. But now they can: they have the spirit. In the miracle of Pentecost, the Church which has mastered all languages begins its course into the world. In the symbolism of the Holy Trinity, whose festival follows Pentecost, it raises on its own behalf the standard rallying its apostles as they swarm forth.

FESTIVALS OF REDEMPTION

But withal it remains no more than a preview of redemption. Redemption itself still has no place in the Church year thereby. To redemption there ought to correspond a third kind of festival, a kind of its own, much as the Days of Awe are added to the Sabbath and Pilgrim Festivals with us. Up to this point there were Christian festivals to correspond to those of the Jewish calendar. What then is the type of festival which would correspond to the Days of Awe?

None. The Church year—it, not the calendar—lacks anything to correspond to these festivals in our calendar. The only one which one could perhaps mention would lie within the sphere of the three festivals of revelation. It was, indeed, noteworthy that Christmas did not conform to a holiday of the Jewish calendar like Easter and Pentecost. Moreover, it is known that it is coordinate with a turning point in the annual orbit of the sun; here the unvanquished solar deity of the cult of Mithra celebrated his annual rebirth. But starting from this alien root, the festival has nonetheless undergone a development, and especially in the principal nation of Christendom and in its most recent centuries, which has brought it into a degree of proximity to the Jewish festivals of redemption. The house opens up to admit free nature. The hospitality of a warm room is extended to the snow-covered Christmas tree, and this opening up of the house to admit nature, and the manger in the strange stable in which the redeemer comes into the world, have their exact counterpart in the open sky admitted by the roof of the tablernacle-hut in memory of the tent of meeting which granted rest to the eternal people during its wanderings through the desert.

But beyond this, there has developed a correspondence with the actual festival of redemption which has already been alluded to before. Christmas is to the Sundays as the Day of Atonement is to the Sabbaths. Without necessarily falling on Sunday, it is the Sunday *par excellence*, that is to say it is, as birthday of the Church year, that which Sunday is for the week: a new beginning. Just so the Day of Atonement, as the day of the entrance to eternity, is for our year what the Sabbath means for the week: consummation. And so it is that both days underwent the same process, namely, the emergence of the eve of the holyday to equal significance with the day of the festival itself. The evening service of the Day of Atonement is the sole one which shows the congregation in the festive garb otherwise reserved for the principal morning service. The evening service turns the Day of Atonement into a "long day" just as Christmas Eve and its "long night" does with Christmas. Only a day consisting of night plus day till night has again completely fallen—only this is a whole day. For the day lies between two midnights only the first of which is truly night; the other is light. And to spend such a long day with God thus means to live wholly with God, to experience the Nought posited before life, and life itself, and the Star which rises over the black of the night beyond life. The Christian lives this kind of a whole long day on the day of the beginning, we on the day of the end. Thus both festivals have grown beyond their original significance. The Day of Atonement became the highest festival of all, something that could not have been foreseen when it was instituted. Already in the days of Philo of Alexandria, exactly like today, even those who were otherwise lukewarm and rarely appeared in the house of God, streamed there in crowds on this day and found their way back to God in praying and fasting. And Christmas, contrariwise, has turned from a church holiday to a popular holiday, forcing even the de-Christianized elements of the people, yea even the non-Christian ones, under its spell. The Day of Atonement, anticipating the end, has thus become a symbol for our people's internal capacity to preserve itself through its faith, and Christmas, the day which renews the beginning, for Christianity's external capacity to expand over life.

Thus the festival of the beginning of revelation is the only one within Christianity which to some extent is on a par with our festival of redemption. There is no festival of redemption as such in Christianity. In the Christian consciousness, everything congregates around the beginning and for beginning, and the clear distinction which exists for us between revelation and redemption is obscured. Redemption has already taken place in Christ's earthly sojourn, at the very least in his crucifixion, properly speaking already at his birth. Christ is called savior and redeemer not only after the resurrection but already at his virgin birth. With us the ideas of creation and revelation contain a compulsion to merge in the idea of redemption for whose sake, in the final analysis, everything prior has occurred. In Christianity, correspondingly, the idea of redemption is swallowed back into creation, into revelation; as often as it erupts as something independent, just so often it loses its independence again. The retrospect to cross and manger, the eventuation of the events of Bethlehem and Golgotha into one's own heart, there become more important than the prospect of the future of the Lord. The advent of the kingdom becomes a matter of secular and ecclesiastical history. But it has no place in the heart of Christendom which pumps the lifeblood through the circuit of the Church year.

THE SECULAR FESTIVALS

But if it has no place in the eternally recurring cycle of the Church year, it does have one in the secular calendar which alters its anniversaries from century to century and which unites with the Church cycle on New Year's Day. Here is room for all those historical anniversaries on which mankind becomes conscious of its passage through time. Such dates change with the changing centuries; they differ from place to place, from government to government. But as long as each one is celebrated, it is filled with human rejoicing in the secular present and with the hope of a still better, still richer, in short a growing life in the future. In our case, the few memorial days of our national history have, because that history is past, turned into permanent fixtures.[1] All three are unknown to the Torah: the day of mourning for the destruction of Jerusalem, the festival recalling the deliverance recorded in the Book of Esther, and that of the rededication of the

[1] Note, however, that a large number of others, attested for the period of the Second Temple or later, have since gone out of use. (Tr.)

defiled sanctuary after the victory of the Maccabees. All three are distinctively commemorative festivals. Accordingly, their dates are coincidental, conditioned only by history. In rank they cannot compare with the other festivals, not even the day of mourning for Jerusalem. Now they recur annually, having become rigid, though they are historical festivals—as rigid as the history of our people. It is otherwise with the historical memorial days of the nations. The celebrations of their wars and victories scarcely outlast the event by half a century ere they are displaced by others. Royal birthdays change as royalty itself changes. Constitution-days and liberation holidays last as long as the constitution or at most the state. And withal they satisfy the nation as symbol of its durability through time precisely in their change and temporality.

THE CHURCH AND THE SECULAR CALENDAR

Now the Church plunges in here and joins the celebration. It grows into the people and its history by accompanying its memorial days with its blessings. It is a piece of its mission to the heathen which it is pursuing here. By casting its light of glorification over the branches of national life, it renders a service on the path of redemption, for redemption is never other than the sowing of eternity into the living. Where the Church is constituted according to the boundaries of a country, it establishes days of repentance and prayers annually or for the great occasions of the national life. Festivals of thanksgiving for the harvest, celebrations of the beginning of a war or its triumphant conclusion—everywhere the Church has to add its word. But it has its own history too, and this too must be celebrated. Thus the Lutheran Church celebrates its Festival of the Reformation, while the Catholic Church annually proclaims its unabated antithesis to the heretics in the procession of the festival of Corpus Christi. And the Catholic Church in particular has missed no opportunity to weave its own life directly into the Church year in a series of festivals. In general it does so in those festivals which mirror the existence of the Church itself in the course of the life of Mary. Furthermore it does so particularly in the saints days which, given the Church's limitless capacity for change, adaptation, and growth, make possible a very intimate alliance between it and the local, the social, and even the personal interests of the world. Thus it repeatedly incorporates this temporal-secular element into the eternal circle which in any case has long ceased to remain a circle; rather, in such festivals as these which change according to time and place but which belong to the eternal path of redemption through time and place, this circle opens up into a spiral.

But whether they be ecclesiastical or secular, sub-ecclesiastical or super-secular, how are these festivals of redemption celebrated? We have already encountered the festivals of communal listening and of the communal meal. But these festivals of redemption cannot be festivals of common genuflection. Common genuflection had already found its place in Christianity previously. Christendom has already knelt at the manger with Mary and Joseph, with the shepherds by night and the three magi of the East. In the breathless stillness before the transubstantiation, into which only the Church bell sounds quietly, Christendom kneels before the sacrifice on the cross newly represented in the sacrifice of the mass. Thus it again incorporated the ultimate silence of the redeemed in the celebration of the initial origin and the ever renewed presence of the Lord. Between creation and revelation it again becomes unmindful of the coming redemption. And the festivals with which the Church itself brings redemption into the Church year have no place for that ultimate devotion.

How then are these festivals to be celebrated? 'That to God every knee must bend' remains the true form for the celebration of redemption, but only we celebrate it in this true form in festivals of its own. For only with us can the sacred year form a closed circle in its own festivals of redemption; only we live a life in the eternity of redemption and thus can celebrate it. Christianity is only on the way. It celebrates eternal redemption only in festivals of time and thus not in its own peculiar form of the communal genuflection. Then what, in Christianity, is the temporal form which corresponds to this eternal form of the celebration of redemption? How does art prepare man to celebrate these festivals?

SOCIOLOGY OF THE DRAMATIC ARTS: MIRACLE PLAY

Poetry was that art form which created a sphere for itself beyond pure space and pure time. Man is, after all, more than the spatiality of the body, more too than the temporality of the soul: he is a whole man. And thus it remained for the poetic arts to emerge as the arts of the whole man over and beyond the fine arts and music. The element in which poetry moves is the idea, and as conception, the idea unites in itself the spatiality of the perceptual and the temporality of feeling, and turns them into one whole. Poetry's content is the world as a Whole, and its little god, man the microcosm. And thus poetry might be expected to supply man with the mood for finding his way to that ultimate redemptive silence which should have appeared to him in the secular festivals of redemption at least as prospect and promise.

But the way into the life of the community seems even longer when regarded from poetry than it did from fine arts and music. The latter were at least preserved and performed in public halls, in houses of their own. But poetry's home, its prison cell, is the bookcase. The space between the two covers of a book is the only place where poetry is truly "pure" art; there it is in its pure world of ideas, each work in its own one. As a picture creates a "pure" space for itself in its frame, and a piece of music its pure time, so every poem creates its own "ideal" world. The very act of reading it aloud already forces it out of this pure world of its imagination and makes it somehow common. And if one goes so far as to present it on stage as drama, then its esthetic "ideality" is entirely forfeited. The proper drama is the drama in book form. To call a drama theatrical is to condemn it in the esthete's terms; though he may inconsistently pardon it in Shakespeare, he counts it heavily against Schiller and Wagner. Surely there will come a day—it has already come for Schiller—when one will cease to reproach Wagner for writing theatrically for the theater. And yet the theatre, even the theatrical theatre, remains pure art, though it is not entirely able to escape the influence of the assembled multitude: the hybrid effect of the theatre derives precisely from the conflict with the real world of the assembled audience into which the ideal world of the drama is necessarily plunged. Obviously poetry too would have to be freed from the bookcovers of its ideal world and introduced to the real one ere it could guide masses of humanity into the realm of communal and mutual silence. Then it would no longer be only a matter of bodies being together in the same space, as under the spell of the architecture of physical concentration, of tongues being united into the chorus of the equal rhythm and the identical word, as under the magic wand of music, the guide of souls. But then all men would be near to each other and as one, in word and

To be used thus, however, poetry itself would first have to learn silence, for in the word it is still tied to the soul. It would have to learn to free itself of the concept of a configuration already present in the world. It would itself have to bring forward a configuration; it would have to become gesture. For only gesture is beyond word and deed—not, to be sure, the gesture which attempts to say something— for this would be but a pitiful substitute for discourse, a mere stuttering; nor that gesture which only seeks to elicit action on another's part, for this would be a pitiful substitute for one's own deed; but that deed and beyond word and deed.

gesture which has become wholly free, wholly creative, and which is no longer directed at this or that person or thing, a gesture which perfects a man wholly for Being, for his humaneness and thereby for humanity. For wherever man expresses himself wholly in gesture, there the space separating man from man falls away in a "wonderfully still" empathy. There the word may evaporate which had tumbled headlong into this divisive interval in order to fill it with its own body and thus to become a bridge between man and man by its own heroic self-sacrifice. Thus gesture perfects man for his full humanity. It must burst the space into which architecture had placed a multitude of others, and whose interstices music had filled in and bridged. This is accomplished on our festival of redemption by that prostration which is the ultimate gesture of all mankind; this prostration bursts every space and erases all time. The Talmud mentions this too among the miracles of the sanctuary in Jerusalem: the multitude assembled in the enclosed forecourt crowded so close together that there was not the least room left, but at the moment when those who were standing prostrated themselves on their faces, there was endlessly much room left over.

Dance is that form of art in which poetry thus emerges from between its covers, transposing itself from the ideal world of conception into the real world of exposition—dance and all that develops out of it, all such self-expositions as have no spectator or by rights should have none, as have only participants who, at most, may occasionally rest and relieve each other by turns. A people recognizes itself in festive processions and parades, in tournaments and pageants. Here too belongs that art which seeks the open air in monuments, or accompanies the roving spectator on calvary, or welcomes a gathering in a speech, or brings people together as a drinking song or marching tune. Cologne at carnival time is such a place where a multitude of dancers are involved, and so is a sports terrain, an Olympic stadium, a Bayreuth stage. Yet the dance of the individual remains the first thing and even within the dance itself it remains the simplest gesture, the glance. The power to dissolve all that is rigid already inheres in the glance. It is a power which remained unattainable to the deed, a power for whose sake the word sacrificed itself if only to master it at this cost for the brief pause before the answer. A word forgets itself and is to be forgotten; it wants to perish in the answer. The power of the glance, however, does not perish with the moment. Once an eye has glanced at us, it will glance at us as long as we live. When Aphrodite danced before the blissful gods at the wedding of Amor and Psyche, she danced at last only with her eyes.

THE SACRAMENT OF BAPTISM

But the dance does not find its way into the Church, at least not in its simplest form, the form which catches up the individual directly and attunes him for community. Again it is a fact that the closed space of the Church can no more accommodate the idea of redemption than did the closed circle of the ecclesiastical year. The idea of redemption opens the circle and turns it into a spiral; it bursts the locked gate, and the procession proceeds into the city. It is not without reason that Corpus Christi became the festival of processionals *par excellence*. The gates of our Jewish houses of worship may remain closed, for when Israel kneels, there is suddenly room for all mankind in what was hitherto a confined space. The circuits of the Torah take place only on the inside of our houses of worship, especially that great circuit which marks the end of the festivals of redemption on the day of the Rejoicing of the Law. But here redemption is celebrated directly in the closed circle of the congregation as of the year; here the dance too could develop as a cultic act, to wit in the dance of the Hasid, who "praises God with all his limbs."

Dance thus finds a place in the religious service itself only among us; the architectural power to create space and the musical power to fill space are first consummated in the gesture of dance as it bursts space. The Church must export its cult into the world for the sake of redemption, and supplement it by worldly festivals; it is here still only on the way, in the clearest possible sense. The space of the Church radiates outward into the exterior which surrounds it; its times define the segments of the stream of time that flows past it; but it can win its world only by means of the world outside. It does not simply export its world like the laws of its space and time. Rather, by going out to all the peoples, it first receives its own law on the outside, by virtue of working under the law of the world. The end is not inside its walls: always it but stands at the beginning, but travels the path.

Accordingly the sacrament by which the Church completes the preparation provided by those folkloristic spectacles, those offshoots of the dance, can only take the form of a consecration of the beginning. Genuflection, which means and is the final redemption, remains alien to the Church. But it can consecrate the individual for entry into the world as the way of redemption. That is the remarkable double meaning of baptism: performed on the individual, the newborn, at the beginning of his life, it vouchsafes him, in the minority of his life, the consummation of his life, his redemption. In baptism, Christianity consummates redemption; it allows the defenselessness of the minor child, unconscious of itself, to count as the defenselessness of the supreme consciousness of silent adoration. And this is what keeps Christianity on its way once and for all. But at the same time it makes it mistress over the way. No one can here compete with it. No one can dispute with Christianity this its final assurance of victory which lets each individual first step every time serve as the last. With the exception of the Eucharist, the sacrament of revelation, all the seven sacraments search out man in certain hours and relationships of his natural, moral, social way of life. Among these sacraments, baptism can thus really substitute for the other five sacraments of the way of redemption. In this sense, Protestantism has undertaken to simplify matters, if it had to be done at all, at the right point. For by consecrating the beginning of the way in advance with the consecration of redemption, all subsequent life is subsumed under it; every subsequent hour which the Christian may live as a Christian means simply a renewal of the covenant of baptism which, at this very entrance into world, co-opted him among the definitively redeemed. Baptism lets us recognize completely what we first recognized in Christmas: for Christianity the beginning replaces redemption, the beaten path replaces consummated life. Every baptism renews the adoration of the divine infant. Christianity is wholly young. For in every individual, in every soul, it begins anew.

The Image of Heaven: Christian Esthetics

WORLD AND SOUL

Christianity is young—but not the Christian world. Baptism may have consecrated the individual for the Christian world, but this world itself is not consecrated. The circle of life which for us Jews is closed in the people, for the Christian is only closed in one's own soul. Only the soul is vouchsafed eternal life in baptism; perpetuation and renovation alternate eternally only in the soul. The world is not endowed with eternal life. The circle of individual life bursts apart in the world, and flows into the spiral of a history in which the secular progress of the world regularly wins power over the eternal perpetuation and renovation of the soul. The ecclesiastical year is rounded off only for the individual; for him it is a home. But for the world, and its years and anniversaries, the ecclesiastical year is no more than an inn; it may be open to all guests, but every guest has yet to leave it again. The eternal people already reposes in the house of life: the nations of the world remain on the way. Only the soul has already found its way home. She knows that her 'redeemer lives,' with no less certainty than she knows it in the eternal people. For her, the circle of the year closes.

CHILD OF THE WORLD AND CHILD OF GOD

For the soul, the year is closed in the alternation of perpetuation and renovation. The Christian world, and already the Christian people live in the spiral of world history. Both know that their anniversaries are milestones of its path and that they change with the centuries. But the individual's glance does not reach so far. He is content if his own name-day recurs annually on the calendar. The divine and the wordly directions cross in the single ecclesiastical year. Their general point of intersection is New Year's Day, while the individual himself stands at their personal point of intersection—he himself to whom it is said that all is his, but he is Christ's. For him, the crossing of the two directions means precisely the closing of the circle of his life. He knows himself whole only in this duo-unity of his essence. And the proof of this unity, the bond that unites in him both the child of the world and the child of God, is the circle of the year in which alone he experiences both realms, that of the Church and that of the world, as an ever recurring unity.

AGES OF MAN

His very life only becomes unified thereby, for it is not so inherently. From one decade to the next it passes through many ages. But before God, all the ages are alike. To him, man is ever the child. Only the world draws distinctions. For it, the ages of man are not indifferent. Child, youth, man, elder—to each it assigns different tasks, to each, too, it shows itself different. Before God there are no minors; in the people there are. Before God there are no aged; in the people there are. If a man lived only among the people, he would constantly have to appear different to himself. But by being with God, he knows that he remains ever the same. The unity of his life is that he ever remains the same while ever changing, and this unity within him of perpetuation and renovation, this unity of his life in the alternation of time, this is first assured to him by the year which itself ever recurs in this alternation, the year which embraces in its ambit both perpetuation and renovation, both the festivals of eternity and the festivals of time. The year does not conceal the contradiction between the two, between eternity and time, between Church and world, neither has it overcome the contradiction; it simply presents it as it is. Precisely on that account it allows man to experience his own unity. In the ever-recurrent circuit of the year, man as God's unaging child forever merges into man as the child of the world who grows from youth to old age, and back again; each quality perpetuates and renovates itself in the other.

THE STRUCTURING OF THE PASSION

In the Christian, those forces intersect which elsewhere appear to cancel each other out. Christianity affords them no refuge beyond these contradictions. It absorbs them all within itself and inserts the Christian into their midst, into a middle which—for him who stands there—is at the same time a beginning. The cross neither negates the contradiction, nor annihilates it; rather it articulates it as structure. Structure is not created by fiat, nor is it brute force. Structure must be shaped, brought forth, constructed. The way of the Christian is at every station a crossroad. Jewish life was at the goal with every moment, in competition with the state and its incessant definition of goals, with its battle cry endlessly blared into time and space: thus far and no further; the eternity of the eternal people is drowned out by the sword which keeps time for the epochs of the nations. But the Christian's way of the cross is in competition, within his soul, with a different power. It is the only power which similarly overcomes the contradiction by structuring it, not by denying it, namely art. Art was already effective in preparing the soul for entering the way. It was capable of fulfilling this function because it too, in its own realm, knew the crossroad of the soul: Prometheus already hung suspended from the rock half a millennium before the cross was raised on Golgotha.

Art, too, overcomes only by structuring passion, not by denying it. The artist knows himself the one to whom it is given to say what he is suffering. The muteness of the first man is within him too. He attempts neither to pass over suffering in silence, nor to shout it to the rooftops: he depicts it. In the depiction he reconciles the contradiction that he himself exists and that suffering too exists all the same; he reconciles it without diminishing it in the least. All art is "tragic" in its content; it depicts suffering. Even comedy thrives on this sympathy for the ever-present poverty and deficiency of existence. Art is tragic in content just as it, and all art, is comic in form. It simply depicts—even the most monstrous—with a certain romantic-ironic levity. Art as depiction is tragic and comic in one. And truly the greatest depicter is at once comedian and tragedian, as it was discussed at the dawn of the symposium celebrating Agathon's dramatic triumph. Like Janus, art has two faces: it makes life's sufferings harder at the same time that it helps man to bear it, and this is what entitles it to accompany him through life. Art teaches man to overcome without forgetting. For man is not to forget; he is to remember everything in his very members. He is to bear sorrows, and to be consoled. God consoles him together with all who are in need of consolation. The tears of the mourner will be wiped from his face as 'from every face.' [But] until the great renovation of all things, they will gleam in his eyes. Till then, his consolation is to be disconsolate. Till then, the soul is quickened by the durability of suffering. Till then, its renovation takes the form of perpetuation. Till then, it gathers new strength from the remembrance of its earlier days. Past pains, not past joys, are the delight of the soul in every present moment. It renews itself in itself. And art forges this ring of life for it.

ART AND THE CROSS

Art indeed appears to replace the cross in the fullest measure. Why should the soul still need the cross if it finds perpetuation and renovation within itself? Yea, it wears the ring of life, which art forged for it, within itself, but it wears it as a hard metal band around its heart. The band must burst if the pliable heart is to learn to beat once more in unison with all hearts. The cross which art taught men to bear was only each and everyone's own cross. Even he who did not imbibe misanthropy out of the abundance of love, learned from art only to observe with amazement the thousand springs in the desert by the side of the thirsty. Art did not let him see the thirsty thousands who were with him in the same desert. It did not teach him the unity of all that is the cross. This is experienced by the lonely pagan soul, in whose blood the last unity of the We does not circulate, only in view of the cross on Golgotha. It recognizes itself as one with all souls only under this cross. Here the artificial ring is broken from his heart which always lay there in great pain, for something dear to him always remained enchanted for him in the well.[1] Thus the one pain without equal takes the place of his own pain and every personal pain, and thereby the bond is now forged from soul to soul. The soul which has stood under the cross, and which was quickened by the eternal pain, this soul ceases to seek the circuit of perpetuation and renovation solely in its

[1] An allusion to Grimm's fairy tale of Iron Henry, whose master was turned into a toad. (Tr.)

own breast, there where art makes it beat. In its own interior it now experiences in com-passion that orbit of eternal suffering and eternal joy which motivates the heart that, on the cross, suffered for many and also for it.

SOUL AND WORLD

Thus the soul experiences its eternity along the way, unconcerned with the fact that the world has not yet reached its goal. Let the spiral of the world reopen the orbit and drive it further time and again: for the soul, the circle of eternity has already closed. Eternity has been promised to the world of the nations too, but a greater circle encloses them. The nations are forever reborn out of souls, and thereby they can sense the quickened circulation of the blood, as it emanates from the cross, down to their very veins. But the blood does not circulate in the veins themselves. Rather it flows in an irreversible descent through the landscape of time into the ocean of history. Redemption again and again bursts the circle of the ecclesiastical year. There must be a circle by which the nations as a whole recognize their own will for their own perpetuation and renovation as an eternal fate. Otherwise they might not realize that an eternal will is at work in their personal fate. This great circle of redemption is closed in the year of the eternal people, the bearer, ever unrecognized by the nations, of that prophecy which the nations had to believe already fulfilled in the vicarious suffering of the individual for the individuals. In the eternal people, the nations experience that closed eternity for which they themselves reach out helplessly. For their streams all empty into the sea, and the eternal circulation of the waters under heaven does not take place solely in the river beds. Only one single body of water in the world stands ever circulating within itself, apparently without tributaries and without drainage, that is without earthly tributaries and drainages—a miracle and an affront to all who see it, for it shirks the duty of all waters to seek the sea. The streams do not suspect that, in their eternal circulation, they are presented with a picture of their universal future. Yet all the more quickly they hurry along their own way that will bring them toward this future. For what is it that drives them onward along this eternal way if not the drive for eternal life? Does the tree know that it desires nothing but to produce the fruit which shelters the image of its long-lost seed?

The Realization of Eternity

Here, as at the end of the previous book, it is a metaphor of the great singer of our Diaspora to which we were alluding. Let it be said here in Judah Halevi's own words: 'Thus God has a secret plan for us, a plan like his plan for a seed-grain which drops into the ground and appears to change into earth and water and dirt, till nothing remains of it by which the eye might recognize it; and which nonetheless transforms earth and water into its own essence, which decomposes their elements step by step and converts and adapts them to its own material, till it produces bark and leaves; and once its inner marrow is prepared to receive the embryo of the former seed for new corporeality, the tree produces fruit like that whence the seed first came: thus the law of Moses draws every successor in its train, transforming him in reality even though to all appearances everyone rejects it. And the nations are the readying and preparation of the Messiah whom we await. He will be the fruit, and all will become his fruit and acknowledge him, and the tree will be one. Then they will praise and glorify the root which once they despised, of which Isaiah spoke.'

Thus far the analogy from the *Kuzari*. Building on the [53rd] chapter of Isaiah concerning the unrecognized servant of the Lord and his vicarious suffering for the nations of the world who walk in the bright light of history, it portrays the supreme recurrence, the recognition of the seed in the fruit. It is experience come home to roost, the verification of verity. The truth lies behind the way. The way ends where home has been reached. For though its end lies in eternity, and it is thus eternal, it is at the same time finite, since eternity is its end. Where everything is on fire, there are no more rays, there is only one light. There 'the earth shall be full of the knowledge of the Lord as the waters cover the sea.' In this ocean of light every way is submerged like vanity. But thou, oh God, art truth.

BOOK THREE

The Star

or

The Eternal Truth

The Eternity of Truth

God is truth. Truth is his signet. By it he is known. And will be even
when one day all has come to an end by which he used to make his
eternity known within Time—all eternal life, all eternal way—there
where even the eternal comes to an end: in eternity. For not the way
alone ends here, but life too. Eternal life, after all, endures only so
long as life in general. There is eternal life only in contrast to the life
of those who pave the eternal way, which is always exclusively temporal. The desire for eternity sighs forth out of the well-pits of this
temporality; if it assumes the form of a longing for eternal life, that is
only because it itself is temporal life. Of a truth, in truth, life too
disappears. The way became vanity as the ocean of light engulfed it
in its billows; life, though it does not thus become vanity, dissolves in
the light. It is transformed, and having been transformed, is no more.
Life has gone up in light. The mute darkness of the protocosmos had
found speech in death. And something stronger, love, had overpowered death. Love had chosen life. And as the protocosmos had
found its voice in death, so now life rallies in the silence of the hypercosmos and is transformed into light. God is not life: God is light. He
is the lord of life, but he is no more living than dead. To say the one
or the other of him, with the old [philosopher] that "God has life,"
or with the new one that "God is dead," reveals the identical pagan
bias. The only thing which does not resist verbal designation is that
neither/nor of dead and alive, that tender point where life and death
touch and blend. God neither lives nor is he dead; rather he quickens
the dead—he loves. He is the God of the quick and the dead, precisely

because he himself is neither quick nor dead. We experience his existence directly only by virtue of the fact that he loves us and awakens our dead Self to beloved and requiting soul. The revelation of divine love is the heart of the All.

God (Theology)

THE MANIFEST ONE

We learn that God loves but not that he is love. He draws too nigh to us in love for us to be yet able to say: he is this or that. In this love we learn only that he is God, not what he is. The What, the essence, remains concealed. It is concealed precisely by being revealed. A god who did not reveal himself would not permanently hide his essence from us, for nothing remains concealed from man's far-reaching learning, his capacity for conceptualization, his inquisitive intellect. But God pours forth over us in revelation; with us he turns from stationary to active God. Precisely thereby he forges the fetters of love around our free intellect, which is irresistible for everything stationary. Bound by such bonds, summoned thus by name, we move in the orbit in which we found ourselves, and along the route on which we are placed. We no longer reach beyond this except with the powerless grasp of empty concepts.[1]

THE CONCEALED ONE

If then the Manifest God dissolves in us, his concealed aspect remains with him all the more. True, we now recognize him in the dead and the living: he is the agent who creates the dead and re-creates it, transforms it until it comes to him and lets him quicken it; he is the agent who releases from himself the living, which had heard him summon it for life, and redeems it. But Creator and Redeemer we recognize in this way only after their connection in revelation. We catch sight of the Creator and the Redeemer only from the vantage point of the God of love. We can see what has been and what is to be only to the extent that the flicker of that moment of divine love shines. The purely Prior, the protocosmos created from of yore, is too dark for us to be able to recognize the Creator's hand in it. And the purely Posterior, the redeemed hypercosmos, is too bright for us to be yet

[1] For the play on words (reach, grasp, concept) cf. above, p. 59 (Tr.)

able to see the Redeemer's countenance in it; he thrones above the annually recurring hymns of the redeemed. Only in the immediate vicinity of that heart and center of the All, of the revelation of divine love, is the Creator and Redeemer too manifested to us, to the extent that such manifestation is vouchsafed at all. Revelation teaches us to trust in the Creator, to wait hopefully for the Redeemer. Thus it allows us to recognize Creator and Redeemer too only as him who loves.

THE FIRST ONE

Thus it is the Loving God whom alone we see directly. As such a one, however, God is not the Lord. As such he is active. He is not above his deed. He is within it. He is one with it. He loves. Only as the Lord is God beyond that of which he is the Lord: the Lord of life and death is himself beyond life and death. It is beyond conceiving what he may be as Lord of death, his essence before creation. Revelation extends only as far back as the Creator. Its first word is "in the beginning," its second "there created." Before the beginning there may have been that inner vitality of God which grew out of divine self-creation, self-revelation, self-redemption; we could only depict it analogically, by analogy, that is, to the authentic creation, revelation, redemption, by allowing God to experience within himself what emanates from him. The heathens knew of a God who had come to be in this fashion, and this perhaps gave us a hint that we were dealing with more than a mere analogy. But no word, no term derived from this hint. That vitality concealed within itself concealed this God from us too. The God-become became the God-concealed. To answer honestly what he might be, we would have had to say: Nought. For vitality in the Uncreated, in the realm of the dead, is nought. The heathen God is not dead, but he is Lord of the dead and only of the dead at that, only of Nought. This company of gods wields power only in the realm of the dead. Elsewhere they do not rule, they only live. But as Lords of the Nought they themselves become—Noughts. 'The gods of the heathen are noughts,' exclaims the Psalmist. They are not dead, far from it; the faith of their devotees testifies to that. Gods in whom a living world believes cannot be less alive than this world itself. But in all their vitality they are just as unsteady, just as ephemeral, just as subordinate to the almighty Perhaps as is this world, as are these devotees. They lack the framework of reality, the unambiguous orientation, the fixed position, the knowledge of right and left, above and below, which enters the world only with revelation.

For all their vitality, they are thus "Noughts." And "those who make them are like them; so are all who trust in them." They are created, they live concealed in the shelter of their celestial fortress; and this the Psalmist counters with that which distinguishes his God from these Noughts: he has 'made the heavens.'

THE LAST ONE

What God, the true God, may have been before creation thus defies the imagination. Not so that which he would be after redemption. True, here too our living knowledge tells us nothing about God's essence beyond the Redeemer. That he is the Redeemer is the last thing that we learn by our own experience: we 'know that he lives' and that our 'eyes will behold him.' But God's redemptive function assumed a special importance even within this knowledge that is manifest to us. His creative power and his revelatory wealth both befell something else, something objective, juxtaposed to them. His redemptive function, on the other hand, has only an indirect effect on anything else, redeeming man by means of the world, the world by means of man. Its direct effect is confined to the redemption of God himself. For God himself, redemption is the eternal deed in which he frees himself from having anything confront him that is not he himself. Redemption frees God from the work of creation as well as from his loving concern for the soul. Redemption is his day of rest, his great Sabbath, the day which is but adumbrated in the Sabbath of creation. It is the day when, freed from all that is outside himself, from all that is ever and again compared to him, incomparable though he is, he 'will be one and his name: One.' Redemption redeems God by releasing him from his revealed name. In the name and its revelation there is consummated that delivery of revelation which had commenced with creation. Whatever happens thereafter, happens "in the name." Sanctification of the name or desecration of the name—since revelation there is no deed which does not bring about one or the other. The process of redemption in the world takes place in the name and for the sake of the name. The end, however, is nameless; it is above any name. The very sanctification of the name occurs only so that the name might one day be muted. Beyond the word—and what is name but the collective word—beyond the word there shines silence. There where no other names any longer confront the one name, where the one name is al(l)-one and all that is created knows and acknowledges him and him alone, there the act of sanctification has come to rest. For sanctity is meaningful only where there is still profanity. Where everything is sacrosanct, there the Sacred itself is no longer sacred, there it simply exists. This simple existence of the Highest, such unimpaired reality, omnipotent and solely potent, beyond any desire for or joy in realization, this is truth. For truth is not to be recognized through error, as the masters of the school think. Truth attests itself; it is one with everything real; it does not part in it.

THE ONE

And such is the truth which, as God's signet, announces that he is One at the time when even the eternal people of the one God sank and disappeared. The One—this one name—outlives the people that acknowledges it. It outlives even the revealed name by which this outliving and more-than-living name will become known to the future. For the sake of this outliving which will be the lot of the One in the future, the revealed name must already be silent for the present and for every present. Precisely we Jews, we who know the name, who are called by it, and on whom the name is called, who know it and acknowledge it—we are not allowed to pronounce it. For the sake of our eternity, we must anticipate the silence in which it and we together will one day sink. We must substitute for the name itself that which God is as long as he is still called upon as one name among other names, as Creator of a world of being, as Revealer of a language of souls: The Lord. We call him the Lord in place of a name. The name itself falls silent on our lips and even beneath the silently reading eyes, just as it will fall silent one day when he is al(l)-one in all the world, when he is One.

THE LORD

It is the ultimate silence which keeps silent in us there. This is the true depth of the deity. God himself is there redeemed from his own word. He is silent. Though the God of the protocosmos had not himself been dead, he was, as Lord of dead matter, himself like this a Nought. From creation we learn that the meaning of the protocosmos is death. Just so we learn, from redemption, that the meaning of the hypercosmos is life. The Lord of the hypercosmos is the Lord of life. As such he is not alive, far from it. But just as the Lord of dead matter, though not himself dead, was like the dead and thus nought, or more exactly a Nought, one of many Noughts, so too the Lord of the hypercosmos, though not himself alive, is like the living. That simile of the Psalm applies to him too: like him are those who trust in him.

Since that which believes in him is what lives, therefore he must resemble that which lives. But what then is the nature of this living
matter? What word can capture its essence? For we are aware that
we have here made the leap beyond the world of words, just as we
were still standing before its portals in the protocosmos. The realms
of the dead lay before that portal, and we had recognized its Lord as
a Nought there. For what could be the essence of an Aught prior to
the world other than the Nought? And the Lord of dead matter,
though he is not part of that matter, is in essence akin to it and thus
a Nought like it. What then might be the essence of living matter,
lying beyond the world of words on that side just as dead matter lay
before it on this? The place of the Nought would already be occupied; it is located before words. With what word, then, are we to
designate that which would lie beyond words? It would have to be
just as little at home among words as the Nought. The Aught is at
home in the world of words. But above this world, as little a part of
it as the Nought, there rests the All, to be precise the true All, the
All which does not burst into pieces as in the world of the Nought,
but rather the one All, the One-and-all.

This is the essence of living matter. Like death in creation, it is the
last word in redemption. As such it points beyond words, like death.
It designates redeemed matter as death designates uncreated matter.
And as the Lord of life, God would be equal in essence to this essence. He would be the Lord of the one-and-all. And just this, this
lordliness over the one-and-all, is meant by the sentence: God is truth.

Truth (Cosmology)

GOD AND THE TRUTH

Only Noughts can reign over the multipartite Nought, over the one
All only a One who still has room beside and above it. But what else
still has room beside the one All as the consummate reality except—
truth? For truth is the only thing which is wholly one with reality
and, while no longer separating in it, nevertheless is still distinguished
from it as a whole. Truth is enthroned above reality. And is then
truth—God?

No. Here we ascend the pinnacle seen from which the entire traversed path lies at our feet. Truth is not God. God is truth. To go on
from the latter proposition first: it is not truth itself that sits enthroned above reality, but God, because he is truth. Because truth is

his signet, he can be One above the one-and-all of reality. Truth is the scepter of his dominion. Life is consummated in the one-and-all; it becomes wholly alive. Truth is the essence of this wholly alive reality to the extent that it is one with it; to the extent that it can nevertheless separate itself from this reality—without in the least suspending the connection—truth is the essence of God.

TRUTH AND REALITY

If then God is truth, reality is nonetheless also truth. Even its ultimate essence is truth. The proposition "reality is truth" claims equal status with the other one, "God is truth." Thus truth is the essence of reality as well as of God. We recognized it as such in the all-embracing concept at the end of the course of reality. Already for this reason it would be impossible to reverse the proposition. One cannot say that truth is God, because it would then equally well have to be reality. In that case God would be reality, hypercosmos one with the world, and everything would be fused in one mist. Thus God has to be "more" than the truth, just as every subject is more than its predicate, every thing more than the conception of it. And even if truth is really the last and the only thing one can still declare of God and his essence, still there remains to God a surplus beyond his essence. How then does he compare to his essence? After all, the proposition "God is truth" differs from other propositions of the same kind, even from the proposition that reality is truth, since its predicate is not the general concept under which the subject is subsumed. But in that case what could the truth be? What is truth?

QUESTIONING THE TRUTH OF TRUTH

Truth is supposed to be the only thing that cannot be gainsaid, cannot be doubted. Or so philosophy teaches. It is a fundamental notion of Idealism that truth authenticates itself. Every doubt about it is supposed to presuppose its indubitability. The proposition "There is truth" is supposed to be the sole indubitable proposition. If that were true, then obviously a proposition such as "God is truth" would be inadmissible, since it would tie truth to something else here when in fact it is only supposed to bind itself. Truth could only form the subject of a sentence, not its predicate. The very question "What is truth?" would constitute lèse majesté. Rather the proposition which we rejected above would be valid: that truth is God. What is then really the situation with regard to this self-authentication of truth?

THE FACT OF TRUTH

To begin with we must concede the fact that the validity of truth is indubitable. It would really not do to say that there is no truth, for then it would have to be true, at a minimum—that there is no truth. This will not do, in fact. But what have we admitted herewith except —a fact? And what is the basis for the respect which this fact enjoys? The respect is undeniable, so much so that philosophy does not hesitate to establish the certainty of this undeniability on it, on the mere fact that truth is undeniable. But is this factuality then even more deserving of respect than—the truth? Woe to "Idealism" if that be so! For Idealism set out to put the truth on its own two feet, and is it now to end by anchoring it to a—belief in a matter of fact?

THE TRUST IN TRUTH

But what else is actually to be expected? Can anything stand without having something to stand on? And if it were to stand on itself, would not then "itself" be the ground on which it stood? For then it would, after all, not be standing on its own standing, but on "itself." Only if it stood on its own standing, then it would indeed be without a where-upon. But the fact of the undeniable validity of truth is no such standing on its own standing at all. For one does not trust this fact of undeniability after the manner of matters of fact in general. If that were the case, then indeed the fact of the truth would stand on its own standing. But it is not the case. For otherwise why should one trust just in this fact? Just in this and none other. No one denies, after all, that there is error. Error is just as undeniable as truth. By admitting the fact that the existence of truth is undeniable, one also admits that there is untruth. As facts, the undeniability of truth and the undeniability of untruth are inseparable. Why then does one trust just the former undeniability while the undeniability of untruth is depressed to a fact of second rank? Because that undeniability of truth appears to us as a—true fact, and the undeniability of error is an—untrue one. The criterion of truth is directly connected with this fact, so directly that it appears to us as itself a fact. The undeniability of truth is a true fact, but a fact.

Thus it is not the fact in which we trust, but its trustworthiness. The fact as such, truth's standing upon itself, would mean little to us if it were only a standing on its own standing. It is, however, really a case of standing on itself: the undeniability of truth is itself true. It is not the fact of undeniability which already commands belief, but only the truth of this fact.

All trust in the truth thus rests upon an ultimate trust that the ground on which truth places itself with its own two feet is capable of supporting it. Truth is itself the ultimate presupposition of truth, not as truth which stands on its own feet, but as fact in which one trusts. Truth itself is a fact even before the fact of its undeniability. The fact of its undeniability would in and of itself still be a mere fact. But by virtue of the factuality of the truth which precedes it, sealed by the trusting Truly of belief, the fact of the undeniability of truth stands really established. The self-confidence of the intellect, which is customary with the masters of philosophy, is quite justified. But it is justified only because it rests on the confidence of the whole man, of whom intellect is but a part. And this confidence is no self-confidence.

TRUTH AND GOD

Thus the factuality of truth is the last thing that truth itself has to tell us about itself. This last thing is that it demands confidence in itself as a fact. And thereby it acknowledges precisely this: that it is not God. Not truth is God, but God is truth. And for its truth, the truth must appeal to the fact—not that it be truth, let alone God, but that God is truth. Truth is from God. God is its origin. If truth is illumination, then God is the light whence springs its illumination. That God is the truth, the concept with which we had to designate the essence of God, is the last thing which we recognize in him as Lord of the Last, of the one life which is consummated in the All of the hypercosmos. And this last concept of his essence dissolves in our fingers. For if God is the truth—what does this tell us about his "essence"? Nothing but that he is the primeval ground of truth and that all truth is truth only by virtue of deriving from him. Thus truth becomes a concept which is anything but universal. It is not some concept for elucidating God's essence much as the essence of any given thing might be elucidated, by means of the universal concept under which it can be subsumed. Contrariwise, God is himself the lucid light which elucidates the truth. That which, being true, becomes clear and illuminating, derives its clarity and its illuminative power from him. The proposition "God is the truth" stands all alone among the propositions which seek to elucidate his essence. This divine essentiality is none other than God's revealing (manifesting) himself. Even the "ultimate" that we know of God is none other than the innermost that we know of him, namely that he reveals himself to us. God is the truth—this is the proposition with which we thought we had attained an uttermost of knowledge. But if we look more closely into what truth is, we find that this proposition merely brings us again in different words what we had already experienced as inmost confidence; the apparent knowledge concerning his essence becomes the proximate, immediate experience of his activity: that he is truth tells us in the final analysis none other than that he—loves.

AT THE GATE OF TRUTH

Thus we grasp the ultimate knowledge of God's essence in the light of the hypercosmos only to recognize it as the very same discovery that we had already been able to make daily within the world as his creatures and children. If that be so, this ultimate cognition entitles us to venture one more time back into that pristine noncognition, that cognition of the Nought, which was our point of departure. In this Nought, paganism had directly found an All, the All of its gods, the fortress in which they concealed themselves from the eyes of the world. Paganism was satisfied with these gods and demanded nothing more. Revelation, however, taught us to recognize in these gods the concealed God, the concealed one who is none other than the not yet manifest one. Paganism really had found an All in that Nought. We, who recognized it as Nought, could only hope to find the All in it. The pagan world became protocosmos for us, the life of the pagan gods became for us the concealed prelife of God. Thus the Nought of knowledge of him became a Nought full of content for us, a mysterious prediction of what we have discovered in revelation. The darkness of the Nought loses its independent power, if ever it had it before. That God is the Nought becomes as figurative a proposition as that other one, that he is the truth. Just as the truth turned out to be simply the consummation of what we had already discovered with palatable and visible presentness in the love of God, namely his revelation, so too the Nought can be none other than the prophecy of that revelation. That God is "Nought" can no more hold out against the question into the essence, the question "What is?" than that God is "truth."

DISCOVERING THE TRUTH

What is Nought? The very question rules out the only answer which would allow the Nought to remain Nought, the answer: Nought. For Nought can never designate the essence, can never be predicate. Nought is no concept. It has neither dimension nor content. The concluding sentence of Schopenhauer's main work, "the world is

—nought," is an absurdity in purely conceptual terms. At least it does not explain the world. With regard to the world it really says—nothing. The proposition about the Nought which Schopenhauer had in mind is another matter entirely. This is the Buddhist idea which one may formulate thus: the Nought is God. This proposition is no more absurd than that of Idealism to the effect that the truth is God. Only, like the latter, it is—false. For in the last analysis the Nought, exactly like the truth, is not an independent subject at all. It is a mere fact, the expectation of an Aught, a nought-yet. It is, in short, a fact which is still seeking the ground on which it stands. As the truth is truth only because it is from God, so the Nought is Nought only because it is toward God. Only of God can it be said that he is the Nought. This would be a first, nay the first cognition of his essence. For here indeed Nought may be a predicate, precisely because God is not recognized in his essence at all: the question "What is God?" is impossible. And precisely this impossibility is perfectly indicated in the true proposition: God is the Nought. This, apart from that other "God is the truth," is the only admissible answer to this question. As the answer "God is the truth" brings the mystical question concerning his hypercosmic essence, this ultimate question, back to the living discovery of his actions, so too the answer "he is Nought" leads the abstract question concerning his protocosmic essence, this pristine question, forward to the same discovery. In this discovery there thus is collected from both directions all that we may want to ask. There beginning and end arise out of their concealment into the manifest. We find ourselves in this middle, and find Him, the "First and the Last," by our side, in immediate proximity, as a man finds his friend. Thus the concealed becomes manifest. And seen from here, factuality, proximity, immediacy now fill all the ends of the world; it sleeps in every fragment of the protocosmos, it dwells on all the stars of the hypercosmos. Whether it be truth or Nought, God's essence has vanished in his deed, a deed wholly in-essential, wholly real, wholly proximate, in his love. And this his wholly manifest act of loving now enters space, freed as that is from the rigidity of essence, and fills it to every farthest corner. The Manifest becomes the Concealed.

AT THE GOAL OF TRUTH

Beginning, middle, end thus become equally immediate, that is, equally beyond mediating, beyond median-izing, became themselves already medial. With the beginning and end as immediate as the middle, the All that once broke in pieces has now grown back together

again. By its immediacy, revelation provided the cement for healing
the age-old breach. True, the pure reason of Idealism had ventured to
rhyme the line which begins: "God, man and constellation, in that
equalizing machine of cerebration." But these three, God, world, and
man, cannot be "rhymed." Rather, the first requirement was to accept
them as they were, in their unrhymed factuality. Here as in world
history, revelation cannot open its mouth until authentic paganism—
metaphysical, metalogical, metaethical—has preceded. By undertaking
to equalize and adapt, to rhyme what is without rhyme and reason,
Idealism only destroys the pure factuality in which the three originally
stand each by itself. The stalwart figures of man, world, and God
dissolve into nebulous images like subject, object, and ideal, or I,
object, and law, or whatever other names may be vouchsafed to them.
If, however, the elements are simply accepted, then they can come together, not for "rhyme and reason," but rather in order to produce a
route in their mutual interaction. What becomes immediately visible
in revelation is neither God nor man nor world. On the contrary,
God, man, and world, which had been visible figures in paganism, here
lose their visibility: God appears to be concealed, man secluded, the
world enchanted. What does become visible is their reciprocal interaction. That which is here immediately experienced is not God, man,
and world but rather creation, revelation, and redemption. In them we
experience what it means to be a creature, to be child of the Name
and its believing-disbelieving bearer through the world. But this immediacy of experience no more leads to an immediate relationship to
the All than did that previous immediacy of cognition. Cognition had
everything, true, but only as elements, only in its pieces. Experience
got beyond the piecemeal; it was whole at every moment. But because
it was always at the moment, it did not, though it was whole, have
everything in any of its moments. The All, which must be everything
as well as whole, can neither be honestly recognized nor clearly experienced. Only the dishonest cognition of Idealism, or the unclear
experience of mysticism, can delude itself with having comprehended
it. The All must be comprehended beyond cognition and experience
if it is to be comprehended immediately. And precisely this comprehension takes place in the illumination of prayer. We have seen
how the route here is rounded out to the cycle of the year and how,
with the prayer for this rounding off, the All presents itself immediately to view. In this ultimate immediacy in which the All really
approaches us completely, we are permitted to renew the name with
whose denial we began our work, the name of the truth. We had
been forced to reject the truth as it presented itself to us at the be-

ginning of wisdom, namely as the appointed companion on the pilgrimage through the All. We denied that philosophy which rested on such a belief in the immediacy of cognition to the All and of the All to cognition. Now that our way has taken us from an Immediate via a Nighest to the immediate view of the structure, we find that the truth, which had wanted to press itself on us as the first, is the last there at the goal. In viewing it, we comprehend the eternal truth. But we do not view it, like philosophy, as basis—for us that is and remains the Nought—but rather as ultimate goal. And in seeing the truth there at the goal, it dawns on us at the same time that the truth is after all none other than the divine revelation which occurred to us too who hover in the middle between basis and future. Our Verily, our Yea and Amen with which we answered God's revelation—at the goal it stands revealed as the beating heart of the eternal truth as well. We find our way, find ourselves in midst of the fire of the farthest star of the eternal truth, ourselves in the truth and not—to reject here for the last time the blasphemy of philosophy—the truth in us.

Spirit (Psychology)

IN THE TRUTH

We find ourselves. We find ourselves present. But we must have the courage to find ourselves present in the truth, the courage to say our Truly in midst of the Truth. For so we may, since the ultimate truth is none other than—ours. God's truth is none other than the love with which he loves us. The light with which the truth illuminates is none other than the word to which our Truly makes answer. In the first "Let there be light," there is created not only the light of this world but also that other one which God separated and put aside for the world of consummation. Thus we say our Truly there where we find ourselves present. There is no such thing as mere coincidence. Being born as personality is no coincidence even if it so seems from the metalogic viewpoint of paganism; it is creation. Being reborn as Self when the *daimon* befalls the character is no coincidence even if it so seems from the metaethical viewpoint of paganism; it is revelation. Man finds himself born and reborn. He may not venture to deny the one any more than the other. He must live there where he is placed. For the hand of the Creator has placed him there; he has not fallen there out of the lap of coincidence. He must go where he is sent for he has received direction from the word of the Revealer, not an obscure dispensation from the blind tottering of fate. Position and mission—as he receives them at the located place and the decisive moment of his life as his personal Here and Now, he must say his Truly to both, so that they become truth for him.

POSSESSION OF THE TRUTH

His truth must become the truth because altogether it is truth only as a his-truth. The truth which originates with God we recognized as the essence of truth altogether. Thus it must come to man too as God's truth, and as such he can only discover it by making it his own in the Truly. For only that which one receives as gift teaches one to recognize the giver. That which I merely find counts as owner-less or at best as lost property for me. I experience as the property of the giver only the gift, precisely because and as it becomes mine. Thus the truth counts as God's truth for me only when I make it my own in the Truly. What is it then that I can make my own? Only that which was imparted to me in my inner Here and Now. Whether that be the "whole" truth is of no concern to me. It is enough that it was im-parted to me. It became my part. I can discover that God is truth only in the sense which we have now established, as origin of truth, by discovering that he is "my part," "the portion of my cup on the day that I call upon him."

THE VERIFICATION OF TRUTH

Thus truth must be verified, and precisely in the manner in which it is generally denied, that is, by leaving aside the "whole" truth and by yet recognizing the portion to which one holds as the eternal truth. It has to be thus, for we are dealing with the eternal here. In the eternal, the triumph over death, which is swallowed up in it, is celebrated. The broken weapons of death are exhibited in the triumphal procession. Death meant to mow down all life lest it live on to eternal life. He had presumed that no end could be reached except by dying. But the eternal people is held up to him as a triumphant proof that the end can also be experienced by living. With that the scythe of the grim reaper breaks. Death had galloped up and down every road, sure that all passers-by were to pass on. But on the eternal way it is possible to walk without perishing, for every step takes place again from its beginning. With that the rider's horse breaks its legs. Death had scorned all truth as being tied to a miserable piece of reality and as thereby already denying the truth, so that all must fall prey to him as if by default. Now he is confronted by the banner of a truth which is recognized and acknowledged as eternal by being verified as personally received and imparted, a part, that is, which verifies the whole truth instead of denying it. The mere part is become "my eternal portion." Then the cocksure grin is wiped off the face of old man Death, and he bows to the eternal verdict.

PLACE AND TIME OF TRUTH

The personal is verified as eternal truth: birth and rebirth, station and mission, located Here and decisive Now of life. In paganism, neither the one nor the other is present; instead of the former, there prevails chance, instead of the latter, fate; it is a chance-world and a fate-world without station and without mission. And there really can be no question of verification in this sense at all. There the Own remains own, and verification at best verifies the verity that it is personal. Where revelation occurred and the bridge was erected from heaven to earth, from the eternal to the personal, there both the Here and the Now are fixed at one and the same time. Both space and time are structured out of revelation. But verification occurs in the very own, in the individual life. And the individual life must be rooted in the common ground of revelation; a part of it must reach below the earth. And the question is only which part. Both the Here and the Now can each dwell as well in the common ground as in the individual life. Precisely their inseparability assures the individual plant that it is really rooted deep in the ground. Thus there is a dual possibility of verifying the verity. And in this dual possibility we rediscover the antithesis of nuclear fire and emanations which were described in the two previous books. But this time they are not in simple juxtaposition, but in a reciprocal intertwining which, while it cannot be experienced, can be perceived. It cannot be experienced for, as we have now recognized, the Supreme can be imparted to man only by becoming a part. But it can be perceived.

EXPERIENCING THE TRUTH

True, the whole too can be perceived only where it has become part, and so the whole of the truth, the whole truth can be perceived only by being seen in God. This is the only thing which is seen in God. It is only here that man does not experience directly; rather it is God who experiences while man merely watches. He grasps his part of the truth in the direct unity of experience and observation. But the whole truth, just because it is the whole truth and thus im-parted only to God, a part only for God, this he can observe himself only in God. For he remains a man in life. True, he may experience God—for what else is revelation; but, like the experiencing of another person, of a friend, this means simply that the one understands what the other says to him. It is impossible to experience what another person, even the nighest one, experiences on others. To this and only to this, not to the direct intercourse of men among each other, there applies the hard saying that no bridge leads from man to man.

LIMITS OF HUMANITY

Thus man remains man in life. And even if he can experience God, can hear God's voice, he by no means experiences thereby what God himself experiences. In perception, however, he perceives directly what God experiences, precisely because he here steps ashore from the liquid element of experience. He perceives it in God. God himself experiences it. That makes a great difference. For man it is never more than the truth, for God it is more than the truth. For God it is experience. "God is the truth" means that he bears it within himself, that it is imparted to him. The whole truth is imparted only to God. Man takes part in the truth, and verifies as much with his Truly which is the veritable countersignature to the document, emanating from the Lord of Truth, of his part and office as faithful servant of his lord. To the truth which is God's seal there corresponds the Truly as man's seal. He may and must say his Truly, his Yes and Amen. He is not permitted any if's and but's. In his mouth, "if" is a vile word, and he is entitled to decline to answer to a moralistic cross-examination confronting him with "what would you do if." It is enough for him to know what he must do when any one of these if's has become a "then" for him. "If" is a word of the whole truth, and therefore a right reserved to him before whom it eternally changes into a Then. Man may venture to look the If in the eye only in God, only in this perpetual transformation into the Then, and even then ever in the awareness that it is not for him to concern himself about the If. His province remains the Then, his word the Truly.

CONFIGURATION OF HUMANITY: THE JEW

In revelation, truth coursed into the Here and Now, and there was a dual possibility for it to unite with the Truly of Man. The locus where man was located, the station where he stood, could be found in himself; his nature could be such as was created for and in him at birth, something he could carry around with him, an inner home which he could no more cast aside than the snail its house or, to use a better analogy, a magic circle which he could no more escape than the circuit of his blood, precisely because, like the latter and with the latter, he carries this with him wherever he may go or stand. If then man carries his inner home, his inner station, with him, then the decisive moment, the moment of his second birth, of his rebirth, must lie for him beyond the confines of his personality, before his own life. The rebirth of the Jew—and it is of him that we are here speaking —is not his personal one, but the transformation of his people for freedom in the divine covenant of revelation. On that occasion the people experienced a second birth, and he in it, not he personally as an individual. The patriarch Abraham heard the call of God and answered it with his "Here I am," and the individual only in Abraham's loins. Henceforth the individual is born a Jew. He no longer needs to become one in some decisive moment of his individual life. The decisive moment, the great Now, the miracle of rebirth, lies before the individual life. In the individual life there is found only the great Here, the viewpoint, the station, the house and the circuit, in short all that is granted to man in the mystery of his first birth.

CONFIGURATION OF HUMANITY: THE CHRISTIAN

It is just the contrary with the Christian. In his personal life there occurs to him at a given point the miracle of rebirth, and it occurs to him as an individual. Direction is thereby injected into the life of one born heathen by nature. "A Christian is made, not born." This beginning of his having become a Christian, whence originate ever new beginnings, a whole chain of beginnings, this he carries with him, but otherwise nothing. He never "is" a Christian, although there is a Christianity. Christianity exists without him. The individual Jew generally lacks that personal vitality which only comes to a man in the second birth, with the "intrusion of the self." For although the [Jewish] people has the defiantly demonic self in full measure, the individual [Jew] has it not at all. Rather he is from his first birth on whatever he is as Jew, in a sense, then by virtue of his personality, not of his character. Correspondingly, the Christian loses everything "natural," everything innate, in his Christianity. There are Christian characters, men, that is, in whose features one can read the struggles in which the Christian in them was born. But in general there are no Christian personalities; an artificial expression like "Johannine nature" is the exception that proves this rule. What is Christian by nature has its being outside him, in secular and ecclesiastical institutions; he does not carry it around with him on the outside. The mystery of birth, which occurs in the Jew precisely to the individual, here precedes every individual in the miracle of Bethlehem. There, in the origin of revelation which is common to all, the first birth common to all occurred. The undeniable, the given, the original and enduring being of their Christianity they find, not in themselves, but in Christ. They themselves had, each of them, to become Christian. They are relieved of being-Christian before birth by the birth of Christ, just as, contrariwise, the Jew is relieved of becoming-Jew in the protohistory of his people's revelation, while he possesses his being Jew in himself from birth on and carries it with him.

LAW OF HUMANITY: BIRTH AND REBIRTH

This contradictory relationship of Here and Now, of birth and rebirth, also determines each and every further contrast in effect between Jewish and Christian life. Christian life begins with rebirth. Birth lies outside it in the first instance. Thus it must seek to lay a foundation for its birth and its rebirth. It must remove the birth from the manger in Bethlehem into its own heart. 'Were Christ born a thousand times in Bethlehem, but not also in you, you would still be lost.'[1] This whole Here that is still without, this whole world of naturalness must be drawn into the series of becoming-Christian's which begins with the great Now of the rebirth. Christian life leads the Christian into the outside. The rays radiate evermore, till all the outside shall be irradiated. Jewish life is just the opposite. Birth, the whole natural Here, the natural individuality, the impartible participation in the world—already exists here, and this broad and full existence must be conducted into the narrow instant of the rebirth. This conducting becomes a re-duction, for rebirth precedes the personal and individual birth by time out of mind. The reliving of the quondam common rebirth here takes the place of the transfer of the quondam common birth into the personal reborn heart. Thus instead of the past being made present, the present is conducted back into the past. Everyone is to know that the Eternal brought him personally out of Egypt. The present Here dissolves in the great Now of the remembered experience. The Christian way becomes expression and expropriation and irradiation of the outermost, while Jewish life becomes memory and internalization and inspiration of the innermost.

[1] Cf. above, p. 339. (Tr.)

The Shape of Verification: Eschatology

The rays of the Star thus break forth to the exterior, the fire glows toward the interior, and neither rests till it has arrived at the end, the outermost or the innermost. Both draw everything into the circle filled with their effect. But the rays do so by dividing on the outside, scattering, and going their separate ways, ways which only reunite beyond the outer space of the protocosmos when that has been traversed in its entirety. The fire, on the other hand, does so by gathering and in-gathering within itself the rich multiplicity of existence, in the flickering play of its flame, as contradictions of the inner life, contradictions which likewise find their resolution only there where the flame may be quenched because the world has ceased to glow and no longer provides it with fuel, and the hissing life of the flame dies out in what is more than human-worldly life: in the divine life of truth. For with this we are concerned here, with the truth, and no longer with the bifurcation of the way in the visible world, or with the inner contradictoriness of life. But truth never appears before the end. The end is its locus. For us it is not the given but the result. For to us it is a Whole; only to God it is im-parted. For him it is not the result, but the given, given, that is, by him, gift. But we never see the truth until the end. Thus we must now accompany both the bifurcation and the contradictoriness to the end; we may no longer be content with what we encountered hitherto on our journey of discovery, with life and the way.

THE CHRISTIAN WAY

The forks in the road were threefold, according to the three forms that the All assumed after it had burst into pieces for us. The centrifugal way of Christianity embraced God, world, and man, all three incommensurable as far as intellect was concerned. And wherever the apostles of Christendom drew a portion of the All into Christianity, the old gods, the old world, the old Adam were nailed to the cross, and those born in paganism were reborn in Christianity for the new God, the new world, the new man. The obscure designations which only remained as tablets inscribed by pagan hands at the tops of the three crosses were read by Christianity in their own manifest sense as the concealed God, the secluded man, the enchanted world.

SPIRITUALIZED GOD

The ways of the Father and the Son unveiled the All of the Concealed God. They radiated outward from the Star of Redemption,
but they radiated apart, and appeared intent on constituting themselves the contrast between two persons. In its face, admittedly, paganism collapsed because of its fundamental indefiniteness, and
collapsed each time anew, as each new indefiniteness was caught in
this ever-open Either-Or. The worldly materialistic bases for the
creation of new gods were caught up in the belief in the Father, the
human-personal ones in the belief in the Son. Thus paganism was
really at the end of its wisdom, but Christianity appeared to triumph
over it only by adapting its concept of God to it; it purchased the
end of pagan wisdom only at the cost of the curse of ever having
to remain at the beginning of the way. In the concept of the Spirit,
which emanates from both Father and Son, Christianity itself thus
designates the point where both, Father and Son, will meet again when
once the world has gathered under this cross, beyond the way. The
Christian credo had to accommodate itself to a pagan impulse in order
to win over the pagans, and this impulse is quenched by the worship
of God in the Spirit and the truth, by the promise that the Spirit would
lead Christendom. It is quenched, however, only to make room for a
new danger: a deification of the Spirit or rather a spiritualization of
God. This would forget God himself in favor of the Spirit; it would
lose the living power of God, incalculably creating and quickening life,
in the hope of a glimpse; intoxicated with the hope of seeing him and
with the fullness of the Spirit, it would lose touch with the constantly
growing world and with the soul renewing itself in belief. The Eastern
Church, true to its origin in the Apostle John and the Greek Church
Fathers, assumed the function of the conversion of wisdom; henceforth
it displays the great illustration of this danger of spiritualizing God, seeking refuge in hope and a glimpse from an anarchic world, a chaotic soul.

DEIFIED MAN

The ways of priest and saint disclosed the All of the secluded man.
Though they likewise emanated from the same ray of the Star of Redemption, they too radiated apart, and appeared to constitute themselves into the contradiction which, among men, divides man from
man. And here too paganism, which divided men among themselves
in a hundred different ways, collapsed again and again in the face of
this [single] contrast. For paganism made all its divisions according

to the permanent criterion of shape and color, class and language, or according to the fleeting emotions of the moment, in hate and love. But all these permanent criteria came to nought before the one indestructible character of the priest, a character setting him apart from the laity; all the tempestuous emotions of the moment shattered on the saint's one great passion, his ever-new passion of love. The wealth of pagan forms paled into insignificance before the weight of that [one] form; every caprice of pagan passions disappeared before this [one] passion and came to nought. But the contrast still remained. Though it caught and appeased the pagan frenzy of humanity, the struggle continued between those who now lay there in stillness. Between form and freedom, between priest and saint, peace remained just as unaccomplished in the All of humanity as it did between the single form and the wealth of figures, between the one freedom and the passions. Here again, unity beckoned only there where the two ways met again beyond every way in order to gather mankind under this cross. Thence beckoned the image of him who had said to Christendom: 'I am the truth.' The Son of man was the only one whose high priesthood did not suffer from the servant-form, and whose humanity, on the other hand, was not reduced by his divinity. The figures of priest and saint, always separated in their campaigns of conquest through the country of the soul, were thus united in view of this image of one who would be true man and true God, and in imitation of him. In the duality of these figures, and in all the divisions which this duality in turn posited within the soul, man, who was still and yet as divided within himself as in paganism, could thus shape himself in an image approaching the longed-for image of a unity of the heart, at least in imitation and hope. At least in the longing and hope for a unity of the heart, the last conflict of the pagan soul thus appears to be resolved before the image of the Son of Man. But here too a new danger again threatens: a deification of man and a humanization of God which would forget God himself in favor of man, which threatened to lose the straightforward belief in the superhuman God and the activity-minded love for a figure-poor world in favor of a credulous longing to descend into the still chamber whence spring the manifold rivulets of the soul. The Northern[1] Church, true to its origin in Paul and the German Fathers, had assumed the function of converting the Spiritual, of the poet in man; henceforth it displays the great illustration of that danger of a humanization of God which deifies man, seeking refuge in the still corner of longing and in one's own heart from a world bereft of soul and from the Lord of the spirits of all flesh.

[1] *i.e.*, Protestant. (Tr.)

IDOLIZED WORLD

The ways of state and Church freed the enchanted world from enchantment. These too, though emanating from the one ray of the Star, radiated apart, and appeared to constitute themselves the contrast which, in the world, divided order from order, world from world. And once more paganism which, in the world, divides all from all, state from state, people from people, class from class, each from each, collapsed again and again before this uniform contradiction. Before the one essential division between natural and supernatural order, all the divisions of paganism became inessential. If henceforth they wished to embellish their zeal against one another with so much as the appearance of justification, they had to borrow the reflected glory of a higher justice from that contradiction; they had to attempt to provide power with spiritual content. Thus the pagan 'struggle of all against all' was sublimated into a higher struggle for higher stakes, but it remained a struggle. Only at the end of all history there looms the prospect of a kingdom free of struggle and contradiction in which God will be all-in-all. The fullness of the pagan world would have simply refused to dissolve in a 'kingdom of priests and a holy nation.' To comprehend this wealth fully within itself, Christianity had to walk the two separate but parallel ways, the way of the state and the way of the Church, and these meet there at the end of all history. Thus the two ways cannot unite until the fullness of the pagans has dissolved. But in this prospect of a future one-and-universal world freed from contradictions, of a day when God will be all-in-all, there once more lies a danger for Christianity. It is the last of the three great dangers which are unavoidable because inseparable from its greatness and strength: making the world divine or God worldly. It would forget the One above all in favor of the All-in-All; it would forfeit the pious confidence in the free inner strength of the soul which renews itself, and in the providence of God which goes its own way above all human insight, in favor of the lovingly active unification of what the world has separated into the one-and-universal building of the kingdom. The Southern[1] Church, true to its origin in Peter and the Latin Church Fathers, had assumed the function of converting the visible legal system of the world; henceforth it illustrates that danger of making God worldly by making the world divine, seeking refuge in the act of love which sustains the world and in the joy of the effectively effected [good] work from a freedom of the soul which it mistrusts and from a God whose sway is beyond finding out.

[1] *i.e.*, Roman Catholic (Tr.)

THE CHRISTIAN DANGERS

Threefold was the division of the way, threefold the reunification which is always in the Beyond, threefold the danger. That the Spirit leads onto all ways, and not God; that the Son of man be the truth, and not God; that God would become All-in-All and not One above all—these are the dangers. They originate at the end points of the way, in the Beyond where the rays at last unite which never meet in the Here of God as of the soul and of the world. Thus they are dangers which Christianity never overcomes—spiritualization of God, apotheosis of man, pantheification of the world—just as it never overcomes the division of the churches into the Church of the spiritual truth, that of the Son of Man, and that of the kingdom of God. Each of these, immersed respectively in hope, faith, and love, must neglect the other two forces in order to live all the more strongly in the one, and in order to administer its portion in the work of bringing about the rebirth of the protocosmos which was born in paganism. Christianity radiates in three divided directions. It presses toward an Outermost in pursuing its self-expropriating course to the outside, but this Outermost is not something simple. Like the protocosmos in which the pagan finds himself, it is something threefold. Revelation bridged the gap between those three Alls of the protocosmos, connecting the three points in the one immovable order of the Day of the Lord. But Christianity completes its expropriation into the All, and the rays which were scattered on their way through time gather together again by making God spiritual, human, worldly, and these three points can no longer be connected, as we shall see. Though they are in a fixed order with respect to each other, unlike the three points of paganism, and the Perhaps has long ago fallen silent forever, yet Christianity no longer offers them a fluent interconnection which would again lift these three separated ones too into a unity, at least not completely. Before we turn to this ultimate understanding of the rays which are radiated into the outside, let us now return to contemplate the glow with which the flame of the fire glows in itself.

JEWISH LIFE

The flame too flashed in threefold blaze. In three contradictions of its own burning life, it internalized the tripartite life of the outer All. The might and humility of the Jewish God, the election and the redemptive vocation of Jewish man, the this-worldly and eschatological character of the Jewish world—in these three flashes, the flame gathered, mirror-like, all possible contradictions into its interior as simple contradictions. For in contrast to all earthly flames, it does not simply burn out its warmth by radiating outward. Rather, because eternally feeding on itself, it simultaneously gathers the blaze into its innermost interior as supreme perfervid fire. And by thus gathering its blaze inwardly, it in turn smelts the blazing, flashing contradictions more and more into a unitary, still glow.

THE GOD OF THE [JEWISH] PEOPLE

The contradiction between creative power and revealing love is itself still inherent in the original transformation from the concealed God of paganism to the manifest God of revelation. It is Jewish in the narrower sense only in the fitful and unpredictable transitions between his two aspects. In the inner warmth of the Jewish heart, this contradiction is melted down in the invocation of God as "our God and God of our fathers." This God is indistinguishably the God of creation and of revelation. He is not invoked here by his revealed name, but as God in general. Yet as God in general he nonetheless becomes "our" God. And this his quality of being ours is in turn made to root in his very beginning so that the revelation whereby he is our God is based in its own creative origin in the revelation to the Patriarchs. Precisely this whole intricate structure of belief is a perfectly simple emotion in the Jewish heart. It is no ultimate unity; it is not an Outermost which emotion can just barely attain. It is something inner, a simple, inner unity. It is not something supreme; it is the Jew's everyday consciousness of God. So far from being something supreme and ultimate, it is on the contrary something extremely "constricted." The whole constriction of direct, naïve Jewish consciousness consists in this ability to forget that there is anything else in this world, indeed that there is any world outside of the Jewish world and the Jews. Our God and God of our fathers—of what concern is it to the Jew at the moment when he thus invokes God that this God is the "king of the universe," the One God of the future, as he otherwise again and again says and knows. In this invocation he feels himself entirely alone with him in the most constricted circle, and has lost consciousness of all wider circles, not perchance because he only has him in the way in which God revealed himself to him and God's creativity thus remains outside for him; no, for the creative power is quite there with him. But the Creator has constricted himself into Creator of the Jewish world, and revelation only occurred to the Jewish heart. The paganism which had been embraced by the ways of Christianity, radiating outward and then radiating back together again, is here left entirely behind, entirely outside. The glow which glows inward knows nothing of the darkness that surrounds the Star on the outside. Jewish feeling has here poured creation and revelation entirely into the most intimate space between God and his people.

THE MAN OF ELECTION

Like God, man too constricts himself for Jewish feeling when this seeks to unite him into a unitary glow out of the dual consciousness, still flaming into one another, of Israel and the Messiah, of the gracious gift of revelation and the redemption of the world. One concept leads from Israel to the Messiah, from the people that stood at the foot of Sinai to that day when the house of Jerusalem 'shall be called a house of prayer for all peoples.' This concept emerged under the prophets and has governed our inner history since then: the remnant. The remnant of Israel, the faithful remnant, the true Israel within the people, this is at every moment the assurance that a bridge connects the two poles. For the rest, Jewish consciousness may well flicker back and forth in hot-blooded transitions between those two poles of life which were determined in the original inner conversion of the secluded man of paganism into the determined and disclosed man of revelation, the poles respectively of the personal discovery of divine love and of the dedicated effectuation of love in the sanctity of conduct. But the remnant represents both at the same time: the assumption of the yoke of the commandment and that of the yoke of the kingdom of heaven. If the Messiah should come "today," the remnant will be ready to receive him. In defiance of all secular history, Jewish history is the history of this remnant; the word of the prophet, that it "will remain," ever applies to it. All secular history deals with expansion. Power is the basic concept of history because in Christianity revelation began to spread over the world, and thus every expansionist urge, even that which consciously was purely secular, became the unconscious servant of this expansionist movement. But Judaism, and it alone in all the world, maintains itself by subtraction, by contraction, by the formation of ever new remnants. This happens quite extensively in the face of the constant external secession. But it is equally true also within Judaism itself. It constantly divests itself of un-Jewish elements in order to produce out of itself ever new remnants of archetypal Jewish elements. Outwardly it constantly assimilates only to be able again and again to set itself apart on the inside. In Judaism there is no group, no tendency, nay barely an individual who does not regard his manner of sacrificing incidentals in order to hold on to the remnant as the only true way, and himself therefore as the true "remnant of Israel." And so he is. In Judaism, man is always somehow a remnant. He is always somehow a survivor, an inner something, whose exterior was seized by the current of the world and carried off while he himself, what is left of him, remains standing on the shore. Something within him is waiting. And he has something within himself. What he is waiting for and what he has he may call by different names; often enough he may barely be able to name it. But he has a feeling that both the waiting and the having are most intimately connected with each other. And this is just that feeling of the "remnant" which has the revelation and awaits the salvation. The strange questions which, according to tradition, will one day be presented to the Jew by the divine judge, indicate these two aspects of the feeling. The first, "Have you derived sentence from sentence?" means: was the consciousness alive in you that whatever may happen to you was somehow already given to you before birth in the gift of revelation? And the other, "Have you awaited salvation?" means that pointing toward the future advent of the kingdom which is placed in our blood at birth. In this duo-unity of feeling, man has thus wholly constricted himself into Jewish man. Once more the paganism which was embraced by the divergent and finally reconverging ways of Christianity lies outside in the darkness. Jewish man is wholly by himself. The future which otherwise weighs so heavily on his soul has here fallen silent. In the feeling of being the remnant, his heart is wholly at one in itself. There the Jew is Jew alone. The revelation which was his, the redemption for which he has been summoned, both have completely merged in the constricted space between him and his people.

THE WORLD OF LAW

And like God and man, so the world too becomes quite intimately constricted for Jewish feeling so soon as it seeks to escape into the unity of a worldly existence from the flame flickering restlessly back and forth between this world and the world to come. That the world, this world, is created and withal in need of the future redemption is a dual idea whose disquieting character is quieted in the unity of the law. Though as content of revelation and claim on the individual it is commandment, seen as world it is law. The law, then, in its multiplicity and strength ordering everything, comprising everything "external," that is all the life of this world, everything that any worldly jurisdiction may conceivably comprise, this law makes this world and the world to come indistinguishable. God himself, according to

Rabbinic legend, "studies" in the law. For in the law everything of this world that is comprised in it, all created existence, is already given life and soul directly as content of the world to come. Jewish feeling is oblivious to the fact that the law is only Jewish law, that this finished and redeemed world is only a Jewish world, and that the God who rules the world has more to do than merely to study in the law, and this quite apart from whether the law is meant in its traditional sense or whether the old concept has been filled with new life. For even in the latter case, Jewish feeling takes only this world for unfinished, while it takes for finished and unalterable the law that it presumes to impose on this world so that it might be transformed into the world to come. Even if the law appears in the highly modern garb of some contemporary Utopianism, the law then stands in sharp contrast to that Christian lack of law which can and wants to be taken by surprise, which still distinguishes the Christian-turned-politician from the Jew-turned-Utopian, and which endows the latter with the greater power to shake up, the former with the greater readiness to attain. The Jew always thinks that what counts is only to turn his legal doctrines this way and that; sooner or later it would turn out to have "everything in it." The law turns its back on the paganism which Christianity embraces, it knows nothing of it and does not wish to know anything of it. The idea of the transition from this world into the world to come, the idea of the messianic age which is suspended over life as a Today that is ever to be awaited, this idea coalesces here and becomes an everyday object as the Law in the obedience to which the seriousness of that transition recedes, the more complete the obedience. For precisely the How of the transition is already determined. The life of the pious man, like that of God in the legend, may now also be exhausted in the ever more complete "study" of the law. The whole world, that which is created for existence as well as that which is still to be endowed with soul, and which grows toward redemption, is combined into one by his feeling, and poured into the intimately familiar space between the law and his people, the people of the law.

THE JEWISH DANGERS

Everything twofold, everything internally all-comprehending within Jewish life has thus become very constricted and simple for this innermost of Jewish feelings. One would have to say too simple and too constricted, and one would need to detect dangers in this constriction as much as in the Christian latitude. If the concept of God was threatened there, his world and his man appear to be in danger here. By radiating apart to the outside, Christianity threatens to lose itself in individual rays far from the divine nucleus of truth. By glowing toward the inside, Judaism threatened to gather its warmth to its own bosom, far away from the pagan reality of the world. If there the dangers were spiritualization of God, humanization of God, secularization of God—here they are denial of the world, disdain of the world, mortification of the world. It was denial of the world if the Jew, in the proximity of his God, felt himself anticipating redemption, and forgot that God is Creator and Revealer, that as Creator he supports the entire world, and that as Revealer he ultimately does turn his countenance to man as such. It was disdain of the world for the Jew to regard himself as the remnant, and thus as the true man, originally created in the image of man and awaiting the end in this original purity, thereby withdrawing from the very man to whom befell, in his God-forsaken obduracy, the revelation of divine love, and who now had to act out this love in the limitless work of redemption. Finally it was mortification of the world if the Jew, possessed of the law which had been revealed to him and had become flesh and blood in his spirit, now dared venture to regulate the existence of things, renewed at every moment, and their silent growth, or even but to judge them. All three of these dangers are the necessary consequences of an inwardness turned away from the world, as those of Christianity are the consequence of an externalization of the self turned toward the world. For the Jew it is essential to encase himself thus. It is the last step in that internalization, that rooting in his own self, whence he draws the strength of eternal life, just as that evanescence is, for the Christian, the necessary consequence of his unimpeded egress and progress on the eternal way.

HARMLESSNESS OF THE DANGERS

But this rootedness in one's own self is nevertheless something entirely different from the Christian externalization of the self. Granted, for the individual personality our self-encasement may represent a grave danger while the Christian personality need hardly suffer from those dangers of Christianity. But in truth our dangers represent no danger at all for us in the final analysis. For here it turns out that the Jew simply cannot descend into his own interior without at the same time ascending to the Highest. This is, in fact, the profoundest difference between Jewish and Christian man: the Christian is by nature or at least by birth—a pagan; the Jew, however, is a Jew. Thus the way of the Christian must be a way of self-externalization, of self-renunciation;[1] he must always take leave of himself, must forfeit himself in order to become a Christian. The life of the Jew, on the other hand, must precisely not lead him out of himself; he must rather live his way ever deeper into himself. The more he finds himself the more he turns his back on paganism, which for him is on the outside not, as with the Christian, on the inside; the more, that is, he becomes Jewish. For though he is born a Jew, his "Jewishness" is something which he too must first live and experience for himself, something which becomes wholly visible in looks and traits only in the aged Jew. The type of the aged Jew is as characteristic for us as the youthful type is for the Christian nations. For Christian life de-nationalizes the Christian, but Jewish life leads the Jew deeper into his Jewish character.

JEWISH LIFE IN THE MYSTERY OF THE HIGHEST

Thus the Jew internalizes himself into his interior only for the sake of his Most High, for God's sake. And therewith those dangers now prove to be dangerous at most to him as individual. He can, that is, become hard, say, or proud or rigid. But they are no dangers to Judaism. To set up his God, his man, his world as God, man, world in general are three ways of turning his back on the exterior, of turning inward to the interior, practiced respectively on God, man, and the world. But this triple fanning of the flames of his Jewish sentiment is not itself an Ultimate; it does not end there. These are not, like God, world, and man in paganism, three points devoid of relation and order. Between these last three elements, rather, there courses a connecting current, an orbit, that is, comparable to that on which the elements of paganism entered into the relationship which led from creation via revelation to redemption. And in this interconnection, the apparently exclusively-Jewish aspect of this threefold sentiment, apparently constricted and exclusive and isolated, now closes ranks again into the one all-illuminating stellar image of truth.

THE TALE OF THE CHARIOT

Jewish mysticism bridges the gap between the "God of our Fathers" and the "Law" in a manner all its own. It replaces the general concept of creation with that of the mysterious creations, the "tale of the chariot" as it is called in an allusion to the vision of Ezekiel. There

---

[1] Both meanings are inherent in the original's Stelbstentäusserung. (Tr.)

the created world itself is full of mysterious relations to the law, and the law is not alienated from this world but the key to this enigma of the world. The plain wording of the law conceals a hidden meaning which expresses nothing so much as the essence of the world. For the Jew, the book of the law can thus, as it were, replace the book of nature or even the starry heavens from which the men of yore once thought they could interpret terrestrial matters by intelligible omens. That is the basic idea of countless legends with which Judaism expands the apparently constricted world of its law into the whole world, and on the other hand, precisely because it finds this world presaged in its law, already sees the world-to-come in it. All modes of exegesis are pressed into service, especially of course that infinitely applicable one of numerology and reading the letters in accordance with their numerical values. One hardly knows where to begin to give examples. The seventy offerings of Tabernacles are offered for the seventy "nations of the world"—as counted by legend on the basis of the Tabula Gentium in Genesis. The number of the bones of the human body are juxtaposed to the numerical value of a passage in the prayerbook so that the words of the psalmist be fulfilled and all bones praise the Eternal. The revealed name of God is concealed in the words which recount the completion of creation. One could continue endlessly. In itself, this biblical exegesis appears peculiar and even ridiculous to the observer unaccustomed to it. But its sense is none other than that the entire creation is interpolated between the Jewish God and the Jewish law, and that God and his law thereby both prove to be equally all-embracing as—creation.

THE WANDERINGS OF THE SHEKHINA

Mysticism bridges the gap between the "God of our Fathers" and the "Remnant of Israel" with the doctrine of the Shekhina. The Shekhina, God's descent upon man and his sojourn among men, is pictured as a dichotomy taking place in God himself. God himself separates himself from himself, he gives himself away to his people, he shares in their sufferings, sets forth with them into the agony of exile, joins their wanderings. The Torah was thought to have been created prior to the world, and the world for its part on behalf of the Torah; in this conception, the law had become, for Jewish feelings, more than just the Jewish law; it was really sensed as a fundamental pillar of the world, and even the notion that God himself studies his law thus now gained a general, supra-Jewish sense. Just so the pride of the "rem-

nant of Israel" now arrives, in the concept of the Shekhina, at a more
general implication. For the sufferings of this remnant, the constant
requirement to separate and exclude oneself, all this now becomes a
suffering for God's sake, and the remnant is the bearer of this suffering. The idea of the wanderings of the Shekhina, of the sparks of the
original divine light being scattered about the world, this casts all of
revelation between the Jewish God and Jewish man, and thereby
anchors both, God as well as the remnant, in all the depth of—revelation. In mysticism, the expansion of the Jewish to the universal occurred to creation by means of that multiplicity of meanings and
interpretations of the Law. In the same mysticism it occurs to revelation by means of the profound insight which detects in God's self-
dedication to Israel a divine suffering which really should not be permitted, and in Israel's separating itself into a remnant the establishment of a dwelling-place for the exiled God. Precisely this divine
suffering marks the relationship between God and Israel as constricted,
as too slight. Nothing would be more natural for the "God of our
Fathers" than that he should "sell" himself for Israel and share its
suffering fate. But by doing so, God himself puts himself in need of
redemption. In this suffering, therefore, the relationship between God
and the remnant points beyond itself.

THE UNITING OF GOD

But the redemption would then have to occur in the relationship of
the "remnant" to the "law." How is this relationship conceived? What
does fulfilling the law mean to the Jew? How does he conceive it?
Why does he fulfill it? For the sake of heavenly reward? 'Be not as
the servants who serve their masters for the sake of the hire.' For the
sake of earthly satisfaction? 'Say not: I do not like pork; say rather:
I like it well enough, but my Father in heaven has forbidden it.' The
Jew, however, fulfills the endless customs and precepts "for the sake
of uniting the holy God and his Shekhina." With this formula, the
individual, the remnant, prepares his heart, "in awe and love," to
fulfill, "in the name of all Israel" whatever commandment is at the
moment incumbent on him. He will gather the glory of God, dispersed all over the world in countless sparks, out of the dispersion
and one day bring it back home to Him who has been stripped of his
glory. Every one of his deeds, every fulfilling of a commandment,
achieves a portion of this reunion. To confess God's unity—the Jew

calls it: to unify God. For this unity is as it becomes, it is Becoming Unity. And this Becoming is enjoined on the soul and hands of man. Jewish man and Jewish law—nothing less than the process of redemption, embracing God, world, and man, transpires between the two. The fulfilling of the commandment is inaugurated and stamped as an act which brings redemption nearer, with a formula in which the individual elements, such as they are absorbed into this last One, once more resound individually: the "holy God" who has given the law, the "Shekhina" which he expropriated from himself to the remnant of Israel, the "awe" with which this remnant turned itself into the dwelling-place of God, the "love" with which he thereupon proceeded to fulfill the law, he the individual, the "I" which fulfills the law, yet he "in the name of all Israel" to which the law was given and which was created through the law. The most constricted has all expanded into the whole, the All, nay better: has redeemed itself for the unification of the One. The descent into the Innermost has disclosed itself as an ascent to the Highest. The merely Jewish feeling has been transfigured into world-redemptive truth. In the innermost constriction of the Jewish heart there shines the Star of Redemption.

CHRISTIAN ESCHATOLOGY

Here the Star blazes. The Ultimate, the Innermost, the apparently constricted and rigid nature of emotion is set in motion. It coalesces into a structure illuminating the world. By comprehending God, world, and man via creation and revelation through to redemption, it expressed the content of Judaism; now it likewise also illuminates the Innermost of the Jewish soul. Thus the Star of Redemption is the image of being, but it continues to glow also in the inner sanctum of emotion. That is here very different than in Christianity. There too the Star of Redemption designates the content, the inner being, whence it radiates outward into the world of reality as something real. But these rays reunite at three disparate points, at true end points, points which are also goals for emotion. And these points can no longer be interconnected. Mysticism can no longer bridge the gap between these outermost prospects of emotion. That God is spirit stands isolated from the notion that he is all-in-all, and also from the notion that the Son who is the way is also the truth. The idea of creation does not mediate between the former disjointedness, nor that of revelation between the latter. At the most a certain connection is established in mythological images such as that of the 'spirit hovering over the waters' or the pouring out of the spirit in the Johannine baptism. But this remains image; it does not merge into an emotional unity. Only between the two last ideas, the divinity of the Son and the promise that God will be All-in-All, does a bridge arch. The first theologian of the new religion teaches that the Son, when once all will have submitted to him, will turn over his dominion to the Father, and then God will be All-in-All. But one can see at once that this is a theologism. For Christian piety it is meaningless. It depicts a distant, far distant future. It deals with the last things by explicitly depriving them of all influence on time. For the dominion belongs to the Son, as yet and for all time, and God is not All-in-All. It depicts an eternity wholly beyond time. And thus this sentence has never meant more in the history of Christianity than precisely—a theologism, an idea. It was not and could not be a bridge on which emotion might move to and fro between one shore and the other. The two shores were structurally too diverse for this, the one too exclusively temporal, the other too exclusively eternal. True, it was an idea that the Son of Man would one day turn over his dominion, but this does not alter the fact that, within time, he was deified. True, it was an idea that God would one day be All-in-All, but this does not alter the fact that he was granted precious little influence on the Aught-in-Aught of this temporality where his *locum tenens* was lord. Emotion did not step on the bridge. Here as everywhere it confined itself to the individual points in which it gathered its last rapture. The rapture did not carry further than these end and gathering points. Christianity has produced spiritualistic, individualistic, and pantheistic mysticism, but these three did not enter into a mutual relationship. Emotion can find satisfaction in any one of the three, just as a discrete form of the Church corresponds to each of them, and none is made superfluous by the other two. Emotion everywhere attains its goal. And well it may. For where it attains its goal, there a piece of the protocosmos is renewed in death and resurrection: dead is the myth and resurrected in the veneration of the Spirit, dead is the hero and resurrected in the word from the cross, dead is the cosmos and resurrected in the one-and-universal All of the kingdom. That these three, each in itself, imply an attenuation of the truth or, more precisely, that God is Lord of the Spirits, not Spirit, giver of sufferings and not the crucified one, one and not All-in-All—who would want to raise such objections to a faith which marches triumphantly through the world and for which the gods of the nations—national myth, national hero, national cosmos—are no match? Who would indeed!

The Law of Verification: Theology

THE MEANING OF BIFURCATION

And withal: the Jew does it. Not with words, for what would words still avail in this realm of vision! But with his existence, his silent existence. This existence of the Jew constantly subjects Christianity to the idea that it is not attaining the goal, the truth, that it ever remains—on the way. That is the profoundest reason for the Christian hatred of the Jew, which is heir to the pagan hatred of the Jew. In the final analysis it is only self-hate, directed to the objectionable mute admonisher, for all that he but admonishes by his existence; it is hatred of one's own imperfection, one's own not-yet. By his inner unity, by the fact that in the narrowest confines of his Jewishness the Star of Redemption nonetheless still burns, the Jew involuntarily shames the Christian, who is driven outwards and onwards, to the utter dissipation of the original fire, into the outermost reaches of emotion, an emotion which no longer knows of a whole in which it might find itself at one with every other emotion to a truth beyond all feeling, but rather an emotion which itself was already blissful. The uttermost in Christianity is this complete losing oneself in the individual emotion, this immersion, be it in the divine spirit, the divine man, the divine world. No current of action any longer runs between these emotions; they themselves already stand beyond all action. True, that attenuation of emotion is essential, just as its constriction is in Judaism. But whereas the latter finds its resolution in Jewish life itself, in the world-redemptive meaning of a life-in-the-law, the former, the attenuation, no longer finds its resolution in any life, since it itself is already an uttermost experience.

THE ETERNAL PROTEST OF THE JEW

If, therefore, the Christian did not have the Jew at his back he would lose his way wherever he was, just as the three Churches which, after all, are none other than the earthly domiciles of those ultimate three emotions, experience their affinity on the Jew; without him they might at most know it but not feel it. The Jew forces on Christianity the knowledge that that emotional satisfaction remains denied to it. The Jew sanctified his flesh and blood under the yoke of the law, and thereby lives constantly in the reality of the heavenly kingdom; the Christian's constantly profane flesh and blood sets itself in opposition to redemption, and he learns that he himself is not permitted to anticipate redemption emotionally. By anticipating redemption, the Jew purchases the possession of truth with the loss of the unredeemed world; he gives the lie to the Christian who, on his march of conquest into the unredeemed world, has to purchase his every forward step with illusion.

THE TWO TESTAMENTS

Christianity is well aware of this relationship, of the dependence of its own development on the existence—and no more than the existence —of Judaism. It was always the hidden enemies of Christianity, from the Gnostics to the present day, who wanted to deprive it of its "Old Testament." A God who was only spirit, and no longer the Creator who gave his law to the Jews, a Christ who was only Christ and no longer Jesus, a world which was only All and its center no longer the Holy Land—though it would no longer offer the slightest resistance to deification and divinization, there would be nothing left in them to recall the soul from the dream of this deification into unredeemed life; the soul would not just get lost, it would remain lost. And the mere Book would not render this service to Christianity, or rather: it renders this service only because it is not mere book, because our life is living testimony that it is more than a mere book. The historical Jesus must always pull out from under the feet of the ideal Christ the pedestal on which his philosophic or nationalistic worshipers would like to set him. For an "idea" can after all be united with any theory or self-conceit to lend it its own halo. But the historical Jesus, that is precisely Jesus Christ in the dogmatic sense, does not stand on a pedestal; he really walks the streets of life and forces life to submit at his glance. It is exactly the same with the "spiritual" God in whom all those believe gladly and easily who hesitate to believe in Him "who created the world that he might reign over it." In his spirituality, that spiritual God is a very agreeable partner who leaves us entirely free to dispose of a world which is not "purely spiritual" and thus not his but consequently presumably the devil's. And this world itself—how gladly one would like to regard it as All, and oneself as the gloriously irresponsible "speck of dust in the All," rather than as its responsible center about which everything rotates or as the pillar on whose stability the world rests.

THE ETERNAL HATRED FOR THE JEW

It is always the same. And as that ever-present struggle of the Gnostics shows, it is the Old Testament which enables Christianity to withstand this its own danger, and the Old Testament only because it is more than mere book. A mere book would easily fall victim to the arts of allegorical exegesis. Had the Jews of the Old Testament disappeared from the earth like Christ, they would [now] denote the idea of the People, and Zion the idea of the Center of the World, just as Christ denotes the idea of Man. But the stalwart, undeniable vitality of the Jewish people, attested in the very hatred of the Jews, resists such "idealizing." Whether Christ is more than an idea—no Christian can know it. But that Israel is more than an idea, that he knows, that he sees. For we live. We are eternal, not as an idea may be eternal: if we are eternal, it is in full reality. For the Christian we are thus the really indubitable. The pastor who was asked for the proof of Christianity by Frederick the Great argued conclusively when he answered: "Your majesty, the Jews!" The Christians can have no doubts about us. Our existence stands surety for their truth. That is why, from the Christian point of view, it follows logically that Paul should let the Jews remain to the end—till "the fullness of the peoples shall have come in,"[1] that is, to that moment when the Son shall return the dominion to the Father. The theologism from the beginnings of Christian theology enunciates what we have here explained: that Judaism, by its eternal endurance through all time, the Judaism attested in the "Old" Testament and itself attesting livingly to it, that this is the One Nucleus whose glow provides invisible nourishment to the rays which, in Christianity, burst visibly and divisibly into the night of the pagan proto- and hypocosmos.

THE MEANING OF VERIFICATION

Before God, then, Jew and Christian both labor at the same task. He cannot dispense with either. He has set enmity between the two for all time, and withal has most intimately bound each to each. To us [Jews] he gave eternal life by kindling the fire of the Star of his truth in our hearts. Them [the Christians] he set on the eternal way by causing them to pursue the rays of that Star of his truth for all time unto the eternal end. We [Jews] thus espy in our hearts the true image of the truth, yet on the other hand we turn our backs on tem-

[1] Romans 11:25.

poral life, and the life of the times turns away from us. They [the Christians], for their part, run after the current of time, but the truth remains at their back; though led by it, since they follow its rays, they do not see it with their eyes. The truth, the whole truth, thus belongs neither to them nor to us. For we too, though we bear it within us, must for that very reason first immerse our glance into our own interior if we would see it, and there, while we see the Star, we do not see—the rays. And the whole truth would demand not only seeing its light but also what was illuminated by it. They [the Christians], however, are in any event already destined for all time to see what is illuminated, and not the light.

And thus we both have but a part of the whole truth. But we know that it is in the nature of truth to be im-parted, and that a truth in which no one had a part would be no truth. The "whole" truth, too, is truth only because it is God's part. Thus it does not detract from the truth, nor from us, that it is only partially ours. A direct view of the whole truth is granted only to him who sees it in God. That, however, is a view beyond life. A living view of the truth, a view that is at the same time life, can become ours too only from out the immersion into our own Jewish heart and even there only in image and likeness. As for the Christians, they are denied a living view altogether for the sake of a living effectiveness of the truth. Thus both of us, they as much as we, we as much as they, are creatures precisely for the reason that we do not see the whole truth. Just for this we remain within the boundaries of mortality. Just for this we—remain. And remain we would. We want to live. God does for us what we want for so long as we want it. As long as we cling to life, he gives us life. Of the truth he gives us only what we, as living creatures, can bear, that is our portion. Were he to give us more, to give us his portion, the whole truth, he would be hoisting us beyond the boundaries of humanity. But precisely as long as he does not do this, just so long too we harbor no desire for it. We cling to our creatureliness. We do not gladly relinquish it. And our creatureliness is determined by the fact that we only take part, only are part. Life had celebrated the ultimate triumph over death in the Truly with which it verifies the personally vouchsafed truth imparted to it as its portion in eternal truth. With this Truly, the creature fastens itself to its portion which was imparted to it. In this Truly, it is creature. This Truly passes as a mute mystery through the whole chain of beings; it acquires speech in man. And in the Star it flares up into visible, self-illuminating existence. But it remains ever within the boundaries of creatureliness. Truth itself still says Truly when it steps before God. But God himself no longer says

Truly. He is beyond all that can be imparted, he is above even the whole, for this too is but a part with him; even above the Whole, he is the One.

THE TRUTH OF ETERNITY

Thus the Truly, and even the highest Truly, the Yea and Amen jointly recited, by those redeemed for eternal life and on the eternal way, in a chorus in sight of the Star of Redemption, is still the sign of creatureliness, and the realm of nature has not yet ended, not even in the eternity-become-structure of the redeemed hypercosmos; but then the end submerges back into the beginning. That God created, this premonitory first word of Scripture does not lose its power till all be fulfilled. Till then, God will not recall back into his lap this first word to emanate from him. We had already seen the eternal truth sinking back into the revelation of divine love: redemption was altogether none other than the eternal working out of the beginning ever newly posited in revealing love. In love, the concealed had become manifest. Now this ever-renewed beginning sinks back into the secret, ever-enduring beginning of creation. The manifest becomes the concealed. And with revelation, redemption too now merges back into creation. The ultimate truth is itself only—created truth. God is truly the Lord. As such he revealed himself in the power of his creativity. If we call on him thus in the light of eternal truth—it is the Creator from the beginning, it is He who first called "Let there be light" whom we call upon thus. The midnight which, behind the existence of creation, always glitters for our blinded eyes in eternal stellar clarity—it is the same as that which spent the night in God's bosom prior to all existence. He is in truth "the first and the last." "Before the mountains were born and the earth was delivered—from eternity to eternity thou wast God." And thou wast from eternity what thou shalt be unto eternity: Truth.

GATE

Recapitulation:
The Face of the Figure

The Eternal had become figure in the truth. And the truth is none other than the countenance of this figure. Truth alone is its countenance. And be very careful for the sake of your souls: you have seen no figure, only heard speech—as it is said in the revealed world around-and-about. But in the redeemed world above-and-beyond, brought about forcibly by the more powerful blessing recited at the right place, there the word falls silent. Of this world, consummate and pacified, it is said: "May he make his countenance to shine upon you."

GOD'S COUNTENANCE

The truth is this shining of the divine visage alone. It is not a figure of its own, hovering freely, but solely the countenance of God, shining forth. But for him whom he lets his visage shine upon, to him he also turns his visage. As he turns his visage to us, so may we recognize him. And this cognition does not recognize figuratively. Rather it recognizes the truth as it is, that is as it is in God: as his countenance and part. By no means does it become a figurative truth because this countenance is turned toward us, God's portion imparted to us; for even as literal and most literal truth it would be none other than—portion and countenance. In the Star of Redemption, then, in which we saw divine truth become figure, there shines forth none other than the countenance which God turned shiningly toward us. Yea, we now recognize the Star of Redemption itself, as it has at last emerged as figure for us, in the divine visage. And only in this recognition is its cognition consummated.

418

THE DAY OF GOD

For as long as we only knew its course, without as yet seeing its configuration, just so long the order of the original elements remained unfixed. True, the unrestrained to-and-fro fluttering of the Perhaps had long since sunk away powerlessly; God, world, and man had structured themselves in a definite mutual order which came to them on the course; the sequence of the three hours of the day of God had ordained an unalterable relationship among themselves to the elements of the All so that the course was recognized as the course of the constellation to which these elements of the course belonged. But though the Star was thus sighted, it still seemed able to rotate about itself, so that world and man seemed nonetheless still to experience their own day within the already fixed sequence of the three periods of the day of God, with which this day of their own did not simply coincide. Only for God was redemption really the Ultimate. For man, however, his creation in the image of God implied being redeemed for every conceivable consummation, for the world likewise the descent of God in revelation. Thus it seemed as though the three hours were only hours of the day of God, while the day of man and the day of the world would be another [day].

The whole object of the third Part, which dealt with the Eternal of the redeemed hypercosmos, was to prove the contrary. That apparent interchangeability was here itself rooted to the spot in configurations which were assigned their fixed position in the eternal truth of the day of God. In eternal life, admittedly, redemption was already anticipated for the world in revelation which, after all, contains everything; eternal life was planted in the revelation to the one people, so that it itself no longer alters; this eternal life will one day return in the fruit of redemption as it was once planted. So too a piece of redemption is here already really placed into the world, the visible world, and it becomes true that, seen from the world, revelation would actually already be redemption. And on the eternal way, for its part, one really does again begin with man's innate image-of-God character. Here redemption takes place through the new Adam, free of sin, not fallen, and with him it already exists. The miraculous birth of the second Adam renews this creation in the image of God, and man, endowed with soul, here makes it his own and thus becomes heir to redemption, to a redeemedness which is his own from of yore, from creation on and only waits to be claimed by him. Thus it becomes true that, from man's point of view, creation would actually already be redemption.

GOD'S TIME

Thus the relationships of time here find their precise place. For man was created as man in revelation, and in redemption he was permitted and required to reveal himself. This simple and natural temporal relationship, in which being created preceded revealing oneself, now establishes the entire sequence of the eternal way through the world, its own chronology, the consciousness which is found in every present between past and future and on the way from past to future. On the other hand the peculiar inversion of chronological sequence for the world which we have already noticed several times, now receives its graphic confirmation. For to the world, the experience of awakening to its own manifest consciousness of itself, namely the consciousness of the creature, occurs at its creation, and only in redemption is it first properly created; only there does it acquire its firm durability, that constant life in place of the ever-new existence born of the moment. Thus awaking precedes being for the world, and this inversion of chronological sequence establishes the life of the eternal people. For its eternal life constantly anticipates the end and thus turns it into beginning. In this inversion, it denies time as decisively as possible and places itself outside of time. To live in time means to live between beginning and end. He who would live an eternal life, and not the temporal in time, must live outside of time, and he who would do this must deny that "between." But such a denial would have to be active if it is to result, not just in a not-living-in-time but in a positive living-eternally! And the active denial would occur only in the inversion. To invert a Between means to make its After a Before, its Before an After, the end a beginning, the beginning an end. And that is what the eternal people does. It already lives its own life as if it were all the world and the world were finished. In its Sabbaths it celebrates the sabbatical completion of the world and makes it the foundation and starting point of its existence. But that which temporally speaking, would be but starting point, the law, that it sets up as its goal. Thus it experiences no Between for all that it naturally, really naturally, lives within it. Rather it experiences the inversion of the Between. Thus it denies the omnipotence of the Between and disavows time, the very time which is experienced on the eternal way.

THE ETERNAL GODS

Under the signs of the eternal life and the eternal way, the two "views" thus harden from the "viewpoint" of world or man into figures visible in their own right, and enter under the one sign of the eternal truth. And with that the question as to which order of the three hours is required for the eternal truth itself is simplified. For having recognized eternal truth as that truth which will be at the end and which originates with God at the beginning, it follows that only that order does justice to the ultimate truth which presents itself as from God and in which redemption is really the Last. And precisely in this order-from-God, even the orders from the world or from man, which apparently are still at least possible by its side, find their domicile. There they can reside in safety and recite their Truly as essential and visible configurations under the dominion of the eternal truth. Paganism will live on to the eternal end in its eternal gods, the state and art, the former the idol of the realists, the latter that of the individualists; but these gods are there put in chains by the true God. Let the state claim the supreme place in the All for the world, and art for man; let the state dam up the current of time at the epochs of world history, and art try to divert it into the endless irrigation system of experiences—just let them! He who thrones in heaven mocks them. He confronts their bustling activity, which already is at cross purposes, with the quiet effectiveness of created nature in whose truth the deified world is defined and configured for eternal life, where deified man is bent and dispatched on the eternal way and thus both, world and man, are jointly subordinated to God's dominion. In the struggle for time, state and art must destroy each other, since the state wishes to stop the flow of time, while art would drift in it. But even this struggle is settled in divinely ruled nature. World and man find room side by side in the eternity of life and the eternity of the way; there they are deified without being idolized.

THE GOD OF GODS

Thus it is only before the truth that the frenzy of all paganism collapses. Its blind and drunken desire to see itself and only itself, climaxing in the eternal struggle of art and the state, is confronted by the quiet superior power of the divine truth which, because everything lies at its feet as one single great nature, can assign to each its portion and thus order the All. As long as art and the state, each for itself, may both regard themselves as omnipotent, just so long each claims all of nature for itself, and rightly so. Both know nature only as their "material." Only when the truth limited both, the state by means of eternal life, art by means of the eternal way, could it free nature from this double slavery and restore its unity; in this state and art may claim their portion, but no more. As for the truth—whence should it draw its power of carrying the All of nature like a pillar if not from the God who gives himself figure in it and only in it. In the sight of the truth not only does the Perhaps lose its validity—for that had long since disappeared—but in the final analysis every Possibly too. The Star of Redemption, in which the truth achieves configuration, is not in orbit. That which is above, is above and stays above. View points, *Weltanschauungen*, philosophies of life, isms' of every sort— all this no longer dares to show itself to this last simple view of the truth. The points of view are submerged before the one constant sight. Views of the world and of life are absorbed into the one view of God. The ism's retreat before the rising constellation of redemp- tion which, irrespective of whether one believes in it or not, is at any rate meant as a fact and not an ism. Thus there is an Above and a Below, inexchangeable and irreversible. Even the cognizant one may not say If. He too is governed by the Thus, the Thus-and-not-other- wise. And just because there is an Above and a Below in the truth, therefore we may, nay we must call it God's countenance. We speak in images. But the images are not arbitrary. There are essential images and coincidental ones. The irreversibility of the truth can only be enunciated in the image of a living being. For in the living being, an Above and a Below are already designated by nature prior to all theory or regulation. And of living beings in turn there, where self- consciousness is awake to this designation: in man. Man has an above and a below in his own corporeality. And just as the truth, which gave itself configuration in the Star, is in turn assigned within the Star to God as whole truth, and not to man or the world, so too the Star must once more mirror itself in that which, within the corpo- reality, is again the Upper: the countenance. Thus it is not human illusion if Scripture speaks of God's countenance and even of his separate bodily parts. There is no other way to express the Truth. Only when we see the Star as countenance do we transcend every possibility and simply see.

THE FACE OF MAN

Just as the Star mirrors its elements and the combination of the ele- ments into one route in its two superimposed triangles, so too the organs of the countenance divide into two levels. For the life-points of the countenance are, after all, those points where the countenance comes into contact with the world above, be it in passive or active contact. The basic level is ordered according to the receptive organs;

they are the building blocks, as it were, which together compose the face, the mask, namely forehead and cheeks, to which belong respectively nose and ears. Nose and ears are the organs of pure receptivity. The nose belongs to the forehead; in the sacred [Hebrew] tongue it veritably stands for the face as a whole. The scent of offerings turns to it as the motion of the lips to the ears. This first triangle is thus formed by the midpoint of the forehead, as the dominant point of the entire face, and the midpoints of the cheeks. Over it is now imposed a second triangle, composed of the organs whose activity quickens the rigid mask of the first: eyes and mouth. Not that the eyes are mutually equivalent in a mimic sense, for while the left one views more receptively and evenly, the right one fixes its glance sharply on one point. Only the right one "flashes"—a division of labor which frequently leaves its mark deep in the soft neighborhood of the eyesockets of a hoary head; this asymmetric facial formation, which otherwise is generally conspicuous only in the familiar difference between the two profiles, then becomes perceptible also en face. Just as the structure of the face is dominated by the forehead, so its life, all that surrounds the eyes and shines forth from the eyes, is gathered in the mouth. The mouth is consummator and fulfiller of all expression of which the countenance is capable, both in speech as, at last, in the silence behind which speech retreats: in the kiss. It is in the eyes that the eternal countenance shines for man; it is the mouth by whose words man lives. But for our teacher Moses, who in his lifetime was privileged only to see the land of his desire, not to enter it, God sealed this completed life with a kiss of his mouth. Thus does God seal and so too does man.

Prospect: *The Everyday of Life*

THE LAST

In the innermost sanctum of the divine truth, where man might expect all the world and himself to dwindle into likeness of that which he is to catch sight of there, he thus catches sight of none other than a countenance like his own. The Star of Redemption is become countenance which glances at me and out of which I glance. Not God became my mirror, but God's truth. God, who is the last and the first— he unlocked to me doors of the sanctuary which is built in the innermost middle. He allowed himself to be seen. He led me to that border of life where seeing is vouchsafed. For "no man shall see him and live." Thus that sanctuary where he granted me to see him had to be a segment of the hypercosmos in the world itself, a life beyond life. But what he gave me to see in this Beyond of life is—none other than what I was already privileged to perceive in the midst of life; the difference is only that I see it and no longer merely hear it. For the view on the height of the redeemed hypercosmos shows me nothing but what the word of revelation already enjoined in the midst of life. And to walk in the light of the divine countenance is granted only to him who follows the words of the divine mouth. For—"he has told thee, oh man, what is good, and what does the Lord thy God require of thee but to do justice and to love mercy and to walk humbly with thy God."

THE FIRST

And this Last is not Last, but an ever Nigh, the Nighest; not the Last, in short, but the First. How difficult is such a First! How difficult is every beginning! To do justice and to love mercy—that still looks like a goal. Before any goal, the will can claim to need a little respite first. But to walk humbly with thy God—that is no longer goal. That is so unconditional, so free of every condition, of every But-first and Tomorrow, so wholly Today and thus wholly eternal as life and the way. And therefore it partakes of the eternal truth as directly as do life and the way.

To walk humbly with thy God—nothing more is demanded
there than a wholly present trust. But trust is a big word.
It is the seed whence grow faith, hope, and love, and the
fruit which ripens out of them. It is the very simplest
and just for that the most difficult. It dares at
every moment to say Truly to the truth. To
walk humbly with thy God—the words are
written over the gate, the gate which
leads out of the mysterious-
miraculous light of the divine
sanctuary in which no man
can remain alive. Whither,
then, do the wings of
the gate open? Thou
knowest it not?
INTO LIFE

INDICES

IN KEEPING WITH Franz Rosenzweig's plan, the indices refer also to those names and sources which are "unnamed and merely alluded to" in *The Star of Redemption*. For this reason, the literature on which the book is based has been incorporated into the Index of Names. The special Index of Jewish Sources gathers the sources from the Bible, Talmud, Midrash, and Prayerbook.

—*Nahum N. Glatzer**

* The Index of Jewish Sources has been adapted from the Second (German) Edition by the Translator. The Index of Subjects, taken over from the Third Edition, and the Index of Names have both been newly revised by Gertrude Hallo. (Tr.)

ERRATA

The cross-references contained in the Index of Jewish Sources, pp. 427-436, are incorrect. The correct references are supplied below for the following entry numbers:

Entry number	Cross-reference to entry number	Entry number	Cross-reference to entry number
19	152	247	150
22	13	249	198
32	1	252	158
45	39	256	81
48	34	263	50
71	56	264	159
80	18	269	255
93	82	272	85
98	85	276	267
114	13	277	258
127	85	280	109
133	129	282	1
134	82	283	258
151	146	284	259
169	13	285	38
174	144	286	150
175	146	287	203
179	168	288	224
183	91	289	153
184	150	293	177
226	192	294	82
227	144	298	101
231	150	299	195
238	146	305	254
240	152	313	203
242	144	316	144
243	168	318	278
244	182		
245	204		
246	106		

INDEX OF
JEWISH SOURCES

PART I

Entry*   Page

1   4   Cf. Isaiah 25:8: He will swallow up death forever.**
2   26   Genesis 1:1: In the beginning.
3   45   Ecclesiastes 1:9: new under the sun.
4   63   Psalm 139:9: if I take the wings of the morning.
5   63   Ecclesiastes 1:4: A generation.
6   69   Genesis 1:27: in the image of God.
7   69   Genesis 3:5: like God.
8   69   Genesis 3:1-5: the serpent.
9   76   Judges 16:30: Let me die with the Philistines.

PART II

10   94   Exodus 7:8-13: Pharaoh's wise men; the rod.
11   95   Deuteronomy 18:10: a sorcerer.
12   95   Deuteronomy 18:20ff.: the prophet.
13   111   Morning prayer: who renews daily the work of creation (cf. Chagigah 12 b).
14   111   Genesis 1:3: And God said, Let there be light.
15   111   Proverbs 20:27: The spirit of man is the lamp of the Lord.
16   112   Genesis 1: 1ff.: God said. God created. In the beginning.
17   115   Cf. Psalm 118:22: The stone which the builders rejected.
18   117   (Logical deduction) Sifra, introduction: Rabbi Ishmael said: there are thirteen rules of Biblical hermeneutics.
19   117   (Rabbinic theology) Genesis Rabbah XII 15: The Holy one, blessed be he, said: If I create the world on the basis of mercy alone, then its' sins will be great; if on the basis of justice alone, how could the world endure? Therefore, I will create the world on the basis of justice *and* basis of mercy; thus may it endure! (Hence the expression The Lord God; *See below*, number 58.)
20   118   Genesis 8:22: while the earth remains.
21   121   Genesis 1:11 etc.: according to its kind.
22   122   *See above*, number 30: the work of creation.
23   132   *Ibid.*: renews daily.
24   135   Isaiah 40:25: To whom then will you compare me.
25   151   Cf. Isaiah 55:8: neither are your ways my ways.
26   151–155   Genesis 1:1-4, 11, 14, 26, 31.
27   155   Genesis Rabbah XI: Very good—that is death.
28   156   Song of Songs 8:6: Love is strong as death.
29   157   Cf. Psalm 89:16: in the light of thy countenance.

* Entries have been numbered in order to facilitate cross-referencing.

** Biblical citations in this index are generally taken from the Revised Standard Version (RSV). Chapters and verses are numbered as in the Hebrew text. (Tr.)

Entry	Page	
30	157	Cf. I Kings 18:27: perhaps he is asleep.
31	160	Genesis 1:26: in the image of God.
32	164	*See above*, number 9.
33	166	Cf. Exodus 19:20: and the Lord came down.
34	171	Pesikta de-Rav Kahana commenting on Isaiah 43:10: If you testify to me.
35	171	Cf. Psalm 139:9: the uttermost parts of the sea.
36	175	Genesis 1:26: Let us.
37	175	Genesis 3:9: Where are you?
38	176	Genesis 22:1: Here am I.
39	176	Deuteronomy 6:5: And you shall love the Lord.
40	177	Deuteronomy 6:6: I command you this day.
41	177	Cf. Psalm 95:7: On that today you would hearken to his voice!
42	178	Exodus 20:2: I am the Lord.
43	178	Exodus 11:4 *et passim*: Thus says the Lord.
44	178	II Kings 9:26 *et passim*: pronouncement of the Lord.
45	179	*See below*, number 114.
46	179	Liturgy of the New Year: I have sinned.
47	180	Cf. Numbers 14:20: I have pardoned.
48	182	*See below*, number 107.
49	182	Cf. Song of Songs 2:16: My beloved is mine and I am his.
50	183-185	Isaiah 43:1: I have called you by name, you are mine.
51	183	Cf. Soṭah 12a: Rabbi Yoḥanan said: He who marries a wife in the name of Heaven, it is accounted to him by Scripture as if he had begotten her.
52	184	Psalm 22:2: My God, my God.
53	184	Cf. Psalm 66:20: He has not rejected my prayer or removed his steadfast love from me!
54	185	Sanctification (Kedushah) in the Additional Prayer (Musaph): a second time in the eyes of all living.
55	185	Job 14:13 *et passim*: Oh that thou wouldest (literally: who would grant).
56	185	Song of Songs 8:10: then I was in his eyes as one who finds peace.
57	186	Genesis 1:26: image of God.
58	187	Cf. Genesis 2:19: the man (Adam) called every living creature (by a name).
59	197	Genesis 1:1: In the beginning.
60	201	Song of Songs 1:2: better than wine.
61	201	Genesis 1:31: very good.
62	202	Song of Songs 8:6: Love is strong as death.
63	202	*Ibid.*: flashes of fire.
64	202	Song of Songs 1:4: draw me after you.
65	202	Songs of Songs 5:2: open to me.
66	202	Song of Songs 2:10: arise, . . . come away.
67	203	Song of Songs 5:10: distinguished among ten thousand.
68	203	Song of Songs 4:9 *et passim*: my sister, my bride.
69	203	Song of Songs 1:6: Do not gaze at me.
70	203	Song of Songs 1:5: I am very dark.
71	203	Song of Songs 8:10: finds peace in his eyes: (*See below*, number 125).
72	203	Cf. Song of Songs 2:7 etc.: I am his.
73	203	Song of Songs 2:7 etc.: nor awaken love.
74	203	Song of Songs 8:1: O that you were like a brother to me.
75	203	Cf. *ibid.*: Outside I would kiss you.

Entry	Page	
76	204	Song of Songs 8:6: Set me as a seal upon your heart.
77	204	Cf. Shabbat 133b: Abba Saul said: Become like Him; as He is generous and merciful, be thou generous and merciful.
78	205	Leviticus 19:18: love your neighbor as yourself.
79	205	Genesis Rabbah XXIV 7: Ben Azzai said: This is the book of the generations of Adam . . . he made him in the likeness of God (Genesis 5:1)—this is the embodiment of the Torah. Rabbi Akiba said: Love your neighbor as yourself (Leviticus 19:18)—this is the embodiment of the Torah); don't say: because I was despised, my companion shall be despised like me, because I was cursed, my companion shall be cursed like me. Rabbi Tanchuma said: If you have done so, know whom you despise—he made him in the likeness of God (Genesis 5:1).
80	216	(Logical deduction): *See above*, number 37.
81	219	Cf. Isaiah 25:8: God will wipe away tears from all faces.
82	226	Cf. Sanhedrin 98a: (Rabbi Joshua ben Levi) said to (the Messiah): When will you come? He said to him: Today. Elijah said: that is what he said to you: Today—if you hearken to his voice (Psalm 95:7).
83	227	(Coercing the Kingdom): Cf. Baba Metsi 'a 85b: I thought that they would thus become strong in prayer and bring about the Messiah before his time.
84	229	Cf. Isaiah 43:1: I have called you by name.
85	231	Cf. Midrash Tehillim to Psalm 91:16: Rabbi Abahu taught: This is one of the difficult verses in which the salvation of the Holy One, blessed be He, is declared to be the salvation of Israel.
86	231	Psalm 136:1: O give thanks to the Lord for he is good, for his steadfast love endures for ever.
87	232	Psalm 103:1,22: Bless the Lord, O my soul.
88	232	Psalm 148:7: Praise the Lord from the earth.
89	233	Psalm 117:1: Praise the Lord, all nations!
90	233	Psalm 135:20: You that fear the Lord, bless the Lord!
91	234	Cf. Abodah Zarah 7b: Nahum the Mede said: The individual prays for his needs in the (blessing) "He who hears prayer."
92	234	Psalm 136:1: endures for ever.
93	234	See above to [II 179].
94	237-238	Cf. Psalm 139:21: Do I not hate them that hate thee, O Lord?
95	238	Psalm 139:23f.: Lord, judge me.
96	238	Psalm 139:12: the night is bright as the day, for darkness is as light with thee.
97	238	Zechariah 14:1 *et passim*: a day of the Lord.
98	238	See above to [II 185].
99	239	Psalm 136:1: O give thanks.
100	239	Cf. Leviticus 19:18: love your neighbor as yourself.
101	250	Cf Avot 5:22: Turn (the Torah) this way and that, for everything is in it.
102	250	Cf. Psalm 73:1: Truly God is good to Israel.
103	250	Psalm 22:21, 35:17: "soul" and "solitary one" in parallelism.
104	251	Cf. Genesis 12:1: Go . . . to the land that I will show you.
105	251-253	Psalm 115:1, 9-18.
106	252	Cf. Exodus 4:22: Israel is my first-born son.
107	253	Psalm 36:10: in thy light do we see light.

Entry	Page	
108	253	(The light which God separated): cf. Chagigah 12a.
109	253	Genesis 1:4: and God separated the light from the darkness.
110	253	Cf. Song of Songs 8:10: as one who finds peace.
111	253	Berakhot 17a: Rav used to say: the world to come is not like this world. In the world to come there is no eating or drinking, no fruitfulness and multiplying, no buying and selling, no envy, hate or struggle. Rather, the pious sit with their crowns on their heads and taste the splendor of the divine presence.
112	259	Cf. Leviticus 19:18: love your neighbor as yourself.
113	259	Genesis 1:26: in the image of God.
114	261	*See above*, number 30.
115	261	Cf. Job 14:1: Man that is born of a woman.

PART III

116	265	Cf. Isaiah 40:15: Behold, the nations are like a drop from a bucket.
117	265	Cf. Job 25:6: Man, who is a maggot, and the son of man, who is a worm.
118	265	Morning prayer (cf. Berakhot 60b). And bring us not into the power of sin, nor of transgression or evil, nor of temptation, nor of reproach.
119	266	Cf. Avot 4:22: You were created without your consent and born into the world without your choice.
120	266	Cf. Sanhedrin 97b: Rabbi Elazar said: If Israel repents, it will be redeemed, if not, it will not be redeemed.
121	266	Cf. Sanhedrim 65b and Genesis Rabbah XI 5 for the river Sambation.
122	266	Job 2:9: Curse God.
123	266	Avot 6:2: Do not read *ḥārūt* (graven; Exodus 32:16) but *ḥērūt* (freedom); for you will find none free who does not busy himself in the study of Torah.
124	266	Berakhot 33b: everything is in God's hands.
125	267	Cf. Leviticus 19:18: love your neighbor as yourself.
126	267	Psalm 13:4: lighten my eyes.
127	272	(Self-redemption): *See below*, number 185.
128	272	Cf. Exodus 3:14: "I am who I am," or "I will be what I will be."
129	272	Cf. Psalm 69:14: my prayer is to thee, O Lord, at an acceptable time.
130	275	Psalm 90:1,17: A prayer of Moses.
131	275	Psalm 65:3: O thou who hearest prayer! To thee shall all flesh come.
132	284	Cf. Isaiah 40:31: They who hope for the Lord shall renew their strength, they shall mount up with wings like eagles.
133	288	(Accelerating eternity): *See above*, numbers 17-22.
134	289	*See below*, number 179.
135	291	Cf. Genesis 1:16: And God made the two great lights.
136	291	Genesis 8:22: seed time and harvest.
137	291	(Analogy of creation): cf. Exodus 20:8-11.
138	292	(Symbol of human freedom): cf. Deuteronomy 5:14-15.
139	293	Cf. Psalm 26:12: In assemblages I will bless the Lord.
140	295	Cf. Psalm 36:10: in thy light do we see light.
141	296	Zephaniah 3:9: For then I will turn unto the peoples a purified speech (literally, lip).
142	296	Zephaniah 3:11: On that day you shall not be put to shame.

Entry	Page	
143	297	Berakhot 58a: Our Rabbis taught: On seeing the sages of Israel one should say: Blessed be he who has imparted of his wisdom to them that fear him.
144	298	Benediction after reading from the Torah: Blessed art Thou. (Cf. Soferim 13:8).
145	298	Genesis 15:5: So shall thy seed be.
146	298	Cf. II Samuel 7:23: Who is like your people Israel, one nation in the land; and Sabbath prayer.
147	300	Cf. Genesis 12:1: Now the Lord said to Abraham: Go from your country and your kindred.
148	300	Genesis 23:4: a stranger and a sojourner.
149	300	Leviticus 25:23: The land is mine.
150	304	Cf. Pesachim 10:5 (quoted in the Haggadah for Passover): in every generation a man is obliged to regard himself as having come forth from Egypt.
151	305	(The One People): See above, number 49.
152	305	Cf. Genesis Rabbah XXXIII 3: Wherever the text uses the divine name YHWH, it indicates the attribute of mercy; wherever it says Elohim (God), it indicates the attribute of justice.
153	306	Cf. Jeremiah 10:10: He is the living God and the king of the universe.
154	307	Cf. Psalm 2:11: Serve the lord with fear, with trembling.
155	307	Cf. Genesis Rabbah XLIV 12 to Jeremiah 10:2: In the days of Jeremiah the Israelites wished to entertain this belief [in wondrous signs], but the Holy One, blessed be he, would not permit them.
156	307	(Majesty and meekness): Megillah 31a to Deuteronomy 10:17-18, Isaiah 57:15, Psalm 68:5-6.
157	307	Cf. Amos 3:2: You only have I known of all the families of the earth; therefore will I punish you for all your iniquities.
158	307	Cf. Isaiah 45:23 (quoted in the Aleinu-prayer): To me every knee shall bow.
159	307	Psalm 22:4: enthroned above the praises of Israel.
160	307	(Suffering servant): Isaiah 49-50, 52-53.
161	307	Cf. Isaiah 19:25: Blessed be Egypt my people, and Assyria the work of my hands.
162	307	Cf. Genesis 2:7: God formed man of dust from the ground, and breathed into his nostrils the breath of life.
163	307	Cf. Isaiah 11:1: There shall come forth a shoot from the stump of Jesse.
164	307	Isaiah 49:6: that my salvation may reach to the ends of the earth.
165	307	Avoth 2:2: Excellent is the study of Torah when combined with a worldly occupation.
166	308	(Share in the world to come): cf. Sanhedrin 10:1.
167	311	Exodus 31:17: In six days the Lord made heaven and earth.
168	311	Sanctification of the Sabbath (Kiddush-prayer): memorial of the work of creation.
169	311	(Daily renewal): See above, number 30.
170	311	Genesis 2:1: and the heaven and the earth.
171	312	Exodus 33:11: face to face.
172	312	Cf. Deuteronomy 34:10: And there has not arisen a prophet since in Israel like Moses, whom the Lord knew face to face.
173	312	(Elect through the gift of the Torah): cf. Berakhot 11b.
174	312	(Eternal life implanted): See above, number 48.
175	312	(The "one and only" people): See above, number 49.

Entry	Page	
176	313	Cf. Deuteronomy 6:4: Hear, O Israel: the Lord our God, the Lord is one.
177	313	Cf. Berakhot 2:2: Rabbi Joshua ben Karcha said: why does the paragraph beginning "Hear (O, Israel)" precede that beginning "And it shall be, that if you hear . . . (Deuteronomy 11:13-21)" (i.e. in the Reading of the Shema)? So that one will assume the yoke of the kingdom first, and only after that the yoke of the commandments.
178	313	Cf. Solomon Ha-Levi Alkabetz, Lekhah Dodi: Come, my beloved, to meet the birde; hymn for welcoming the Sabbath (cf. Shabbat 119a).
179	314	(Commemorate the work of the beginning): See above, number 64.
180	314	Cf. Exodus 20:9: Six days you shall labor and do all your work.
181	314	Cf. Isaiah 58:13: (If you honor the Sabbath) by not pursuing your business nor speaking thereof.
182	314	Cf. Deuteronomy 5:14: that your manservant and your maidservant may rest as well as you.
183	314	(Individual requests): See below, number 189.
184	316	See above, number 56.
185	317	Sanctification of the Sabbath (Kiddush): reminder of the exodus from Egypt (cf. Deuteronomy 5:15).
186	317	Cf. Deuteronomy 10:19: Love the alien therefore, for you were aliens in the land of Egypt.
187	317	Pesachim 10:4 (quoted in the Haggadah for Passover): What distinguishes this night from all (other) nights?
188	318	Cf. the Haggadah for Passover: Not just one alone arose against us to destroy us.
189	318	Cf. the Passover hymn Dayyenu, (It would have been) sufficient for us.
190	318	(Reading of the Song of Songs): on the Sabbath afternoon during the Passover week; or at the conclusion of the Passover Seder.
191	318	(Isaiah's prophecy): Isaiah 11:1-10, part of the Prophetic portion for the eighth day of Passover.
192	319	Cf. Malachi 3:23-24: Behold, I will send you Elijah.
193	319	(Revelation linked with creation): cf. Shabbat 88a commenting on Genesis 1:31: Rabbi Simeon ben Lakish said: this teaches us that the Holy One, blessed be He, made a stipulation with the work of creation, saying: if Israel accepts the Torah, you will endure, but if not I will make you formless and void again.
194	319	(Revelation contained in creation): cf. Pesikta Rabbati 21:19: The Ten Commandments were intended to be paired off with the ten words whereby the world was created. "I am the Lord your God" (Exodus 20:2, Deuteronomy 5:6) is paired with "And God said, Let there be light" etc.
195	319	(Ezekiel's vision): Ezekiel 1, the Prophetic portion for the first day of the festival.
196	319	(Habakkuk's song): Habakkuk 3, the Prophetic portion for the second day of the festival.
197	320	Cf. Numbers 14:35: in this wilderness they shall come to a full end, and there they shall die.
198	320	I Kings 8:56: Blessed by the Lord who has given rest. . . . From the Prophetic portion for the eighth day of the festival.
199	320	Zechariah 14:9: And the Lord shall be king.

Entry	Page	
200	320	(Solomon's concluding words): I Kings 8:60-61.
201	320	(Chapter from Ezekiel): Ezekiel 38:18-39:16, the Prophetic portion for the Sabbath of the week of Tabernacles.
202	321	Ezekiel 38:23: Thus will I magnify myself.
203	323	Numbers 16:22: the God of the spirits in all flesh.
204	323	Leviticus 23:32: It shall be to you a sabbath of sabbaths.
205	323	Cf. Yoma 6:2 (quoted in the Additional Prayer for the Day of Atonement): When they heard the ineffable name pronounced by the High Priest they knelt and prostrated themselves.
206	323	Aleinu-prayer: When every knee shall bow. (cf. Isaiah 45:23).
207	324	(This prayer): the Aleinu-prayer (Adoration).
208	324	(Day of judgment): Rosh ha-shanah 16b.
209	324	Cf. the New Year liturgy: on the New Year you will be inscribed, and on the fast-day of atonement you will be sealed.
210	324	Cf. Pesikta Rabbati 40:5: Why then do I suspend execution for ten days? So that Israel may yet be moved to penitence.
211	325	Introduction to Kol Nidrei (liturgy of the eve of Atonement): we declare it lawful to pray together with the sinners.
212	325	Morning service: The soul which you, my God, have given me, is pure (cf. Berakhot 60b).
213	325	Cf. Yoma 86b: Rabbi Simeon ben Lakish said: Great is repentance, for what was done with premeditation thus becomes something done in error.
214	326	(Jewish by birth): cf. Rashi to Kiddushin 68b.
215	327	Numbers 15:26 (quoted in the liturgy of the eve of Atonement after Kol Nidrei): And all the congregation.
216	327	Yoma 8:9: The Day of Atonement atones for transgressions between man and God; it does not make amends for transgressions between man and his fellow-man until he has satisfied his fellow-man.
217	327	Cf. Midrash Tanchuma to Leviticus 4:2: it is the soul that sins.
218	327	Cf. Psalm 22:2: My God, my God, why hast thou forsaken me?
219	327	Exodus 34:6-7: The Lord, the Lord, a God merciful and gracious.
220	327	(Mercy on him who repents): Yoma 86a to Exodus 34:7.
221	327	I Kings 18:39: The Lord is God; serves as the very last sentence of the service of the Day of Atonement.
222	330	Cf. Deuteronomy 20:15: Thus you shall do to all the cities which are very distant from you.
223	331	Cf. Sifre to Deuteronomy 20:17: When the text says, "as the Lord your God has commanded you," it means to add the Girgashites [to the six nations mentioned].
224	331	Exodus 19:6: and you shall be to me a kingdom of priests and a holy people.
225	334	Cf. Joshua 10:13: And the sun stood still, and the moon stayed, until the nation took vengeance on their enemies.
226	335	(This turning of the hearts): See above, number 74; Malachi.
227	335	(Blessed art Thou . . .): See above, number 48.
228	336	Cf. Isaiah 55:8: For my thoughts are not your thoughts, neither are your ways my ways.
229	336	Cf. Daniel 11:14: Men of violence among your own people shall lift themselves up to fulfill the vision, and shall stumble.
230	336	Zephaniah 3:9: Yea, at that time. . . .
231	341	(God led every individual . . .): See above, number 56.
232	341	Deuteronomy 29:13-14: I make this covenant.

Entry	Page	
233	343	Exodus 12:16 *et passim*: sacred convocation.
234	343	Cf. Exodus 12:6 *et passim*: the whole assembly of the congregation of Israel.
235	347	Cf. Genesis 23:17: I will multiply your descendants as the stars of heaven and as the sand which is on the seashore.
236	347	Cf. Isaiah 11:9: for the earth shall be full of the knowledge of the Lord as the waters cover the sea.
237	347	Psalm 8:3: Out of the mouths. . . . Cf. Shabbat 119b *ad loc.*: Rabbi Judah ha-Nasi said: The word exists only by virtue of the breath of school children.
238	349	(The one people): *See above*, number 49.
239	349	Isaiah 44:7: the eternal people.
240	349	(Justice and mercy): *See above*, number 58.
241	355	Cf. Micah 5:1: But you, O Bethlehem Ephrathah, who are little to be among the thousands of Judah.
242	358	(Eternal life): *See above*, number 48.
243	359	(Remembrance of the work of creation): *See above*, number 64.
244	359	(Man-servant and maid-servant): *See above*, number 68.
245	359	(Greater . . . Sabbath): *See above*, number 81, Exodus 23:32.
246	364	(First-born of God): *See above*, number 211.
247	365	(The Exodus): *See above*, numbers 56, 68.
248	365	Psalm 37:31: The law of his God is in his heart; his steps do not slip.
249	365	(Ultimate rest): *See above*, number 76.
250	366	Cf. Berakhot 31b: Rabbi Akiba said: The Torah speaks with the language of men.
251	367	(Day of Atonement . . . instituted): cf. Leviticus 16; 23: 26-32.
252	370	(Every knee . . .): *See above*, number 59.
253	372	Cf. Avot 5:5: Though the worshippers stood serried they could freely prostrate themselves.
254	373	Cf. Psalm 35:10: All my bones shall say, O Lord, who is like thee?
255	375	Job 19:25: For I know that my Redeemer lives.
256	377	(The tears of the mourner): *See above*, number 169.
257	380	Isaiah 11:9: For the earth shall be full.
258	380	Cf. the Amidah-prayer of the High Holydays: For thou, Lord God, art truth (based on Jeremiah 10:10).
259	381	Shabbat 55a: Truth is his signet.
260	381	Cf. Song of Songs 8:6: Love is strong as death.
261	381	Cf. the Amidah-prayer: author of life and death (based on I Samuel 2:6).
262	381	Cf. Hosea 11:4: I led them with cords of compassion (text: of man), with fetters of love.
263	381	(Summoned by name): *See above*, number 122.
264	382	(Thrones above . . .): *See above*, number 59.
265	382	Genesis 1:1: In the beginning, there created God.
266	382	Cf. Psalm 96:5: For all the gods of the peoples are idols.
267	383	Psalm 115:8: Those who make them.
268	383	Psalm 96:5: but the Lord made the heavens.
269	383	(The Redeemer lives): *See above*, number 148.
270	383	Cf. the Amidah-prayer: May our eyes behold thy return to Zion (Based on Micah 4:11).
271	383	Zechariah 14:9 (quoted in the Aleinu-prayer): On that day the Lord will be one and his name one.
272	383	(Redemption redeems God): *See above*, number 185.
273	383	Cf. the Adoration (Aleinu-prayer): And all the children of flesh shall invoke thy name.

Entry	Page	
274	384	Cf. Deuteronomy 28:10: you are called by the name of the Lord.
275	384	Cf. Pesachim 50a to Exodus 3:15: The Holy One, blessed be he, said: I am not invoked as I am written. I am written IH (the tetragrammaton), I am invoked as AD (Adonai, Lord).
276	384	(Simile of the Psalm): See above, number 158.
277	385	(God is truth): See above, number 154f.
278	390	Isaiah 44:6: I am the first and I am the last.
279	392	Genesis 1:3: Let there be light.
280	392	(The light that God separated): See above, number 213.
281	393	Adon Olam hymn: the portion . . . (based on Psalm 16:5).
282	393	(Death is swallowed): See above, number 9.
283	395	(God is truth): See above, number 154.
284	395	(God's signet): See above, number 155.
285	396	(Here I am): See above, number 113.
286	397	(Everyone is to know . . .): See above, number 56.
287	400	(Lord of the spirits . . .): See above, number 80.
288	401	(Kingdom of priests . . .): See above, number 91.
289	403	(King of the universe): See above, number 59.
290	404	Cf. Exodus 19:17: and they took their stand at the foot of the mountain.
291	404	Isaiah 56:7: for my house shall be called a house of prayer for all peoples.
292	404	Isaiah 10:20 etc.: the remnant of Israel.
293	404	(Assumption of the yoke): See above, number 67.
294	404	(Today): See above, number 179.
295	404	Isaiah 11:11: the remnant of his people that will remain.
296	405	Shabbat 31a: Raba said: When man is led in for judgment [in the world to come], he is asked: . . . did you hope for salvation, did you engage in the dialectics of wisdom, did you derive one thing from another?
297	406	Cf. Avodah Zarah 3b: Rabbi Judah said in the name of Rav: the day has twelve hours; for the first three hours the Holy One, blessed be he, sits and busies himself with the Torah.
298	406	(This way and that): See above, number 209.
299	408	(Vision of Ezekiel): See above, number 75.
300	408	(Tale of the Chariot): Chagigah 11b etc.
301	409	(The seventy offerings . . .): Numbers 29:12-38.
302	409	(Counted by the legend): Sukkah 55b.
303	409	(Tabula Gentium): Genesis 10.
304	409	Cf. Midrash Tanchuma to Leviticus 19:2: There are 248 words in the Reading of the Shema (Deuteronomy 6:4-9; 11:13-21; Numbers 15:37-41), corresponding to the number of human limbs.
305	409	(All bones praise . . .): See above, number 146.
306	409	Cf. Psalm 91:15: I am with him in distress, and Exodus Rabbah 115 ad loc: Just as in the case of twins, if one has a pain in his head the other feels it also.
307	409	Cf. Megillah 29a: Rabbi Simeon ben Yochai said: Come and see how precious Israel is to the Holy One, blessed be he: every place to which they were exiled, the Shekhina was with them.
308	409	Cf. Pesachim 54a: Seven things were created even before the world was created, namely: the Torah.
309	409	(World on behalf of the Torah): cf. Genesis Rabbah I.
310	410	Avot 1:3: Do not as the servants.

Entry	Page	
311	410	Sifra to Leviticus 20:26: Say not.
312	411–412	Genesis 1:2: and the spirit of God was hovering over the face of the waters.
313	412	(Lord of the Spirits): *See above*, number 80.
314	412	Cf. Kiddushin 40b: Thus the Holy One, blessed be he, dispenses suffering to the righteous of this world.
315	413–414	Cf. Avot 3:5: Rabbi Nechunya ben Hakanah used to say: whosoever assumes the yoke of the Law, they remove from him the yoke of government and the yoke of worldly affairs.
316	415	(Eternal life): *See above*, number 48.
317	417	Aleinu-prayer: It is for us to praise . . . the Creator-from-the-beginning.
318	417	(The first and the last): *See above*, number 168.
319	417	Psalm 90:2: Before the mountains were.
320	418	Cf. Deuteronomy 4:12: You heard the sound of words, but saw no form; there was only a voice.
321	418	Numbers 6:25: The Lord make his countenance.
322	418	Cf. Numbers 6:26: The Lord lift up his countenance toward you.
323	421	Psalm 2:4: He who thrones in heaven laughs; the Lord has them in derision.
324	423	Cf. Deuteronomy 32:52: For you shall see the land before you; but you shall not go there.
325	423	Cf. Deuteronomy Rabbah XI 10: At that time the Holy One, blessed be he, kissed him and took away his soul in the kiss of his mouth.
326	423–424	Exodus 33:20: For no man shall see me and live.
327	424	Cf. Psalm 89:16: they walk, O Lord, in the light of thy countenance.
328	424	Micah 6:8: He has told thee, oh man.

INDEX OF NAMES

Aaron, 252

Abelard, Peter, (*sic et non* . . . 'Scholastic model'), 173

Abba Shaul, 204

Abraham, ("Here I am"), 176; (the father of Israel), 300; 396

Abraham, ibn Ezra, (the ancient Jewish Dogma), 96

Adam, 69; 166; 398

Aeschylus, (language of tragedy; "simple word of truth"), 43; (the heroes of Attic Tragedy), 73; 77; (Attica), 78; (the silence of the tragic hero), 81; (he, the measure of all things), 85; (the heroic man), 89; (a simple Being of truth), 120; (the chorus in classical tragedy), 207; (heroes), 213; (Prometheus already), 376

Agathon, 376

Akiba, Rabbi, ("Talmud," not based on a "Bible"), 166; (The Song of Songs . . . "mystical"), 199; 205; 216; 366

Alkabez, Solomon Halevi, (as the bridegroom . . . bride), 313

Allah, 117-118; 122-124; 165-166; 181; 215; 216; 225

Ambrose, (the Latin Church Fathers), 401

Angelus Silesius, (*see* Translator's note: "Were Christ . . . lost"), 340, 397

Apuleius, (Aphrodite), 372

Archimedes, (fixed point), 135

Aristotle, (political animal), 32; (antiquity), 38; 53-54; (political animal), 71; (classical man; polis), 73; 77; 80; 84; (enlightenment of antiquity), 97-98; (hybris; *daimon*; Greek theoretician of tragedy), 167-168; 220

Al-Ashari, (caprice of the Creator), 115; (orthodox philosophy within Islam), 122-124

Athanasius, (the Greek Church Fathers), 399

Augustine, (*Credo quia absurdum*), 62; 94; 97; 146; (*Fac quod jubes*), 214; 280; 284; (*fides* and *salus*), 330, 331; 358; (*see* Translator's note: the Latin Church Fathers), 401

Augustus (Emperor), 56; 224; (was enthroned), 278

Averroes, ibn Rushd, (dual truth . . . reason . . . faith), 280

Bach, J. Sebastian, 360

Bacon, Francis [of Verulam], 132; (self-confidence of the intellect), 388

Ben Bag Bag, ("Everything is in it"), 250, 406

Balzac, Honoré, 149

Basilius [the great], (the Eastern Church: the Greek Church Fathers), 399

Beethoven, Ludwig von, 100; 149

Boethius, A. M. Severinus, (*nunc stans*), 281-283

Boehme, Jacob, 26

Bonaventura, (Scholasticism), 98; (*Summa theologica*; Scholastic philosophy), 107

Boniface ["Apostle of Germany"], (The envoys of the successors of Peter), 279

Brandes, Georg, 244

Brockhaus, F. A., (the publisher), 8

Bruno, Giardano, (Enlightenment . . . Renaissance), 98

Buddha, 36; 37; 58-60; 75; 339

Buelow, Hans von, 197

Caesar, 278; 352

Calé, Walter, ("No bridge as yet leads"), 81; (a bridge between man and man), 366, 372; (no bridge leads from man to man), 395

Calvin, (the German Fathers), 400

Canterbury, Bishop Anselm of, (beginning of the Middle Ages), 62

Charlemagne, 352

Cherbury, *see* Herbert

Chrysostomus, (the Greek Church Fathers), 399

437

Cicero, (Roman orator), 329
Cohen, Hermann, 20; 21; (the most determined philosopher), 102; (belief wholly the content), 103; (bearers of the two about-faces), 104; (picture album of the idealistic world), 132; (as antiquity saw it), 135; (our great master proclaimed), 253; 299; (idea . . .), 414
Confucius [Kung-Futse], (Classical China), 36; 59; 73-74
Constantine [Emperor], (Moved . . . from the seventh day to), 358; 365
Copernicus, Nicholas, (Enlightenment . . . Renaissance), 98
Cusanus, see Nicholas of Cusa

Damian(i), Peter, (handmaiden of theology), 104
Daniel, 336
Dante, 18; (that great lover), 160; 287
David, (the psalmist), 250; 307; 348; (the psalmist), 383
Descartes, René, (De omnibus dubitandum), 42; (beginning of modern times), 62; (Enlightenment . . . Renaissance), 98; (the Enlightenment), 108; (self-confidence of the intellect), 388
Dostoevsky, Fydor, (Alyosha Karamazov; from the Russia of Karamazov), 285
Drews, Arthur, (denied the historical Jesus), 102
Duns Scotus, John, 12
Dürer, Albrecht, (Being-full-of-form), 43; (inwardly full of form), 150; ("being full of configuration within"), 192; (inwardly full of form), 248

Ehrenberg, Hans, 14; (beginning of the nineteenth century), 62
Eckhart, Meister, (mystical term), 25; 26; (sombre basis; abyss of the deity), 29; (sombre foundations), 125
Einstein, Albert, (general relativity), 256
Elazar Ben Zadok, (giver of sufferings), 412
Elazar Ha-Kappar, (though he is created), 266
Elijah, 319
Empedocles, (For philosophy . . . beginnings), 254
Epicurus, (the heathens), 125

Esther, 369
Euripides, (the heroes of Attic Tragedy), 73; (Attic Tragedy); Attica; Phaedra), 78; (the silence of the tragic hero), 81; (the heroic man of tragedy), 89; (Alcestis), 156; (the chorus in classical tragedy), 207
Ezekiel, 319; 320; 409

Fichte, Johann Gottlieb, 3-6; (German Idealism), 12-13; (Ding ar sich; pre-metalogical philosophies; Idealism), 47; 50-53; (Kant's successors), 70; (basic concept of philosophy), 94; (historical enlightenment), 98; (new epoch . . . 1800), 99; (About 1800), 104; (idealistic philosophy), 135, 137; (GENERATION; the I of Idealism; subject; thing in itself; system), 137-142; (Kant and his followers), 217; (not the generation of), 224; ("synthesis"; Idealistic movement), 229; (Idealism's infinity), 255; (German Idealistic Movement), 281; (subject, object, ideal), 390-392
Flaubert, Gustave, 149
Frederick II of Prussia, ("Your Majesty, the Jews!"), 415

Galilei, Galileo, (Enlightenment . . . Renaissance), 98; (new science of the world), 221
Ghazali(al), (creation ex nihilo), 119, 120, 138-140; (Islam), 171; 172
Geibel, Emanuel von, (recover if the essence), 330
Gibbon, Edward, 98
Goethe, Johann Wolfgang von, 4; 8; 18; 22; (Mephistopheles), 25; (realm of the mothers), 26; (Mephistopheles cherishes), 28; ("distant until the stars"), 32; "sound and haze"), 39; ("the prospect 'cross . . .'"; plentitude of visions; sunlike quality of the eye—Xenien), 44, 45; (as on the day), 49; ("He can endow the moment with permanence"—Das Goettliche; "hover in vacillating appearance"), 63, 65; ("You still stay ever what you are."), 68; ("greatest gift of mortal men"), 68; 71; (miracle . . . the favorable child), 93, 99; ("the kingdom of the noble"), 102; ("a fool in love"), 102; (dearest child), 108; ("a simple word of truth"),

121; ("already in existence"; crafts-man . . . his due), 131; ("darkness which at first"), 137; (higher, purer, unknown), 143; 149; (Faustian age), 156; (Islam means resigned to God—*West-oestlicher Divan*), 171; (sound and fury—*Faust I*; to name the name), 188; (merely a simile—*Faust II*; turn from the eighteenth to the nineteenth century), 199; (All . . . transitory . . ."; perpetual negation; sensual—super sensual), 201; (*From* "For Charlotte vom Stein"), 203; (MODERN TRAGEDY), 209-211; (*Sturm und Drang*), 244; (*see* Translator's note), 247; ("never read"), 247; 257; 258; ("endowing it with duration"), 259; 275-278; 283-288; (permission to complete the labor), 293; (the man of life), 296; (man's own spirit), 366; (to say what he is suffering), 376.

Grabbe, Christian, (one of the first), 210

Grimm, Wilhelm, (*see* Translator's note), 377

Habukkuk, 319

Harnack, Adolf von, (theology of the nineteenth century), 101-105, 106; (the gnostics), 414 415

Hassler, Leo, (head full of blood and wounds), 365

Hegel, Georg W. F. (philosophy, Idealism), 3-7; 6-7; (the post-Kan-tians), 10; (*Weltanschaung*), 11; (German Idealism; from Ionia to Jena), 12; 13; 15; 16; 17; 19; (mere epigone of a movement which had run its course), 20; 21; (philoso-phy), 41; 44; (pre-metalogical phil-osophies), 46, 47; (Idealisms), 50-53; 52; 53; (Kant's successors), 70; (basic concept of philosophy), 94; (historical enlightenment), 98; (new epoch . . . 1800), 99; (About 1800), 104; (Idealistic philosophy; GENERATION), 135-136; (the I of Idealism; subject; thing in itself; system), 137-142; (Kant and his fol-lowers), 217; (not the generation of), 224; 226; ("synthesis"; Ideal-istic movement), 229; (the All of the philosophers; Idealism's con-cept of generation), 238, 239; 254; 255; (German Idealistic Move-ment), 281; ("ideal"—in "transcen-dentalist" terms), 355; (subject, object, ideal), 391

Heim, Karl, (the bearers of the two about-faces), 104

Heraclitus, 71; ("You cannot step twice"), 332; 359

Herbert, Edward, Baron of Cherbury, (Enlightenment), 98; 100

Herder, Johann, Gottfried v. (explain miracles away), 99; (turn from the eighteenth to the nineteenth cen-tury), 199

Homer, (pathos; moira), 31; (*plesios allos*), 218; 261

Horace, (*si fractus*), 76

Huch, Ricarda, (*see* Translator's note), 149

Hume, David, (percursors in England), 146

Hus, Johann, (the German Fathers), 400

Isiah, (*see* Translator's note), 4; (the servant of God), 211; (first-born son), 252; (the command of the prophet), 314; 318; 379; 404

Jacob ben Moses, Halevi ("Maharil"), (God consoles him), 376

Judah [Jehudah] Ha-Levi, (ancient Jewish dogma), 96; (the seed of eternal life), 355; (the Kuzari), 379; (mysticism), 395

Jerome [St.], (the Latin Church Fa-thers), 401

Jensen, Peter, (pan-Babylonianists), 102

Jesse, 319

Jesus, 102; 166; 172; ("love me"), 205; ("among you"), 226; ("coerce the kingdom"), 227; (Lead us not into temptation), 265; 277; ("be as the children"), 284; ("unto all the world"), 287; (the man of the cross), 329; 338-345; 347; (SON AND FATHER), 349-351; 352; (birth in the flesh; the only begotten; that cir-cumcision), 364; (the three kings of the east; the cross and not the manger; head full of blood and wounds), 365; 366; (virgin birth), 368; (knelt at the manger), 369; 374-375; (the cross on Golgotha), 376-377; (the miracle of rebirth), 396; (the manger in Bethlehem), 397; (tablets . . . of the three crosses), 398; (the Son; the Son of man), 399-400; (the Son; the word from the cross; the crucified one), 411-412; 414-415

Job, 78; 97; 266

John, the evangelist, 285; 399
John, the Baptist, (pre-Christian name-sake), 285; 396; 411
Jose bar Chanina, (as living creatures can bear), 415
Joshua, 320
Judah Maccabee, 367
Justinian, (codification of civil law; delineation . . . private . . . sphere), 277-278; (end of Patristics), 280

Kant, Imanuel, 3-7; 10; 17; 19; ("*Ding an sich*"), 21; (the sage of Koenigsberg), 23; ("*Ding an sich*"), 41; 62; 67; 70; 101; ("A priori" . . . "experience"), 103; ("*Ding an sich*"), 127; (Idealistic philosophy; GENERATION), 135-136; (the I of Idealism; subject; thing in itself; system), 137-142; ("fine arts"), 146; 147; 217; (datum), 224; 225; ("synthesis"; Idealistic movement), 229; (the All of the philosophers; Idealism's concept of generation), 238-239; (philosophy's view), 255; (a priori heirlooms), 294; ("Ideal" —in "transcendentalist" terms), 355; (as the schoolmasters think), 384; (philosophy; "There is a truth"), 386; Idealism; philosophy; subject, object, ideal), 391
Kierkegaard, Sören, 7; 18
Kleist Heinrich, von ("rigid as antiquity"), 209; 247
Klinger, Friedrich, M. von, ("*Sturm und Drang*"), 244
Kohelet, 44; 63; 201-202; 320
Körner, Theodor, (*see Translator's note*), 149

Lagerloef, Selma, (*see Translator's note*), 149;
Lao-tzu, (The Tao), 37; 60; 75
Lasson, Georg, (Epigones . . . of German idealism), 103
Leibniz, Gottfried, W. von, (contingency of the world), 12; (Enlightenment), 98-99, 107, 108
Lenz, Jakob, 382
Lessing, Gotthold Ephraim, 98; 211; 244; 245; (Freemasonry), 285
Li-Po, 75
Locke, John, 14; (Enlightenment), 98-99, 107, 108; (percursors in England), 146
Louise [Queen of Prussia], (great words of a queen), 228

Luria, Isaac, (doctrine of the Shekhina), 409
Luther, Martin, 97-100; 107; 173; ("Here I stand"), 268; (faith alone), 281; 284; 368; (Protestantism), 374; (the Northern Church; the German Fathers), 400

Macchiavelli, Niccolo, (neo-pagan ethics), 172
Mohammed (Muhammed), 115; 116-118; (Kismet), 122; 164-166; 171-173; (master of the great plagiarism), 178; (Islam's acknowledgment), 181; (Allah), 215, 217; (the way of Allah; the prophet; Ijmā), 225-227
Moses, 94; (the true prophet), 178; 275; (the man of God), 296; 312; 379; 423
Maimonides, 115; (creation . . . from nought; *creatio ex nihilo*), 119, 120, 138, 140; 121; ("special providence"), 123; (Rabbinic concept of the Oral Law), 226; (*see* Translator's note), 336; (delays notwithstanding), 365
Marcion, (the gnostics), 414
Mary, the Virgin 345; 368; 369
Marcus Aurelius, (neo-pagan ethics), 172
Melanchthon, Philipp, (Protestantism), 374; (the German Fathers), 400
Menenius, Agrippa, 344
Meyer, Conrad Ferdinand, (Faustian age), 156
Michelangelo, Buonarotti, (Prospero), 190; 206
Moerike, Eduard, (what is beautiful), 38

Napoleon, (neo-Frankish emperor), 352
Nechunya, Ben Hakana R., (under the yoke of the law), 413
Newton, Isaac, (Enlightenment), 98, 99, 107, 108; (new science of the world), 221
Nicholas of Cusa, (contingency of the world; certain medieval tendencies), 12; 23; 181
Nietzsche, Friedrich, 8-11; 62; 105; 286-287; (with the new one), 380
Novalis (Friedrich von Hardenberg), 45

Occam, *see* William of Occam
Origen, 98

Parmenides, 12-13; (from the Iionians on), 15; (beginnings in Ionia), 19; (pre-metalogical philosophies), 47; 52; 94

Paul, Apostle, 100; (apostles of Christianity), 277; 278; 281; 284; ("everything belongs . . . Christ"), 344; (brothers in the Lord), 345; ("festival from the seventh day . . ."), 358; ("everything belongs . . ."), 374; 400; (God all-in-all), 401; (the first theologian), 411; 414

Peter, Apostle, 279; 281; 345; (the apostles of Christendom), 398; 401

Peter Damian, see Damian

Philo, (Septuagint), 218; 367

Philoponus Johann, (creation . . . from nought; creatio ex nihilo), 119, 120, 138, 140

Plato, 20; (antiquity), 38; 53-54; (daimon), 71; (polis), 73; 84; (enlightenment of antiquity), 98, 99; 103; 146; 148; (Eros), 156; (daimon; personality), 212; 220; 229; 246; (Agathon's triumph), 376; (daimon), 392

Plotinus, (neo-Platonic school), 53; (emanation), 135; (doctrine of emanation), 142; 146

Protagoras, (THE SOPHISTS), 57; (Sophist theories), 73; (he, the measure of), 85

Ramanuya (the Indians' love for God), 39

Ranke, Leopold von, (pure historian), 227

Rashi, 152; 325

Rav, (creator from the beginning), 417

Rava, ("All that is . . . acknowledges"), 384

Reimarus, Hermann Samuel, (explain miracles away), 99

Rembrandt van Rijn, 414

Reventlow, Franziska von, (the gnostics), 414

Rilke, Rainer Maria, 43-44; 149; 192-193; 247-248

Ritschl, Albrecht, 101; 103

Sacharja, see Zechariah

Salomo Halevi Alkabez, see Alkabez

Samuel (Shmuel) Bar Nachmani, (God of . . . justice . . . mercy), 306; 349

Samson, 76

Saul, 76

(Al) Shafii, ("Imam" and "Ijmā"), 226

Schelling, Friedrich W. von, 3-6; (the post-Kantians), 10; 12; 14; 18; 26; (philosophy), 41-42; 45; (pre-metalogical philosophies), 47; (Idealism), 41-53; 52; (basic concept of philosophy), 94; (historical enlightenment), 98; (new epoch . . . 1800), 99; (About 1800), 104; (Idealistic philosophy; GENERATION), 135-136; (the I of Idealism; subject; thing in itself; system), 137-142; (not the generation of), 224; (philosophy's view; Idealism's infinity), 255; (German Idealistic Movement), 281; (subject, object, ideal), 391

Schiller, Friedrich von, ("Man is created free. . . ."), 32; ("God ethereal . . ."; wisdom of wise men), 33; (Gods of myths), 36; ("Ever of yesterday"; "Universally Common"; infuriated rebel), 46; (century not yet eternal; Credo of Beethoven's Missa Solemnis), 100; (has "done its duty . . ."), 101; ("lonesome Master of the world"), 114; ("stands ever at rest"), 131; ("modestly hide behind eternal laws"), 162; (a moment gone like an arrow), 201; (MODERN TRAGEDY), 209-211; 219; 247; (eternal laws), 258; (it's a day in history), 284; (moment gone like an arrow), 289, 303, 337; 370

Schleiermacher, Friedrich, (explain miracles away), 99; 100-101

Schopenhauer, Arthur, 5; 8-9; 10; 12; 338

Schroeder, Ludwig von, (one has observed), 57

Schweitzer, Albert, 101; (bearers of the two about-faces), 104

Shakespeare, William, (Richard III), 16; ("a Woman in this humor woo'd"; "Juliet's fortune"), 78; (Prospero; some Stratford), 190; (MODERN TRAGEDY), 209-211; 244; 370

Simon Ben Yohai, (the master of the Kabbalah), 171; 181; 409

Socrates, (the pious pagan), 273

Solomon, 202; 320

Sophocles, (the heroes of Attic tragedy), 73; (Attic tragedy), 76; (Attica; Oedipus), 77, 78; (the silence of the tragic hero), 81; (the heroic man of tragedy), 89; (the chorus in classical tragedy; heroes), 207, 213

Spener, Phil. Jacob, (pietistic mysticism), 99; (pietism), 281

Spinoza, Baruch, 17; (Enlightenment), 98; 107; 108; 200

Spitteler, Karl, 193

Stael, Mme. De, 14

Stahl, Friedrich J. (and not only he), 7

Stein, Charlotte von, ("my sister, my bride"; in times gone by . . ."), 203

Strauss, David Friedrich, (theology of the nineteenth century), 101-103; ("historical" theology), 106

Tertullian, (*credo quia absurdum*), 62; (Patristic literature; disciple of Greece), 98

Thales, (*Weltanschauung*), 11; (All is water), 15-16; 19; 94

Thomas Aquinas, 98; (*Summa contra gentiles*); Scholastic philosophy), 107

Traub, Friedrich, (the gnostics), 414

Uddalaka Aruni, (Upanishads), 37

Voltaire, François, 98; (idea of progress), 100

Wagner, Richard, 244; 371

Werfel, Franz, (wonderfully still), 371

Wetzstein, Johann Gottfried, ("It was . . . discovered"), 201

William of Occam, (Anti-Thomists), 98; ("dual truth . . . reason . . . faith"), 280

Winckler, Hugo, (pan-Babylonianists), 102

Wolff, Christian, (idea of progress), 100

Xenocrates, (the *daimon*), 71; (*daimon*; Personality), 213; (the *daimon*), 391

Xerxes, (king of Persia), 323

Yajnavalkya, *see* Uddalaka Aruni

Zechariah, 320

Zeno, 56

INDEX OF SUBJECTS

The Subject Index does not claim to be completely comprehensive. In order to serve its purpose and not to grow boundlessly, it had to be limited to those captions and key-words which appeared most important to me as the editor. The basic subjects CREATION, REVELATION, REDEMPTION, GOD, WORLD, MAN are omitted because they constitute, page after page, the theme of the book.

Professor Nahum Glatzer, Boston, Massachusetts, and Mr. Achim von Borris, Zurich, Switzerland, helped me with the compilation of the subject index.—Edith Scheinmann-Rosenzweig

Ages of man, see Life
The All, 3-22, 47-48, 83-87, 144-145, 188, 238, 254, 306, 311
Antiquity (classical), 53-57, 60-61, 73, 89-90, 98, 220
Art, 33-46, 230-231, 242
Art, Artist, 38, 60, 80-82, 145-150, 189-197, 242-249, 354-358, 360, 370-372, 377, 420

Baptism, 373
Belief, 6, 63, 93-94, 97-103, 107-108, 265, 282, 342-343
Belief-hope-love, 284, 424
Birth (see also Rebirth), 49-50, 70-71, 222

China, 35-37, 57-59, 74-76
Christianity (see also Church), 277-289, 328-329, 339-379, 396-397, 398-402, 411-415
Chronology, see Time
Church (see also Christianity), 342-344, 351-352, 354-358, 369-371, 372-373, 398, 400
Church (Johannine, Pauline, Petrine), 278, 283, 284-285, 288
Church (Eastern), 285, 399
Church (Protestant), 400
Church (Roman Catholic), 401
Church year (Christian), 353, 366-370, 372, 375

Christmas, 363-364, 367
Easter, 365
Pentecost, 366
Secular festivals, 368-369
Sunday, 359-360
Clerical year (Jewish):
Day of Atonement, 323-328, 367
New Year's, 323-325, 364
Pessach, 315-319
Sabbath, 310-314
Secular festivals, 368-369
Shevuot, 318
Sukkot, 319, 327
Coercion, 333
Commandment, 349-350, 386-388
Community, see Oecumene
Creation (in idealism), 50, 132, 134-139, 141-142, 188
Creature, 118, 123, 221
Cross, 347, 265, 376-378

Dance, 372-373
Death, 3-5, 70-72, 74, 76, 155, 164, 201-202, 252-253, 273, 303, 325-326, 381, 382, 393
Defiance (see also Soul), 68, 76, 166-167, 170, 211

Emanation, 134-136
Enlightenment, 97-98
Eternal life, 258, 298-335, 354

Eternity, 164, 224, 226, 234, 239, 252-253, 258-261, 288-290, 291-293, 298, 300, 302-303, 324-325, 334-335, 341-342, 353, 376, 378-380, 412, 417
Ethics, 10-12, 14-15, 55, 172
Existence (see also Creation, Creature), 119-124, 131-133, 221-222

Faithfulness, 168-171
Freemasonry, 286

Generation, see Creation
Genesis, 151-155
Genius, 149, 191-192, 249
Gods, 33-34, 383, 388, 420-421
Grammar, 28, 108-109, 126-131, 139-140, 151-155, 165-166, 186, 228-229, 232-234, 294

Hebrew, see Holy language
Hero, see Tragedy, Tragic Hero
Holy land, 300
Holy language, 300-301
Hope, 320, 332, 347, 363
Humility, 167-171

"I" (me) (see also Self), 3, 62, 136-137, 154, 178
"I" and "you", 155, 173-175, 186, 198, 199-203
"I" and "we", 251
Idealism (see also Philosophy), 4-5, 11-12, 47, 50-51, 52-53, 56, 136-147, 188, 223, 239, 250, 386, 389-392
Immortality, 78-79, 225, 240
India, 35-36, 37, 39, 57, 59, 73-74
Islam, 116-118, 122-124, 164-166, 172, 181, 215-217, 225-227

Judaism, 403-417
    Jew, 286, 306, 347, 395-396, 412-413
    Jew-hatred, 412, 414
    Jewish people, 299-300, 328, 330, 335, 347
    Jewish world (see also Holy land, Holy language), 307-308
Judgment (verdict), 237, 324-325

Kingdom (of God), empire, 185, 219, 222, 223-228, 234, 239, 242, 252, 271, 274-275, 288, 293, 335, 352-353, 368
Knowledge (science), 6-7, 62-63, 273-275, 355

Language, 25-26, 78, 109-111, 125-132, 141-142, 145, 148, 150-151, 186, 198, 200, 231, 260, 295, 300-302
Law (see also Commandment), 14, 72, 176, 302-303, 332-333, 405, 408-410
Life, 70-71, 155, 222-226, 240, 347
    Ages of man, 375, 381, 398, 423-424
Listening, 309-310, 314, 321
Logic, 12-15, 145
Love, 156, 159-161, 161-164, 168-173, 176-185, 198-204, 211-215, 239-240, 267-269, 325, 381, 390, 392
Love of neighbor, 205, 213-214, 218, 239, 269

Marriage, 203, 240, 325
Mathematics, 19-21, 125, 254-255, 295
Meal, 315-316, 322, 363
Messiah, 307, 336, 347, 364, 380, 404
Metaethic, see Ethics
Metalogic, see Logic
Metaphysics, 16-18, 39
Miracle, 93-111, 183, 197, 294
Missionary activity, 278, 281, 288, 341
Moment (instantaneousness, instant), 65, 66, 121-122, 160-164, 176-177, 197-198, 201, 211-212, 222, 251-253, 289-290, 292, 334, 340-341
Music, 194, 197, 231-232, 245, 360-362, 371
Mysticism, 130-131, 272, 273, 391, 408-409
Mythology, 34-38, 302, 329

Name, 7, 39, 176, 187-188, 383, 391
Nations, see Peoples
Neighbor (see also Love of neighbor), 218, 228, 235-236, 239, 252, 259, 267, 270-271
Nought, 4-5, 20-29, 35-38, 42-44, 57-58, 60, 62-63, 65, 75, 113, 119-120, 157, 382-383

Oecumene (community), 41, 250, 278, 321, 341-342

Pagan, paganism, 87, 158-159, 172, 280, 283, 350, 382, 388, 390-393, 399-401, 421
People, "The," see Judaism
Peoples (of the world), 283, 299-301, 304, 328-333
Philosophy (see also Idealism), 3-12, 16-22, 41-42, 51-52, 103-108, 140, 254, 296
Poetry, 193-194, 245-246, 370-371
Prayer, 184-185, 233-234, 252, 265-268, 270-275, 283, 285-288, 292-294, 296-297
Pride, see Defiance
Priest (see also Saint), 350-351, 399-400
Prophet, 95, 178

Psalms, 250-252
Psychology, 62

Reality (*see also* Truth), 14, 189-192, 385, 415, 420-421
Realization, 236
Rebirth (*see also* Birth), 396
Reformation, 97
Remnant, 404, 410

Sabbath (*see also* Clerical year), 383
Sacrament, 358, 362, 372-373
Saint, 211-213, 217, 345, 351, 399-400
Scholasticism, 98, 280
Scripture, *see* Testaments
Science, *see* Knowledge
Self (*see also* "I"), 67-72, 73-75, 77, 206-208, 211-212
Shekhina, 409-410
Silence, 76-80, 260, 296, 307, 321-322, 352, 358, 383
Sin, sinner, 39, 179-180, 221-222, 272-274, 324-325, 327
Song of Songs, 198-205
Sophists, 57
Soul (*see also* Defiance), 79, 166-171, 176, 178-185, 198, 205, 207, 229, 235, 239-240, 267, 282, 353-354, 374, 378, 401
Space, 134, 354-358

State, 55-56, 278, 331-335, 351-352, 364, 376, 400, 420

Talmud, 117
Temptation (of God), 265
Testament, Old and New, 97, 117, 413-414
Thanksgiving, 232, 239
Theology, 17, 23, 41, 52, 94, 101-105, 106-108, 140, 190, 298
Time (chronology), 226-227, 272, 276, 289-292, 302-303, 330, 337-340, 346, 360-361, 419-420
Torah, 302-303, 326
Tragedy, 76-78, 168, 206, 208-209
Tragic hero, 73, 76, 81, 207, 208-210
Trust, 252, 387, 424
Truth (verification), 14, 381, 383, 385-387, 398, 415-416, 421

Verdict, *see* Judgment
Verification, *see* Truth
Volition, 66, 69, 213

War, 329-330, 333
"We" (*see also* "I"), 236-237, 251-253, 298, 325
Word, 358, 383

"You" (*see also* "I"), 412